D1614328

The History of the Maghrib

An Interpretive Essay

Abdallah Laroui, who has taught as Visiting Professor at the University of California at Los Angeles and at Harvard, is Professor of History at Muhammad V University.

Princeton Studies on the Near East

CHOICE

History, Geograp

Travel

Middle East &

North Africa

DT 194
L 3613

LAROUI, Abdallah. The history of the Maghrib: an interpretive essay, tr. from the French by Ralph Manheim. Princeton, 1977. 431p maps (Princeton studies on the Near East) bibl index 76-20679. 22.50 ISBN 0-691-03109-6. C.I.P.

An English translation of a book that was originally published in France in 1970. The subtitle, "an interpretive essay," is extremely important — anyone looking for an organized and comprehensive history of the Maghrib will be disappointed. Laroui's main thesis is that French and American historians have not given an accurate picture of the Maghrib and that he, as a Maghribi, can give an accurate account. He accuses non-Maghrib historians of seeing the early history of North Africa only as Roman history. This criticism ignores books such as Bernard Hoffman, *The structure of traditional Moroccan rural society* (1967), which gives a very comprehensive view of Berber tribal society in Morocco. Laroui does not even include Hoffman's book in the bibliography although it was published three years before the French edition of this book. Other significant books that do not fit Laroui's thesis are also ignored. While this book gives some historiographical information that the specialist on North Africa will find useful, it is a book that would confuse the undergraduate.

ABDALLAH LAROUI

The History of the Maghrib

An Interpretive Essay

Translated from the French by Ralph Manheim

Princeton University Press, *Princeton, New Jersey*

LIBRARY
MAR 6 1978
UNIVERSITY OF THE PACIFIC
341255

Copyright © 1977 by Princeton University Press
Translated from Abdallah Laroui, *L'Histoire du Maghreb: Un essai de synthèse*, Paris, Librairie François Maspero, 1970
Published by Princeton University Press, Princeton, New Jersey
In the United Kingdom: Princeton University Press, Guildford, Surrey

All Rights Reserved

Library of Congress Cataloging in Publication Data will be found on the last printed page of this book

This book has been composed in Linotype Baskerville

Printed in the United States of America
by Princeton University Press, Princeton, New Jersey

To the Memory of My Father

Contents

The History of the Maghrib

An Interpretive Essay

Introduction

Why this book?

A familiar theme in the histories written during the colonial period is that the Maghrib has been unfortunate: unfortunate in not having recognized the Roman conquest as a bringer of civilization, unfortunate in having been forced to accept Islam, unfortunate in having undergone the Hilālian invasion, and unfortunate in having served as a base for the Ottoman pirates. . . . But might there not be more reason to speak of a very different misfortune? That of always having had inept historians: geographers with brilliant ideas, functionaries with scientific pretensions, soldiers priding themselves on their culture, art historians who refuse to specialize, and, on a higher level, historians without linguistic training or linguists and archeologists without historical training. All these historians refer the reader back to each other and invoke each other's authority. The consequence is a conspiracy which puts the most adventurous hypotheses into circulation and ultimately imposes them as established truths.[1] True, the Maghribi historians have served us hardly better: torn between political leaders,

Full bibliographic data for references cited throughout the footnotes are given in the bibliography.

[1] A clear illustration of this strange habit among historians of deferring to each other is provided by Jérôme Carcopino, who in *Le Maroc antique* (p. 300) justifies his own adventurous hypotheses by referring to the "brilliant intuitions" of Gautier. This leads him to write that Mas'ūdī lived in the fourteenth century instead of the tenth (p. 138) and that the Khārijite revolt broke out in 657, i.e. before the conquest of the Maghrib (p. 299). Courtois, who in *Les Vandales et l'Afrique* (p. 364) rightly ridicules these "brilliant intuitions," nevertheless (p. 318) pays George Marçais the same kind of respect when he finds it convenient. In countless instances an author, in order to support a daring conclusion, refers the reader in a note to a work that is itself hypothetical in the highest degree: the prehistorians refer the reader to the medievalists, the authors of modern history to the historians of antiquity, and vice versa ad infinitum.

schoolteachers, and imitators of medieval historians, the reader can only console himself with the thought that, after all, the serene certainty of these men is no more unfounded than that of their adversaries, of whom as it happens they are more respectful than they should be.[2] By the very nature of the available documents, we shall doubtless have to put up with such aberrations for a long time to come, since to establish a scientific historiography much more is needed than abstract criticism.[3] Why then am I writing this book?

Essentially because my experience as a teacher at an American university has convinced me that merely disregarding the colonial literature on the history of the Maghrib does not prevent it from exerting a profound influence on scholars avid for knowledge but very poorly equipped to exercise their own judgment. Theses which even their authors present as partial or provisional are mistaken by hurried readers for total and definitive conclusions. American scholars, for the most part young, ignorant of Arabic or Berber, interested chiefly in the present, and seeing history as no more than a convenient introduction, required by the academic curriculum, to studies in sociology and political science, tend to overestimate everything written in French, and this is true of not just an isolated few.[4] Consequently it has seemed to me worthwhile to present the viewpoint of a Maghribi concerning the history of his own

[2] See Allāl al-Fāsi, *Al-Harakāt al-Istiqlālīya fī al-Maghrib al-ʿArabī*, and his polemic in the introductory chapter against Ernest Gautier, whom he calls "most learned" (*ʿallāma*).

[3] This criticism can be leveled against Sahli, in *Décoloniser l'histoire*, who seems to think that to decolonize history it suffices to demonstrate the political presuppositions of colonial history. This is undoubtedly a necessary step, but it is not sufficient. Though following in Sahli's footsteps, I differ from him insofar as I hope to provide not a radically decolonized history but only a "reading" of history. I feel certain that at the worst my reading will be no more ideological than that of the colonials.

[4] E.g. Nickerson, *A Short History of North Africa*; Gallagher, *The United States and North Africa*; Zartman, *Morocco: Problems of New Power*; and Barbour, ed., *A Survey of Northwest Africa*, which is a translation of French articles.

country, even if I were to provide few new findings and differed from the colonial historians only in my way of interpreting certain facts.

But this is not my only reason: even young Maghribis are too preoccupied with the present—economics, sociology, politics; they look on the study of the past as a largely unprofitable investment and leave this task to foreigners without stopping to ask whether the resulting picture of their past may not in the long run shape their present. Taken in conjunction with other factors, this helps us to understand why the effects of decolonization have been less felt in history, especially that of the pre-nineteenth-century past, than in other fields. Economists, city planners, geographers, even writers and artists have incorporated this essential phenomenon of the mid-twentieth century—the end of the colonial empire—into their vision and their methods. Only the historians of the Maghrib, particularly those dealing with premodern periods, have in large part escaped this influence.[5] To be convinced of this one has only to attend one of the scholarly congresses periodically held in the Mediterranean countries. The lack of interest on the part of Maghribis is assuredly more to blame than the intellectual laziness of foreign historians.

And yet our political experience, once the passions have died down, makes us more and more keenly aware of the burden which inherited structures and past generations have imposed on us. Each day we see more clearly the necessity of questioning the past concerning the two phenomena that haunt our political and intellectual life: our historical lag and its conscious compensation, that is, the revolution. In the following pages I shall criticize so many foreign historians so severely that I feel obliged to announce at the outset the questions I shall continually be asking of Maghri-

[5] The history of black Africa has suffered less in this respect, because, having been neglected during the colonial period, it has had fewer taboos and prejudices to overcome. It started with decolonization and so bore its mark from the outset.

bi history: what is the extent, the genesis, the anatomy of what at a certain moment became a "lag requiring to be made good"?[6]

Along with its necessarily pedagogic aspect as a critical review of what has already been written, this book will be a "reading" of the Maghribi past. Perhaps that will make it somewhat uneven; in places the tone will vary, but the central question will remain unchanged throughout. It will not so much retrace history as such, though this cannot be entirely avoided, as attempt to determine what the attitude of a Maghribi concerned with his future should be toward his past as a whole. In a sense this study will continue, in a precisely delimited sphere, to describe the connections between continuity and discontinuity that I have sketched elsewhere.[7] Accordingly, the dominant consideration will be: the Maghribs vis-à-vis their past.

It is very difficult to justify an individual undertaking where a joint effort is required. When a genuine institute of historical sciences is established in the Maghrib and scholars, combining an intimate knowledge of the country and local sources with a critical mind and enthusiasm for the new perspectives of a global history, succeed in giving the history of the Maghrib the new direction for which we are all hoping,[8] it will no longer be possible for a historian

[6] See Laroui, *La Crise des intellectuels arabes*, chapter 5; and "Marx and the Intellectual from the Third World," pp. 134ff.

[7] Laroui, *L'Idéologie arabe contemporaine*, pt. 2.

[8] Up until now this has been the role played by Julien in his *Histoire de l'Afrique du Nord*; no one writing on the subject can escape having to define his attitude toward this book. Its importance must be recognized, for Maghribis as well as non-Maghribis have long used it as a reference work. It is difficult, however, to pronounce judgment on Julien's work because of the need to distinguish between the original version of the book published in 1931, and the new edition published in 1951. It is true that no Maghribi, young or old, can fully appreciate the intellectual courage it required for this man, as militant and historian, to publish such a book at the time when the centenary of the capture of Algiers was being celebrated with pomp and circumstance. A cursory comparison with a book such as *Histoire et historiens de l'Algérie* (1931), which presents the official point of view, suffices to

to operate with the old individualistic methods. In the meantime everyone who is willing to take the risks is entitled to question the past with a view to forming a picture of a possible future.

The Idea of the Maghrib

Any idea that we can open the curtain on the beginnings of Maghribi history, that we can pretend to put ourselves in the place of the first Maghribis and witness the birth of their history by starting, as is usually done, with a description of the country, its inhabitants, society, etc., is illusory. When such an exposition is based on established findings it amounts to natural history, and when it is hypothetical, as is ordinarily the case, it is fraught with all the ideological prejudices of the colonial period.

---

show the enormous novelty of Julien's approach. True, this approach is in every way reformist; in the debate that he carries on throughout the book with the leading historians of the day—Gsell, Gautier and Albertini—he accepts their conclusions and merely tries to prove that these same conclusions necessitate a new vision of the future and a change in political attitude toward North Africa. But at the time the vast majority of nationalist leaders held the same views. Any judgment on the Julien of 1931 is necessarily a judgment on Bourguiba, Ferhat Abbas, and the Moroccan authors of the reform plan of 1934, and that is no small homage to a non-Maghribi. Be that as it may, history often plays tricks on historians, and though the political thinker in Julien evolved in pace with events, as an author he clung to his work; he was unwilling or unable to rid himself of certain judgments which were justified by the situation of the Maghrib before 1939, but which had become utterly anachronistic twenty years later. This was well understood by the editors of the second edition, who brought the facts up to date, but carefully preserved these same obsolete judgments. The two editions can rightly be regarded as two different works even though they bear the same title; our criticism of the work of Charles Courtois and Roger Le Tourneau, our absolute rejection of the ideology that inspires them do not seem to us to be incompatible with the great friendship we still feel toward Charles-André Julien, the liberal humanist and anticolonialist militant who to most of us was a master and a friend. Volume 3 of the second edition, to be published under his sole responsibility, will undoubtedly help us to form a definitive judgment on his work as a historian.

Indeed, difficulties arise from the very start. What shall we call the part of the world we are dealing with: North Africa, a term criticized by the geographers; Northwest Africa, a term that is geographically more correct but dictated by present political considerations; Barbary, a malleable term that has undergone varying fortunes since the beginning of modern times and has finally been abandoned because of its political or even racial implications; or finally the Maghrib, a vague Arabic term, which even restricted by the adjective Arab or Moslem cannot be used in Arabic, but is possible in a European language, because then it becomes a foreign word?[9] Some writers have come to the conclusion that this difficulty indicates the artificial character of the undertaking. Still, when we see the sometimes absurd aberrations of present Moroccan, Algerian and Tunisian historiography, such as raising rival claims to an emperor or author, or considering decisions involving territories beyond borders that have not yet been established as relevant to foreign policy,[10] we realize that local perspectives are no less arbitrary than the overall view.

The ideal, of course, would be to start with a history of historiography; to trace the genesis of the concept of the Maghrib and discover how it ultimately took on an objective definition. Such an historiographical history, to be sure, is no simpler an undertaking than the kind of history that claims to center on the historic act itself: it is sometimes impossible to follow in its meanders and implications; but at least it is honest enough not to conceal the fact that it is

9 The term Maghrib will be used throughout these pages, except where the context requires the geographical term North Africa; similarly, the adjective Maghribi will be given preference over all other adjectives except where the context makes it necessary to employ the adjective Berber, especially in the pre-Islamic period.

10 The most frequent examples are the Almohade Abd al-Mu'min, claimed by both the Algerians and the Moroccans, and the historian Ibn Khaldūn, claimed by the Algerians, the Moroccans and the Tunisians. Henri Terrasse considers Almoravide or Almohade policy in Andalusia as if it were a foreign policy defined by the canons of nineteenth-century diplomacy.

itself the prisoner of a certain history and that it has no claim to permanence or exclusivity.

I have decided, nevertheless, not to adhere strictly to this program, chiefly because it is premature, but my chosen plan of exposition is inspired by it and consequently imposes upon the entire book this conception of history as historiography. The term Maghrib, chosen for want of a better one, will be used not in a geographical, but rather in an essentially historical and dynamic sense: in each period a distinction will be made between a center and a periphery, between a history and a protohistory, as it were. In each period our vision will be confined to a city (Carthage, Kairouan, Fez), to a province (Ifrīqiya), to a monarchy or an empire (the Almohade Empire), leaving a large part of the geographical northwest in the realm of the unperceived and unknown. True, the historical field will gradually widen, until in the twentieth century it covers the entire region, but prior to this period all Maghribi history is by definition an incomplete history, if only from the standpoint of extension, not to speak of comprehension. This is regrettable, but we must resign ourselves to it; and we must also make it clear at every step that this is so, for often a part is taken for the whole, or a whole that is thus far unknown to us is compared with a part that can at least be known.[11] This cleavage between the historic field and its nonhistoric hinterland springs from the fact that history was not born in this part of the world, that "civilization" came to it from outside; such a cleavage can be said to exist only in a perspective that overestimates history. This overestimation, as the prehistorians and ethnologists call it, will not be questioned in the present book. Other Maghribis may do so some day, and then the total history of the Maghrib will be rewritten. In the meantime, I shall adhere to this history

[11] Gabriel Camps does this and we shall have occasion to criticize him a number of times in what follows. There is a history and protohistory of the Maghrib, but at first they merely indicated a stage in our knowledge and only later took on a structural significance. Neither of them should be overestimated.

oriented toward the Mediterranean East; in this light, it takes on the appearance, for long periods, of an object-history, the history of a country that is conquered, exploited, and "civilized"; and the opposition between history and protohistory will coincide with the opposition between the part of the Maghrib that has been conquered or merely subjected to control, and the uncontrolled part; neither part, however, will be overestimated at the expense of the other.

Thus we can distinguish a long period during which the Maghrib is a pure object and can be seen only through the eyes of its foreign conquerors. When narrated directly and uncritically, the history of this period ceases to be anything more than a history of foreigners on African soil; much as this history may tell us about one conqueror or another, remarkable as it may be for its wealth of documentation, literary qualities and dramatic moments, there can be no doubt that up until now it has enjoyed more privilege than it deserves.[12] However we may date the end of this period (I propose the middle of the eighth century A.D.), the Maghrib ceased to be an object when it recognized itself in an ideological, religious movement that gave rise to city-states, principalities, and finally empires. Up to the fourteenth century, the history of the Maghrib was, to all intents and purposes, the history of such ideological movements. Historiography in the restricted sense developed with the monarchies that owed nothing to religious schisms; it first dealt with the life of the capitals of these monarchies (Fez, Tlemcen, Tunis) and then dispersed into local history: the history of provinces, of secondary towns, of brotherhoods and families. At the same time, relations with a new and increasingly threatening world were reflected in ac-

[12] It is a subtle but serious distortion to attribute as much importance (according to the number of pages devoted to them) to the ancient history of the Maghrib as to the history of the Moslem period, as C.-A. Julien does, for whatever one may say to the contrary, the two periods do not carry the same weight.

counts of travels, of captivity, of embassies. In the nineteenth century, two mutually hostile historiographies, the one colonial, the other nationalist, came into being, and developed in opposite directions—if not in all their aspects at least in their view of reality. Colonial historiography treated its subject most adequately in its beginnings, while that of the nationalists acquired its content at the end of the process.

It will be necessary, of course, to show, period by period, discontinuity and continuity, and above all the identity we have postulated between the evolution of historiography and the historical development; it will also be necessary to make sure that the periods we distinguish are indeed periods, in the sense that they enable us to differentiate successive levels of economic and social development, of political organization, culture and psychology; these points will be discussed in our partial conclusions. In any event, such an exposition will enable us to avoid certain pitfalls.

The first of these is to juxtapose epochs in accordance with a geographical, dynastic or racial criterion, for example, to set up a sequence such as Punic, Roman, Vandal, Byzantine, Arab, Turkish, and French—the objections to which are obvious. The second is more subtle, and indeed most writers and their readers have fallen into it; it might be called the ternary myth. Originating in the universities, it serves ideological purposes. Its academic source is to be found in the sacrosanct classification of antiquity, the Middle Ages, and modern times, the first ending with the barbarian invasions and the second with the Renaissance. This scheme is applied to the Maghrib with the help of manipulations, some relatively harmless and others more serious: the Arab conquest of the seventh century replaces the fifth-century barbarian invasions; the Turkish conquest at the beginning of the sixteenth century or even the nineteenth-century French invasion takes the place of the Renaissance. Of course this methodology conceals a political bias: the Maghrib is represented as an area of conflict between two entities, always present and never defined: the occident and the orient, of which Christianity and Islam and the Latin and Arabic languages are merely reflections.[13] The Maghribis also accept this ternary classification, but confine it to the period of Islamization and reverse it: thus they distinguish a long classical period extending from the seventh to the fourteenth century and subdivided into periods of preparation, apogee and decline, followed by a long period of eclipse marked by defeats in Spain, foreign encroachments on the coasts, dislocation of the states and cultural lethargy; these last are followed in turn, and redeemed as it were, by the cultural renewal at the end of the nineteenth century, which diverts attention from the burdensome presence of the colonizers. These two chronological systems, it is true, bring out real discontinuities of rhythm, which will be analyzed, but to represent them as in any way self-explanatory would be to denature them. Basically, every ternary system retains some trace of its mystical implications, and these must be avoided at any cost.

While awaiting the development of an economic and social historiography, it seems worth our while to experiment with this periodization of political historiography as a means of classifying history itself, and to expose it, if only in order to rid ourselves of this mythology of flowering and decadence, which only too often degenerate into fall and redemption. It goes without saying that there can be no question of confusing the logic of exposition with the logic of the facts themselves.

13 This idea will be refuted several times in the following pages. Allāl al-Fāsī takes it up, but with a variation in opposing the Latin spirit to the Greek, which was essentially the same as that of the great civilizations of the Mediterranean orient. This point is not sufficiently brought out by Von Grunebaum in his analysis of al-Fāsī (*Modern Islam*, pp. 328-330). Berque also subscribes to the same myth in *French North Africa* when he speaks of "eternal dreams of reconquest" and compares the Maghrib to an "Andalusia twice lost" (p. 395).

PART I
The Maghrib under Domination

1. The Search for Origins

It is well known that the knowledge of history develops in the opposite direction from the course of events; it is the period of Maghribi history most remote from us, the period preceding the first Phoenician establishments at the end of the second millennium B.C., that was last to enter the field of empirical study. It has also been the uncontested monopoly of colonial historians. The Maghribis, ancient or modern, have very little to say on the subject; this is to be expected, since the science of the origins of man is less than a century old.

For a long time the study of this epoch was ancillary to that of classical antiquity; up to the time of the First World War, when Stéphane Gsell became recognized as the foremost authority on the pre-Islamic history of the Maghrib, the methods developed by the students of prehistory and their findings in respect of the Maghrib served only as a means of verifying literary documents. After 1930 the study of Maghribi prehistory advanced by leaps and bounds, and Lionel Balout succeeded to the position of preeminence formerly occupied by Gsell. Nevertheless, though there was a change of perspective, though archeological findings began to supersede the authority of literary documents, the two currents remained united by so many ideological ties that it is not possible to speak of a true renewal. A number of preconceived ideas, which are responsible for many distortions of Maghribi history and which we shall have frequent occasion to criticize in what follows, owe their survival to the specialists of that period; this again is perfectly normal, because archeology is a relative newcomer to the sciences.

Students of Maghribi prehistory tend to ask the following questions: Has there been a change in the climate of North Africa? Where did the Berbers come from? What is the origin of their language? What is the origin of their culture?

Each of these questions and the answers to it respond both to scientific and to ideological considerations, and it is both easier and safer to cite ideological than scientific grounds in attempting to account for the theories put forward.

At the very outset Gsell makes his ideological motivation clear: "We must try to determine whether the chief cause of this prosperity [of the Roman period] was a climate more favorable to agriculture than the present-day climate, or whether it was due primarily to the intelligence and energy of men; whether we should confine ourselves to regretting a past that will never return or whether on the contrary we should look to it for lessons that may be profitable at the present time."[1] This question remained in vogue until the eve of the Second World War, and by and large the answer given was that which Gsell, very circumspectly to be sure, had formulated, namely, that there had been very little change—an answer that fell in with ideological prejudice. The increasingly frequent discoveries, beginning in the thirties, of cave paintings which tend to prove that at least certain parts of the Sahara were relatively green in a not too distant epoch (thousands rather than tens of thousands of years ago) obliged certain students, despite radical disagreement as to how the Saharan sgraffiti and paintings should be interpreted, to recognize that there has been a decrease in humidity.[2] But this proof is far from having convinced everyone, and the specialists are no longer interested in the question; only amateurs continue to busy themselves with it. It should be noted, however, that these two successive attitudes reflect two more basic attitudes that we shall encounter in other connections, namely, an optimism concerning the destiny of North Africa, followed by a profound pessimism.

The same development can be observed with regard to

1 Gsell, *Histoire ancienne de l'Afrique du Nord,* vol. 1, p. 40.

2 See Gautier, *Le Sahara,* pp. 59-69; Lhote, *A la découverte des fresques du Tassili*; Briggs, *Tribes of the Sahara,* pp. 38-39; Capot-Rey, *Le Sahara français.*

the origin of the Berbers.[3] In the colonial period there were two conflicting schools: one linked them with the populations of Europe, while the other sought their origin in the Middle East. Despite a considerable margin of uncertainty, anthropological studies and archeological finds now tend to prove both the antiquity and diversity of the Maghribi population. Today no one believes in recent arrivals of negroid and "blond" elements, or holds that the anthropological diversity described at the beginning of the century reflects successive waves of invaders in the none too remote past. The idea that seems to be gaining general acceptance[4] is that the bulk of the population consists of a mixture, stabilized in the neolithic era, of an old paleo-Mediterranean stock with two Mediterranean groups which both came from western Asia but entered the Maghrib by two different routes, the one via the northeast, where it tended to grow whiter, and the other via the southeast, after a long detour through East Africa, where it crossbred with blacks. Whatever the scientific value of this theory may be, we observe that it no longer takes a positive stand in favor of a western or eastern origin of the entire population; it recognizes the present diversity and projects it on prehistoric times.

Research into the language and culture of the ancient Berbers, however, has argued an eastern origin. As far as the language is concerned, only dilettantes continue to venture hypotheses; the specialists, especially those who know Berber, take refuge in silence. They believe that there is at present no possibility of elucidating either the origin or extension of Libyan, or even the existence of other languages in the prehistoric Maghrib. Libyan inscriptions, even when bilingual, have not been deciphered to any significant degree, and this has prevented scholars from determining

3 The question is discussed in the article "Berbères" in the *Encyclopédie de l'Islam*, 2nd ed., pp. 1208ff. and in Camps, *Monuments et rites funéraires protohistoriques*, pp. 14ff.

4 Summed up by Julien in *Histoire de l'Afrique blanche*, pp. 17-18. Details in Briggs, *The Stone Age Races of Northwest Africa*, pp. 72-75.

the origin of the Libyan alphabet. Nevertheless, students of general linguistics tend to confine the area of research to the proto-Semitic, especially to southern Arabic. This thesis, if accepted, would tend to show that the section of the population coming from East Africa is dominant; some writers believe, however, that toponomy argues in favor of the Mediterranean group which entered from the northeast. Thus a balance seems to have been restored.[5]

As for Berber culture, the habit of attributing all the discoveries that the prehistorians amalgamate under the head of neolithic revolutions to the Phoenicians was gradually abandoned. Gsell wrote: "The natives of this region did not wait for the arrival of Syrian(!) navigators before breeding cattle and engaging in agriculture."[6] But he added —and this is the question that the prehistorians have continually raised: "Was some of their progress due to their own intelligence and initiative? We do not know." These neolithic and aeneolithic acquisitions are now assigned to the Maghribi past, but the credit continues in large part to be given to foreigners: neighbors, merchants from foreign countries, invaders or others. It is recognized more and more that a neolithic civilization developed locally, but one so poor, it is added, as hardly to deserve the name; the decisive changes were introduced by people who came from Asia by way of Upper Egypt.[7] Despite the revision of ideas on points of detail made necessary by archeological discoveries, the overall perspective remains unchanged. Gsell wrote that wheat, certain varieties of trees, and the horse had been introduced from the east at a relatively recent date (the

[5] Camps, *Monuments et rites*, p. 31, n. 2, where he cites the authority of Gsell, after having observed that volume 1 of the latter's *Histoire* was so outmoded that no one read it any more.

[6] Gsell, *Histoire*, p. 239. Note the tendency to apply modern nomenclature to the political geography of the ancient world.

[7] The famous Caspian man as opposed to the Ibero-Maurusian (Oranian) man. There is still a tendency to suppose that the two coexisted up to the first millennium B.C., in other words that the neolithic did not extend to the entire Maghrib. See Camps's critique of this thesis in "Massinissa ou les débuts de l'histoire," p. 164.

horse in the course of the second millennium B.C.); he also wrote, but with many qualifications, that the neolithic era continued up to the beginning of the first millennium and that the Maghrib passed directly into the age of iron, which was introduced by the Phoenicians, without having known a copper or bronze age[8]—a notion that became a commonplace, transmitted from book to book. The discovery of copper and tin deposits, which refuted one of Gsell's arguments, the knowledge that chariots, which could hardly have been built without metal, existed well before the arrival of the Phoenicians, and finally the discovery of cave paintings in the High Atlas,[9] dealt a severe blow to the theory that the copper and bronze age was skipped. It has gradually come to be recognized that while the great neolithic discoveries were introduced from the southeast, the discoveries of the age of metals were introduced from the west, essentially under Iberian influence. Thus the historic-leap theory has been replaced by the notion of colonial action: copper and bronze objects were introduced from outside, but not metallurgy itself. The great controversy between those who attributed a western and those who attributed an eastern origin to the Berbers and their culture, the former trend predominating among the amateurs and the latter among the specialists, has given way, in the course of unceasing new discoveries, to the recognition of a diversity of origins and of the essentially fragmented and passive character of the Maghribi past.[10]

8 This idea is taken over without discussion in Julien, *Histoire de l'Afrique du Nord*, 2nd ed., vol. 1, p. 44: "The absence of an aeneolithic period is indeed one of the characteristic features of North African prehistory"; and in a more guarded form in Julien, *Histoire de l'Afrique blanche*, p. 15: "While the west imported copper and bronze from the Iberian peninsula, the east had[!] to acquire iron directly from the Phoenicians, without having known bronze." See also Furon, *Manuel de préhistoire générale*, pp. 348f. and 460.

9 Cf. Camps, "Les Traces d'un âge du bronze en Afrique du Nord," pp. 31-55, interpreting the discoveries of Malhomme.

10 This is the general idea propounded by Camps in his work, as follows: "The Maghrib has been fragmented since the neolithic, sub-

The study of Maghribi antiquities was developed by the colonial administration; governors and residents general took a personal interest in it, and during the greater part of the colonial period the Department of Fine Arts was attached to the Department of the Interior.[11] Thus it is only natural that this study should have been directly influenced by the general ideology of colonialism. Propagated by military men, functionaries and certain publicists, the thesis that links the Berbers to Europe sprang directly from an assimilationist, fundamentally racist policy typical of men profoundly attached to the ideas of the nineteenth century;[12] they were all convinced that assimilation could hope to succeed only if the Berbers shared a common origin, however remote, with the Europeans, that otherwise it was condemned to failure. It was only when this policy began to lose its appeal, toward 1930 to be exact, that the thesis of an Asian origin began to acquire influence, thanks to scholars who were at last able to harmonize their findings with the prevailing pessimism.[13] It is no accident that the first official scientific expression of this thesis is contained in a report submitted to the governor general of Algeria in 1949.

---

ject from the second millennium on to the colonial action of various civilizations, Iberian in the west, south-Italic in the east and Saharan-Nilotic in the south, the central Maghrib being a transitional region without distinct characteristics of its own."

11 To be convinced of this one need only leaf through the acts of the learned societies of North Africa or the summaries of journals such as *Revue africaine* (Algiers), *Revue tunisienne* (Tunis), *Hespéris* (Rabat), etc.

12 Faidherbe declared as early as 1867: "The Berbers are related to the ancient population of western Europe" (quoted by Camps in *Monuments et rites*, p. 29). Brémond's thesis is expressed in the title of his book, *Berbères et Arabes, la Berbérie est un pays européen.*

13 This observation applies particularly to Gautier. Behind his condemnation of the Maghribis there lies a profound pessimism as to the future of French colonization. He was a Cartierist before the fact. (Raymond Cartier of *Paris-Match* was the first right-wing public figure in France to argue that the colonies should be abandoned because they were too expensive and could not in the long run be defended. "Cartierism" stands for anticolonialism on economic rather than ethical grounds.)

This report, based on systematic anthropological and archeological investigations, dashed all hopes of definitively integrating the Maghrib with Europe.[14] Lionel Balout wrote in 1948 and repeated in 1955: "Thus it was in the remote prehistorical past that the countries of the Maghrib, rooted in Africa and the orient, but capable of an opening toward Europe, took on this character which prevented them from the outset from building a civilization of their own, whose center they would have been, or from integrating themselves definitively with the cultures that came to them from three different directions and successively colonized them."[15] Camps expresses the same idea in 1960: "Neither completely African nor entirely Mediterranean [North Africa] has oscillated down through the centuries in search of its destiny."[16]

The Maghribis have offered no opposition to these conclusions, which seem to be protected against all criticism by the armor of science and technology.[17] Actually the Maghribis have no scientific arguments to offer; the classical Arabic documents are useless in this respect, and the modern universities seem to take no interest in a period the study of which is regarded as too closely identified with the cultural policy of the colonial period. Only the Tunisians have moved at all in this direction, and even their efforts would seem to have been motivated more by a desire to encourage

[14] Report by Dr. Vallois, later incorporated in the revised edition of Boule, *Les Hommes fossiles* and in Balout, *Préhistoire de l'Afrique du Nord*.

[15] Balout, "Quelques problèmes nord-africains de chronologie préhistorique," pp. 255 and 262.

[16] Camps, *Monuments et rites*, p. 571.

[17] Only the authors of schoolbooks—because they are obliged to—take an interest in this period. Their accounts are often based on theories that the colonial scholars themselves have discarded. See al-Mashrafī, *Ifrīqiyā al-Shamālīya fī al-ʿAṣr al-Qadīm*; Ibn ʿAbd Allāh, *Tārīkh al-Ḥaḍāra al Maghribīya*, vol. 1, who accepts and stresses the theory of the oriental origin of the Berbers because it falls in with his preferences; Ayache, *Histoire ancienne de l'Afrique du Nord*, who tries to put forward a new point of view, but not for the prehistoric period (pp. 9-15).

tourist trade than by scientific curiosity. With reference, then, to this period, it is not possible to present a nationalist ideology in opposition to the colonial ideology, as we shall be able to do in connection with subsequent periods. Unfortunately, such a lack of interest is fraught with consequences, for it is in the study of this area of the Maghribi past that all the distortions originate, and in all likelihood it is there as well that the most reliable techniques of historical investigation are forged: archeology, linguistics, and anthropology. Thus it would be disastrous for Maghribi culture if we were to confine ourselves, as we have done hitherto, to written documents, conducive as they are to unconscious errors and intellectual laziness, not to say dishonesty.

Nevertheless, although the spirit of the University of Algiers, the center of French colonial ideology, is bound to dominate interpretation of the prehistoric period for some time to come, its ideological bias is so obvious that one need not be a specialist in prehistory to perceive it. Any candid reader can easily detect the discrepancy between the research findings and the adventurous conclusions drawn from them, and is entitled to ask the investigators of Maghribi prehistory to observe at least as much caution as they themselves (and others) practice in dealing with other parts of the world. Yet these same investigators are the first to point out the difficulties in exploiting their three principal sources: the Libyan inscriptions, which thus far have proved indecipherable and would seem to have little information to offer; the Greco-Latin literary sources, which are hard to interpret because of their predilection for allusion, paradox and exoticism; and finally the archeological sites, which continue to suffer from the devastation brought about by numerous amateurs, so much so that it seems questionable whether it will ever be possible to rectify the errors—some of them made in good faith—of the colonial period. And this is not the end of the difficulties: another is the lack of coordination, often criticized in the past, between classical and Arabic scholars, or among prehistorians (mainly archeologists), protohistorians (mainly ethnologists and linguists), and specialists in antiquity (mainly philologists). In their syntheses or interpretations of their findings, one group, with a view to gaining time, affects to accept as definitive conclusions what another puts forward as mere hypotheses. It was thanks to such canonization by scholars of each other's often partial and contestable findings that colonial ideology was able to impose itself at every level of historical research. To be convinced of this, one has only to read Gsell and note how cautiously and hesitantly he put forward judgments which were subsequently accepted far and wide as definitive scientific truths. And when we think of the medievalists who are neither archeologists nor classical scholars and of the present-day writers on the Maghrib (Americans in particular) who are neither Arabic scholars nor classical scholars nor historians, and whose sole access to their subject is through the sweeping generalizations of the popularizers, we see what ravages can result from the slightest carelessness in the formulation of an opinion.[18]

It cannot be denied that the prehistorians are incautious. They ought at least to consider the consequences of their extrapolations. The gravest of these tends to place Maghrib history as a whole in a false perspective. Camps may be taken as a representative of this trend; for him prehistory, protohistory and history are not simple chronological divisions or stages in our consciousness, but structural divisions encompassing geographical, anthropological, socio-cultural, and of course methodological aspects. To his mind the Sahara and its fringe come under the head of prehistory and can be studied only with the help of archeology and ethnography; protohistory, which extends from the neolithic to urban civilization, still applies to the majority of the rural

[18] E.g. Gallagher, in *The United States and North Africa*, characterizes the Maghrib as "no idea producing area" and gives it credit for only six thinkers of any importance, three in antiquity, three in the Islamic period—no doubt because he himself feels rich in the possession of all Greek, Latin and modern European culture, which he appropriates without the slightest difficulty.

population, the study of which must therefore be based on cultural anthropology; while history proper ceases to be anything more than the study of intruding urban civilizations from the Phoenicians to the French.[19] This perspective is the expression in terms of technology of a current thesis regarding the persistence of the neolithic, which in terms of social organization is reflected in the notion of a "tribal history," which we shall discuss below. The grossly ideological character of this view is so obvious that a critique of it would be futile, especially if, as in my case, one cannot base one's critique on irrefutable archeological proof. This much may be said, however: if the conclusions implied by its authors are to be drawn from this thesis, it will be necessary to prove that the situation of the Maghrib is unique, shared by no other region in the whole world—a difficult undertaking, to say the least—and above all to prove that a cultural lag can never be made good.[20] Camps concludes: "An industrial revolution similar to that which transformed Europe in the nineteenth century is now in process in Algeria. The Chawia shepherd playing a few notes on his reed flute, the Kabyle potter decorating his vases with age-old motifs possess the serene certainty that they will endure forever; they do not suspect that they belong to an archaic world on its way to extinction."[21] Very well; but if this is true of the industrial revolution, why would it not be still more true of the neolithic revolution, and, above all, how in a world that two revolutions will soon have changed completely, can we hope to rectify the mistakes of past in-

19 As usual, this ideological deformation has an objective foundation. See the discussion of the tripartite Maghrib, below.

20 G. Bailloud writes in Leroi-Gourhan, *La Préhistoire,* after having cited several examples of a lag in one field being easily compensated in others: "These examples show how closely imbricated the neolithic, the chalcolithic and the bronze ages become as soon as our vision rises above local limitations" (p. 335). It would seem as though the students of Maghribi prehistory had little desire to rise above local limitations.

21 Camps, *Monuments et rites,* p. 571. He takes a different point of view in "Massinissa ou les débuts de l'histoire" (p. 164).

vestigation by ethnological methods? The remark about the Chawia shepherd contradicts all the studies on prehistory and protohistory on the basis of which Camps and his school are trying to justify a view of Maghribi history which is nothing more than the old colonial ideology adjusted to the tastes of the day.[22] This criticism, to be sure, is purely formal; it is directed against unwarranted conclusions, not against the research findings as such; in the course of its progress, science itself, as it has often done in the past, will explode such brilliant and irresponsible theories.

The second consequence of the extrapolations of which I have been speaking is to impose a linear and mechanistic view of all Maghrib history, thus making it more difficult to adopt the more fertile perspective of an uneven progress, which we shall have occasion to put forward several times in the discussion that follows. Even if the Maghrib had gone through a long neolithic period, even if it had bypassed the copper and bronze age (a thesis now repudiated by most specialists), the consequences would not necessarily have been what the prehistorians, faithful to the evolutionist ideas of the nineteenth century, believe; cultural lag can always be compensated, its negative aspects do not necessarily predominate on every level of social life. Just this has been brought out by Germaine Tillion, an ethnologist, in

[22] The dilemma that certain writers wish to impose on us is the following: either you deal with history of the foreign invaders, or you confine yourself to prehistory and protohistory. It is possible to reject both propositions, and that is what I shall attempt to do. It cannot be denied that civilization came in large part from outside the Maghrib, a fact that is not peculiar to this region. The essential point is that the Maghrib accepted certain elements and rejected others. The distinction between protohistory and history can be justified as reflecting the stages in the development of our historical knowledge and providing a general chronological framework, but not as a structural schema, which would have no other foundation than a method arbitrarily judged to be the only one possible. The actual motive concealed behind this circular reasoning is a rejection of the particular form of civilization adopted in the Maghrib. Those who deny the Maghrib a history wish to eliminate this form of civilization because they regret that a different form did not prevail.

a book which unfortunately did not receive the attention it deserves, because it seemed to deal with too specialized a subject.[23] Actually, it provides a new interpretation—one that takes contradictory aspects of all evolution into account—of archaic Maghribi society, precisely that society which others would like to relegate to an undefined protohistory.

[23] *Le harem et les cousins*. An acute and highly original work and an important contribution to historical understanding. But because it runs counter to accepted ideas and because its author, thanks to the internal logic of her search for reality, rediscovered the most fruitful aspects of the dialectic of history, it seems to have been regarded as a mere sketch. But if all non-Maghribi historians rejected the simplist linear development as Tillion does, we should not have to waste our time criticizing so many time-worn prejudices.

2. Colonizer Follows Colonizer

I

In dealing with the long period that begins at the end of the second millennium B.C. and ends in the seventeenth century of the Christian era, in the course of which Phoenicians, Greeks, Romans and Vandals entered the Maghrib, established settlements, and in some cases made their way far into the interior, one essential fact must be made clear at the outset: this period is known to us only through Greco-Latin literature. The people of the Maghrib are described by geographers and travelers, sometimes in relating historical events that have nothing to do with them. But peoples such as the Carthaginians and Vandals are also described from outside, so that what knowledge we gain of the Berbers is doubly indirect: seen through the eyes of the Carthaginians who are in turn seen through the eyes of Romans, they become mere supernumeraries in a history enacted on their soil. Though it is idle to deplore a state of affairs so frequent in the annals of mankind, we must nevertheless call attention to its consequences. The modern historian is first of all a reader, and as a reader he is always pressed for time. It is only at the cost of superhuman effort that he can rid himself of a general view acquired, sometimes in spite of himself, from the necessity of investigating one people's past through that of another. Sometimes without knowing it he relates the history of the second people in the belief that he is speaking of the first, especially if he is moved by the fascination of a grandiose epic. In our case such a historian may give the impression that the Maghribi is no more than a secondary character whose intermittent appearances merely express the perils of a remote and thankless land. In short, almost all the books devoted to this period speak exclusively of Rome.[1]

[1] On the basis of an optical illusion, these books make the Roman presence last a minimum of ten centuries; which leaves the reader amazed at the rapidity with which its imprint was effaced.

But, it may be argued, literature is not our only source; what of the more and more numerous epigraphic, archeological and numismatic finds? Once we look beyond the summaries of the popularizers, we soon discover that those nonliterary documents that present no difficulty as to dating and interpretation add nothing to the literary sources, while those that might enrich our knowledge are hard to date and interpret.[2] Roman ruins of a civil or military character, coins, funerary steles and monuments commemorating victories throw light on Roman cities, hence on the political, military and social organization of the Romans. As for the so-called Berber ruins, it has not been possible to date even the funerary monuments, to which prolonged study has been devoted, with certainty.[3] And since one lends only to the rich, all finds are automatically accredited to the Romans; whenever a building, a tomb, an aqueduct, a coin is discovered, the guiding principle is to look for a Roman origin or imprint, and often, with the help of a forced interpretation, one is found. From time to time, to be sure, there is a reaction to this tendency, but will it ever be possible to catch up with the Romanizers? In spite of everything, the classic literary tradition remains preponderant, and the reader must be warned against the almost unconscious distortions to which it gives rise.[4]

Need it surprise us under these circumstances that our

[2] See the well-founded criticism of Camps in "Massinissa," chap. 1, and Courtois, *Les Vandales et l'Afrique*, pp. 334ff. and n. 2. It is unfortunate that the prestige of Carcopino and the authority still enjoyed by Gsell prevented Camps and Courtois from including them in their criticism.

[3] The following is one example among many of the type of reasoning used in support of certain judgments that no one dares to question. Concerning a page in Gsell's *Atlas archéologique de l'Algérie*, Carcopino writes ". . . Berber ruins which we do not dare to date but which are so numerous that we are justified in connecting them with the general destruction caused by the tidal wave of Arab invasions that descended on the Maghrib between the seventh and ninth centuries" (*Le Maroc antique*, p. 291).

[4] With minor differences the same is true of early Arab historiography, discussed below.

present knowledge—which was obtained very quickly, for recent research has accomplished little more than to clarify conclusions arrived at early in the century—relates almost exclusively to Greco-Roman history: wars and revolts, conquests, administration, and religious development. Let us consider this secure knowledge under three heads: military history, Roman administration, church history.

Military History

In this perspective, North Africa enters the field of history in the sixth century B.C. in the course of the Greco-Phoenician struggle for domination of the Mediterranean. With the elimination of Phoenicia as an independent power, Carthage, the new Tyrian city, took up the Greek challenge, this time in the western Mediterranean. The Greeks of Sicily established their supremacy on the northern, the Carthaginians on the southern shore. It was in connection with the continual struggles between them, in particular when the expedition led by Agathocles (310 B.C.) carried the war to Africa, that we obtain our first direct accounts of the native populations. The Sicilians were followed by the Romans; first Regulus (236 B.C.), then the two Scipios followed the example of Agathocles. While some light was thrown on the Libyans living in the Carthaginian territory by the campaign of Agathocles, Scipio's campaigns during the Second Punic War brought knowledge of the Carthaginians' western neighbors, the Numidians,[5] who were divided into two main groups, the Massyles and the Massaesyles under their kings Massinissa and Syphax. The long history of Massinissa is the story of the shadow cast by Rome, though it is still matter for discussion whether he served the Romans or made use of them. In any case, the whole story was enacted under the eyes of the Roman senate, which was in a position to stop any move it regarded as dangerous on the

[5] The meanings and evolution of the terms "Libyan," "Numidian," "Moor," etc., will be discussed below.

part of the Carthaginians or Numidians. The exploits of Massinissa as recorded by Polybius even seem to belong to the family legend of the Scipios.[6] After the fall and destruction of Carthage (146 B.C.), the history of North Africa as we know it is an integral part of the long death agony of the Roman republic. Massinissa's successor was chosen by the senate and this choice provoked an uprising. The history of the long war waged by the Roman armies is as much the history of the inner contradictions of the Roman republic, exacerbated by a long and difficult war, as of Jugurtha's revolt.[7] Jugurtha's action may or may not have been a conscious effort to unite all the Berbers in a patriotic war; Sallust's account offers no proof either way, since to him Jugurtha was a mere pretext for airing a moral judgment on Rome and its leaders.[8] Again in the course of the last century B.C. an intermittent light was thrown on the kingdoms of Bocchus in the west and of Hiempsal II in the east in connection with the Roman civil wars. The Berber princes let themselves be drawn into alliances with the leaders of the warring Roman factions. These factional struggles led to the suicide of Juba I, the successor of Hiempsal II, in 46 B.C., to the enlargement of the Roman province, and to the ruin of Bogud, heir to Bocchus I, king of western Mauretania. After the death of Bocchus II, the second heir, the whole of North Africa was administered by Roman officials (33-25 B.C.). The last two Massyle kings, Juba II (25 B.C.-23 A.D.) and Ptolemy (23-40 A.D.) were clients of the Caesars far more than autonomous princes.

For two centuries after the annexation of Ptolemy's Mauretania, the history of the Maghrib is indistinguishable

6 Though the conclusions drawn by Camps in "Massinissa" are questionable, his criticism of the use made of the Numidian king's legend is fully justified.

7 An instance of a modern historian taking over an ancient historian's perspective is provided by the account of the Jugurthine War in C.-A. Julien, *Histoire de l'Afrique du Nord*, 2nd ed., vol. 1.

8 Obviously Sallust's failure to mention any such motivation (Jugurtha's Berber nationalism) is no proof that it did not exist.

from the history—marked by continual revolts—of the Roman army in Africa. The series begins with the revolt of Tacfarinas in Numidia in 17 A.D., even before the annexation of Mauretania, which however took part in the revolt.[9] What has been called the peaceful period of Roman domination is that in which the revolts were limited to the west and affected Numidia only intermittently. It should be borne in mind that the historians mention only those revolts that were regarded as abnormally severe; in other words, revolts were a permanent feature of the period. After 180, northern Morocco broke away from the empire, and the Berbers of that region made incursions into Baetica. The revolts became increasingly frequent and in 235 the eastern part of the province, taking advantage of the crisis then shaking the empire, joined in. From 235 to 285 the anarchy was general, even in the interior of the territory under Roman control. Recognizing the fact, Diocletian evacuated the western half of North Africa, but the same causes continued to produce the same effects in the eastern region. When we read that in 372 Firmus led an uprising in Mauretania, the term at that time denoted eastern Algeria. Firmus was defeated after four years of struggle. Twenty years later the revolt was resumed by his brother Gildo, who had served the Romans from 385 to 393 as commander of the African army. Revolting in 396, he carried out a genuine agrarian reform at the expense of the Roman landowners, foremost of whom was the emperor. The story of this uninterrupted succession of revolts can be told from the point of view of the army, in which case it becomes a record of its glorious victories, or else from that of the rebels, in which case it becomes a saga of fierce resistance culminating in the slow reconquest of a lost homeland. We must not forget, however, that we possess only the reports of the generals, who

[9] In reading the account of this revolt in Tacitus one often has the impression that he is simply plagiarizing Sallust. We are hardly justified in inferring real permanence from the traditionalism of the historians. The same observation is valid for the historians of the Moslem period.

offer a rational view of their own actions and represent those of their adversaries as anarchic. We never know the aims and motives of the rebels. Consequently we cannot accept the conclusions of the Roman generals and their heirs, who represent the history of all those years as a struggle between good and evil, ending with the deplorable but inevitable victory of barbarism over civilization, of instinct over reason. Yet we find such judgments in the work of modern historians who seem to do justice to the Berbers' desire for independence but actually celebrate the glory of Rome!

Roman Administration

The study of the Roman military organization in Africa throws light both on the policy which made the army an instrument of Romanization and on the position the African provinces held in the general economy of the empire. Thanks to the discipline it inculcates, the language it imposes, and the privileges it confers, every army is a means of integration with the dominant class. A Berber who enlisted in the army obtained citizenship after twenty-five years of service; as a veteran he was then entitled to settle in a colony and exploit a piece of land granted him by the state. Thus the army became an instrument of colonization as well as Romanization. After the organization of the provinces was consolidated under the Flavians,[10] the army, in the course of the second century, enlarged the territory under Roman control, especially to the southeast, penetrating deep into the Sahara, which was less arid than it is today. Modern students are coming more and more to regard the *limes* not as a mere defensive measure, but as a system of colonial expansion and stabilization; its chief purpose may well have been to prepare soldiers for their future life as colonists faithful to the designs of Rome, for as has long been

[10] See Marcel Leglay, "Les Flaviens et l'Afrique," pp. 201-246, an example of how little progress has been made since the last century.

known, Africa interested the Romans only as a producer of wheat. In the first century it was the only crop encouraged, since Italy was still capable of growing the other foodstuffs it needed; not until the second century do we find, hand in hand with the extension of the growing of wheat to the high plateaus in the south, a return to the intensive cultivation of olive trees and vineyards. Barley was needed as fodder for horses and wood for heating the baths; undoubtedly both the forests and the soil suffered in consequence. Whatever may be the value of the indirect methods used to evaluate the wheat production of Africa and the share of the crop appropriated by Rome,[11] we can be certain that the exploitation was severe, leaving the African population barely enough to subsist on. This exploitation was not diminished by the weakening of the imperial power in the third century, for the wheat of Numidia and the Preconsular Province had then become more necessary than ever to Rome, for the Egyptian production (which seems to have been about half as great as that of North Africa) had been diverted to Constantinople, the capital of the eastern empire, and Sicily was in a state of utter disintegration. It was only during the periods when communications with Italy were cut, as they were during Gildo's revolt at the end of the fourth century and especially under the Vandals, that the Africans enjoyed a respite.

The legislation concerning land tenure and taxation provides an idea of the social situation and above all of the extraordinary concentration of landed property in the hands of the emperor and the great patrician families.[12] All the wars—against Carthage, against Jugurtha, Juba I, Tacfarinias, Aedemon, etc.—resulted in, and all the revolts of the Numidians and Mauretanians were caused by, the confiscation of enormous tracts of land for the benefit of Ro-

[11] See the figures given by Charles-Picard, "Néron et le blé d'Afrique," pp. 163-173, which differ from those of Saumagne in "Un Tarif fiscal du IVe siècle."

[12] Van Nostrand, *The Imperial Domains of Africa Proconsularis*; Charles-Picard, "Néron et le blé d'Afrique."

mans, most of whom were foreign to Africa or who, if they were born there, had taken advantage of their first promotion to leave it. In the parts of the country that had long been Romanized, these lands were administered by agents and worked by serfs or day laborers; in the newly acquired regions, freemen, probably the former owners, were allowed to settle on the public lands, for which privilege they paid rent. The free and semifree smallholders paid ordinary and extraordinary taxes in addition to rent, and in the course of the fourth century the big landowners, having inherited a large part of the powers of an enfeebled state, shifted their share of the *annona* (a tax paid in kind for shipment to Rome) to the backs of the smallholders. Not only, as we have seen, did the bulk of the produce go to Rome; Romans were also the beneficiaries of the distribution system, for all trade in wheat, oil, pottery, etc., was controlled by *negociatores*, forming corporations whose principles of organization are known to us.

The study of Roman legislation, even of laws applying to the empire as a whole, gives some idea of the economic and social life of North Africa, or at least of the part which had been conquered at an early date; we must guard, however, against the mistake, often made by historians of Rome none too familiar with the laws of economics,[13] of identifying production and trade figures with standard of living. Experience has shown that in subjected countries whose economies are not highly diversified a constantly favorable trade balance can go hand in hand with a constant deterioration of the individual living standard. The influx of money from Rome, demonstrated by numismatic finds and records of

[13] The most striking example of this is Albertini, "Un témoignage de saint Augustin sur la prospérité rélative de l'Afrique au IVe siècle." In *Les Vandales de l'Afrique*, Courtois cites laws of modern capitalist economics as if they could be applied unmodified to the Roman economy (see p. 109 and n. 4). He writes (p. 106) ". . . Roman Africa was a wheat-exporting country par excellence, which indicates that production greatly exceeded the requirements of consumption" [!!]. A serious mistake in spite of note 3, p. 321.

expenditures for luxuries in the large and medium-sized cities, denotes a superficial Romanization, not any material or moral improvement in the life of the people. From the legislation we can perhaps infer the theoretical situation of the native landowners or day laborers, but it must be borne in mind that this is a negative inference and that we have at present no possibility of consulting the Maghribi himself on the "civilizing" accomplishments of Rome which are still lauded with unrestrained lyricism.

The History of the Church

In many respects the Christian church took over the function of the Roman administration from the third century on. The Christian apologetic literature, the martyrologies, the conciliar documents and religious laws of the empire have been amply used as means of sounding the African soul, of evaluating its degree of attachment to Christianity, and of describing the specific aspects of the African church. From Tertullian to Augustine, the Christian literature of Africa shows a development, which was that of the church as a whole, from violent opposition to the imperial power, symbolized by refusal to serve in the army, to a concordat in which the two powers supported one another, each enjoying absolute authority in its own domain. During the second century, it is generally believed, Christianity spread inland from the coastal cities of the east and was carried by the army to the small towns of the interior at a time when the Roman organization was functioning most efficiently, that is, when the exploitation of North Africa was at its height.

Whatever part we may assign to the common people of the towns and country in this movement, we cannot help observing a distinctly anti-imperial tendency among the Christians and an intense striving for autonomy among their bishops. It was precisely when the episcopacy made its peace with the empire at the beginning of the fourth century that the majority of Christians in Africa, faithful to their tradition of independence from Rome, enthusiasm for martyrdom, and absolute opposition to the Emperor-Antichrist, rushed into the Donatist schism, ignoring the concept of catholicity central to all brands of Christianity that accommodate themselves to social inequalities, and giving their church a distinctly nationalist coloration. In 412, after a century of struggle, St. Augustine, leader of the Catholic forces, was finally victorious, thanks to the power of the state and perhaps also to the big landowners' fear of the social consequence of the schismatic movement. But this victory was short-lived, for beginning in 439 the Vandals promoted the Arian heresy with the very weapons the Catholics had forged, and after the Byzantine reconquest, for which the church was largely responsible, the North African church definitively lost the autonomy it had claimed since the days of Cyprian.

It cannot be denied that our knowledge of the period extending from the third to the seventh century is very much indebted to the study of Christian literature, inscriptions, and archeological documents. They are our only source for the part of the Maghrib abandoned by Diocletian, that is, the western half. What little we know of the humble inhabitants whom official history neglects has been gleaned almost exclusively from the lives of the martyrs, the pitfalls in which have been made apparent by modern criticism.[14]

Nevertheless, whatever use is made of this literature, whether the spirit is glorified[15] or the betrayal by the episcopacy of the poor people's hopes deplored,[16] it should not be forgotten that in it Africa is seen from the point of view of the church, just as previously it was viewed from that of the empire. In answer to those who insist on characterizing the Christianity of the second century and the Donatism of

[14] Arabic scholars might benefit by studying the enormous Moslem hagiographic literature and by employing the methods used by classical historians.

[15] Carcopino, *Le Maroc antique*, p. 301.

[16] On this point Courtois remains faithful to the Julien of 1931.

the fourth century as opposition movements, a traditional historian can point to the urban, bourgeois and highly Romanized character of those pseudorebels against the empire. As for those who look for Berber traits in Tertullian, Augustine, and such, they need only be reminded that it has not been possible to trace the genealogies of those exceptional men with any degree of precision, and moreover that every religious culture tends to create uniformity. It is always difficult to infer from the history of a religious schism a real picture of the social situation that caused it. To do so, e.g. to infer the existence of a national or social movement from the Tertullianist or Donatist ideology, one must subscribe to the sociological theory of ideologies (Marx, Weber, Mannheim) which very few historians accept. In any event the Christian authors' perception of national and social currents is negative, and whatever their intention they wrote church history rather than the history of the Christian Maghrib.[17]

Ultimately all the historical documents at our disposal deal with imperial history. Archeology (Roman roads, *fossatum*, army camps, milestones), numismatics (municipal or imperial coinages), epigraphy (religious and commemorative inscriptions, treaties) are all confined to the area of the military occupation. We are best informed about the big landowners, the *negociatores*, the churchmen, and the veterans, slaves, servants and artisans of the cities. As for the native inhabitants, we sense their presence, working in the fields, paying the *annona*, confined to the Aurès Mountains or driven beyond the *limes*, but we never see them. We should doubtless be grateful that a shadow of their presence endures, but let us not be dazzled by false riches: Roman history is not the history of the Maghrib.

[17] This is demonstrated by the great difference in tone and content between the two books by Jean Pierre Brisson based on the same documents: *Gloire et misère de l'Afrique chrétienne*, which is a pure glorification of the church, and *Autonomisme et christianisme dans l'Afrique romaine*, which is full of negative judgments.

II

The facts summed up above may be accepted as long established; the archeological and epigraphic discoveries that fill the specialized periodicals merely provide new details, but it is these details that lead the reader to ask: have these facts really a bearing on the history of the Maghrib? How much influence, in extension and depth, was exerted by the successive waves of colonizers?

Extension

The present tendency, encouraged by the enormous progress of Phoenician archeology since the Second World War, has undoubtedly been to overestimate the Carthaginian influence. Though positive proof is still unavailable, it is often claimed that by the last third of the second millennium B.C. the Phoenicians had established a chain of trading posts extending from Sabratha to Mogador (now Essaouira), and that these were regularly visited. The foundation of Carthage is still dated at the beginning of the ninth century B.C., but there is said to have been a settlement on the same site three centuries earlier.

In the sixth century, it is believed, the Phoenicians who had settled in North Africa began to recognize Carthage as their capital. Large towns such as Hadrumete, Tipasa, Lixus and Mogador, and numerous lesser trading posts, which were to become important cities in the Roman period, were integrated into a commercial empire under the leadership of Carthage, which after a period of spectacular expansion girdled all North Africa from Sabratha in Tripolitania to the island of Cerné off Rio de Oro, these being the two termini of the trans-Saharan trails. In most of what has been written on the subject we find this picture of a Carthaginian commercial empire developed with a lyricism that is sometimes alarming: "The economic and colonial conceptions of the Carthaginians were several thousand years in advance of their times," writes Madeleine Hours-Miéden.[18] Is this picture justified by recent archeological finds? Archeological investigations carried on in Phoenicia, on the islands, and along the coasts of the western Mediterranean have advanced our knowledge of the Phoenicians, their cast of mind, religion, and daily life. It has been inferred that their thinking was "oriental" and their religion marked by "colonial" archaism, that they were eminently practical and lacking in esthetic sense.[19] But the few discoveries made in Lixus and Mogador are difficult to date and provide no basis for a radical revision of our previous knowledge. The picture of a commercial empire is still based, as it was in Gsell's time, on the written literature, especially that brief, enigmatic text, *Hanno's Voyage*.

The Phoenicians, as was already known, went to the western Mediterranean in search of metals. Since the trade in Iberian tin had been demonstrated, the proponents of the commercial empire theory looked for an African companion piece to it, and thought of gold. The hypothesis was plausible enough; often repeated, it took on the weight of a certainty, and when it was put into form by Carcopino, few dared to question it in its entirety.[20] But a reader of this author's exposition can hardly fail to observe, under his weighty erudition, an argument so feeble as to make one wonder how it can ever have been taken seriously. Apart from certain fruitful insights in matters of detail, the whole is a perfect example of empty, abstract reasoning: on page after page he demonstrates the possibility of a trade in gold, but never the actual existence of such a trade, which would of course require a good number of archeological finds to establish. To show that this hypothesis can advance our understanding of an enigmatic text is the work of a philologist,

[18] M. Hours-Miéden, *Carthage*, pp. 114-115.

[19] Charles-Picard, *La Vie quotidienne à Carthage*, p. 68.

[20] Carcopino, *Le Maroc antique*, pp. 73-163. For a discussion of the reality of Hanno's voyage, see Rousseau, "Hannon au Maroc," pp. 161-232, and Germain "Qu'est-ce que le Périple d'Hannon . . . ," pp. 205-248.

not of a historian; the real problem would be to determine whether the Carthaginians carried on this trade on large enough a scale to justify us in speaking of a Carthaginian gold market. If there is to be a market, there must be roads, convoys, storehouses, and business transactions; of all this the author, intent on his reasoning *a contrario,* tells us nothing. The question is further complicated when we are told by other scholars that though the Greeks invented coinage in the sixth century B.C., the Carthaginians took no advantage of it for two centuries thereafter.[21] For if this African gold was shipped directly to Carthage and hoarded, it seems impossible to speak of a gold market in Morocco or elsewhere. Thus the maritime traffic is hypothetical; but what of the overland traffic? Our theorists refer to certain none-too-clear texts, mentioning taxes levied in the Tripolitanian region, which brought the Carthaginian treasury a talent a day in the second century, and conclude that this was a tax on the Saharan commerce, controlled by the Garamantes, between Bornu and the coastal towns. Other facts cited are the occupation of the Germa oasis in A.D. 70 and the Roman military expedition which after a four months' march reached an oasis (Agisymba), presumed to have been situated in the Sudan. Here again we find a probability of commercial relations (ostrich feathers, slaves?), but no proof is provided of their importance or regularity or of the role played in them by gold. It is not hard to see (and the second part of Carcopino's book shows clearly) that the theory of a Carthaginian commercial imperialism, far from being based on unimpeachable evidence, archeological and otherwise, is merely a projection upon the past of another, well-known imperialism, to wit, that of the Portuguese in the fifteenth century. Until we have proof to the contrary, we shall continue to regard Carthage as "a ship anchored off the coast of Africa," exerting some influence on other coastal establishments but not the total though indirect control

[21] Charles-Picard, *Vie quotidienne,* pp. 176-177.

over the life of the Maghrib that has too hastily been imputed to it.

But what of its territorial extension? From the fifth century on, we are told, Carthage became a land power when it found itself unable to resist the vast maritime counter-offensive of the Greeks marked by the victories of Salamis and Himera (480 B.C.). It denounced its treaties with the Berber princes, overcame their resistance, and conquered the northern part of present-day Tunisia. The area of the territory that became Carthaginian has been estimated at 30,000 square kilometers. But the information on which this figure is based dates from the beginning of the second century B.C., when the border disputes between Carthage and Massinissa were brought to the attention of the Roman senate; thus we have no way of knowing how much territory was actually conquered. We can form some idea of the north-eastern region, extending from Tabarca to Cape Bon and across the Sahel to the seaports of Tripolitania; but outside of this fringe, the archeological finds, which thus far have not been dated with any degree of certainty, are of no great help to us, nor can we be sure that the boundaries of the Roman province in 146 were those of the territory under direct Carthaginian control.

Roman Africa, to be sure, is better known, but not enough to dispel all doubts. Courtois puts forward the figure of 350,000 square kilometers out of a total of 900,000, excluding the Tripolitanian desert and the Sahara. In the light of the evidence he himself supplies, this figure seems exaggerated, for he takes the second-century *limes* as the boundary of the Roman territory, which was not necessarily the case. If we subtract the mountainous regions and others unsuited to the production of wheat and olives, the area actually exploited by the Roman Empire at the height of its power would seem to have been 240,000 square kilometers, the figure commonly put forward for the post-Diocletian period. This area was reduced by half under the Vandals and still more under the Byzantines, who controlled only the fortified cities and their environs.[22] If we reject the hasty generalizations of the pro-Roman writers, we observe a highly unstable territorial situation throughout the era of foreign (Punic, Roman, Vandal, Byzantine) pressure. A short period of expansion is almost immediately followed by a Berber reconquest. By the middle of the second century B.C. the Carthaginians had lost the territories acquired since the fifth century; the Romans succeeded in stabilizing their control for a hundred and fifty years, but began to lose territory by the end of the second century A.D. This movement continued until the final defeat of the Byzantines. In this light the hundred and fifty years of firm control seem to be the exception rather than the rule in the long history of foreign expansion in North Africa.

Depth

The northeastern part of the Maghrib has always been the most densely populated; if foreign influence was intensive in this region, doesn't this compensate for the small size of the territory? An affirmative answer is given by most colonial historians. These are divided into two camps, the pro-Carthaginians and the pro-Romans. What is denied the Carthaginians is accredited to the Romans, or vice versa. The Maghribis themselves have no place in the discussion. Even Massinissa is regarded merely as a client of Rome. Is the Maghrib indebted to the Phoenician-Carthaginians for metals, agriculture, the wagon, the alphabet, arboriculture and urban organization? After a period of eclipse, Punicophilia has come into fashion again. However, the linguistic evidence adduced has become more and more questionable,

[22] We should have no illusions about the attempts by Saumagne, Courtois and Charles-Picard in particular, to arrive at figures (area of Roman Africa, 350,000 km^2; population, 3,500,000; wheat production, 9 million quintals; yield of *annona*, 250,000-300,000 quintals) because individual preferences are implicit in the methods of calculation, and undoubtedly varying economic relationships are assumed to be permanent. However, Saumagne's calculations are the most circumspect.

for it implies an unspecified oriental origin, and archeology shows that neither wheat, nor the olive tree, nor the fig tree nor the vine were imported from Phoenicia. Agricultural settlements were in existence well before the first millennium, and the development of hydraulic installations owes no more to the Phoenicians than to the Romans. On the basis of written documents and archeological findings, which he checks against each other, Camps confirms Gsell's conclusion: "Indeed, all indications are that agriculture developed in North Africa at the same time as the organization of Berber society," and explicitly condemns the basic assumption of all the Punicophiles: "Are we to suppose that all the simplest agricultural techniques were alien to the Berbers and that this people was utterly lacking in initiative?"[23] The same conclusion is valid for the alphabet and urban development, which were influenced by the Carthaginians but not introduced by them.

Some writers speak of a "back to the land" movement in fifth-century Carthage and cite the name of Mago, a former general, who seems to have tried to encourage his aristocratic compatriots, who were no longer able to support themselves by trade, to turn to agriculture. For their benefit he wrote a book on agronomy, which was later translated into Latin by order of the Senate; the original was inherited by Micipsa after 146 B.C. The development of agriculture in North Africa is alleged to have originated with this "back to the land" movement. If we accept the idea that the territory of Carthage consisted of the immediate environs of the city (shura, or common property), where arboriculture was developed with the help of an enslaved population, and of a hinterland, where under the supervision of Carthaginian officials, whose main function it was to collect taxes and levy auxiliary troops, the Libyans were allowed to remain on their land in return for the payment of rent (a quarter

[23] See Camps, "Massinissa," pp. 70-90. Camps also has his preconceptions, but since they are of a different nature they enable him to see those of other writers.

or a half the harvest), it seems likely that political pressure was indirectly responsible for the increase in the production of grain (the only crop permitted up to the end of the first century A.D.). It was also in all likelihood the Carthaginian threat that impelled the neighboring Numidians to organize themselves into a kingdom, which in emulation took to growing grain and trading with the enemies of Carthage, until in 50 B.C. the Numidian surplus was twice what that of the Carthaginian territory had been a century before.[24] It was not the introduction of a new technique but political competition that obliged the Numidians to enlarge their grain fields by encroaching on their pasture lands and the territories of the south. It was probably this development, which was the acceleration of an existing movement rather than an innovation, which led Polybius to write some years later that Massinissa had sedentarized his people, an obviously fanciful contention. The numerous revolts of the Libyans (396, 379, etc.), the war of the mercenaries in 240, the conflict with Massinissa which from 207 to 148 erupted every ten years—all these disturbances have been characterized (with the help of the dubious pun Numidian-nomad) as opposition to forced settlement; but they can equally well be interpreted as revolts of a conquered, mistreated and exploited population of longtime farmers. The notion that the Phoenician colonists civilized the Maghrib through commerce and farming techniques is based not on unimpeachable archeological evidence, but on the texts of ill-informed ancient authors, whose taste for the picturesque and exotic has often been stressed. Carthaginian influence on social and religious life is undeniable, but oddly enough has been demonstrated only for the Roman period, though we do not know why the Romans should have encouraged such a process of Punicization. There is no reason to project this direct or indirect consequence of Roman policy very deeply into the Carthaginian period.

24 Charles-Picard, *Vie quotidienne*, p. 184.

And what of the Romans? In general the historians have little to say of the Roman contribution to the material civilization of North Africa; at most they tell us that though aqueducts were already in existence, more of them were built under the Romans. Albertini writes: "The Romans of the imperial epoch worked, consciously or not, to develop and organize the entire world, to lead every part of it to civilized life and well-being."[25] Development, organization —in other words, the generalized application of other people's inventions. The problem of Romanization can be reduced to the question, How much did the Romans contribute to the development of the cities? To what degree was the Latin language adopted? and What was the role of the army? True, some historians have painted a glowing picture of an Africa more Latinized, more urbanized and more prosperous than Spain or Gaul; but the reader can only be skeptical, because no distinction is made between Romans settled in Africa and Romanized Africans. These same historians tell us that there were few Romans or other Italians in Africa, that the vast majority of the city-dwellers and soldiers were Berbers; and they stress the role played by Africans in the political, administrative and intellectual life of Rome as an indication of the advanced Romanization of Africa. But the reader would like something more than generalities, something more than references to cases that well may have been exceptional.[26] The strength of the army has been estimated at twenty-seven thousand. With its twenty-year enlistment period, its Romanizing influence cannot have been very rapid or widespread. And those soldiers who

[25] Albertini, *L'Afrique romaine*, p. 19.

[26] If there is such a thing as sociological laws, one might actually draw the contrary conclusion from them. It is in a not very Romanized society that the few Romanized individuals would attain to the highest careers. Compare the Moslem Iran of the second and third centuries H., where the political, administrative and intellectual role of the Arabized Iranians in the Abbāsid Empire was out of all proportion to the degree of Arabization of a country which from the fourth century on recovered its national language.

served outside of Africa can no longer be regarded as Romanizers. True, the impressive ruins uncovered by the archeologists indicate the great wealth of a propertied class, many of whom in all likelihood spent little of their time in Africa.

And what of the cities? How many military colonies were there, how many artificial settlements, how many predominantly Berber towns responding to geographico-economic needs? The figure advanced by Courtois, who calculated that sixty percent of the population lived in the cities, seems more than startling.[27] Even supposing that the cities of the interior were inhabited chiefly by Berbers, to what degree did the Latin language enter into their daily life? The inscriptions that have survived present the official aspect of social life, not the quantitative relation between the languages spoken. All in all, the indications that have been cited can be accepted as proof of a Romanization of Africa only if they are interpreted in accordance with the logic of a much later period. Still, it cannot be doubted that along with the plebs of the cities, a class made up of the petit-bourgeoisie and of well-to-do peasants lived in the shadow of the Roman ruling class and underwent a process of Romanization. But was this class large enough to carry appreciable weight? And above all, to what degree did this class achieve its ambitions in a highly stratified Roman society? Though certain exceptions have been cited, it would seem that there was little social mobility and that this class obtained satisfaction very late, perhaps too late. Albertini asks whether the edict of Caracalla (212) conferring citizenship on all free men throughout the empire may not have been premature. Far from being premature, this concession undoubt-

27 Courtois, *Les Vandales et l'Afrique*, p. 111. Courtois himself found the figures surprising and consulted the geographers, who speak of new countries with a sparse indigenous population, which was not the case in Roman Africa. Actually, the whole question of the urbanization rate in an ancient country is meaningless, since it is next to impossible to determine the juridical, economic and sociological aspects of the urban phenomenon at this early date.

edly came too late, long after the great disorders in the western, and only twenty years before those in the eastern, Maghrib. The municipal structure of the province (a hierarchy of cities and a hierarchy of urban groups) gives a clear picture of the social rigidity that prevailed at a time when the empire was strong and the local population was eager for integration; by the time the state took action to correct this rigidity, the big landowners had become so powerful as to make the reform irrelevant and deserted the cities, thus escaping integration with the African bourgeoisie. There is reason to believe that first Christianity, then Donatism were propagated largely among the African bourgeoisie. Must this not be taken as a protest against the delay in Romanization? Thus Rome seems not only to have exploited the majority of the Berber population, but also to have disappointed the well-to-do minority that might have been won over to its "organizational genius."

This of course is not the opinion of the colonial historians, who regard Christianization as the culmination of Romanization.

Beginning in the middle of the second century A.D., they tell us, this Christianization was so successful that according to Tertullian, writing in the middle of the third century, the adherents of the new religion formed the majority of the population of all the cities. The great persecutions of the middle of the third century and the beginning of the fourth, with their large numbers of martyrs and of apostates as well, show that Christianity, though perhaps none too deep-rooted, was widely disseminated. The long struggle between Catholics and Donatists definitely indicates the social importance religious problems had assumed, even if the causes of the conflict were elsewhere. The heroic resistance to the Arianism of the Vandals, especially during Huneric's persecution (482-484), and a wealth of archeological and epigraphic finds relating to the Vandal and Byzantine periods, bear witness to a deepening of Christian sentiment among the Berber population. Thus Africa would seem to have been a privileged breeding ground of Christianity, perhaps even more so than Spain or Gaul. But this impression is entirely qualitative; we have no means of obtaining a quantitative evaluation. As we have already pointed out, the documents now available are very meager. The Acts of the Martyrs and the records of the church councils enable us at the most to circumscribe the milieu favorable to Christianity geographically (the northeast) and sociologically (the medium ranks of the urban bourgeoisie). The remains of the churches throw some light on the wealth of the pious absentee landlords, but little on the fervor or number of the faithful. In any event, these remains date from a late period and are rare outside the region of Carthage. The greatest number of large churches and Christian inscriptions have been found in the city of Carthage; once again, our evaluation of Christianity hinges on the cities. The contention that the silent Christianity of the countryside may have played a more important role finds no justification in what we know of the propagation of other monotheistic religions. Statistics, we are told, suggest that the Berbers formed a majority in the Christian community and thus represented a good part of the total population. But this again falls short of conclusive proof. The large numbers of apostasies recorded in the middle of the third century would tend to prove, at least for that date, that Christian propaganda was active among the wealthy, that is, the Romans. But doesn't the Donatist schism provide conclusive evidence? Yes, but only if we can prove that its rural wing (the *circumcelliones*) was really Donatist and not merely an occasional ally. All this goes to show that we should be very cautious in attempting to estimate the numerical strength of the African Christians. Few writers exercise such caution, and the use of Christian epigraphy is at the source of many adventurous judgments. The historians of this period work on three assumptions: (1) every prince who employs an architect presumed to be Christian is himself a Christian; (2) every prince presumed to be Christian is necessarily at the head of a Christian kingdom; (3) every individual presumed to be Christian necessarily lives in a Christian community. But these principles, on which all interpretations of epigraphic finds have been based, are far from self-evident. A single example of this method will suffice: Carcopino's account of the development of Christianity in the western Maghrib from the third to the sixth century.[28] He starts by noting two facts: first that more inscriptions have been found in Volubilis and the region of Oran, which at that time were outside the empire, than in Tangiers, which still belonged to it, and more to the west of the Chéliff than to the east, though the latter region is closer to Carthage, and secondly that all these inscriptions are of late origin (450-651 in Oran, 599-655 in Volubilis). Instead of finding a motive for caution in these seemingly startling facts, he cries out: "What religious fervor in Mauretania!" and concludes that Christianity developed in spite of the weakening of the imperial power. The four inscriptions at Volubilis bear the names of three Juliuses and one Julia. Were they Berbers, foreigners or Romans? Carcopino claims they were Berbers, because a prince of the Baquates, the neighbors and protectors of the city, took the name of Julius at the end of the third century. The documents concerning these Baquates are few and mutually contradictory, but this does not prevent Carcopino from writing: ". . . the Baquates of Volubilis, unswerving in their fidelity to Christianity [which brand of Christianity?], to which their ancestors had been converted four centuries earlier."[29] Nor does he stop there; on the strength of the fourth inscription cited, dated 655, which mentions one Julia Rogativa, originally from Altava (Oran region) but adopted by the citizens of Volubilis (western Morocco), he

[28] *Ibid.*, pp. 288-301.

[29] The same reasoning is used by the Sunnite historians when they speak of the Idrīsids. Terrasse ridicules them in his *Histoire du Maroc.* Would he have exercised the same critical rigor toward his colleague Carcopino?

brushes in a picture of a hypothetical confederation of Christian cities and tribes extending from Oran to the ocean. With what proof? "Geography demands it," he says. The linguistic facts he cites may merely signify that the defunct or the author of the inscription hailed from Oran, not necessarily that the two regions were in permanent contact. And he concludes with a hymn of praise to those Berbers, abandoned by their empire and forgotten by the church, who clung to their Christian faith until the seventh century. It is no accident that scientific reasoning is replaced by rhetoric, and in the light of such an example we begin to doubt even conclusions that might have seemed more plausible, such as the existence in the Tiaret region in the fifth and sixth centuries of a dynasty whose princes, to judge by the tombs (13 *djedars*) generally attributed to them, must have been Christian.

Thus the chronology of Christianization, the socio-racial structure and finally the numerical evaluation of African Christianity remain beyond our reach. Yet, this does not justify an immediate conclusion that the phenomenon was superficial. The fact that Christianity was Roman before it was Berber, urban before it was rural, and espoused by the rich before the poor, does not by any means preclude the possibility that in one way or another it gained the support of the poverty-stricken masses in search of hope.

Religious problems would not have occupied so important a position in imperial legislation and daily life if the majority of the population had been indifferent to them. It is here that the problem of characterizing this Christianity arises. Even if we knew how many Christians there were in Africa, we should still have to determine the nature of their Christianity. What was the Catholicism of the third century and what was the Donatism of the fourth?

What sort of Christianity developed in the part of Africa abandoned by Diocletian and not reconquered by the Vandals and Byzantines? The quality of this faith can no more be judged by the faith of St. Augustine than can the number of the faithful by the situation in Carthage. Without an answer to this question, we should be unable later on to account for the de-Christianization of the Maghrib.

III

So many statements have been put forward as true that are at best barely probable! And so much of what has been learned about Carthage, Rome and the church has so little bearing on North Africa as a whole! Under these circumstances one can scarcely be surprised to find hardly a single historian who does not invoke hypotheses and reconstructions, not to mention political and moral judgments, in order to conceal the meagerness of our knowledge. Political and cultural bias is everywhere, and it goes without saying that such bias defines itself in terms of the one question held to be essential: why the ultimate failure of Roman civilization in the Maghrib? According to how much one stresses political or social elements, arbitrary blunders or necessary contradictions, one arrives at a colonialist or liberal view.

The colonial view is the most widespread, since it benefits from a long tradition, public support, academic prestige and, one might say, a certain self-evidence, for how can anyone living in a colonized Maghrib be expected to escape the natural tendency to understand the past through the present: to see Jugurtha through 'Abd al-Karīm, the Roman laws through those of the July monarchy, and the Moslems of earlier periods through the taxpayers of Muqrāni? Almost involuntarily such rhetorical comparisons become explanations.[30] The structure and logic of the present become means

[30] Numerous examples in Julien, *Histoire de l'Afrique du Nord*, 2nd ed., vol. 1, pp. 117, 129, 130, 320; Carcopino, *Le Maroc antique*, pp. 36, 326; F. Richard, in his notes to the French translation of Sallustius Crispus, . . . *Guerre de Jugurtha* (1968 ed.), p. 214, n. 187. Julien's criticism of this same aberration in the Algerian nationalists is obviously one-sided; it did not originate with them.

of ordering the facts of the past, so providing a ready-made system of interpretation.

The Maghribis, we are given to understand, were vegetating in an impoverished and retarded neolithic stage when the Carthaginians brought them into contact with oriental civilization; this influence was slow and did not really make itself felt until the third century B.C. Though highly gifted in practical matters, the Carthaginians were backward in the esthetic and religious fields; their civilization was not comparable to that of the Greeks, which Rome was to adopt and develop. When the Romans arrived in Africa, the Maghribis were far from having acquired the foundations necessary for integration into the Roman community; a period of apprenticeship was indispensable. For three centuries this apprenticeship was carried on under the aegis of the traditional chiefs, the kings of Numidia and Mauretania (this propaedeutic was carried on by way of Punic civilization, considered as an introduction to the only true civilization, the Greco-Roman; the Punic library given to the Numidians after the destruction of Carthage is interpreted as a symbolic gesture). The state, the life of the cities, art, religion, writing—all underwent a rapid process of Punicization. Massinissa, indeed, entered into relations with Greece, his son triumphed in the Panathenaea; but obviously a direct influence was impossible; the propaedeutic was not yet complete. It became so at the beginning of the first century A.D., and annexation was decided on, but annexation did not mean immediate Romanization. Through its army and administration, Rome generalized sedentarization, populated the country, extended agriculture; and within this territory pacified by urban organization, Romanization was rewarded. An individual mounted the ladder of civic rights as he assimilated the language, customs and civic genius of Rome; in time this ladder was shortened, until by the edict of 212 only nomads refractory to organized social life were excluded from citizenship. Why then the wars and revolts? Barbarian obstinacy. And what were the motives of the

Romans? Altruism and sense of duty. All this would be idyllic if not for the way it ended. From the third to the sixth century Roman civilization suffered a long death agony—a fact chiefly explained on the basis of psychology and political blunders. "The servitude of routine has never weighed more heavily on a people," writes Gsell, and adds, "From antiquity on we see them [the Berbers] as they have always been, restless, mobile, turbulent, quick to anger and revolt."[31] Moreover, we are told, Rome made the political blunder of not occupying the entire Maghrib. Rome, Albertini believes,[32] did not conquer enough, did not populate enough territory. An artificial *limes* is always vulnerable, and the withdrawal of 285 was the crowning blunder, leaving the Romanized Berbers exposed to the contagion of barbarism. Later on a skepticism arose among the historians, at first vague, then clearly expressed: Could Rome have succeeded? Thinking of the twentieth-century present, Gsell wrote in his conclusion: "Thus the moral conquest of the country proves to be as necessary as its political conquest. Woe to the masters of North Africa who fail to understand this"—meaning that the Romans offered the Maghribis a superior civilization, but did not convince them of its value to the individual. Albertini is more explicit: "It was the economic crisis [extreme poverty] that drove the people back to their original savagery."[33] In other words, Rome brought wealth to the community and misery to the individual. At this point the incurable admirers of Rome are obliged to abandon their initial theory and reproach Rome for not having extirpated the Carthaginian influence. Having won men's souls, especially in the rural districts, and found a new youth in Christianity, an oriental religion, Punic civ-

[31] Gsell, *Histoire ancienne de l'Afrique du Nord,* vol. v, p. 137, vol. vi, p. 278.

[32] Albertini, *L'Afrique romaine,* conclusion.

[33] Albertini, *op. cit.*, pp. 120, 126. It is easy to see why Jacques Soustelle, then governor general of Algeria, ordered the republication of this book written in 1922, since its conclusions supported his own policy.

ilization raised an insurmountable barrier to the occidental spirit represented by Rome. "The influence of Carthage was the source of the attraction that Asia exerted on the Berbers despite the proximity of Europe," writes Gilbert Charles-Picard.[34] Thus the failure was inevitable. Clearly Roman colonization in North Africa is interpreted in the light of French colonial policy, which first aimed optimistically at complete integration of the North Africans and later declared them to be racially incapable of such a development.

We have cited chiefly the admirers of pagan Rome, who regarded Christianity merely as a new means of propagating Roman civilization. Others have tried to take the point of view of the conquered and tended to regard Christianity as a criticism of Roman imperialism. The egoism and exploitation of this "system of organized pillage" does not escape them. It goes without saying that they have taken a different view of the continual revolts, which are no longer interpreted as outbursts of insufficiently controlled barbarism, but as expressions of national or social strivings.

In this second view everything takes on a different meaning. The period of Punicization ceases to be a necessary propaedeutic and becomes the consequence of political calculation: Rome destroyed Carthage to prevent Massinissa from seizing it and becoming a Mediterranean power. The Roman senate supervised, intrigued, and fomented internecine wars in order to weaken the Numidian kings and make them into docile clients. As long as Rome needed wheat and Massinissa's successors provided it, indirect control was the most economical system; when the civil war, the culmination of insurmountable social contradictions, broke out, the Romans needed land, and annexation was decided upon. The exploitation of this land meant spoliation, and the *limes* was not so much a boundary of civilization as a flexible frontier between the dispossessed, who were thrust out into the desert, and the needed workers, who were enslaved

[34] Charles-Picard, *Vie quotidienne*, p. 252, harking back to an idea of Gautier.

and crushed with taxes. The rebels are specified: the Moors were dispossessed peasants who chose freedom; the Numidians were free peasants and farm workers who periodically avenged themselves on their exploiters. It was on the one hand a national, on the other a social, protest. Roman development of the land brought not only forced sedentarization, but also exhaustion of the soil, deforestation and social debasement. While the Jugurthine War (112-105) was an attempt to oppose direct Roman conquest and assumed a character of national struggle, that of Tacfarinas a century later (17-24) was the first protest against the expropriation of the pasture lands.[35] But for a century and a half the *limes* held firm; the Moors in the west were able to cross it only intermittently, while the Numidians (serfs, seasonal farm workers, *cultores*) were kept under tight control and severely exploited. How were they to protest? By adopting Christianity, a new religion, which under the given circumstances took on a special character of vengeance against the rich and against the empire. The two trends, Moorish and Numidian, subsisted until the end of the Byzantine period; after 285 the abandoned region became Moorish again and pressure was resumed against the new *limes*; within it, in a reduced territory, the increasingly exploited Numidians formed defense groups: the *circumcelliones*,[36] who were themselves free men but rose to the defense of those who were exploited more severely than themselves and attacked the masters of economic life, the *domini, possessores* and *creditores*. What was their social status? Were they Berbers or semi-Berbers, Catholics or Donatists? We cannot say for sure. What is certain is that they controlled the African countryside from 300 to 347 and between 380 and 400, and that they made use of the religious controversy to advance their own aims. They made a tactical alliance with the Donatists, but the Donatists held

[35] See Ronald Syme, "Tacfarinas, the Musulamii and Thubursicum," pp. 113ff.

[36] "Storehouse prowlers" (Saumagne) or "Chief among the saints" (Frend)?

their long-term aims in abomination. In the end the Catholic church, joining forces with the big landowners and the army, destroyed the Donatists and *circumcelliones*, but during a brief intervening period the logic of this movement was clearly revealed. Gildo, who had allied himself with the Romans during the revolt of his brother Firmus (371-375) and later been appointed commander of the African army, revolted in turn in 396, seized the fleet transporting the *annona*, confiscated the imperial lands and distributed them among the *circumcelliones* and his troops.[37] To be sure, he was defeated in 398, but by locally selling the wheat intended for Rome and confiscating the large landed estates, he showed clearly that the aim of these continual revolts was the recovery of the confiscated lands, a policy that could not succeed as long as the Roman empire remained a reality. Seen in this light, the failure was not that of the Roman exploiters, who were condemned in any event, but of the church which, by allying itself with the property owners, disappointed the hopes of the poor and thus caused the best aspects of the Roman presence to be engulfed in the final catastrophe. Regrettable as this may have been for Africa, the Africans cannot be held responsible. In this perspective the absentee landlords and the church are impeached, and the hopes of the poor and the déclassé are glorified in accordance with the laical and democratic tastes of the anticolonialist left.

It is important to recognize the mediate character of this view: the Maghribis are represented as the victims of all oppressive systems; everything is seen in the light of the traditional republican myth: *circumcelliones* and farm laborers are seen in the guise of Jacobins and *sans-culottes*, Donatists and Catholics as low and high clergy. Just as the Maghribis are merely the negative expression of an oppressive system, the revolts denote neither national nor social

[37] See Courtois, *Les Vandales et l'Afrique*, pp. 144-146; for the opposite view, MacMullen, *Enemies of the Roman Order*, pp. 200-207.

consciousness. Outside the *limes*, freedom signifies barbarians without a future; inside it, a blind protest against misfortune. C.-A. Julien has always refused to regard Jugurtha as an autonomist leader, and Brisson says of the Donatists, "It was not because they were Berbers, but because the Berbers were the most unfortunate part of the North African population, since those who had remained nomads were more and more hampered in their natural economy and those who had accepted a relative sedentarization suffered increasingly from the general crisis induced by the intensive exploitation of the country." Courtois admits that Donatism incorporated all those who were opposed to the Roman power, but nevertheless refuses to use the words "nationalism" and "revolution," which he finds anachronistic, though they denote exactly what he is trying to describe.[38]

According to this liberal point of view, Rome failed because of the contradictions in its policy, not because of any Berber reaction to it. The church could have made a better choice, it could have saved both Christianity and Roman civilization; it would have played in the past the role played today by Social Democracy. Despite the truths this perspective may reveal, despite its anticolonial character in certain details, it is merely the negative expression of the viewpoint discussed above. In it the Maghribis play no positive role; looked upon as a danger beyond the *limes* and as victims within it, they are always seen from outside.[39]

All these perspectives are colonial in a positive or negative sense, and in this realm the nationalist ideology has con-

[38] Brisson, *Autonomisme et christianisme dans l'Afrique romaine*, p. 28; Courtois, *Les Vandales et l'Afrique*, pp. 147-148.

[39] It is easy to see why there is no difficulty in passing from one perspective to the other and why in this point Courtois is able to see eye to eye with C.-A. Julien. It is also easy to see why the psychology of the Berbers is regarded as essentially negative. I, too, employ the concept of negativity (below), but in a different sense. Julien thinks this negative attitude on the part of the Berbers was a matter of deliberate choice; I shall try to prove that in the Roman period the Maghribis were deprived of all freedom of choice.

tributed nothing new. Is it possible to restore the specific weight and color of the past? Possibly not, but in that case we must admit as much and criticize all the distortions that have arisen from seeing the past in terms of the present.

IV

The Maghribis of the present day have taken no interest in the period under discussion. This is a grave mistake. As opposition to the glorification of Rome, they have been content to vindicate Carthage, so making themselves heir to the myth of a Maghrib eternally torn between the orient and the occident.[40] Today the oriental origin of Maghribi civilization can be argued more plausibly than ever, but if we go far back, beyond the Phoenicians, to an epoch when all civilization in the Mediterranean West was of oriental origin, the contention becomes meaningless. As for the Carthaginian period, it is difficult, despite all the revolts and struggles of which echoes have come down to us, to contend that the Libyans and Liby-Phoenicians had the same ambitions. True, we can contest the facts recorded by the Greco-Romans, but what positive proof have we to the contrary? What we must actually reject is the entire colonial point of view, according to which the Maghribis were nothing more than alien and unconcerned onlookers at a history enacted on their soil. It is futile to espouse the point of view of one foreigner as opposed to another, for the abstract approach which systematically subscribes to the contrary of what the colonial historians have said prevents us from getting to the heart of the matter and perpetuates a weakness in both our political thinking and our scholarship. Maghribi scholars have neglected any number of techniques (epigraphy, philological critique, the interpretation of religious texts, etc.) that might prove useful to them, and this makes it difficult for them to undertake a radical critique of the colonial

[40] Especially Madanī, *Qarṭajanna fī Arba'a Uṣūr.*

perspectives. This lack of interest can only be attributed to cultural and national immaturity.

What makes it all the more deplorable is that today there is a real possibility of approaching the history of this period from a new angle. What definite knowledge have we of the ancient Maghrib? Very little, and precisely this admission can be a source of progress. For a century historians have painted a picture full of medieval reminiscences and have felt justified in characterizing all Maghribi history as, in the words of Gsell, "a history of mud and gore."[41] We must recognize once and for all that the few accounts by classical authors give us nothing but names, our readings of which are not always certain and whose forms change as they pass from Libyan to Greek to Latin, and that we can never be sure either of their sociological content or of their geographical localization. If it is still possible to correct the geography of the Jugurthine War, which we thought we knew well because the Roman account was sure to be comprehensive, what shall we say of other texts whose authors were not restrained by any concern for precision?[42] It is futile to draw up a geography or paint a social picture of the Maghrib on the basis of ancient texts; this will never produce anything more than a nominalist description. Consequently we must reject once and for all the classical conception of a North Africa entering history as a half-savage country sparsely populated with shepherds. If we are to take anything seriously in the ancient accounts, it can only be the trend they indicate, which seems to have been toward increasing social dispersion. We pass from nations in Herodotus, Polybius and Sallust to confederations in Strabo, Taci-

[41] It would be easy to list the examples of circular reasoning (interpreting ancient history in the light of medieval history and then concluding that nothing has changed) in Gsell, Julien (*Histoire de l'Afrique du Nord,* 2nd ed.), Carcopino, and even in Camps (see his "Massinissa," p. 261).

[42] A. Berthier, *Le "Bellum Jugurthinum" de Salluste,* which moves the entire theater of the war to the Tunis-Algerian border (pp. 88f. and 95-96).

tus and Ammianus Marcellinus, and finally to tribes in Procopius and Corippus. The accuracy of the terms is not certain but there is no doubt about the tendency to dispersion, which is the essential fact. Still, there can be no question of accepting it as a permanent state of affairs, for it has never been definitely proved. It has been widely spoken of for the last century, but a prejudice repeated a thousand times remains a prejudice. What idea can we form of Maghribi society in the light of this tendency to dispersion? It is here that archeology becomes important, for it seems more and more to contradict the picture derived from the ancient texts.[43]

The hypothesis of a Libyan people, coming from the east by way of a not yet arid Sahara and imposing a homogeneous civilization on North Africa through its language and culture, is no more proved today than it was is Gsell's time. Nevertheless, it is permissible to take such a cultural unity as a starting point, and the passage from prehistory to protohistory can then be defined by the superimposition on this basic unity of a certain diversity resulting from protracted relations with the countries of the Mediterranean—a very relative diversity to be sure, since the cultures of these countries were themselves of oriental origin. In any event the Maghrib ceased to be a cul-de-sac opening only on the southeast. This slow differentiation between two Maghribs, the one Saharan and Nilotic, descended directly from the neolithic, and the Mediterranean remained a dominant trait, reaching from protohistory into history and expressed in the opposition between Libyans and Gaetulians. It was the Mediterranean Maghrib that entered into history in the course of the three last millennia B.C.; the society that developed there was comparable in its essential features to that living on the shores of the Mediterranean. As Camps points out, everything in the monuments, furniture, weapons, clothing and rites—the remains or memory of which

[43] Camps, "Massinissa." It is regrettable that whenever this author punctures an old prejudice he seems to introduce a new one.

have been preserved by archeology and the art of the caves —suggests a sedentary agricultural population and nothing points to a life of nomadic shepherds. There are no offensive weapons, the clothing is without ornament; on the other hand, we find porridge bowls indicative of agriculture and large necropolises implying a dense population. Camps observes that while beef bones are abundant everywhere, very few bones of sheep or wild animals have been found, which would be strange in a country inhabited by nomads.[44] This sedentary society grew the most essential crops, concentrated in villages, traded with the opposite shore of the Mediterranean, and created or adapted the Libyan alphabet. What was its social and political organization? Camps believes that since the main aspects of its economic base have been determined, we can infer a certain permanence and deduce a social structure of a kind known to us in history and in some instances existing down to our own times.[45] This deduction is no more acceptable today than it was in Gsell's time, for it is based on circular reasoning. It would be more judicious to take the protohistoric Mediterranean societies rather than historical Berber society as our frame of reference, or else to resign ourselves to ignorance. Since what interests us is the overall movement, static pictures based on reconstructions are not indispensable.[46]

In this perspective, the contact between this sedentary society and the Phoenician seafarers at the end of the second century is no longer a meeting between barbarism and civilization, but rather between urban commerce and an agricultural society; its essential consequence was to cut this agricultural society off from the western Mediterranean. This helps us to understand the implantation and mediating role of the Phoenicians. Undoubtedly their urban organization

[44] Camps, "Massinissa," p. 117.

[45] Here he reverts to Gsell and becomes more and more ambiguous.

[46] Such arguments drawn from archeology can never be absolute, but they nevertheless seem to carry more weight than obscure and unverifiable statements by ancient authors.

influenced the Berbers and their towns. But its most important consequence was the formation of monarchies in the very regions where the old avenues of movement were cut off: in northern Morocco, where the traces of a powerful kingdom are preserved in imposing funerary monuments, and in the east where the names of ancient kings have come down to us. The creation of these kingdoms as early as the sixth century B.C. should be regarded, not as the culmination of a normal development, but as a reaction to Phoenician pressure and a consequence of the diversification noted above. The famous "back to the land" movement in fifth- and fourth-century Carthage was aimed at the destruction of the eastern kingdom, which was then replaced by another further west. In the genesis of this Numidian state in which two groups (Massyles and Massaesyles?) vied for supremacy, the policy of the Carthaginians played as important a role as the determination of the Berbers to resist their advance. The anti-Carthaginian movement as a whole, as manifested by the monarchies, failed, but the circumstances of this failure were to be of the utmost importance later on. The Numidian monarchy came close to attaining its end (the integration or destruction of Carthage) only when another foreign power was on the point of taking over. As events were precipitated, the Numidians defended themselves against the most immediate danger by playing off one foreign power against another, because it was no longer possible to resist them both at once. Time lost and irretrievable, an ambiguity of attitude imposed by the situation—these are recurrent motifs in the history of the Maghrib.

During the two hundred and fifty years that the kingdoms lasted, Rome, intentionally or not, thwarted the natural movement of unification. The Moorish kingdom of Baga and the two Bocchuses incorporated the Carthaginian ports and resumed relations with Iberia; but the centuries-old aim of the Numidians, to retake Carthage, was not achieved. On the contrary, Rome imposed or encouraged the partition of the Numidian kingdom, played on the hostility between Numidians and Moors, invested these kingdoms on every side with its colonists, merchants and soldiers, and finally annexed them both. If Carthage exacerbated the differences between these kingdoms, Rome brought them all into open conflict. The monarchic unification, which was the positive form taken by opposition to the foreign invaders, was now condemned; once halted, the movement could not resume on the same basis. During the two centuries of Roman domination, the opposition was negative: first retreat to mountain strongholds or flight to the Sahara, then religious schism—two negative expressions of a certain will to survival. The universality offered by Rome and later by the church was a universality of servitude; freedom became the name for a return to protohistory. This was not a deliberate choice, it lay in the nature of the situation, and it is also a qualitative threshold of Maghribi history.

True, none of all this is absolutely certain; we can neither be sure that a single family ruled over northern Morocco from the fifth to the first century B.C. nor that Massinissa really aimed to conquer Carthage, nor that Jugurtha wanted to get rid of all the Romans. The essential, however, is that a trend should be plausible, and this one is, for through it we can more readily explain the subsequent developments. What is this trend? Toward a tripartite division of the Maghrib, not in a political and vertical, but in a sociohistorical, horizontal sense, which deprives the names of peoples and kingdoms of all geographical significance. In the eyes of the Carthaginians, the subjugated Libyan was opposed to the unsubjugated Numidian; in the eyes of the Romans, the African, or Romanized Numidian, was opposed to the subjugated Numidian within the *limes*, and both to the independent Moor. If Moor means western, the meaning is socio-political, for the center of the world was the Mediterranean, and the Atlantic Ocean was the wall behind which there was nothing. The Moor was the untractable man of darkness; first localized in the region of Volubilis, he reappeared in the fourth century A.D. in eastern Algeria, and in the sixth century before the walls of Carthage.

Before the arrival of the foreigners, the Phoenicians and Romans, a linguistic and cultural unity was accompanied by an economic duality—agriculturalists versus pastoralists. Foreign pressure led to tripartism, first socio-political, then, after a process of consolidation, extending itself to every aspect of life: economic, cultural, linguistic, geographic. The first division was social: assimilated subject, nonassimilated subject, and free natives; later it became geographical (cities, country, desert), economic (commerce, agriculture, nomadism) and possibly linguistic (Latin, Punico-Berber, Berber). More important than the division itself was the inversion of values that accompanied the development from one sphere to another. In the economic sphere, the gradation from nomadism to urban commerce is positive; in the political sphere this same gradation must be regarded as negative; evolution went hand in hand with involution. The phenomenon we must try to understand is not so much nomadism (a prehistorian's problem) as re-nomadization (a strictly historical problem); what is difficult to interpret is not a lag, but a regression that in some instances is symbolic. The farmer who has reverted to nomadism thinks only of returning to his land, his eyes are forever on the *limes*, though he knows that the desert is his only defense against an unconquerable enemy. This brings us to the problem of the tribe. To say that the whole history of the Maghrib is a "history of tribes"—an expression dear to all colonial historiography—is meaningless, for it is well known that there are essential differences between the tribe of the camel-driving nomads (total tribal organization, the only possible one in a specific geo-economical setting), the clan of the mountaineers (balanced organization determined by socio-economic factors) and the symbolic taxonomy of the agricultural plains and plateaus. Those who start from an abstract or constructed notion of the tribe as the basic organization, which they then proceed to discover unmodified at every stage of Maghribi protohistory and history, will, to be sure, have the pleasure of rendering this history "obscure," as Courtois puts it, but at the same time they will forgo all possibility of grasping the dialectic of the Maghribi development. The phenomenon of the tribe must be regarded primarily as a "return to the starting point" in a particular historical situation, as the consequence and expression of an arrested history, which, rigidified and institutionalized, would serve as an explanation for all subsequent arrests. We do not know where Maghribi history began, but we do know what it was unable to arrive at, and this interrupted journey has a name: the tribe.

Because this contradictory aspect of the matter has not been understood, the tripartite division of the Maghrib has been taken in a physical sense: Moors, Numidians, Gaetulians, and later Maṣmūda, Ṣanhāja and Zanāta; it is useless to situate them on the map or to reconstruct them from smaller groups; this division must be regarded as an ideological formulation of a reality that lies elsewhere.

Can we go further and try to determine the social organization of the early days on a local level? Is it permissible to make use of what we know of later periods to this end? No one claims to know exactly how social life was organized in the area under Carthaginian or Roman rule, and there is no reason to believe (as has been asserted without proof)[47] that the tribal system was shattered under foreign domination and later reconstituted. What we know of the kingdoms that succeeded the imperial power in the territories abandoned by Rome does not give this impression. Even supposing that a tribal structure as we know it from later periods existed in the fifth and sixth centuries in the regions of Volubilis and Oran, and in the Aurès Mountains,

[47] The circular reasoning of Gsell, Julien and Courtois is evident. First they describe the initial society, investing it with medieval characteristics. After that there is no difficulty in representing all evolution as a return to the archetype.

and formed the foundation of the monarchies of the time, the phenomenon of a "return" to the tribal system, considered as a means of defense, should be investigated and not assumed a priori.

The tribal system, in all its aspects and with all its subsystems, must be described at the moment when it appears or reappears in history, after the Roman conquest, and not preconceived as a basic system at the very source of history. Its lasting importance in the Maghribi past is not that it conditioned an evolution or stagnation, but that it was a dialectic response (whether new or revived is of secondary importance) to a blocked historical development. This accounts for its twofold aspect: on the one hand, permanent as a means of self-defense and guardian of tradition, and on the other hand, transitional, as a provisional solution in the expectation of recrossing the *limes*. It endures because the provisional situation endures. It can be understood only in reference to other situations of blocked development, that of the Celts for example.[48]

Herein lies the importance to the modern Maghribi of the period under discussion; it is in this period that a situation which was to be repeated with increasingly grave consequences first appears in the full light of history. In disregarding it, in failing to wrest it from the grasp of colonial ideology, the Maghribi condemns himself willy-nilly to propagating phantasms that prevent us from understanding and from acting.

[48] As is often the case, we find the profoundest insights into this problem in Berque. See his "Qu'est-ce qu'une tribu nord-africaine?" pp. 261-271.

3. Conqueror Succeeds Conqueror

I

With the fifth century and the coming of the Vandals, a period of false regularities and deceptive constancies begins for the Maghrib: secular rhythm, cycle of three generations, government by a foreign minority, the dream of reviving the Carthaginian Empire. And underlying all this, one permanent reality: tripartite Africa.

The facts are known, at least from the Byzantine point of view, and nothing substantially new has been added since the beginning of the century.[1] In a Roman empire divided among various Germanic groups, it was inevitable that North Africa should fall a prey to the first arrivals: these were the Vandals, who were already established in Spain. Led by Genseric, they crossed the Straits of Gibraltar and carved out a kingdom, first in what had been Numidia, then in the vicinity of Carthage, which they took in October 439. The old Africa of the Caesars was reconstituted. This the western emperor recognized, resorting as usual to a juridical subterfuge, which consisted in pretending that the conquerors were merely asking for hospitality. But Genseric, who embarked on his adventure very late, at the age of forty—a frequent phenomenon in the subsequent history of the Maghrib—and lived until 474, was not satisfied with what the Romans had granted. With his eyes fixed on the center of the empire, he took advantage of every crisis and gradually built up a maritime empire encompassing the Balearics, Corsica, Sardinia and Sicily. After a disastrous attempt, in 468, to stop the Vandal advance, the Byzantine emperor, the only effective ruler after the sack of Rome in 455, recognized the fait accompli by the treaty of 474.

All Genseric's conduct indicates a will to inherit the im-

[1] In most cases, Procopius and the Arab chronicles are paraphrased. Even Courtois supplies more interpretations than new facts.

perial authority;[2] he did not pass beyond the confines of Roman Africa and made no change in the existing structures. As an heir, he also inherited the difficulties of the declining empire, which in the fifth century enjoyed the support only of the big landowners and high clergy. Genseric dispossessed the former and alienated the latter with his Arian heresy.

Illegitimate heirs, the Vandals were combated outside their African realms by the empire, and inside it by the church, which, injured in its interests and deprived of its dominant position, looked to Byzantium for help and engaged in intrigues while awaiting its hour of revenge. This revenge, however, was not initiated in the east, but within the Maghrib, for the Vandals, having inherited the *limes* along with the country it delimited, were under continual attack as the Romans had been before them. After several defeats, it became clear that they could not win out, and it was only then that, by promising miracles, the church prevailed on the emperor to send an expedition. And a miracle came to pass: the victory of Justinian's army surprised everyone including Belisarius, the general in command. But long before the expedition of 533 we observe a Byzantinization of the Vandals, and it was their attempt to halt this process of peaceful reconquest that precipitated the crisis.

Actually it was not so much a reconquest as a restoration; a section of the former propertied class, and first of all the church, recovered its lands. Roman landowners were given the right to demand the restitution of property which in some cases had not belonged to their families for as much as three generations. As a century before, the conquerors took over the lands, women and servants of the

2 This aspect accounts for the a posteriori view of the Vandals' motivation. But it seems absurd to speak of a "design" on Genseric's part. The same sort of "design" could then be observed in the Aghlabids. See Courtois, *Les Vandales et l'Afrique*, pp. 205-214. His notions of barbarian psychology are rather elementary.

conquered. And along with the spoils, the Byzantines inherited the usual political and military difficulties. Regaining its place in the empire, North Africa was to share its troubles: schisms in the church, revolts in the army, rivalries and jealousies in the administration. Justinian issued laws as if nothing had happened in the fifth century, but after his death (565) the change became evident: with the connivance of the generals and the high officials, the landowners became the real masters of Africa. The fortifications around the cities, abundant traces of which still exist, bear witness to a disintegrating authority, intensified exploitation, and the steadily increasing opposition between the governing and the governed, the landowning and the landless classes. In this respect the situation was the same as in the eastern provinces of the empire: when in the middle of the seventh century the empire's southern neighbors, the Arabs, uniting in a state and creed, sallied forth from their desert peninsula, they too conducted themselves as heirs. They would arrive in the Maghrib as successors, and once again it was this logic of inheritance that prevailed. In the end they were to imitate the Byzantines, employ the same methods and encounter the same difficulties.

From 429 to 533, from 533 to 649, from 649 to 741: Vandals, Byzantines, Arabs; easy victories over the foreign rulers, difficult conquest of the indigenous population; one master replaced another and in the end was content with the same domain that the Maghribis had long been accustomed to cede to foreigners. We have spoken of a false regularity, a false continuity—false because their sole basis is one foreigner's point of view concerning another. Each successive foreigner vilifies his predecessor and promises to liberate the indigenous population. But what does the population say? Or rather, what does it do? The essential phenomenon of these three centuries is the consolidation of the tripartite division: three regions, three historic levels, each determining the others.

The Sahara

It was in the light of this tripartite Maghrib that the Saharan fringe acquired its historical importance; it would be a mistake to drown a chronologically determinate problem (second to seventh century) in another much broader problem that is a matter of geography.[3] Three points require discussion in connection with this historical Sahara: its economico-social organization, symbolized by the famous problem of the camel; the nature of the population; and finally its relation to the Maghrib as a whole. Gsell put forward an organic theory, according to which the imperialist policy of Rome drove the Maghribis into the desert and the Maghribis in turn drove the Ethiopian blacks before them with the help of the newly arrived camel, which from the first century A.D. on enabled them to transform the Sahara into a vast inland sea. Gautier tries to make the Romans, who are mildly criticized in the preceding thesis, appear in a more favorable light. In his version, the Romans deliberately populated the Maghrib with men and animals. These last unfortunately included the camel, which gave rise to the destructive nomad. Courtois rejects both these explanations, denying that the camel could have been absent from the Sahara in any part of the historical period[4] or that the Gaetulians and Ethiopians ever ceased to coexist; the new development, according to him, was the appearance in Tripolitania, from the third century on, of nomadic tribes (Luwāta) from the Upper Nile; these tribes, says Courtois, were the cause of the evacuation decreed by Diocletian.[5]

[3] See Capot-Rey, *Le Sahara français*; Briggs, *Tribes of the Sahara*; UNESCO, *Nomades et nomadisme au Sahara*.

[4] Courtois, *Les Vandales de l'Afrique*, pp. 99f. In criticizing Gsell and Gautier on this point, he is criticizing a whole method of utilizing ancient literature. See also Demougeot, "Le Chameau et l'Afrique du Nord Romaine," pp. 209-247.

[5] It is evident that Gsell's model was the policy of *cantonnement* (confining the indigenous population to prescribed areas) in Algeria and that of Courtois is the Hilālian invasion.

These three theories, which along with certain variants have gained wide acceptance, all go far beyond the available facts which are themselves uncertain since they depend very largely on the more than hazardous interpretation of the Saharan cave paintings. Thus far it has been impossible to determine why the camel disappeared from this region during the neolithic (if it did), nor at what date it was reintroduced, and in what numbers; furthermore, historians have continually changed their minds about the drying out of the Sahara: was it a process covering hundreds or thousands of years? The fundamental question, however, seems to be, Which came first, the camel or the nomad? All the authors we have cited assume that the camel was responsible for nomadism and that the nomads must have come from outside. This geographic determinism, whose most resolute proponent is Gautier, conceals all manner of political implications and above all indicates a total failure to understand the complexity of historical processes. It is perfectly possible that the camel had always existed on the northern fringe of the Sahara, but that over a long period men had no need to make use of it. Nomadism is not a state of nature or an invariable trait, but a mode of social organization. Over an entire epoch the population may well have shifted back and forth between agriculture and pastoral nomadism; there is no need to assume that an outsider must have come from the east. All in all, Gsell's view, as is usually the case, seems infinitely more acceptable than the later ones with their increasing concern for ideological justification. It seems probable that the bulk of the Maghribi population were renomadized; that, driven beyond the *limes* and taking possession of the northern Sahara, they found camels already present in small numbers and bred more of them. There is no proof (except for the gratuitous hypothesis of a first Hilālian invasion) that the Luwāta of Tripolitania came from the east or that the blacks were driven out of the Sahara. The classical texts provide no assurance that the Ethiopians were really blacks or that the blacks and Berbers were always in close contact. Nor is there any reason to suppose that trans-Saharan trade always existed or concerned the greater part of the Maghrib. The only trade presenting some degree of probability is that between Bornu and the Tripolitanian trading posts; but neither its magnitude nor regularity can be determined. Moreover we have no assurance that the Maghrib was involved in it. All reconstructions by western historians are basically projections of later situations.[6]

The problem of the Saharan Maghrib is not one of zoology or climatology, but is in essence historical. It was when a part of the indigenous population took refuge in the desert, reverting to nomadism though determined to return north at the first opportunity, that the Sahara took on a specific significance; it retained this significance only during a very definite period, beginning with the Roman exploitation of North Africa and ending when the Sahara became a true connecting link between Black Africa and the Maghrib, a development which in all likelihood occurred in the eighth and ninth centuries and not four centuries earlier. It was this Sahara, the Sahara as a place of refuge, that exerted a negative influence on the history of the Maghrib from the third to seventh centuries. Any attempt to seek its causes in extraneous, geographical, zoological or human (migration) serves only, in the last analysis, to obscure its significance as an involuntary return to protohistory.

The Middle Maghrib

This is the free Maghrib of the kingdoms, pushed back to the south and west, crushed and subjugated during the two centuries of Roman rule, and slowly reconquered from

[6] The book to which the reader is regularly referred, Bovill, *Caravans of the Old Sahara*, is closer to the historical novel than to history. The proof that is offered, the discovery of Roman coins in Mauretania, would have to be corroborated a dozen times to carry conviction. See Maung, "Le Périple de la mer Erythrée."

the third century on. The consequences of this setback were fragmentation and regression, as is clearly shown by a comparison of the kingdoms preceding and those following the apogee of the Roman occupation.

We have little information regarding these kingdoms despite the numerous hypothetical reconstructions based on a few inscriptions and monuments,[7] most of them late, dating from the fifth or early sixth centuries, and providing no basis for inferences with regard to the third century. Yet despite our ignorance of the stages of the Berber reconquest, two facts seem established: the fragmentation of the communities, and the extreme caution of the chiefs despite their manifest desire to return to the northeast. Systematizing the indications provided by Procopius and Corippus in their accounts of the Byzantine wars, Courtois distinguishes nine kingdoms, which he names. They are the Baquate kingdom around Volubilia, the kingdom around Altava in the Oran region,[8] the kingdoms of the Ouarsenis Mountains, of the Hodna region, of the Aurès Mountains, of Nemencha, of Capsus (not located), of Antalas in northern Tunisia, and of Cabao in Tripolitania. Two of these, those of Capsus and of Nemencha, are problematic in the opinion of the author himself; others are no less so, for in interpreting inscriptions Courtois extrapolates as unjustifiably as Carcopino did, and when he employs literary sources he runs the risk of mistaking the chiefs of armed bands on the frontiers of the Vandal or Byzantine territory for real political leaders. The kingdoms that merit our attention because they throw light on many subsequent events are those of Volubilis and Oran, which were independent and had few ties with the successors of the Romans, and those of the Aurès Mountains and of Antalas which bordered on

[7] See especially Courtois, *Les Vandales de l'Afrique*, pp. 334f., where the whole question is recapitulated.

[8] The chief of the Oranian kingdom was the famous Masūna, to whose family the thirteen *djedars*, funerary monuments of Christian inspiration, are generally attributed. The word *jidar*, which means "wall" in Arabic, is used in the Koran.

Roman territory and carried on the old policy of Massinissa—extreme caution, combined with determination to allow no further westward advance on the part of the invaders. The Berber chiefs offered no opposition when the northeastern territory changed hands, but when Genseric's successor, disappointed in his Mediterranean ambitions, tried to extend his control to the Maghrib, the inhabitants of the Aurès revolted (477-484) and inflicted defeats on the Vandals that gave the persecuted Catholic Church new hope. Similarly after 535, when the victorious Byzantines tried to reconstitute Roman Africa, they were blocked by the same kingdom of Aurès under Yabdas, who resisted for four years, took refuge in the west, and resumed the struggle in 546. The kingdom of Antalas in northwestern Tunisia also resisted the Vandals, and defeated them in 530. This defeat sounded the death knell of the Vandals' power in Africa, for it revived the courage of the Catholics and of the Byzantine emperor. Recognized by the Byzantines, Antalas helped them in their war against the Yabdas; treated cavalierly when the Byzantines thought they had no further need of him, he revolted, defeated the Byzantines in 545 and was defeated in turn the following year by John Troglita. The same resistance was offered when the Byzantines tried to extend their territory southward or eastward into Tripolitania. The details of these almost incessant struggles are not known, but their significance is clear: the Berber chiefs were willing to recognize the theoretical sovereignty of the masters of Carthage, whoever they might be, but opposed any return to the past, that is, any offensive action on their part. The Berber kings were motivated neither by hatred nor duplicity nor inconstancy, but by a patient, stubborn policy, the old policy of Massinissa, carried out with the same methods: it consisted in shutting up the Byzantines in the Carthaginian redoubt and by-passing them to the south and east. The final episode of Byzantine history in the Maghrib bears the marks of extreme despair: lies, betrayals, acts of vengeance, surprise attacks, all the stratagems of the besieged.[9] As usual, once the masters realized that their exploitation of the country was nearing its end, they intensified it beyond all measure and so brought about new revolts.

Concerning the number, organization and degree of unity of these kingdoms, we are without information. But can we at least know their general character? Did the Latin language and Roman organization survive in them? Was Christianity preserved? On the basis of inscriptions, some historians reply in the affirmative. But even if we accept the Christianity of these princes as proved, what kind of Christianity was it? The generalized and virtually permanent insurrections under the Byzantines indicate that the Berbers drew a clear distinction between Christianity and the imperial power and held aloof from the Catholic Church because it was allied with the Empire. When long after the death of Justinian the church finally turned against the emperor in the Monophysite controversy, we find no indication of any popular enthusiasm for the church. Mention is made of a Donatist revival toward the end of the sixth century; mention is also made of Jewish proselytism after the persecuted Jews had been driven out of Byzantine territory. All this means only one thing: that the Christianity of this middle Maghrib, which developed without contact with the church, gradually took on the form of an abstract monotheism capable of accommodating itself to any dogma whatsoever. This point takes on decided importance if we recall that it was in this part of the Maghrib, which had been autonomous for two centuries, that the Arabs first attempted to implant their new religion.

The Subjugated Maghrib

This is the part of the Maghrib that the Romans retained to the end of their domination and that was inherited successively by the Vandals, Byzantines and Arabs. Under the

[9] For example, the execution, mentioned in all contemporary accounts, of the defeated Berber chiefs, Antalas, Cutzinas and Garmul.

Vandals it was reduced to an area of one hundred thousand square kilometers[10] and under the Byzantines to the coastal regions and to the cities and their environs. Its territorial expansion, however, is of little importance; what we are concerned with here is its historico-social structure. The masters changed; their race, religion and language changed, but not so the structure. The large estates belonged to the state, that is, to the master or suzerain of Carthage; the medium-sized estates of the north were distributed among the conquering soldiers, who when the division was unjust revolted, which was far from a catastrophe for the indigenous population. In the eyes of the serf, the day laborer, the tenant farmer paying rent to the landlord or the state, and of the landowner subject to the territorial tax, the master's identity meant little; the share of the harvest that was taken away from them increased steadily and attained intolerable proportions in the second half of the sixth century under the Byzantines. Despite the studies based on private or public documents of the time, in particular contracts dating from the end of the Vandal period[11] and Justinian's law of restitution, the social structure of the period is far from clear. This much is certain, however: the inhabitants of the Carthaginian region, the richest in the Maghrib, who should have been the backbone of the entire social edifice, were the poorest and most exploited of all. In their eyes the society represented by the imperial state and the church and symbolized by Carthage became a synonym for misery and injustice; it gave them nothing, and the famous peace emphasized by the historians, presided over first by the Romans, then by the Vandals, merely provided the possibility of more intensive exploitation. We read that Rome introduced the state to the Maghrib and that the Maghrib subsequently lost this state to its great detriment. What content can we impute to this "state" for the fourth or sixth

10 See Courtois, *Les Vandales de l'Afrique*, p. 184.

11 *Tablettes Albertini.* They are generally believed to have been hidden during an attack by Antalas's Moors.

century? The state is above all a power relationship. From the third century on, the power of the state became increasingly that of the landowners and bishops; once this power was diluted, no one was able to centralize it or give it full legitimacy again. The subjugated Maghrib did not regard the continual skirmishes of the middle Maghrib as a misfortune; on the contrary, they provided a breathing spell. At the beginning of the sixth century, the "Moors" of Antalas drove the Roman landowners out of western Tunisia, and the joy of the Berbers enslaved to the landowners can easily be imagined. When the Byzantines were obliged to fortify the cities and establish a defensive ring around the Aurès, when early in the exarchate of Gennadius (587) the Tripolitanians appeared before the walls of Carthage, it seems more than likely that these victories of the "Moors" owed a good deal to the help of the serfs, laborers and smallholders, who must have been glad to be freed for a time from rent, forced labor and taxation. Since the Catholic Church had thrown in its lot with the established power, it seems reasonable to infer that the community of interests between the Berber "Romani" and the "Mauri" outweighed all cultural or even linguistic differences between them. In the long run, however, the most important consequence of this "dispersion" of political power was the revival of local groupings, especially of the clan whose defensive function required it to be as large as possible. When "public life" as the foundation of the Roman system is contrasted with the "private life" that became the dominant element in the Moslem period, it must be remembered that the weakening of the Roman empire was accompanied by the decadence of "public life."

Thus far most writers have attributed this turn toward private life, toward the endogamous clan, to an eternal tribal structure, without bothering to look into the situation at the apogee of the Roman power. Perhaps the time has come to consider it as a response to clearly defined problems. Later on this solution would come to be regarded as a model of behavior in times characterized by a diffuse authority without recognized legitimacy. But when a historian encounters it for the first time, he is in duty bound to perceive its freshness and specific character, even though subsequent research may some day thrust its origins further into the past. The phenomenon, of course, is by no means peculiar to the Maghrib; what is specific is a certain similarity between this "regressive" evolution of the subjugated Maghrib and that of the two other Maghribs—a kindred destiny transcending geography and time. But similarity does not mean unity. The clan model of the kingdoms and the tribal model of the desert nomads performed the same function, but there is no justification for lumping the two together and speaking of an identical tribal structure. The clan model is more territorial than has been thought; in the long run genealogies and memories change as a group moves from place to place; the group becomes an agglomeration of men of diverse origins, united by their presence in the same locality. How can this fact, which has been recognized time and time again, be accounted for unless we start from the principle that the group is a product, not of subdivision and dispersion but of a defensive pact among individuals, whose permanence is guaranteed down through the generations by the "name" which has been chosen and which no member of the group is free to abjure? And if this is true, what point can there be in attempting to draw a historical map of the tribes?[12]

Once established, this model was to endure in the Maghrib as long as the problems of exploitation and illegitimate power had not been solved. The consequence was the isolation of the fortified cities and the inexorable decadence of the countryside. For this no doubt the continual wars were to blame, but also the indifference of the population toward something that had ceased to belong to them.

A tripartite Maghrib united in defensive regression, a

12 Compare the reasons for rejecting the "positivist" theories given by Berque in his article "Qu'est-ce qu'une tribu nord-africaine?"

dispersed, impoverished society: these were the consequences of a history—not a geography—that began when the movement initiated long before Massinissa was crushed. The people of the Maghribi have asked, "What did Rome bring us?" It was neither strong enough to control the whole country nor weak enough to abandon it; a sterile equilibrium was established between the three Maghribs and above all within the middle Maghrib, none of whose kingdoms was able to gain the upper hand without outside help. At the same time the people of the Maghrib became accustomed to waiting for outside or supernatural help against foreign rulers; this attitude consolidated the structures of the middle Maghrib and helps us to understand why the victory that often seemed so close always vanished at the last moment. The Maghribis approached Carthage, their goal, only when other conquerors knocked at the door. A prisoner between sea and sand, the middle Maghrib vegetated, waiting for a chance that came too late. But its aim never varied: to retake Carthage, reach the sea, and unify the kingdoms of the center.

In this perspective the third conquest, that of the Arabs, brought no innovation. After an initial period, when it looked as though they might evade the forces we have described, the Arabs gave in to them; in the middle of the eighth century the tripartite Maghrib was reconstituted.

II

The conquest of the Maghrib by the Arab armies over a period of some fifty years is known to us almost exclusively through Arab texts. These draw a distinction between reconnaissance raids and organized conquest.

In 640/18 'Amr conquered Egypt and pushed on to the west; Barqa was taken two years later and Tripoli fell. In 647/26, under the Caliph 'Uthmān, an expedition was organized and 'Abd Allah b. Sa'd b. Abī Sarḥ, governor of Egypt, was put in command. Reinforced in Tripolitania, the expedition entered Byzacenia. Byzantine Africa was under the authority of the patriarch Gregory, who had taken advantage of the religious dissensions between the church and the emperor to declare himself independent; giving battle at Sbeitla (Sufetule) to the Arab army, whose strength has been estimated at twenty thousand, he was defeated and killed. The Arabs then sent out raids in all directions, but seem to have had no intention of attacking the cities of the north. The Byzantines (meaning no doubt the big landowners who had now been deprived of their leader) offered to pay tribute, and the Arabs eagerly accepted. Are we to conclude that at this stage they were interested solely in loot? It should be remembered that the countries they had thus far conquered had been familiar to them for three centuries, whereas the Maghrib was an unknown quantity. At the most they may have heard some vague mention of it in Syria, as of a rich Byzantine province. This ignorance accounts for the Caliph 'Umar's reluctance to embark on the adventure and suggests that 'Uthmān, his successor, had given exact orders concerning the tactics to be pursued.

A second reconnaissance raid was made in 665/45, at the end of the great crisis that had shaken the Moslem community after the assassination of 'Uthmān. In the meantime the internal situation of Ifrīqiya (Arabic transcription of the Latin Africa) had deteriorated steadily as a result of the religious struggles. This had not gone unnoticed by the Arabs established in Tripolitania, who sent an appeal to the new Caliph. This second raid, led by Mu'āwiya b. Ḥudayj, was directed against the cities of the north. Sousse (Sūsa) was besieged and taken, reportedly by 'Abd Allah b. Zubayr, and Jalūla by 'Abd al-Malik b. Marwān. In this second raid the Arabs showed a better knowledge of the terrain and of the Byzantines' tactics. It had now become possible to organize a real campaign of conquest.

This was to be the work of 'Uqba b. Nafi', who was already familiar with Africa, having conquered the Ghadames oasis in 662/44 and taken part in the first raid. Having worked out a strategic plan, he arrived in southern Tunisia in 670 with an army estimated at ten thousand horsemen. Employing tactics that 'Umar had recommended to earlier Arab conquerors, he chose a large plateau in the center of the country and there founded Kairouan (674/55). Then, instead of proceeding northward, he followed the central plateaus, so breaking with the traditional plan of conquest, i.e. to start at the coast and move southward. In the center there were few garrisons of well-armed and well-trained Byzantines, but on the other hand this was the middle Maghrib, which had been independent for centuries. After an interim, during which he was replaced by Abū al-Muhājir, who succeeded by a policy of moderation in gaining the confidence of the local chiefs, especially Kusayla, who later led the Berber resistance, 'Uqba recovered his command in 682/62 and resumed the conquest, taking the route from Lamis to Bagaiya to Ṭāhart. It seems certain that he passed through the Tlemcen region and reached the sea, whether the Mediterranean or the Atlantic it is hard to say.[13] He gathered information about northern Morocco and may even have sent out some reconnaissance expeditions, but it would be hazardous to speak of a true conquest of northern Morocco. It seems well established that on his return march, probably over the same route, he divided his army. Attacked by Kusayla,[14] he was defeated and killed in the Biskra region in 683/64. His chief mistake no doubt was to bypass the cities of the north in the belief that it would be easier to conquer the middle Maghrib. In any event this policy was modified.

The Arabs regrouped their forces in Tripolitania and waited for the second crisis of the caliphate, brought about by the revolt of 'Abd Allah b. Zubayr in Mecca, to be re-

[13] See Brunschvig, "Ibn Abd-al-h'akam et la conquête de l'Afrique du Nord par les Arabes," pp. 108-155; also Lévi-Provençal, "Nass Jadīd," pp. 193-224, and its French translation.

[14] Some writers speak of the Byzantine allies of Kusayla (Kasīla): these were probably armed groups operating on their own account after the weakening of Byzantine authority at the end of the sixth century.

solved. A first attempt to resume the offensive under the command of Zuhayr b. Qays al-Balawī was only partially successful. Kusayla was killed at Mems in 686/67 and Kairouan retaken; but a Berber counterattack obliged Zuhayr to evacuate it once more, and shortly afterward Zuhayr died at Barqa. A second attempt, led by Ḥasan b. Nu'mān, was more fruitful. He recaptured Kairouan in 691/72[15] and marched on to Carthage, which he took by storm the following year, but it was probably retaken by the Byzantine army some time before 695. Ḥasan went on fighting with some success in the northern regions around Bizerte (Benzert). But then he encountered the opposition of the Berber mountaineers, now united under the Kāhina, chief of the Aurès Mountains, and aided by armed groups of Byzantines. Defeated in the Baghai-Tebessa region, Ḥasān withdrew to Tripolitania, where he waited for the caliph to send him reinforcements. Immediately after this victory, the Roman or Byzantine landowners seem to have withdrawn their recognition of the Auresian leadership, just as a century before they had tried to get rid of Antalas after defeating Yabdas. The determination of the Kāhina and her sons to preserve the unity of command was interpreted as a desire to carry out a scorched-earth policy. Be that as it may, Ḥasān, informed of these dissensions, resumed the offensive in 695/76. Carthage was retaken and the Byzantines driven out for good. In 698/79 the Kāhina was defeated. This meant the end of armed resistance, and Mūsā b. Nuṣayr, the new governor, drew the consequences.

Appointed in 704/85, Mūsā, for the first time, held his authority directly from the caliph and was independent of Egypt. He crossed the central Maghrib to northern Moroc-

15 See the story of Ḥassān's arrival in Kairouan, cited in al-Nāsirī, *al-Istiqṣā*, vol. I, p. 82: "He asked the Afāriqa, 'Who is the mightiest of your kings?' 'The master of Carthage,' they replied." In this text Afāriqa means "inhabitants of Ifrīqiya," without specification of any kind.

co; following 'Uqba's itinerary, he entered Tangiers and sent his two sons, 'Abd Allah and Marwān, on reconnaissance to the south. His policy was one of great moderation; the Berber chiefs embraced the new religion and as hostages gave the Arabs their sons, whom Mūsā established in Tangiers. Did Mūsā's sons go beyond the Volubilis-Tangiers region? It seems doubtful in view of the fact that in 709/91 Mūsā began to make preparations for a Spanish expedition, command of which he entrusted to a Berber, Ṭāriq b. Ziyād.

The foregoing facts seem established, though the conquest as a whole presents many obscure points. The sources are late and based on highly divergent traditions; but their main flaw is inherent in the nature of the documents themselves. The books of Maghāzī (Moslem conquests) are often the work of jurists who wished to show under what conditions the various provinces had embraced Islam, because the juridical status of the territories and their populations were determined accordingly. Wishing the people to enjoy the most liberal regime, the jurists accepted the most contradictory accounts. Gautier, who was not an Arabist, expresses his astonishment at this, but fails to understand that the chroniclers refused to choose between contradictory accounts because they wished to see the people enjoy the most favorable legal status. These juxtaposed versions were then taken over intact by the annalists, giving rise to disturbing fluctuations in chronology. It seems unlikely that this situation can be remedied even if older Arabic texts are discovered; only new Byzantine texts or numismatics might help. On the basis of the confused chronology at their disposal, western historians have drawn questionable conclusions with regard to the slowness of the conquest. We must take into account the various crises of the caliphate, which several times brought the movement to a halt, and still more, the distance of the Maghrib from the Arabs' base of operations, which was Egypt, since Tripolitania was never more than a stopping place. The Arabs confronted diverse enemies; the texts speak of Rūm (Byzantines), Afranj (Romans), Afāriqa[16] and Berbers. A great deal has been written in attempts to define these terms. It would seem most plausible to regard the distinctions as socio-economic, the Rūm being the representatives of military and administrative power, for the most part Byzantines, the Afranj being the landowners, for the most part Roman or at least Romanized, the Afāriqa the African city dwellers, probably bilingual and Christianized, and the Berbers the rural indigenous population. It is certain that each group had its own strategy of resistance, which did not make things easier for the conquerors. Undoubtedly the saying quoted by Ibn Khaldūn about the twelve apostasies of the Berbers[17] is nothing more than a rhetorical formula symbolizing the slowness and difficulty of a conquest that was very different from the Arabs' previous conquests. But the slowness and difficulty seem to have resulted less from the attitude of the Berbers, than from the situation in the caliphate and the tactical error of bypassing the cities, so leaving the Byzantines bases from which they could easily foment revolts in the rear of the Arab armies.

One attempt to account both for the vicissitudes and consequences of the Arab conquest is a theory originating with Gautier and handed down from book to book.[18] Those who

[16] Gautier's theory that the Afāriqa were Phoenicians must be rejected.

[17] "Abū Mūḥammad b. Abī Zayd al-Qayrawani maintains that the Berbers apostatized twelve times between Tripoli and Tangiers; they were lastingly converted only when Mūsā b. Nuṣayr crossed the straits to Spain, accompanied by a large number of Berber chiefs, who settled there; it was then that the Maghrib was definitively won to Islam" (quoted by al-Nāṣirī, *al-Istiqṣā*, vol. 1, p. 80). This passage should probably be interpreted in the light of the social mobility introduced by the Arabs—which it implies.

[18] One formulation of this theory occurs in Gautier, *Le Passé de l'Afrique du Nord*, p. 297: "Throughout the history of the Maghrib, we encounter the mutual attraction of the Berber and Arab nomads. The similarity in their modes of life and feelings outweighed the difference in their languages. The legend of the Kāhina seems to show

criticize it, William Marçais for example, have failed to take note of its twofold—cultural and economic—character. In the cultural sphere, Gautier distinguishes between the Romanized populations of the cities and the Punic populations, and in the economic sphere between the sedentary, Christianized, and the nomadic, Judaized, populations. According to this thesis the sedentary populations (Kusayla) opposed the Arabs at first, but the Punic majority among these populations were oriental, hence assimilable, whereas the nonassimilable Romans required order; after the first Byzantine defeats, the sedentary populations had two different but compatible reasons for accepting the new yoke provided that order was restored. The nomads, for their part, were favorable to the Arabs from the start because of their identical modes of life (hence the almost immediate Islamization of a fraction of the nomads), but insisted on their right to go on pillaging. When the Arabs occupied the cities and were obliged to restore a certain amount of order, the nomads turned against them and the consequence was the Kāhina's desperate revolt. Because of this double contradiction, those who resisted assimilation were inclined to accept the new order and those who were opposed to all order were easily assimilated. These circumstances favored the conquerors. But in this form Gautier's thesis is merely an abstract formulation of the events of the conquest, without explicative value. It is evident that the two generals whose conquests were most enduring, Abū al-Muhājir and Mūsā, carried out the same policy as the earlier conquerors of the Maghrib, that is, to occupy the cities and leave the indigenous Berber masses under the authority of their chiefs. The conquest may well have been retarded less by the crises

the influence of this unspoken sympathy, and this at a time when unlike the nomads the sedentary population realized the advantages of the Caliphate, a regular government and administration, and a certain degree of order . . . in short, of all those things without which a city cannot exist."

of the caliphate than by the contrary policy of intense proselytism zealously pursued by 'Uqba. Moreover, this explanation fits in with the subsequent developments.

After 711/93 the Maghrib became theoretically a province of the Arab empire, providing soldiers and slaves, and paying tribute to fill the coffers of the caliph at Damascus. The administration that took form at Kairouan, the capital of the new province, was a copy of that set up by 'Umar I and 'Abd al-Malik b. Marwān; it consisted essentially of a judiciary and of the *dawāwīn* (offices) devoted to the collection of taxes and recruiting for the army. But the new empire was based on a religion and a language. What was the influence of these in the new province? Islam does not advocate forced conversions, especially in the case of "people of the Book," Christians and Jews. What was the attitude of the conquerors toward the Berbers? In view of the extreme ideological confusion prevailing among the Berbers, it may be conjectured that the Arabs were particularly cautious in their approach to the populations of the middle Maghrib, all of whom were most probably under the influence of monotheism in one form or another. From the start the problem was more political than religious, and this would account both for the fierce armed opposition of the inhabitants at the start and for the ease with which they were converted later on. It is more than likely that their conversion took the form of a recognition of sovereignty, quite comparable to the recognition with which Belisarius had contented himself in 533. But it seems possible that a large part of the western Maghrib was not affected by this formal recognition. The military expeditions probably followed the more traveled routes, leaving vast regions, especially in central and southern Morocco, untouched.

To speak of an Arabization of the Maghrib at this stage would be even more hazardous. True, Kairouan, a new capital created ex nihilo, must have been an Arab city from the start; as a haven for fugitives from the destroyed cities, it may even then have played its role as a cultural nucleus.

But even taking account of the ease with which city dwellers change languages for politico-administrative reasons, we cannot be sure that the process of Arabization was rapid; indeed, the numismatic finds argue to the contrary, since the inscriptions on coins long remained bilingual. It is true that Arabic quickly replaced Latin as the administrative language. But if Latin seems to have disappeared with surprising rapidity, the explanation may well be that its implantation was far less extensive than is generally supposed. Genuine Arabization would presuppose a recession of the Berber language, a process that had certainly not begun in the eighth century.

The conquest, which consisted essentially in the imposition of Arab sovereignty, meant neither Islamization nor Arabization.[19] Arabization required many centuries and Islamization was the work of the Berbers themselves. Even the recognition of Arab sovereignty was ambiguous since the authority of the local chiefs was also recognized. The fact that Mūsā b. Nuṣayr, after his easy victory, invited the Berber chiefs to share in the glory and advantages of future conquests, would seem in the long run to imply a certain form of local autonomy.

III

In recapitulating these facts, it is hard to refrain from asking what was new in the Arab conquest. And yet, how many pseudoproblems the colonial historians raised, and how many pseudoanswers they gave! The long resistance? The resistance to the Byzantines and the Vandals was no less long.[20] The failure of Rome and success of Islam, the apostasy of the Berbers? This prevailing view argues a strange

[19] The situation was very different in Syria and Iraq where the process of Arabization had been going on for two centuries at the time of the conquest.

[20] It seems plausible to suppose that the accent put on this Berber resistance by the colonial historians conceals a desire to minimize the difficulties of the French conquest.

historical myopia. Certain writers speak of a "historical scandal," and scandal indeed there would be, if we supposed that the Maghrib was Christian in the same sense as nineteenth-century France and from one minute to the next turned Moslem as it is today. If the terms of reference are the Rome of Augustus and nineteenth-century Islam, one may reasonably speak of a deliberate regression from civilization to barbarism. But if we ask what sort of Roman civilization, what form of Christianity, what degree of Islamization—what we observe is not an abrupt break but a process of imperceptible change. It is an imposture to take Rome at the highest level of social organization and Islam at its lowest, and the "scandal" is purely subjective, for men do not pass from a remembered golden age to an anticipated decadence, but on the contrary from a real decadence (that of the Byzantines) to the hope of better things. Once we change our perspective, we are struck by the continuity of the process.

Once we pose a pseudoproblem, we become lost in pseudo-explanations:[21] the drying out of the Sahara, the coming of the camel from the east, the spread of nomadism, the sleeping Carthaginian, the dormant savage in the Maghribi mind; or all these monsters concurrently, plotting the ruin of Rome from the first century B.C. on and so preparing the way for the Arab conquerors. In reality we find a process of slow, continuous change. It is only in the long view that the Arabs or Islam can be termed successful. The conquest of the middle Maghrib was a failure; what succeeded was the conquest of that Maghrib which all the preceding conquerors had controlled, often with less difficulty. In other words, the success of the Arabs was no more immediate than that of their predecessors. Here there is nothing new. And as for factors that later redounded to the benefit of Islam, some of these were indeed new, while others had long

[21] The last chapter of Julien, *Histoire de l'Afrique du Nord*, 2nd ed., vol. 1, which recapitulates Courtois's article "De Rome à l'Islam," pp. 24ff., is an anthology of these pseudoproblems.

been at work. A desire to settle in the country, which was not always present among the Phoenicians and Romans but greatly benefited the Vandals before the Arabs; the limited number of colonists; the nonexistence of an exploiting church; the relatively quick disappearance of vassaldom toward a distant sovereign; some of these factors had favored the Vandals, whose yoke was found more bearable than that of the Romans and who were regretted when they were gone. Social mobility?[22] This was certainly the most effective factor, one that had never before been present on so large a scale, but it was only after 711 that it took on its full force and even after that there were violent resurgences of an exclusive caste system. The existence of a national schismatic movement, Khārijism? Donatism might have played the same role if the state and the church had not crushed it. There is nothing scandalous or miraculous about the Arab conquest; it proceeded along the same lines as those that preceded it.

Very soon the Arabs were forced to content themselves with the part of the Maghrib that had been ceded to foreigners ever since the Carthaginian period. True, the religion of Islam spread to the middle Maghrib and the Sahara, but in the course of a slow process and for reasons that will be studied at the appropriate moment, i.e. when we deal with the time of their greatest effectiveness. There is no reason to marvel at the success of Islam nor to be scandalized by it; nor is there any reason to attribute to the Arabs a capacity for innovation they did not possess. They merely introduced into the Maghrib a particular way of worshiping God, and we cannot even be sure that the Berbers felt it to be so very new. Like the Vandals, like the Byzantines, the Arabs were heirs, and the discontinuity they are alleged to have introduced is merely a pretext for unfounded judgments.

22 Fostered principally by the *Walā'* (contract of clientage), an institution well known to the Arabs, which enabled many Berber princes to become integrated with the Arab aristocracy.

4. The Winning of Autonomy

The history of the eighth century (700-800/81-184) as recounted in the Arab chronicles is, like that of the two preceding centuries, a history of Berber insurrections. The military conquest had solved nothing. In none of these insurrections was the name of Christianity invoked, unless we suppose, as seems unlikely, that the later Moslem traditions erased this aspect of the problem.

The chroniclers wrote chiefly about battles, most of which took place in the east and in the regions of Tlemcen and Tangiers, which formed the main axis of conquest. Did this axis coincide with an important avenue of communication that an army of occupation was obliged to control? Was it, rather, a line of least resistance for the Arab armies, as opposed to the plateaus and mountainous regions? Or was it simply what we have termed the middle Maghrib, for it is interesting to note that most of the fifth- and sixth-century principalities were situated in this region. Here the Berber populations found a seasoned organization capable of leading them. The coastal cities seem to have been calm and the Arabs were not interested in the Sahara.

Apart from what we can reconstitute on the basis of the chronicles, we possess little information about the populations, political structures and methods of warfare of this period. The conjectures attempted by many western historians must be judged for what they are: hazardous hypotheses.

Though the events remain obscure because the internal situation of Maghribi society is unknown to us, some light is thrown on them by the events of the Arab orient.[1] During the eighth century North Africa was part of the empire of

[1] This fruitful approach was adopted by Georges Marçais in his *La Berbérie musulmane et l'Orient au moyen âge*, the best book on the period.

Damascus and felt the repercussions of events in its center. These events themselves, however, are not clear: struggles between Arab clans, the Muḍarites and Qaysites, amplified by quarrels over the Caliphate between Qurayshite clans, between the Umayyads and the Hāshimites, and within the Hāshimite camp between 'Abbāsids and 'Alīds. The soldiers who went to the Maghrib to fight brought with them the ideologies that served to justify these quarrels. The history of the Arab empire at this period is undoubtedly more helpful to us in understanding certain events in the Maghrib than was the internal history of Byzantium in a similar situation, because Arab influence, comparable to that of the Catholic church in the third century, was far more widespread than Byzantine influence in its day. Still, it would be a mistake to suppose that everything that happened in the Maghrib can be explained by the internal development of Islam. Certain factors remain, and perhaps will always remain, obscure.

I

Because of the rapidity with which the Arab state had developed, its central organization was weak; the Moslems were not subject to regular taxation (the *zakāt* was a legal form of alms), and the state derived its funds from the head tax (*jizya*) and the land tax (*kharāj*) on non-Moslems, and from the spoils of war. The center grew rich at the expense of the provinces, and under these conditions it was impossible to build up a stable organization in the Maghrib. Once the expansionist drive had died down, it was only natural that the state should undergo a crisis. The transformation of an oligarchic emirate to a world empire had created a need for reforms and raised enormous problems. A struggle for power had ensued; its three protagonists were 'Uthmān, 'Alī and Mu'āwiya.[2] Two choices were open: ei-

[2] See Ṭaha Ḥusayn, Introduction to *al-Fitna al-Kubrā*, vol. 1 (*'Uthmān*).

ther to build a conventional state in the image of other world empires—this policy necessitating an innovation (*biḍ'a*), namely regular taxation, was the one finally chosen by the Umayyad family representing the commercial aristocracy; or to perpetuate the system of egalitarian oligarchy. The latter was in the long run impossible, hence the desperate character of the partisans of this policy, exemplified by Khārijism and by Shī'ism in its beginnings. In the end realism won out, and an empire was built, first on the model of Byzantium, then on that of Persia. This development led to grave difficulties in the distant provinces. What form did the crisis take in the Maghrib?

Proselytism played an important role. It has often been said that Islam was tolerant for fiscal reasons. But it should not be forgotten that proselytism was also necessary to Islam. Proselytism may indeed have been contrary to the interests of the Umayyad state, but this was not the first time in history that an expansionist movement had suffered from its own internal contradictions. The Arabs who converted the Berbers to Islam were not all favorable to the ruling family; on the contrary, most of the *fuqahā'* were hostile to it. Moreover, in the struggle between the Umayyads and the 'Alīds, the Khārijites had combated the 'Alīds, their former friends, more bitterly than they had the Umayyads. In the course of the first century H. the Khārijites' relations with the masters of Damascus improved, but since the Khārijites remained a source of disturbance, the caliphs tended to send them to fight in the provinces in the name of God. Many went to the Maghrib. Strict and ardent in their piety, they were men of the desert, full of resentment against the wealth of the cities.[3]

Political exigencies both in Damascus and Kairouan im-

[3] It would be interesting to compare the content and tone of Commodianus with those of the Khārijite literature, if we could be sure that Commodianus was an African Donatist. See Brisson, *Autonomisme et christianisme.*

pelled the amirs to organize the western province, to put the people back to work and make them pay a territorial tax.[4] The measures that the Arab historians and others after them regarded as tyrannical now seem necessary to the establishment of an organized state. The ensuing revolt is explained by the fact that a large part of the population had been beyond the control of any central power since the beginning of the fifth century or earlier. The struggles of the next half century were merely a continuation of those carried on by the Berbers in the fifth and sixth centuries against every non-Berber central power, especially when it strove to go beyond the traditional area of foreign occupation in the northeast. Another reason for the present revolts was that the Umayyads had revived the old caste pride of the Arabs as a principle of government. True, under ʻUmar I, there had already been an aristocracy, but one based on seniority of conversion to Islam; under the Umayyads the old social barriers were revived and the army, which had provided the Berbers with a means of rising in the world, ceased to play this role. Everything conspired to reduce them to the condition they had been in under the Byzantines, and this the Berbers sensed well before the tendency to Byzantinization was symbolized by Governor Yazīd's establishment of a pretorian guard.

It is necessary to distinguish between the motives for revolt and the motives for adopting Khārijism as a justifying ideology, and here the factors inside and outside the Maghrib overlap.

II

The Umayyad caliphs appointed eight governors in all after Mūsā. The first few continued to wage war and to proselytize, especially the second, Ismāʻīl b. ʻUbayd Allah b. Abī

[4] On the relation of the *kharāj* to the general history of Islam, see Levy, *The Social Structure of Islam*, p. 310.

al-Muhājir, appointed in 718/100 by 'Umar II. It is frequently stated by the Arab historians that Islamization was completed—meaning that of the Berber chiefs.

In 720/102 Governor Yazīd b. Abī Muslim resolved to put the population back to work and make them pay taxes; he set up a personal guard modeled on that of the Byzantine governors, having learned these methods of government in the employ of his master, al-Ḥajjaj, in Iraq. He was assassinated, but this was only a straw in the wind.

The real revolt began in the west, in northern Morocco. In 734/116 'Ubayd Allah b. al-Ḥabḥāb, who had proved himself in Egypt, was appointed governor. He delegated his powers to sub-governors, among them 'Umar b. 'Ubayd Allah al-Murādī, who was sent to Tangiers. It should be noted that in this period the Arab armies were still advancing along the Mediterranean coast and in the Sous,[5] and it was essential to keep a secure hold on the bases of operations (Ifrīqiya and northern Morocco). Al-Murādī, we are told, tried a tax of one-fifth on the Berbers, a good part of whom had been converted to Islam.[6] In 740/123 he was assassinated. The revolt was led by Maysara, who had been a water peddler in Kairouan. He was a Sofrite (uncompromising Khārijite), a man of great piety and not of low estate. His revolt was concomitant with others which broke out in Arabia, Yemen and Iraq and put an end to the Umayyad dynasty. Should this conjunction be regarded as mere chance or the consequence of concerted propaganda?

The rebels were victorious. Returning to Tangiers, they immediately became involved in the internal dissensions common to all Khārijite groups. Maysara was killed and replaced by Khālid b. Ḥamīd. The governor of Kairouan sent an army made up of soldiers brought back from Spain and Sicily. In the ensuing battle the imperial army suffered a crushing defeat. At the news the east revolted. A second

5 Throughout this period, Sous means Morocco south of the Sebou.

6 Possibly they were not very thoroughly Islamized, which would account for the attitudes of both parties.

army (of twelve to seventy thousand men?) sent from Damascus under the new governor Kulthūm b. 'Iyaḍ was decimated the same year on the Sebou River and the survivors fled to Spain. After these two battles, all of northern Morocco was lost to the Caliph's authority. The Berbers of Spain had revolted at the same time, but were defeated. Further battles were fought in southern Constantine, on the marches of Ifrīqiya. But before going under, the Umayyad dynasty had time for a slight revenge. An imperial army under Ḥanzala b. Ṣafwān inflicted severe defeats on the Khārijites of Ifrīqiya in two battles (al-Qarn and al-Asnam, 741/124).

At this date the Maghrib may be said to have won its autonomy; indeed, it had returned to the Vandalo-Byzantine situation, but this time under the banner of an Islamic sect. This choice must certainly be attributed to the Berber chiefs, who wished to establish or reestablish their kingdoms in the middle Maghrib.

In the series of events related in the chronicles, which from now on concern only the eastern Maghrib and Spain, the desire of certain Arab aristocrats to carve out principalities for themselves is clearly discernible, an obvious indication that their ties with the center of the empire were by now extremely relaxed. The descendants of 'Uqba b. Nāfi' tried to do so in defiance of all legality. The first, 'Abd al-Raḥmān b. Ḥabīb (745-755/127-137), took possession of Kairouan, but his venture failed because of family dissensions, the Khārijite forces on the border of Tripolitania, and finally because of the intervention of the 'Abbāsid caliph al-Mansūr. The second attempt, this time with the consent of the caliphate, was made by 'Umar b. Ḥafṣ (768-771) and Yazīd b. Ḥātim (771-788/156-173), descendants of al-Muhallab b. Abī Sofra, a famous general who had fought the Khārijites in Iraq. In the belief that he had pacified southern Tunisia, 'Umar advanced into the Tobna region. Encircled by a coalition of the Khārijites, he escaped only thanks to dissensions in the enemy camp. His successors continued his efforts but recognized the hopelessness of any attempt to go beyond the borders of Ifrīqiya. One of them, Rawḥ b. Ḥātim (787-790) concluded a pact with a Khārijite chief, Ibn Rustum.

Though the al-Muhallab family failed to carve out a principality for themselves in Ifrīqiya, the Aghlabids, who had been their lieutenants, succeeded. Al-Aghlab b. Salīm al-Tamīmī, who had defended the Zāb against the Khārijites, arrived in Ifrīqiya in 759/142 and served as governor for two years (765-767); his son Ibrāhīm b. al-Aghlab obtained the title of amir in 800/184 and handed it down to his heirs. Thus it was with the consent of the caliphate that the eastern Maghrib achieved its autonomy—independently of the Khārijite schism but thanks to it.

III

The political content of the Khārijite movement can be summed up in two points: rejection of a Byzantine style state based on exploitation and inequality, and inability to set up a counterstate based on the organic development of already existing institutions. The same situation had prevailed before the coming of the Arabs, but it seems possible that the outcome of the old struggles against the Romans and Byzantines well outside the Carthaginian redoubt had doomed all subsequent attempts to forge an autonomist movement in the middle Maghrib. The Maghribis were now constrained to organize within the framework of Islam. Khārijism seemed capable of leading to the desired goal, but in practice it proved an interim solution because it implied unremitting hostility to a system that had to be maintained if opposition was to continue to be fruitful. Without the system to combat, the Khārijites turned on themselves and devoured each other. By the end of the eighth century Khārijism had fulfilled its role, which was to assert the autonomy of the Maghrib, but it had not given the country the national state to which it aspired.

Can Khārijism be identified with a specific socio-economic

structure? True, it found its most ardent supporters in the least urbanized parts of the Umayyad empire (Jazīra, Yamāma, Yemen, etc.), but to infer from this, as Gautier does,[7] that its ideology was a typically nomadic one is venturesome. In view of its asceticism, frugality and democratism, and above all its subsequent development in the cities of the Mzab, one might equally well characterize it as typically urban, strangely comparable to a kind of Calvinism. There is indeed reason to suppose that the middle Maghrib became impoverished and that its cities declined during the eighth century, but there is no reason to believe that the sole cause of this was the Khārijite war. In any case we know so little about the economic situation that it is wiser to abstain from any judgment.

It is certain, on the other hand, that Khārijism extended the area of Islamic influence by its inner dynamism and its character as an opposition movement. It served as a banner for Berber autonomism but carried within itself the seeds of endless conflicts: uninterrupted criticism, deposition of caliphs, assassinations, theological controversy, all ruinous to the stability required for the organization of a great state. Small states whose history is little known to us were established on the basis of the Khārijite ideology: those of the Barghwāṭa of western Morocco (744/127), of the Midrārids in Sijilmāsa (757/140), and of the Rustumids in Ṭāhart (761/144).

Can this be called a return to the Byzantine situation? Yes, in a sense, but under different conditions. The subjugated Maghrib also won its autonomy, keeping for itself the greater part of the wealth which previously had found its way to the east. Though still divided into principalities, the Middle Maghrib was now animated by an oppositionist ide-

[7] This thesis of Gautier—"Khārijism was essentially a Zanātī phenomenon, i.e. destructively nomadic," is even weaker than his theory of the conquest, especially since the author himself recognizes that the Khārijite revolt resulted in the foundation of the kingdoms of Ṭāhart and Fez (which incidentally, is untrue) and in the development of the oases on the fringe of the Sahara.

ology which denied the legitimacy of the power established in the northeast. The Saharan Maghrib had ceased to be a historic redoubt, and had been opened to the commercial activity of the Middle Maghrib. To a certain degree, these positive aspects had been present in all the preceding periods, but never all together or definitively. The Donatist schism had been crushed, the Vandals had been unwilling to confine themselves to Africa and the Byzantines to sever their ties with the center of the empire. At the end of the eighth century the elements of autonomy were established, and this perhaps accounts for the definitive Islamization of the Maghrib.

So ends the first part of Maghrib history, in which the Maghrib always expresses itself negatively. If we look at that history from the outside, it is easy to represent it as the story of foreign exploits on African soil.[8] Seen from the inside, it is a series of refusals expressed by the desire to return to a past situation: on the social level through a revival of tribalism, on the political level through the reconstruction of the Middle Maghrib kingdoms, on the religious level through innumerable schisms, and on the geographical level through repopulation of the Saharan redoubt. The most essential determinant in the history of this period is perhaps the fact that the Maghrib was a "Finistère," a dead end, where human groups stopped and became isolated because they could go no further. Given this historical situation, which lasted long enough for provisional solutions to become durable components, it is easy to adduce determinants of all sorts—racial,[9] psychological,[10] social,[11] geographical—but these are mere facets, and not essential causes. The central level of the social structure, which reflects the dialecti-

8 Camps, *Monuments et rites*, p. 8.

9 Charles-Picard, *La Civilization de l'Afrique romaine*, p. 116: "The possibility is not excluded that African man is by nature hostile to technical activity."

10 Gsell, *Histoire ancienne*, pp. 116 and 274-285.

11 *Ibid.*

cal evolution of internal and external factors, becomes a permanent datum that explains everything, a smooth mask on which the passage of foreign civilizations leaves no trace.

Non-Maghribi historians raise questions that seem legitimate. "Who are the Berbers?" the prehistorians ask. "How did they develop from barbarism to civilization?" ask the protohistorians and classical scholars. "Why did they espouse Islam?" ask the medievalists. But behind these questions others, far less innocent, are concealed. Did they miss the age of metals?[12] Did agriculture come to them from the Phoenicians? Did they fail to appreciate the political organization of Rome?[13] Actually these are barely veiled assertions, beneath which lies the same old horrified outcry: What a scandal that they should have been converted to Islam![14] During the period of triumphant colonization this was thought to be a simple, easily corrected, error; when the Berbers refused to be persuaded that they had missed the boat with the Romans and had better not make the same mistake in their dealings with the modern colonizers, the concept of the Berber as the eternal laggard of the Mediterranean world, always a bit behind,[15] became popular. This in turn lost its appeal and was replaced by the theory that the Berber lacked "authenticity," that he was always untrue to himself. In the first century B.C., we are told, Massinissa's Maghrib had the chance to be itself, but preferred to be Carthaginian;[16] this was the unpardonable mistake. It is safe to say that this idea will win numerous adherents, even among Maghribis.

[12] Julien, *L'Histoire de l'Afrique du Nord,* 2nd ed., vol. I, p. 444; Furon, *Manuel de préhistoire générale,* p. 458.

[13] "For Africa this was a disaster . . . , which gradually reduced the Romanized natives to the elementary civilization from which the ambitious egoism of the Caesars had so opportunely raised them" (Courtois, *Les Vandales et l'Afrique,* p. 214).

[14] *Ibid.,* pp. 64, 358, 359.

[15] Gsell, *Histoire ancienne,* pp. 236, 274.

[16] "A curious example of Berber nationalism, Massinissa, a client of Rome, was the propagator of Punic civilization" (Camps, "Massinissa," p. 301).

But this notion that the Berbers were lacking in will to be themselves is no more tenable than the idea of a backwardness clinging to them like a curse from neolithic times. From the first century B.C. to the eighth century A.D. the will of the Berbers to be themselves is revealed by the continuity of their efforts to reconstitute the kingdoms of the Carthaginian period, and in this sense the movement was crowned by success. The only remaining problem, an important one to be sure, is the time factor. The reconstitution took too long, with the result that temporary structures solidified and lost all malleability. Camps' hypothesis is worth considering,[17] provided two observations are taken into account as follows. First, Massinissa did not himself choose to be Carthaginianized; the situation forced his hand, and that situation is called Rome. We read in Julien: "If our minds were not haunted by the heaps of ruins created by the invasion of the Hilālian Arabs, we should feel less admiration for the work of Rome."[18] A purely subjective haunting, for the Maghrib of the seventh century could not foresee the future; the Hilālians undoubtedly come in handy, serving to justify Bugeaud as well as the Roman consuls. Secondly, it is always futile to reconstitute historical events that did not take place, for even if Massinissa had developed a genuine Berber civilization, would Rome have spared it? Other peoples whose civilizations were thousands of years old at the beginning of the Christian era did not escape the leveling pressure of Rome.

Behind all these brilliant hypotheses we invariably find the same assertion—that the Maghribis never knew where their true interests lay: confronted by Rome, they turned to Carthage, their enemies of the day before; dominated by the Arabs, they took refuge in Islam; conquered by France, they turned to Arabism. And this eternal naughty child is reminded that he must once and for all choose correctly, meaning of course the Mediterranean community. If this logic were to be accepted, there would be no end to the repri-

17 Camps, *Monuments et rites*, p. 274.

18 Julien, *Histoire de l'Afrique du Nord*, 2nd ed., vol. I, p. 232.

manding of the peoples of the earth, for all of them in one way or another have at some time made a bad choice. If a Maghribi were to rewrite the history of France or England from the point of view of the Celts, stressing their negativism and inauthenticity, he would be laughed at; yet that is what many learned scholars do, page after page, and on the pretext of friendship. This is "colonialized history," or the endless telling to certain peoples what they ought to have done in the past.

The immutable datum we must take as our starting point, while constantly analyzing its dialectic, is the Berbers' increasingly violent rejection of foreign exploitation and their determination to resume the course interrupted by the Roman conquest. This goal was attained in the eighth century under the banner of an Islamic schism. Failure of Rome, success of Islam—these are moral or subjective judgments. The reality consists of elements that must be analyzed: the halting by Rome of a natural development of the Maghrib and the long, too long, wait before the movement was resumed; a period of waiting which consecrated a structure that was itself the result of an arrested history. This consolidated structure had a character of permanence, since every subsequent setback gave it new youth. It was neither a curse nor inevitable: Rome might have dominated Africa as far as the Niger or might have abandoned the Maghrib much earlier than it did. In either case, everything would have been different. As it was, the Maghrib had to wait for centuries before resuming its arrested march. That is the essential fact, and it is futile to look elsewhere—in an unavowed desire to justify Rome—for the primary cause of the subsequent developments. Once we accept this truth, we realize why the people of the Maghrib have always regarded their Islamization as a victory[19] and not as a defeat. And we can avoid posing problems as futile as they are insolvable.

[19] "Their [the Berbers'] hearts opened to the call of Islam because in it they saw a means of national liberation and territorial independence, and at the same time a guarantee, for the mind and the heart, against all servitude" ('Allāl al-Fāsī, *Al-Harakāt al-Istiqlālīya*, Introduction.

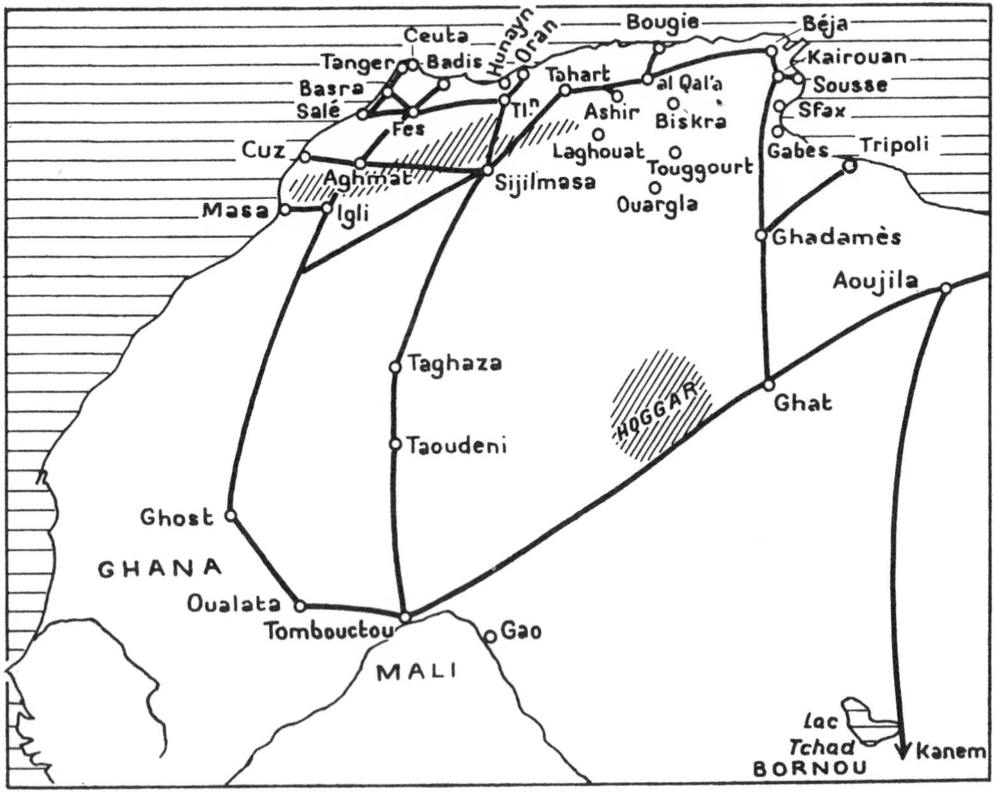
Ceuta
Tanger
Badis
Hunayn
Oran
Bougie
Béja
Kairouan
Sousse
Sfax
Gabes
Tripoli
Basra
Salé
Fes
Tl.n
Tahart
Ashir
al Qal'a
Biskra
Laghouat
Touggourt
Ouargla
Cuz
Aghmat
Sijilmasa
Masa
Igli
Ghadamès
Aoujila
Taghaza
Taoudeni
HOGGAR
Ghat
Ghost
GHANA
Oualata
Tombouctou
Gao
MALI
Lac
Tchad
BORNOU
Kanem

PART II
The Imperial Maghrib

The period from the ninth to the thirteenth century has a a unity of which all historians, early and modern, have been more or less clearly aware, essentially because in this period a drive toward empire building developed and because after several unsuccessful attempts the Maghrib was united for the first time. This unification did not last, but we should not conclude a posteriori that it was doomed to failure. These centuries might also be characterized as the period in which, at least for a century and a half, the Maghrib dominated the western Mediterranean. From the standpoint of our major concern—the emergence of a Maghribi personality, as history reveals it—the essential fact about the period is that the unification was accomplished in the name of a religious idea. An orthodox doctrine had not yet been clearly defined;[1] all Islamic doctrines were successively tried: Khārijism, Zaydism, Shī'ism, Mālikite militantism, Almohadism; only in the thirteenth century was orthodoxy definitively victorious. In this part of its history, then, the Maghrib is perceived through a succession of religious movements, and for a time its history becomes their history. Are we to generalize and say that all political action in the Maghrib was in essence religious?[2] It would be naive to reduce these movements to their religious dimension; they are to be seen, rather, as twofold in aim—religious and political—and with a simultaneous, schismatic and national growth of consciousness. True, the factor of religious mediation is of

[1] This point, essential to the understanding of the politico-religious movements prior to the fifth century H. has never been brought out in Moslem historiography. (See Laoust, *Les Schismes de l'Islam*.)

[2] This is the point of view of most orientalists and Arabic scholars. Yet Ibn Khaldūn, whom they are so fond of quoting, says the exact opposite in his *Muqaddima*, to wit, that religious doctrine is necessary to political action, but as a condition of success, that is, as a means, not as an end.

the utmost importance, but the political aim pursued must not be minimized, even though from our vantage point it can only be inferred.

Yet even when the motives of a political movement, the general conditions under which it operated, are well understood, they tell us nothing about the means by which the movement achieved success, and it is here that our knowledge is deficient. We strongly suspect that all these movements depended in large part on the trade routes, especially those of the Sahara (it is important to note that in our opinion the trans-Saharan trade did not become crucially important to the Maghrib until the ninth century), but it is a long way from such hypotheses to a cogent proof. Without losing sight of the true line of development, we are obliged for the moment at least to stress the politico-religious factor, for it is this aspect that can best be studied on the basis of documents at present available, though we are fully aware that such a study can provide at best no more than a half-truth.[3]

[3] On the pretext that only economic history can be regarded as explicative, which is true though such history is almost beyond our reach at the present time, the ideological history, which is perfectly accessible, has been neglected. There is not a single book about the development of Mālikism in North Africa. Dragué (pseudonym for Spillmann), *Esquisse d'histoire religieuse du Maroc* is not very useful.

5. Islam and Commerce: The Ninth Century

I

The ninth century was a century of Islamization. The process has not been studied in detail, but it seems certain that this Islamization went hand in hand with commerce. The commercial colonies established by Arabs at the crossroads of an alien world provided a model for public and private life, and since this commerce covered a wide territory, it enabled Islam to penetrate the entire Maghrib.[4] It determined not only the content of the "states" that now came into being but also the relations between them. Even Khārijism, that ideology of opposition, was taken up by the commercial community. Let us first take a look at the political map at the beginning of the ninth century. It will provide us with a typology of state organizations.

The Western Maghrib

This is the region about which least is known; what little information we possess is of late origin, which is only natural since the caliphate lost all hold on northern Morocco after the battle of the Sebou.

The Barghwāṭa[5]

To the south of the Sebou, on the Atlantic plains, the embryo of a state took form; it is believed to have been founded about 744/127 by Ṣāliḥ b. Ṭārif. Taking the genesis of Islam as his model, Ṣāliḥ declared himself a prophet,

[4] We can form an idea of this process by observing the most recent developments in Black Africa. See Levtzion, *Muslims and Chiefs in West Africa*.

[5] The Barghwāṭa have often been identified with the Baquates of the Roman period. This is pure speculation.

wrote(?) his Koran in Berber, and instituted a fast, prayers, dietary laws, etc. We do not know how much this religion derived from local traditions and how much from Islam or other monotheistic religions. The Barghwāṭa state was long-lived, surviving until the middle of the eleventh century; it was known to the Andalusians (in particular to al-Bakrī, d. 1094/487), for in the eleventh century it established relations with the Umayyad caliph.

Ṣāliḥ's prophetism has been attributed to vestiges of an earlier Christianity; more probably it was an offshoot of the Shī'ite ideology, for there is no reason to believe that Khārijism was the only Islamic sect active in the Maghrib. The significant fact, in any case, is the modification of the Koranic ordinances. The wish to Berberize Islam and adapt it to the Berber past was only natural, but to modify it rather than reject it altogether implied recognition of Islam as a civilizing force. The question remains, however: why did this Berberized Islam spread neither to the north nor to the south, where in fact there was nothing to stop it?

Apart from this Barghwāṭa state, we have no precise information about southern Morocco. The Arab chroniclers use the term *Sūs* (Sous) to designate this region, with frequent variations in meaning.[6] The little information we have concerns the Rif region. In the Ghomāra region south of Tetuán, a prophet, Ḥamīm, aided by his aunt Ṭangīt, established another variety of Berberized Islam.

Two independent political powers were established in two Mediterranean ports. The first, founded in Nakkūr (near Mellila) by a certain Ṣāliḥ b. Manṣūr, an Arab immigrant who had fought the Khārijites, was recognized by al-Walīd, the Umayyad amir of Spain and lasted from 809 to 917; the other, founded in Ceuta by a Berber family, the Banu 'Iṣām, survived until 931. These, however, do not seem to have modified the message of Islam in any perceptible way.

6 See al-Nāṣīrī, *al-Istiqṣā*, vol. 1, p. 139, in which, citing Ibn Abī Zar', he speaks of a hither-Sous beginning on the west bank of the Moulouya, so treating the term Sous as synonymous with Morocco.

Other more ephemeral powers may have existed, but the chroniclers give the impression that economic conditions were not yet ripe for the building of a really structured state. The country as a whole was wooded, populated (sparsely perhaps) by sedentary farmers, with relatively few cities except on the northern fringe. Islam was opening up the country and, through the cities it founded or restored, preparing the way for unification; even the travesties of Islam prevalent in farming communities still relatively untouched by commerce worked in the same direction. The qualitative leap occurred under the leadership of the Idrīsids.

The Idrīsids

The history of this dynasty is hard to write, chiefly because the city of Fez which it founded achieved undisputed political primacy by the fourteenth century and the historians writing at that time, most of them natives of the city, saw the past in terms of present splendors. Hence there are all kinds of distortions that are difficult to evaluate objectively. Ibn Khaldūn, who knew the central better than the western Maghrib, systematized the work of those historians and lent it the support of his great authority. The Andalusian chroniclers, who wrote before the fourteenth century, at a time when the legend had not yet taken form, seem more reliable.

Like many others before him, a descendant of ʿAlī, of the Ḥasanid branch, fled from the tyranny of the ʿAbbāsids. Seeking refuge in the Maghrib, he found suitable conditions in northern Morocco. Contrary to what we read in the chroniclers, we learn from al-Ashʿarī's history of the schisms that Idrīs b. ʿAbdallah was sent to the Maghrib by his brother Muḥammad b. ʿAbdallah, who had revolted against al-Manṣūr (d. 775) long before the battle of Fakh (786/169), which is generally supposed to have been the reason for Idrīs's departure. Here we also read that his second brother, Ibrāhīm, who also revolted against al-Manṣūr, in Baṣra, was surrounded by a group of Mu'tazilites and Zaydites.[7] It seems possible that at the end of the eighth century, the Shī'ites tried to organize their propaganda in the Maghrib concurrently with the Khārijites. But by then Shī'ism had split into a number of schools, and al-Ash'arī speaks of Zaydism. This was the most moderate of these schools, closely connected with Mu'tazilism (thanks to the relations between Wāṣil b. 'Aṭā' and Zayd b. 'Alī, and many of its tenets were later incorporated into the orthodox system. The old historical texts speak of Idrīs as a Mu'tazilite and Shī'ite; later writers call him orthodox, because in the meantime the character of Shī'ism had changed.[8] It seems likely that Idrīs belonged to a more or less pronounced Zaydite tendency, and that before he went to the western Maghrib his group had already sent emissaries, as it had to Yemen and other regions. This hypothesis would enable us to understand certain aspects of Idrīsid policy that have remained obscure.

The ground having been prepared, Idrīs arrived in 788/172 under the emirate of Rawḥ b. Ḥātim and settled in Oulili (Volubilis). The region, relatively urbanized compared to the rest of the country, seems to have been converted to Islam, but not so the surrounding territory, which leads us to doubt the importance if not the existence of 'Uqba's expeditions and still more the Khārijite character of the revolt of 740. Maysara was probably a Khārijite, but what of his troops? For it is difficult to believe that in Khārijite surroundings Idrīs would have concealed his sentiments. If we suppose on the contrary that northern Morocco had been scarcely touched by Islam, we understand more readily why it should have tempted the Zaydite emissaries, known for their proselytizing zeal. The existence of an emissary (possibly Rashīd) is made all the more plausible by the political acumen we discern in the Idrīsid state from the very start.

7 Al-Ash'arī, *Maqālāt al-Islāmīyīn*, vol. 1, p. 145.

8 Terrasse failed to understand this point; hence the misplaced polemicism of his chapter on the Idrīsids (*Histoire du Maroc*, vol. 1, pp. 107-199).

The typical title of imam that Idrīs conferred on himself as well as the fact that his assassination has generally been imputed to a known Zaydite, Sulaymān b. Jarīr, may be regarded as further indications of his Shī'ite leanings.

Idrīs seems to have had two preoccupations: to establish a capital and to proselytize; his son and successor, Idrīs II, born of a Berber mother, pursued his program. The city of Fez, the most durable result of the dynasty's policy, was built in several stages, before 808, the date usually given. The city, which was double from the start (Fez and al-'Aliya), developed rapidly, reinforced by several waves of Arab immigrants, first from Cordova in 814 after the so-called revolt of the rabaḍ (suburb) against al-Ḥakām I and later from Kairouan. These emigrations had a political explanation: the opposition of the 'Alids both to the Umayyads and to the 'Abbāsids. There is evidence of an Idrīsid coinage from 801 on. Having secured a political base, Idrīs I and later Idrīs II sent expeditions first against Tlemcen (which was attacked for the first time in 790) and then to the south, where Chella, on the border of the Barghwāṭa principality, was taken, and finally to Sous, where the city(?) of Nfīs was taken in 812. These three towns were of political and above all economic importance, since they controlled the main routes from the Sahara to the north and east. It seems at first surprising that the Barghwāṭa should so easily have let themselves be encircled by the new dynasty. As the chroniclers of the Marīnid period were to attest, the Idrīsids converted the greater part of the country to Islam. In any event it was they who brought the teachings of Islam to the Berber population in regions which 'Uqba's soldiers had in all likelihood merely traversed.

The Idrīsid state was rudimentary, amounting to little more than a locally recruited army, paid out of the spoils of war and taxes levied on non-Moslems. Idrīs I was wholly dependent on those who had adopted him (the Awriba), and when Idrīs II recruited five hundred Arabs, immigrants from Andalusia and Ifrīqiya, the result was a political crisis

(808) which soon put an end to his attempt to seize power.[9] Idrīs II seems to have acted far more as a religious leader (imām) than as a true political leader. At his death (828/213) his eldest son Muḥammad divided the conquered territories among his six brothers, retaining only the title of imam and rule over the capital. It is difficult to interpret this decision. Was it a Berber custom as the Arab writers believe? (According to them the decision was suggested to him by Kanza, his grandmother.) Or was it taken for geographical reasons, because the territories were not contiguous? Or was the reason simply that the Idrīsids were regarded primarily as religious leaders, whose main duty it was to proselytize—a theory that would be in keeping with the Zaydite doctrine? The consequence in any case was continual disputes among their descendants. Rich as it is, the chronicle of the military operations is full of gaps, because the chroniclers were interested only in the city of Fez and mention the Idrīsids only when they take possession of the capital. But the effect of the Idrīsid period is clear: a rapid Islamization of the controlled regions. Their Arabization, however, is much less certain, for in the eleventh century we encounter distant Shī'ite descendants of the Idrīsids engaged in the struggle for power in Andalusia after the fall of the Cordova caliphate, and they were thoroughly Berberized.[10] Up to the arrival of the Shī'ites at the beginning of the tenth century, the numerous dispersed heirs of Idrīs II carried on the essential work of their dynasty, namely, the Islamization of the western Maghrib.[11] Though less particularist than the Barghwāṭa, they enjoyed equal autonomy.

9 This part of the chroniclers' account seems to be a mere projection of the relations between the Anṣār and the Prophet—a common feature of Islamic historiography.

10 See 'Inān, *al-Dawla al-'āmirīya*, p. 160.

11 The following judgment is typical of colonial historiography: "By creating and developing the great center from which Islam, its oriental-type civilization and its language were diffused, the Idrīsids weighed heavily on the history of Morocco" (Terrasse, *Histoire du Maroc*, vol. 1, p. 134).

The Khārijite Principalities

Three attempts were made to found a state in the Khārijite territory, extending from the Moulouya to the Zāb. The first was that of Abū Qurra in Tlemcen, which served as a rallying point for all the Khārijites engaged in fighting the Arab armies that came from Ifrīqiya. Abū Qurra was essentially a military leader. He played an important role under the three governors 'Abd ar-Raḥmān b. Ḥabīb, Muḥammad b. al-Ash'ath, and 'Umar b. Ḥafṣ. He succeeded in uniting the population of the whole central Maghrib as far as Tobna in a concerted military action. As soon as the armies of the caliphate gave up trying to cross the Zāb, the chroniclers seem to have lost interest in him. It seems probable that his attempt to establish a state failed because of the proximity of another city-state, that of Ṭāhart. His power, in any case, was crushed by the Maghrāwa of Muḥammad b. Khāzir, who took Tlemcen in 786/170, before the Idrīsid conquest.

Further to the south, to the east of the Atlas, the city of Sijilmāsa was founded or restored in 757/140 by a group of Sofrite Berbers, led by 'Isā b. Yazīd al-Aswad (an Arab mawlā we are told). In all likelihood he was a foreign Khārijite, but the true leader was Abū al-Qāsim b. Samkū, who founded the Midrārite dynasty (from the name of the fourth amir, Midrār b. l-Yasa'). This dynasty reigned for more than two centuries, and its history in its broad outlines has been related by Ibn Khaldūn. It is characterized by continual struggles between Khārijite factions, especially the Sofrite and the more moderate Ibāḍite factions, which last finally won out and prepared the way for the adoption of Sunnite orthodoxy at the end of the tenth century under Amir Muḥammad b. al-Fatḥ b. Maymūn. The chronicle also mentions the excellent gold coinage struck in Sijilmāsa. The presence of gold may explain why the city was built on this particular site and the increasing wealth of the community may account for the development of a less austere morality. Long before this date, we are told, Abū Mansūr al-Yasa'

(d. 823/208) levied a tax (1/5) on the operation of the mines of the Dra' (Dar'a).[12]

The third power, the most important and best known, was that of Ṭāhart,[13] founded by a man of Persian origin, 'Abd al-Raḥmān b. Rustum, who seems to have been brought up in Kairouan. When the attempt of the Banū 'Uqba to carve themselves a principality failed and Kairouan fell into the hands of the Berber Khārijites (758/141), another Khārijite, an Arab, came from Tripolitania, drove out the extremists and left Ibn Rustum as sub-governor. When the city was retaken by the army of the caliphate in 761/144, Ibn Rustum fled to the Berbers with whom he had formed an alliance (*ḥilf*), and together they founded the city of Ṭāhart (six miles west of present-day Tiaret). Fifteen years later he was promoted to the dignity of Khārijite caliph, an honor which remained in his family until 908/296.

The little information at our disposal indicates that this city-state, which concluded a peace with Kairouan in 787/171, represented the politico-religious ideal of the moderate Khārijites. Its population included non-Khārijites and probably Christians, who participated to some extent in its political life. In principle the imam was elected and was expected to meet with the canonical requirements of knowledge, courage and piety. His powers were wide, but he was closely controlled by the community. Political life hinged entirely on theological problems. Controversies often ended in schisms (e.g. the Nukkarite schism under the second imam) and interdynastic struggles (e.g. that between Abū Ḥātim and Ya'qūb in 894/281). But more worthy of note than this politico-religious life of which we know little, is the medi-

12 These amirs of Sijilmāsa did not bear the title of imam. Was this a case of forgetfulness on the part of the Sunnite chroniclers, or are we to infer that the only true imam was the imam of Ṭāhart? It should be noted that al-Yasa' married his son to the daughter of Ibn Rustum.

13 We possess two texts on the imams of Ṭāhart: the chronicles of Abū Zakariyā' and of Ibn al-Saghīr. Summarized in Bekri, "Le Kharijisme berbère," pp. 55-108.

ating role played by the city: first with the Orient (Khārijite scholars came from the East to study the practical application of their doctrine and brought with them novelties such as the ideas of the Mu'tazilite Wāṣil b. 'Atā'), and later with the Umayyads of Spain (two of Ibn Rustum's sons went to Cordova). And even more important was the role played by Ṭāhart as a rallying point for all the Khārijites of the Maghrib from the Nafūsa of Libya to the Sadrāta of the desert. But this influence was purely ideological. Without regular army, administration or system of taxation, the imams of Ṭāhart made no attempt to expand. All indications are that the city's geographical situation made for a flourishing economic life; the presence of rich Persian merchants and of Christians suggests extensive commercial relations both with the Orient and with Andalusia,[14] and there seems to be little reason to doubt the existence of ties with Sijilmāsa. When Ṭāhart was occupied by the Fāṭimids in 908, the survivors took refuge with their books of Ibāḍite theology in a southern oasis (Sadrāta), whence they moved to Mzāb, where the sect has survived to this day.

Thus throughout the ninth century we find city-states throughout the western part of the Maghrib. Their relations with the surrounding country were extremely varied. The geographer al-Ya'qūbī gives us an idea of the situation when he describes several communities dependent on no outside power and consequently paying no taxes. Conditions in the eastern Maghrib were very different.

Aghlabid Ifrīqiya

The dynasty of the Banū al-Aghlab (801-909/185-296) is the best known of those reigning in the ninth-century Maghrib, chiefly because it remained subject to the 'Abbāsids.

[14] See Georges Marçais, *La Berbérie musulmane*, n. 111. This however is an impression. There is no concrete proof. See Lewicki, "L'Etat nord-africain de Tāhert et ses relations avec le Soudan occidental," pp. 513-535.

All the eastern Arab historians speak of it at length in connection with the empire. Throughout this period, the high point of the Baghdad civilization, 'Abbāsid Iraq and Aghlabid Ifrīqiya maintained constant relations. Hence a parallelism between the histories of the two dynasties; at almost the same time the one succumbed to the assault of the Fāṭimid Shī'ites and the other became a protectorate of the semi-Shī'ite Daylamites (945). Ifrīqiya had won its autonomy with the consent of the caliph. This was the first step toward the politico-administrative dismemberment of the empire, soon followed by the granting of autonomy to Egypt and Khurasān. Writing of these concessions, later historians distinguished between a governor who could be recalled at any time and an autonomous amir who was free to designate his successors as he pleased. The caliph's suzerainty was symbolized by the *khutba* (Friday sermon) delivered in his name and the payment of an annual tribute (800,000 dirham for Ifrīqiya according to Ibn al-Athīr, 130 millions and 120 carpets according to Ibn Khaldūn).[15] The amount of this tribute may have varied, but it was never annulled, for the amir might always have need of the caliph's power or prestige. The territory granted to Ibn al-Aghlab was not delimited; theoretically it covered the entire Maghrib from Cyrenaica westward, including any new territories he might conquer. He was expected to fight the enemies of his sovereign (Umayyads and 'Alids), but experience had made the master of Kairouan cautious, and he contented himself with a territory roughly coinciding with the Africa of the Caesars. To the east Tripoli controlled the road connecting the autonomous province with the center of the empire; to the west, fortresses (in many cases renovated holdovers from the Byzantine era) in the Hodna and the Zāb defended the

15 Levy, *The Social Structure of Islam*, p. 320, gives this last figure, taken from Jahshiyārī, who is probably Ibn Khaldūn's source. Since this refers to the reign of ar-Rashīd, during which the Aghlabids were trying to gain recognition, it seems likely that the figure rose very quickly to that cited by Ibn al-Athīr.

territory against incursions from the Aurès, and others in the Bône region against attack from Kabylia. The Aghlabids had no more designs on the west than the Vandals or Byzantines before them. The Aghlabid state was modeled on that of Baghdad. The amirs distrusted the army composed of Arab immigrants, which grew in numbers because of the anti-Khārijite wars, and surrounded themselves with a personal guard of black slaves, comparable to the Turks whom the 'Abbāsids had taken into their service. Also like their suzerains, they peopled the bureaucracy with Mawālī or natives (Afāriq), many of whom had remained Christians. We find the same functionaries as in Baghdad: a vizier, a chamberlain (*ḥājib*), a master of posts and intelligence (*ṣāḥib al-barīd*), numerous secretaries (*kuttāb*) serving in the various offices (taxation, army, mint, official correspondence, etc.). This administrative apparatus, much less differentiated than that on which it was modeled, was superimposed on a largely Berber society. The number of Arab immigrants concentrated in the army and the cities, chiefly Kairouan, has been estimated at one hundred thousand.[16] Most of them had come not from Arabia, but from Syria and Iraq, regions which from the start had supplied numerous emigrants to the Maghrib. Many Rūm (Byzantines) and, it goes without saying, Afāriq (probably bilingual natives) had remained in the cities; in addition numerous Persians had come with the various Arab armies. All these groups had some share in the political power, but not so the majority of the Islamized Berbers who, because of their Khārijite tendencies and the ties they preserved with their compatriots in the rural regions, were looked upon with mistrust. The rural population, still Christian, as there is reason to believe, in the north, and Khārijite in the center and south, had only intermittent relations with the central authority.

[16] See William Marçais, *Articles et conférences*, p. 177. The figure is comparable to the one hundred thousand advanced for the Vandals and is equally plausible; the "Arab" immigration, however, was much more varied.

Every aspect of this structure, at once simple and compartmented, recalls that of the Vandalo-Byzantine period, which it seems merely to have perpetuated and perfected. Nor is this the only point that shows continuity with the past.

The political life of the Aghlabid state was dominated by two series of events, one of which was the consequence of the other. First, the amirs were obliged to combat numerous revolts of the army, which became increasingly turbulent once the Khārijite Berbers ceased to be a threat. The Arab soldiers from the east felt cramped in little Ifrīqiya. As often happens in such cases, partisan quarrels ended in revolts, some of them serious, especially under the first amirs who in the eye of the army were no more than lucky generals. In 802/186 Ḥamdis al-Kindī, surnamed Khuraysh, revolted near Tunis; no sooner was he overcome than ʿImrān b. Mujālid, the general who had defeated him, revolted in turn and took Kairouan; but it was in 824/209, under Ziyādat Allah I, Ibrāhīm's second son, that the most dangerous of these revolts broke out when the amir attempted to impose the common law on the army. Manṣūr b. Naṣr al-Tunbudhī, a man of high prestige, rose up with the support of the whole army, gained control over all Ifrīqiya, and minted his own coinage. Driven into the southern region, between Sous and Tripoli, the Aghlabid amir saved his power only by enlisting the help of the Berbers of the Khārijite Jarīd. Once peace was restored, it lasted until the end of the dynasty, when the cruelties of Ibrāhīm II, an amir of unstable character, provoked a general revolt (893/280) which was put down by the amir's guard of black slaves.

It was in part the first revolts that impelled the Aghlabids to conquer Sicily, and indeed the conquest ushered in a long period of internal peace. In addition, to be sure, the Aghlabids were fired by the example of the ʿAbbāsids in the east and of the Umayyads in the west. Planned years before, the conquest had been delayed not by reinforcement of the Byzantine defenses but by the Khārijite revolt in the eighth century. Numerous raids had been made soon after the conquest of Ifrīqiya, under Mu'āwiya and 'Uqba (666 and 669) and again under Mūsā b. Nuṣayr in 705; a great naval battle in 734/116 seems to have opened the way to conquest, but then came the Khārijite revolt and it was not followed up. In 827/212 an expedition was finally organized by Ziyādat Allah. It left Sousse under the command of a religious leader, the qadi Asad b. al-Furāt. Apparently the dynasty found it necessary to consolidate its legitimacy by giving the undertaking a conspicuously religious character. The campaign was carried on methodically. Palermo fell in 831, Messina in 843; then the army crossed over to Italy and reached Rome in 846. This was the period when the whole western Mediterranean was under Arab domination.[17] Despite the weakness of the eastern and western empires, several towns resisted, and the conquest was not completed until shortly before the fall of the Aghlabid dynasty. Taormina was taken in 902/290.[18]

We can gain some idea of the society that developed in Ifrīqiya, and eminently in Kairouan, in the eighth and ninth centuries from biographies, hagiographic works, and economic treatises.[19] The first of its kind in the Maghrib, it was taken as a model in the centuries to come. It was a mercantile society; commerce, prices, weights and measures figure prominently in its politics, its laws, and even its literature. The quality of the coinage was the constant concern of its rulers and jurists; Ibrāhīm II carried out a monetary reform aimed at eliminating impure silver coins, and the gold dinar (4.20 grams) was not devaluated until shortly before the end of the dynasty. Several trade routes converged in Kairouan; here cereals and oil were stored and slaves

[17] The dawn of nationalism in Tunisia and in the Maghrib as a whole has led to a revival of interest in this period.

[18] On the organization of the island, especially the legislation on land tenure and taxation, an important text was published by Ḥ. Ḥ. 'Abd al-Wahhāb and F. Dachraoui in *Études d'orientalisme dédiées à la mémoire de Lévi-Provençal* (Paris, 1962), vol. II, pp. 405-427.

[19] Such as the piece by Ibn 'Uman al-Andalusī, "Aḥkām al-Sūq," studied by 'Abd al-Wahhāb; see also *idem, Waraqāt*, vol. I, p. 127.

from the Sudan were assembled before being sent eastward to Alexandria. Thanks to this commercial development, the city grew in size and beauty (the famous aqueducts built during the reign of the sixth amir, Abū Ibrāhīm Aḥmād, bear witness to its prosperity). In the cultural sphere two learned types emerged, the jurist (*faqīh*) and the religious scholar (*'ābid*) tinged with mysticism and busying himself with the hadith and occasionally with history. There is no more striking example of the interaction between outside influence ('Abbāsid Iraq) and local character based on socio-economic development than the culture of Aghlabid Kairouan. At the end of the ninth century (third century H.) Islamic orthodoxy underwent a significant development in Baghdad, largely as a result of the bitter struggle against Mu'tazilism. This doctrinal development is echoed in Ifrīqiyan biographers,[20] who tell us of scholars come from the orient to seek their fortune in the Maghrib and of Maghribis who went to the orient to meet the leading Islamic thinkers. Mu'tazilite theology found adepts among them, and Ziyādat Allah I seems to have gone over to Mu'tazilism in imitation of his suzerain al-Ma'mūn. But it was the juridical sciences that won the largest following. The two schools, of Abu Ḥanīfa and of Mālik, had their representatives in Kairouan. At first Ḥanafism was predominant, doubtless under the influence of Baghdad, but in the end, for a number of reasons that have not yet been fully studied, Mālikism won out. A striving for cultural autonomy, the desire to found a tradition, must have played a part, but the triumph of Mālikism is perhaps best explained by the fact that Ḥanafism had originated in the more complex society of Baghdad and was ill-suited to the more rudimentary conditions in Ifrīqiya. In any event, this development was to have important consequences, since Kairouan was to exert a unifying influence on the thinking of the entire Maghrib, especially of the cities. Qadi Asad b. l-Furāt (559-829/142-214) inclined definitely to Ḥanafism. His disciple Saḥnūn ('Abd al-Salām

20 Al-Tamīmī, *Ṭabaqāt*; al-Mālikī, *Kitāb Riyād an-nufūs.*

b. Sa'īd) (776-854/160-240) created the vulgate of North-African Mālikism in his *Mudawanna*. Most of the scholars whose names have been preserved disregarded the other schools that flourished in Iraq, a fact that suggests that the Arabization of Ifrīqiya was not very far advanced. Side by side with the *faqīh* we find the *'ābid*, or ascetics, gloomy men like Ḥasan al-Baṣri, always ready to weep over the misfortunes of mankind. Their prototype was Buhlūl b. Rashīd (d. 799/183), who despised money and declined the post of grand judge. By virtue of their independence and prestige, these pious men were a political force. With their criticism of the amirs, especially in matters of finance and trade, they became objectively the spokesmen of the urban population, and their function was almost institutionalized. Concomitantly, they furthered the movement of Islamization.

A similar symbiosis of outside influence and local tradition may be observed in the art of the Aghlabid period. In his study of mosques, the palaces of the amirs, and military construction, Georges Marçais was able to distinguish the components of a prestigious art, traces of which have been preserved in the mosques of Kairouan and Sousse, the palace of Raqqāda (or what is left of it), the fortresses of Belezma and Baghaï, and the ribats of Sousse and Monastir.[21] In later years Kairouan, the city par excellence of the early Islamic Maghrib, was taken as a model of a commercial center and intellectual capital; its architecture was imitated. The descriptions made of it at the time give us an idea of what Fez or Tlemcen or Bougie were to become.[22]

II

It is frequently maintained that there was a long economic crisis in the Maghrib, supposedly extending from the third

[21] See his conclusion in *La Berbérie musulmane*, pp. 100-101, and Lézine, *Architecture de l'Ifrīqiya*.

[22] 'Abd al-Wahhāb, *Waraqāt*, contains a large number of his studies on Aghlabid Ifrīqiya, especially on Kairouan and environs, Sousse, economic and cultural life, etc.

to the eighth century. Beginning under the Romans with the formation of the large estates, a decline in trade and the continual revolts of the Berbers, it is said to have continued under the Vandals, who by destroying the ramparts of the cities supposedly left them defenseless against the "Moors," and under the Byzantines, who did not have time to rebuild the cities. The Arab conquest and the Khārijite wars, we are told, could only make matters worse. These inferences, it goes without saying, are drawn from political events and not from economic documents, which are nonexistent. They seem to be grossly exaggerated: the century of the Vandals was much less negative than has been said, and, what is more, the economic-crisis theory would be valid only for Roman Africa, that is, essentially the northeast. Elsewhere, a recession in the monetary economy would not necessarily have entailed a collapse of production and hence misery; one might even be tempted to draw the contrary conclusion. Be that as it may, even the colonial historians agree that the ninth century was a century of recovery, during which the states and city-states not only maintained their structure, but also amassed wealth which later enabled more ambitious dynasties to pursue a policy of expansion.

Though explicit documents are lacking and numismatic evidence is rare, we can gain some idea of the economic situation from the Arab geographers. Their testimony must be interpreted, for most of them were functionaries or travelers interested chiefly in cities and itineraries. Still, economic inferences can be drawn from thier observations. For the period in question we can call on Ibn Khurradādhbih (d. 885), al-Ya'qūbī (d. 891) and Ibn Ḥawqal (d. after 977). Georges Marçais made use of al-Ya'qūbī in his study of the eastern and central Maghrib and Lévi-Provençal of Ibn Ḥawqal in his study of northern Morocco (as a zone of Andalusian influence).[23] These authors were Shī'ites; consequently, there is no reason to doubt their favorable judg-

[23] See Ibn Khurradādhbih, *Description du Maghreb.*

ments regarding the commercial and economic policies of the Aghlabids and Khārijites, to whom they were in principle opposed.

On arriving in Ifrīqiya, al-Ya'qūbī was struck by the flourishing appearance of the countryside; he describes the orchards extending along the seaside for a hundred miles from Qamūda to Sidi Bouzīd, the olive groves of the Sahel, the vineyards of Cape Bon, famous for their *nabīd* (wine), the orchards of Gafsa, the palm groves of the Jarīd. On the plain of Kairouan, especially near Béja, he was impressed by the grain fields. He also took an interest in the mines and speaks of Majjānat al-Ma'ādin (thirty miles north-northeast of Tebessa), where silver, antimony, iron and lead were being extracted for use in the shipyards, especially those of Sousse. In the cities he was attracted by the development of the crafts—carpets, ceramics, pottery, glass, and state operated manufactures (*ṭirāz*), were active in weaving luxury fabrics. The roads, all converging on Kairouan, were busy and well maintained. As he proceeded into what had formerly been Numidia, the landscape changed. Though wood was available, urbanization was not far advanced; the people lived in villages which are hard to localize. The groups he speaks of, the Banū Barzāl, the Kutāma, the Nafūsa, were farmers and cattle raisers; they seem to have been independent, maintaining no regular ties with any suzerain and paying no taxes to anyone. The situation changed, however, as he approached Ṭāhart, whose politico-religious organization and commercial relations with the surrounding population he describes. From there he went on to Sijilmāsa by a route passing, as he tells us, through the territory of the Zanāta. In this southern region, he was struck by the large palm groves and mineral wealth. Near Tāmdult on the eastern slope of the Atlas, he reports, gold and silver were as abundant and easy to come by as grass. From Sijilmāsa southward to Ghost,[24] a distance of fifty

[24] See Devisse et al., *Tegdaoust*.

stages, he passed through the territory of the veiled Ṣanhāja; on the shore of the Atlantic to the northwest lay the seaport of Masam where wheat was loaded on ships similar to those that "sail from Obella (in Iraq) to China." Al-Ya'qūbī does not seem to have traveled in Morocco; he may have heard what he says about the Idrīsids in Tlemcen. We can make up for this deficiency by consulting Ibn Ḥawqal, though he wrote a century later; it does not seem likely that the situation changed radically in so short a time.

Ibn Ḥawqal distinguishes four regions to the west of the Moulouya: the heavily wooded Mediterranean coast, rich in all sorts of fruit trees and even in sugar cane in the vicinity of Ceuta; the valley of the Sebou near Fez and Baṣra its port —here wheat, barley and even cotton were grown and after Sefrou there were fruit trees and vineyards; the far Sous, a region of small villages and sugar cane—this, he says, is the richest part of the far Maghrib; and finally the Atlantic plains, which he does not describe because they were inhabited by heretics but which, he tells us, produced wheat, since the Barghwāṭa went to Salé, Sijilmāsa[25] and the Sous to sell their cattle and farm produce. He also mentions various mines: asbestos in the Dra' region, antimony near the Moulouya, silver in Taroudant and Tāmdult, gold in Taza, Taroudant and Sijilmāsa, copper in Iglī in the Atlas. To judge by Ibn Ḥawqal's account, there seem to have been no urban artisans at the time; it was an agricultural country, engaged in the exportation chiefly of cereals, wool and leather.

In general the geographical literature gives us the impression that arboriculture and to a lesser degree agriculture were highly developed in the Maghrib, that numerous mines were in operation, and that under eastern influence manu-

25 Ibn Ḥawqal gives the reason for the prosperity of Sijilmāsa. The direct road from the kingdom of Ghana to Egypt had been abandoned because of sandstorms and bandits. Merchants from places as distant as Kūfa and Baṣra then began to appear in the city.

factures were beginning to be implanted (or in some parts of the country reimplanted) with distinctly improved techniques. This production formed the basis of a constant internal trade among farmers, fruit growers and cattle raisers in active centers such as Salé, Aghmāt, Ṭāhart and Kairouan, and of foreign trade with Spain and the Moslem orient, both by land from Sijilmāsa via Ṭāhart and Kairouan to Tripoli, and by sea via a string of ports extending from Māsa in the southwest to Baṣra, Ceuta, Tenès, Bône and Sousse. The most profitable, if not quantitatively the most important, trade was that of the Sahara. Its center of gravity was Sijilmāsa, which had benefited by the decline of the eastern route leading directly to Egypt or branching off toward the Ghadames oasis.

This picture of economic life is well known; the problem is to date it, and here the geographers do not help us. Still, we can set limits to our uncertainty. We can be sure that it does not reach back to the Roman or even the Vandalo-Byzantine period, for conditions in the Maghrib before the sixth century were very different; if the mines had been exploited, we would know it. Gsell concedes, "I am inclined to believe that the most active period in the mining industry in Barbary was the Middle Ages and not antiquity."[26] Commercial relations were certainly not as extensive in antiquity, though the quantity of goods may have been greater in the northeast. Nor would we be justified in claiming that our picture remains valid until the fifteenth century, for there is reason to believe that commercial activity varied in intensity over the following centuries and above all that the trade routes changed. Since the economic and commercial development of the ninth century cannot be accredited to the Arab conquerors, we can only conclude that it was brought about by groups of Berbers in the principalities of the middle Maghrib. The only effect of the Arab

[26] *Hesperis*, VIII, 1928, p. 16.

conquest was to drive them further south, so bringing about the economic integration of the Sahara with the northern Maghrib. This was probably the central phenomenon of the ninth century.

III

What do the colonial historians say of this century, so important for the Maghrib? Some, misinterpreting the Arab chroniclers, distinguish three states, Aghlabid, Rustumid (Ṭāhart) and Idrīsid, and speak of a division corresponding to Tunisia, Algeria and Morocco. Unfortunately some Maghribi historians follow them in this aberration. Carried away by his phobia, Terrasse writes: "No doubt Islam, with its ferments of discord, had brought the hitherto pagan populations firmer rules of moral conduct; nevertheless, the Arab geographers' praises of the virtuous peaceful populations refer chiefly to the cities or tribes of former Roman Morocco, where a Latin and Christian order had been preserved." Faithful to his antinomad passion, Gautier explains(?) both the Khārijism of Ṭāhart and the non-Khārijism of Fez and Kairouan by the destructive drive of the nomads. "In a far corner of the Maghrib, Khārijism culminated in its contrary, a regular government with an urban base." Georges Marçais, with his superior knowledge of the Arab historians, speaks of a ninth-century renewal and cites proofs of it; but he feels obliged to describe the Aghlabid state as a foreign organism, "in which the Berbers were both despised and feared," forgetting to mention the fact (not what hagiography has to say of it) that al-Buhlūl b. Rashīd, the most influential man of his time in Kairouan, was a Berber; which at the very least indicates the considerable social mobility introduced and guaranteed by Islam.[27] The basic mistake of all the colonial historians is to confuse a thin fringe with the whole Maghrib. Even if we suppose

[27] Terrasse, *Histoire du Maroc*, vol. I, p. 208; Gautier, *Le Passé . . .*, p. 316; Georges Marçais, pp. 57-101.

that the coming of Islam was relatively a regression for ancient Africa and the coastal strip (which is far from proved), it was a great step forward for the vast territories of the west and south.

The essential characteristic of the ninth-century Maghrib was the dual—agricultural and commercial—character of the economy. The basic economic-social contradiction was between commerce and agriculture and not between nomadism and agriculture, as Gautier, misled by the colonialist mania for projecting later structures on the past, supposed. In the ninth century there were two kinds of tax, one on agriculture, another, with a far greater yield, on commerce. The typology of the various political organisms was determined by their source of revenue. The Barghwāṭa community and the eastern Algerian communities described by al-Ya'qūbī were supported by agriculture alone; the various Khārijite groups, the Nafūsa in the east and the three Zanāta groups in the west by commerce alone. The city-states of Fez, Ṭāhart and Kairouan were characterized by systems of taxation based on both commerce and agriculture. The question whether a "state" existed in the ninth-century Maghrib—whether one answers in the affirmative, or in the negative with Gautier and Terrasse—is meaningless, especially if one has in mind some immutable and supposedly universal definition of the state. Political organisms vary according to their economic base. There were many kinds in the ninth-century Maghrib, and they must be examined without preconceived ideas. We lack the necessary documents to do so at present, but it is in this direction that we must orient our researches.

The Maghrib remained tripartite in the ninth century, but under new conditions. In Aghlabid Ifrīqiya a "state" was developed on the model of the central Islamic state. This Aghlabid state, which in later years would in turn serve as a model, was Arabo-Berber, Arab in form, Berber in substance. (The same combination was to prevail throughout the Maghrib, but only as a first step, for as the Berbers were

Islamized the Arab cadres tended to disappear.) The continuity with the past is evident, but the Aghlabids may be said to have succeeded where the Vandals had failed, for the Vandals had conducted themselves as the "heirs" of Rome and had never made any attempt to serve the designs of the Berbers; though independent, they had refused to work for the autonomy of the Africans. Whatever the intentions of the Aghlabid amirs may have been, the logic of Islam, which they could not totally obstruct, unified the society of Ifrīqiya, and in the long run the adoption of Mālikism paved the way for the autonomy and moral unity of all North Africa. In this period the middle Maghrib remained a region of city-states, but expanded considerably, northward to the Mediterranean and southward to the Dra' River. In many cases we seem to witness a revival of the third- and fourth-century principalities, which had been shattered by the wars of conquest. The consequence was a remarkable development in commerce, industry (mining) and intellectual life, a glaring refutation of the thesis of Courtois that there was no civilization outside the Roman orbit. The Saharan Maghrib also expanded very considerably, penetrating to the heart of the present-day Sahara; it became essentially the commercial Maghrib, controlled at its two extremities by the Zanāta and the veiled Ṣanhāja. The true opening of the Sahara dates from this period; its inhabitants became the carriers of trade (camel caravans); a particular social structure resulted (lacking, if you will, the character of a state); but the essential and determining phenomenon was the commercial activity and not this particular structure. Of course the significance of all subsequent events can be changed by replacing the economic determinant with other factors, such as social structure or race, and setting up an opposition between the Zanāta (middle Maghrib), the Ṣanhāja (mountaineers in Kabylia and nomads in the Sahara) and the Maṣmūda of the Atlantic plains. A permutation of this kind may appear to be a simple shift of perspective; in reality, even when the high authority of Ibn

Khaldūn is evoked, it reduces the historic process to absurdity.

The new elements by which the ninth century differs from the fifth and sixth were the affirmation of autonomy and the opening up of the Sahara, which ceased to be a "redoubt," or refuge. In a sense the contradiction created in the Roman period and aggravated under the Vandals and the Byzantines was resolved, and the fact that this was done under the sign of Islam accounts no doubt for the slow but irrevocable success of Islamization.

6. Eastern Forces for Unity: The Fāṭimid and Zīrid Ventures

The tenth century (fourth century H.) was the beginning of a period in which the Maghrib participated actively in the history of Islam as a whole. The direct consequence was marked progress in the adoption of Islamic civilization; the indirect consequence was a distinct tendency toward unity based on the state established in Ifrīqiya. The history of this period is fairly well known because during it North Africa was closely involved on the one hand with the Fāṭimid movement and on the other with Umayyad Spain, then at its apogee.

I

Fāṭimid Ifrīqiya

This part of the Maghrib, as we know, was then juridically a part of the 'Abbāsid Empire, which at the end of the third century underwent a grave crisis, provoked by increasingly extremist Shī'ite propaganda (the Qarmatian movement). Under the same conditions and for the same reasons Shī'ite proselytism developed in Ifrīqiya. It is no longer possible to contend that Shī'ism was unknown in the Maghrib before this time; there is good reason to suppose that it had been competing for some time both with Khārijism and with orthodox Islam,[1] with intermittent success. The new element in the middle of the fourth century was the development of Shī'ism itself: the emergence of the Ismā'īlī sect with its secret organization and unified direc-

[1] A careful distinction must be made between the dogmatic orthodoxy which did not take on its definitive form until the fifth century H. and the preexisting save-the-community movement (*Ahl al-Jamā'a*), which provided its social foundation and was essentially characterized by a rejection of all exclusivism.

torate disposing of numerous propagandists (*du'āt*). These propagandists traveled widely, looking for favorable areas in which to recruit. Because of the secrecy surrounding this propaganda, scholars have not been able to agree about the stages of the Ismā'īlī offensive.[2] We do know, however, that it developed simultaneously in Ifrīqiya, Syria and Iraq. Consequently the Aghlabid amir could not hope for any help from his suzerain.

One of these propagandists seems to have been led by a stroke of luck to take a special interest in the Maghrib. Meeting some Kabyles in Mecca and noting their attitude of independence toward the established powers, he quickly grasped the strategic possibilities of their country, situated on the frontier of the Aghlabid emirate. This *dā'ī*, known to us only by his pseudonym Abū 'Abd Allah the Shī'ite, accompanied his new friends on their return journey and settled in Ikjān in 893/280. We possess little information about the beginning of his stay, which, however, cannot have been very different from that of Idrīs I at Oulili or of Ibn Rustum at Ṭāhart. He raised an army, won the population over to his ideas, and built up a political organization. When he thought he was ready, he attacked the fortresses which the Aghlabids like the Byzantines had built on the confines of Kabilya and the Aurès. His first attack (902) was a failure and he withdrew to his base, which was beyond the reach of the enemy. A second offensive, in which he bypassed the Aghlabid territory on the south, was successful: Sétif was taken in 904 and Tobna the following year. The army of Ziyādat Allah III, the last Aghlabid amir, was crushed at Al-Urbus, and Abū 'Abd Allah entered Raqqāda, the amir's palace, in March 909/296. Meanwhile the Qarmatian revolts had been crushed in the east, and in 902 the Mahdī (the true descendant of 'Alī), who had been living at Salamīya in Syria awaiting the outcome, set out for the west by the route long familiar to fugitives from the east

[2] See Laoust, *Les Schismes dans l'Islam*, pp. 140ff. and "Fāṭimides," *EI*[2], vol. II, pp. 870ff.

(Alexandria, Tripoli, Castilya in the Jarīd). He ended up in Sijilmāsa, probably because he had adepts in that city, but the Midrārite amir put him in prison. Thereupon the *dā'ī* went looking for him, took Ṭāhart (August 909) in the process, arrived in Sijilmāsa and freed his master. The master, whose name 'Ubayd Allah is as uncertain as that of his servant, went to Raqqāda, where he revealed himself to be the Mahdī and took the title of amir of the faithful (910/297). Here a government was already in existence, with offices (*dawāwīn*), governors (*'ummāl*), a judiciary and an army. He replaced the army with contingents of his own supporters (Kutāma). At first taxes were reduced for reasons of propaganda, but soon sharply increased to finance the army. The Fāṭimid caliph remained the chief of a sect, bound by ties with an empirewide secret organization, and this was to determine his policy, which remained as intransigently sectarian as before his accession. He appointed a Shī'ite qadi, changed the wording of the call to prayer, the official colors, and so on. The contradictions between the ideological needs of a sect and the broader requirements of a state account no doubt for the conflict between the Mahdī and Abū 'Abd Allah; a similar situation had arisen in the beginnings of the 'Abbāsid empire (the conflict between al-Manṣūr and Abū Muslim), though in such conflicts it is not always possible to determine which party is the intransigent ideologist and which is the moderate politician. Be that as it may, Abū 'Abd Allah and his brother Abū l-'Abbās were executed in July 911. 'Ubayd-Allah began to build up a powerful army and a large war chest with a view to returning and conquering the whole empire. As a symbol of this policy, a maritime capital (al-Mahdiya) was founded between Sousse and Sfax; begun in 912, the work was completed in 921. Three expeditions (913, 919, 925) were sent against Alexandria. None of them succeeded; the time was not yet ripe.

This manifestly partisan policy provoked a series of revolts inspired by the Mālikite jurists and ascetics,[3] supported by the victims of a burdensome taxation, and led by the former beneficiaries of the caravan trade, now controlled by the Fāṭimid army. After the execution of Abū 'Abd Allah in 911, his friends gave vent to their dissatisfaction. Ṭāhart revolted the same year, Tripoli in 912, and Sicily in 915/303 under the leadership of an Aghlabid prince. But the most dangerous of these revolts began in 935/324 in the Aurès. In 943 it spread to the whole country under the leadership of Abū Yazīd, a Khārijite, who succeeded in uniting malcontents of all kinds, and won victory on victory over a period of years. After taking possession of Béja, Tunis and Kairouan, he besieged al-Qā'im, the second caliph, in Mahdiya in November 944. After a prolonged siege the dynasty was saved thanks to a counterattack by the troops of Zīrī b. Manād. Ismā'īl, the third caliph, returned to Kairouan, defeated the army of Abū Yazīd (846/335), pursued him in the Hodna and destroyed him the following year.[4]

Their constant difficulties convinced the Fāṭimids that they would have to choose: either to stay in the Maghrib in the hope of winning it to their cause or to leave it quickly and for good. Probably realizing that the first course was impossible, al-Mu'izz decided to emigrate. In 969/358 he sent his best general, Jawhar al-Rūmī, to conquer Egypt. This he did without difficulty, entered Fusṭāṭ, and laid the foundations of a new capital, Cairo. Three years later the caliph left Ifrīqiya with his treasures, his administrative staff, and the coffins of his predecessors.

[3] In describing the isolation of the Shī'ite minority among the population of Ifrīqiya, H. Mu'nis quotes a passage in a letter from al-Mu'izz to Jawdhar, his confidant: "If corruption had not been rooted in the hearts of these vile barbarians, the light of God possessed by his servants would not have vanished and the lies of God's enemies would not have spread far and wide" (*Etudes d'orientalisme dédiées à la mémoire de Lévi-Provençal*, I, p. 217).

[4] His treatment of the corpse of Abū Yazīd (he had it stuffed and displayed at the gate of al-Mahdiya) shows how much he had feared him.

For Ifrīqiya the period of 'Ubaydite rule had been a mere interlude, but it led to the autonomy of this part of the Maghrib under Berber rule; in this sense it was the culmination of a long process. The inherited state remained Arab in form, but it no longer had Arab cadres and in the years that followed was completely Berberized. The period of Shī'ite domination effaced the last traces of Khārijism and at the same time, by accentuating the opposition of the 'ulama to every form of dogmatic extremism, prepared the way for the Mālikite hegemony which, spreading from Kairouan, was to bring about the moral unification of Islam in the Maghrib. Lastly, the Fāṭimid policy of westward expansion ushered in a period characterized by attempts to create an empire.[5]

The Western Consequences of the Fāṭimid Policy

These were both religious and economic. 'Ubayd Allah proclaimed himself caliph in 910/297. The Umayyad 'Abd al-Raḥmān III waited until the imperialist designs of the Fāṭimids were evident, then in 929/317 he, too, proclaimed himself caliph. The unity of the caliphate, one of the principles of Islamic political theory, was shattered. The consequence was a succession of wars. The Maghrib became a battlefield for the two western caliphs. With their conquest of Ṭāhart and Sijilmāsa, the Fāṭimid rulers had already shown their interest in the central Maghrib, for these two cities, as we have seen, were great commercial centers, dominating the two axes of Saharan and eastern trade. Their economic and financial importance is obvious. We have no precise information about the relations between the two cities and the surrounding country, but it is certain that the local populations played an important role in their commercial activities and derived a substantial profit from them.

[5] Gautier's theory that the Fāṭimid movement in North Africa was an attempt on the part of the Berbers to take revenge on the Arab east is a mere expression of prejudice and of no interest.

The Umayyads of Spain on the other hand seem to have been dependent on the mineral wealth of the western Maghrib and above all on the gold of the Sahara, which was minted in Sijilmāsa, Aghmāt and Fez and sent to Andalusia via Ceuta or Tlemcen (all these places were Idrīsid city-states). This traffic had to be defended against the enemies of the Umayyads, who accordingly allied themselves with all those who were threatened by the Fāṭimids, in particular the Zanāta and the Idrīsid groups. Since the Fāṭimid army was chiefly made up of Ṣanhāja from the eastern Maghrib, many writers have attributed the ensuing struggles to a feud between the Zanāta and the Ṣanhāja, forgetting or minimizing the central issue, which was control of trade routes.[6] Harassed by the Fāṭimid armies, the Zanāta crossed the Taza pass, introducing a new element into the demography of the western Maghrib, which cannot have been very densely populated at the time. But since the designs of the two protagonists, the Fāṭimids and Umayyads, were more economic than territorial, and since they preferred to act through intermediaries rather than directly, the struggle was long and indecisive.

Three Zanāta groups—the Miknāsa, Ifranids and Maghrāwa—lay in the path of the Fāṭimids, who were obliged either to make allies of them, to conquer them, or to drive them out of their country. The general movement was a forced emigration westward and southward.

The Fāṭimids first acted through the intermediary of the Miknāsa. Their chief, Maṣāla b. Ḥabūs, started west from Ṭāhart (917/305), defeated the Idrīsid Yahiā IV and established Mūsā b. Abī l-ʿĀfiya as governor of northern Morocco (between the Rif and the Bouregreg River), leaving the Midrārids in power at Sijilmāsa. But since the army was far from its bases, it could not win a complete victory and the Idrīsids did not disarm. A second expedition was organized in 921/309; on this occasion the Idrīsids were driven

[6] Terrasse, *Histoire du Maroc*, vol. I, pp. 175-179; C.-A. Julien, *Histoire de l'Afrique du Nord*, 2nd ed., vol. II, p. 58.

from Tlemcen and the Mediterranean ports, and al-Ḥajjām's attempt at an Idrīsid restoration (after the deposition of Yaḥiā IV) failed (925/313). But at that point, impelled by their own interest and the intrigues of the Umayyads, the Maghrāwa, whose territory was in the rear of the Miknāsa, revolted and killed Maṣāla. The Fāṭimids sent an army under Abū al-Qāsim, the Mahdi's son, which defeated the Maghrāwa, drove them out of their territory and went on as far as Tlemcen (927-928/315). But in 929/317 Mūsā b. Abī al-'Āfiya, who now found himself too close to the Umayyads, began to think of changing sides, which proves that the Miknāsa had fought for the Fāṭimids out of necessity rather than conviction. In 931-933 the break was consummated, and, at the behest of the Fāṭimid caliph, the Miknāsa of Ṭāhart, led by Ḥāmid b. Yslitan, Maṣāla's nephew, turned against Mūsā and drove him out of Fez. 'Ubayd Allah died in 934/322. Thereupon Mūsā retook Fez and the Maghrāwa returned to the central Maghrib. Thus a direct expedition became necessary. It was organized in 935/323 under the command of the eunuch Maysūr; out of necessity the Idrīsids, who had been deposed and frequently defeated by Mūsā, allied themselves with the Fāṭimid army. The situation of the Idrīsids was desperate in any case; they had no choice but to lose their power or become governors for one or the other protagonist; one of them, al-Qāsim Jannūn, was appointed governor by the Fāṭimids.

The revolt of Abū Yazīd threatened to reverse the situation. Mūsā reconquered northern Morocco, the Idrīsids were driven out, and even the Miknāsa of Ṭāhart thought the time had come for a declaration of independence. The difficulties of the Fāṭimids were not, however, long-lived. After the defeat of Abū Yazīd, Zīrī b. Manād, the savior of the dynasty, was sent west with a powerful army; he retook Ṭāhart (947/336), and subdued the Maghrāwa and the Ifranids. Ten years later a great expedition led by Jawhar reconquered Fez and Sijilmāsa (958-960/347-349). The departure of 'Ubayd Allah for Egypt seemed to open up new possibilities for the enemies of the Fāṭimids, but the armies of Buluggīn b. Zīrī (972/362) crushed the Maghrāwa and Ifranids for good; the Miknāsa and the Idrīsids were obliged to rally to the Fāṭimids.

As recorded by the Arab chroniclers and here summed up, the foregoing events seem very confused. It is difficult to analyze them, as is always the case when wars are waged by mercenaries who serve aims of their own in addition to those of their employers. But despite the profusion of immediate motives (and Ibn Khaldūn, copied by all subsequent historians, was interested solely in these),[7] the effective causes seem to have been relatively simple. All the battles were fought for control of the cities: Ṭāhart, Sijilmāsa, Tlemcen, Fez and the Mediterranean ports. It seems reasonable to suppose that the city-states of the central Maghrib had more or less tacit agreements with the Zanāta groups who controlled the Saharan trade routes. In the tenth century this politico-economic balance between the masters of the cities and the masters of the roads had been disturbed by the new power of the Fāṭimids. The latter, in need of funds for their offensives in the east, tried to obtain them through political and economic domination over this part of the Maghrib, which had formerly been the domain of the Khārijites. The populations reacted in different ways: some rallied to the new masters in the hope of preserving their privileges, others revolted and made common cause with the enemies of the Fāṭimids. The consequence of these long struggles was the economic and demographic decline of the central Maghrib, whose inhabitants moved to Morocco, where their chiefs tried to carve out principalities for themselves at the expense of the Idrīsids. The theory that the war was a mere racial conflict between Ṣanhāja and Zanāta, is based on a racist philosophy of history and not on a realistic

[7] Ibn Khaldūn's account of these struggles bears the mark of events that took place much later (the struggles between Marinīds and Zayyānids); we are under no obligation to accept as historical truths notions that fit in so well with Ibn Khaldūn's theories and Gautier's prejudices.

view of events. Gautier interprets the whole struggle as a feud between the nomadic Zanāta and sedentary Ṣanhāja; he sees the Zanāta as what they became after losing control of the Saharan trade, when, obliged to look for another mode of livelihood, they took to preying on the urban populations. But the pillaging Zanātī as Gautier describes him is only a consequence of the wars; he cannot be invoked as a cause of them. The social structure (in this case nomadism) became a determining factor only when its economic base (the Saharan trade) failed it.

Apart from the weakening of the central Maghrib, another important consequence of the Fāṭimid offensive was the removal of a part of the Saharan trade to the east, and this was one of the principal reasons for the prosperity of Zīrid Ifrīqiya.

Zīrid Ifrīqiya

Zīrī b. Manād had saved the Fāṭimid power from the threat of Abū Yazīd. The caliph al-Qā'im had authorized him to build himself a provincial capital at Ashīr and, thanks to its favorable geographic situation, it grew rapidly. He founded or repopulated three towns, Algiers, Miliana and Médéa, and appointed his sons governors over them. He minted coins in his name. Thus he may be regarded as a true viceroy of the marches of Ifrīqiya. When al-Mu'izz left for the east in 973, Buluggīn b. Zīrī established himself in Manṣūriya (the capital which the Fāṭimids had preferred to the excessively hostile Kairouan) and left Ashir to his son Ḥammād. In 978/368 Tripolitania was retroceded to him (but not Sicily) by al-'Azīz, the second Fāṭimid caliph of Cairo. Theoretically Buluggīn remained a mere governor, but all Ifrīqiya was under his rule, and he had no designs on anything outside the Maghrib, whereas his suzerain had enormous ambitions in the east. Thus a trend toward autonomy was inevitable. Though formal autonomy was not achieved for many years, Buluggīn's allegiance to the caliph had little content, manifesting itself solely in official correspondence and gifts on the occasion of marriages, victories and coronations. Buluggīn's successor al-Manṣūr began to conduct himself in every way like an independent prince, but the caliph still had means of pressure, chiefly those members of his army (the Maghāriba) who had remained in close contact with their Kutāma compatriots. The Kutāma felt obliged to defend their preeminence in the state they had helped to found by preserving its alliance with the Fāṭimid dynasty. Consequently they revolted in 986 and again in 988-991. The movement toward autonomy was halted under Bādīs (996-1016/386-406), but in the course of his squabbles with his uncle Ḥammād, Bādīs soon found out that loyalty to a distant suzerain did not pay, and moved toward a break, which was consummated in 1049/441 by his son al-Mu'izz.[8] At that time, it should be recalled, an 'Abbāsid renewal had long been in progress under the caliphs al-Qādir and al-Qā'im, whereas the Fāṭimid camp had been undergoing a grave crisis. The caliph al-Ḥākim (996-1021) had been killed under obscure circumstances on the occasion of a change in the Shī'ite doctrine, and his successors were not recognized by all the members of the sect, which split into an eastern and a western faction. In the light of these developments, the step taken by al-Mu'izz can hardly be regarded as revolutionary. All the symbols of the Fāṭimid power, the call to prayer, the official color, the coinage,[9] were abandoned in favor of 'Abbāsid symbols.

What was going on in the west during this time?

In the marches of old Numidia, the Zīrids had left their former territory to their B. Ḥammād cousins, who gained their autonomy even more quickly than the Zīrids had done. In 1007-1008 Ḥammād b. Buluggīn had chosen a new capital,

[8] Within the framework of Islamic public law this independence could be symbolized only by the recognition of a suzerainty even more remote and theoretical than that of Cairo. Thus the 'Abbāsid caliph of Baghdad was recognized.

[9] Many historians note that the change was followed by a monetary devaluation.

Qal'a, on the slopes of Jabal Ma'did, and had populated it with the inhabitants of Msila, whom he moved by force: which proves either that the region was thinly populated after the tenth-century wars or that its urban traditions had declined. Later on, the refugees from the cities of Ifrīqiya brought in a certain amount of activity. The Zīrid amir Bādīs, then a young man, encouraged his uncle Ḥammād's autonomist tendencies by putting him in command of his western army, so enabling him to increase his prestige. When in 1014/405 Bādīs, with the consent of the Fāṭimid caliph, appointed his son al-Manṣūr his heir and gave him Constantine, which was part of the Ḥammādid territory, as his fief, Ḥammād rebelled, broke with the Fāṭimid authority, and recognized the 'Abbāsid caliph. Bādīs besieged Qal'a, counting on the help of his suzerain, which was not forthcoming; Bādīs and his son died, and in 1017/408 his successor al-Mu'izz recognized the fait accompli.

In the western Maghrib the Umayyads, taking advantage of the split in the Fāṭimid forces, decided to take direct action. Al-Ḥakam II (961-976) sent out Ghālib (973/362), his best general, who captured Fez and Barṣa, and besieged Ḥajar al-Naṣr, which the Idrīsids regarded as an impregnable bastion. Indeed, the Umayyad army had great difficulty in reducing it, but in the end, Ḥasan b. Jannūn surrendered and all the Idrīsids were deported.[10] For a time northern Morocco was administered directly by the Umayyads. In 979/369 Buluggīn counterattacked, reoccupying Fez, and waged war on the Barghwāṭa. In the meantime Ḥasan b. Jannūn had left Spain and reappeared in Fez. But in 984 Buluggīn died and the Umayyads organized the great offensive of 'Askalāja,[11] reoccupied the northern capital with great difficulty, and finally killed the Idrīsid pretender.

[10] Terrasse goes so far as to write, "Thus the first Sherifian dynasty in Morocco ended with a police operation" (*Histoire du Maroc*, vol. I, p. 180).

[11] His name was Abū al-Ḥakam 'Amr b. 'Abd Allah b. Abī 'Amir; thus he was the cousin of the famous chamberlain al-Manṣūr b. Abī 'Amir.

The Ifranids rallied and for a time the Maghrāwa, under the leadership of Zīrī b. 'Atiya, governed northern Morocco.[12] But just as Mūsā b. Abī al-'Āfiya had asserted his autonomy vis-à-vis the Fāṭimids, so Zīrī rebelled against the heavy hand of the Umayyads. In 996/386 they were obliged to send an army against him and replace him by an Andalusian governor. Later on, Zīrī's son al-Mu'izz was restored to favor and power, but under the tight control of Cordova. After 985 the Zīrids of Ifrīqiya recognized the impossibility of holding northern Morocco as long as there was a strong power in neighboring Spain; now and then the Ḥammādids undertook a western campaign, but apparently without much conviction. As a result of all this warfare both in the central Maghrib and in northern Morocco, the Tlemcen-Ṭāhart-Sijilmāsa axis was destroyed; it was this destruction that made the region the home of nomadism, not the other way round.

II

When we try to picture the Maghrib in the middle of the eleventh century (and of the fifth century H.), what strikes us first of all is the enormous difference between east and west. While the east was shared by two unified, Ḥammādid and Zīrid, principalities, the west, as a result of the struggles between the Fāṭimids and the Umayyads, was divided among a large number of city-states. The Barghwāṭa, though subjected to pressures of all sorts, still held their territory on the Atlantic plains. The Idrīsids succeeded in holding on to commercial centers of Tāmdult, Iglī and Māsa, thanks pre-

[12] It is on this occasion that we clearly perceive the opposition between the exploiting Maghrāwa and the exploited urban population. Ibn Abī Zar' writes, "At that time the inhabitants of Fez dug large cellars in which they took to milling their grain and cooking their food, for fear that the poor among the Maghrāwa would hear the sound of the millstones and seize their food" (*al-Anīs al-Mutrib*, vol. 1, p. 177). It should not be forgotten, however, that these Maghrāwa had become mercenaries in the pay of the Umayyads and were left destitute at the cessation of hostilities.

cisely to the Barghwāṭa buffer zone. At the fall of the Cordova caliphate, they would recover the city of Ceuta, but the newcomers, the Maghrāwa and the Ifranids, were the true powers in the region; the former remained the masters of Fez, which just before the Almoravid conquest experienced a certain urban development under the amir Dūnās (1054-1060/446-452), and also controlled the Haouz in the vicinity of Aghmāt and Sijilmāsa (taken in 976/366 from the Midrārite vassals of the Fāṭimids), which remained in the Banū Khazrūn family until the coming of the Almoravids. The Ifranids governed in Tlemcen (B. Ya'la), in Salé and in the Tadla. Thus the Zanāta maintained in the western Maghrib the system they had known in the central Maghrib (it should be noted that their bases, Sijilmāsa, Aghmāt, Fez, and Oujda, were on an important trade route, mentioned above); the new element was that they now controlled the cities, whereas formerly they had only controlled the roads; since trade was on the decline, they lived and supported their armies by taxes levied on the urban populations.

The Andalusian al-Bakrī (d. 1091/487) gives us an account of the economic situation. He describes at length the country around Fez and Oujda in northern Morocco, a thriving region served by several seaports: Ceuta, Tangiers, Bādīs, Mellila and Nakkūr. Orchards were abundant—pears, pomegranates, and also vineyards; from Tetuán to Fez there were rich meadows, and in the vicinity of Baṣra cotton was grown; the region was also famous for its horse breeding. He also describes the southern region, taking in both slopes of the Anti-Atlas, its main cities being Māsa, Iglī, and the city(?) of Dra'; this was a region of villages and orchards; to the north of the Anti-Atlas the oil-bearing argan tree predominated and sugar cane was grown. To the west of the High Atlas, in the vicinity of Aghmāt and Nfīs, there was an abundance of fruit trees, especially apple trees, while to the east the Sijilmāsa region was rich in minerals as well as date palms. To judge by al-Bakrī's account, the Barghwāṭa country seems to have been open to commerce, for the port of Fedala handled its farm produce. He speaks of numerous busy roads. Fez was connected with Spain via Tangiers and Ceuta, with the central Maghrib via Oujda, and with the Sahara via Aghmāt and Sijilmāsa. From this last city a road led northward via Oujda to the Mediterranean port of Tabaḥrit, and another westward to Māsa by way of Tāmdult and Iglī, not to mention the main road to the Sudan via Awdaghost. There was also a lateral road from Aghmāt along the Tensift River to the ribat of Cūz, which seems to have been the frontier of the Barghwāṭa territory. A lively trade in the slaves, honey, sugar and hides of the south, the sheep of the Atlantic plains, and the horses of the Rif was carried on especially with Spain. To judge by al-Bakrī's description, the country does not seem to have been impoverished by the political struggles, which had been chiefly felt in the north. The transfer of populations from the central Maghrib seems on the contrary to have accelerated the integration of the various regions with each other and with Spain. It was this commercial integration which in the long run put an end to the autonomy of the Barghwāṭa and prepared the country for a political unification which would in turn enable it to play an active role in the destinies of the Maghrib as a whole.

For the present, however, the political power was in the eastern Maghrib; the two principalities, Ḥammādid and Zīrid, formed a unit. Comparing the accounts of al-Bakrī and of al-Ya'qūbī, we see that the population was becoming more homogeneous: the descendants of the Rūm and of the Persians had mixed to such an extent that they were no longer identifiable in the fortresses of the Jarīd and the Constantine district. By then there were very few Afāriq in the cities: Kairouan, Tunis, Gabès and Monastir; there were still some Christians living in Qal'a and Bougie, whither they had no doubt been drawn by the Ḥammādid princes. The Arab immigrants, on the other hand, were not only numerous in the cities, but also merged with the populations of the surrounding country. The majority had remained faithful to Mālikism; the Shī'ite minority, concentrated in the coastal cities, especially in Mahdiya, was gradually losing its prerogatives, while Khārijism was holding out only in the southern marches of Tripolitania and in the Hodna. These accounts give us the impression of a homogeneous population strongly marked by the Arabic language. Thus the situation had changed radically since the days of the Aghlabids.

The historians and even more so the men of letters describe the wealth and munificence of the Zīrid princes in the most glowing terms. The geographers dwell on the great prosperity of the country. The basic crops of Ifrīqiya—wheat, olives (oil) and dates were harvested in abundance; Beja was the great market for cereals, while the thriving oil presses of Sfax were supplied by a veritable forest of olive trees extending to the gates of Kairouan. Tozeur, at the center of the Jarīd, was the great date market. In the northern region of Tunis and Carthage, there were enormous groves of orange, fig and banana trees; the geographer also notes the presence of sugar cane in the Jarīd and at Gabès, and of cotton near Msila and Carthage.[13] The textile industry seems to have been highly developed in Gabès, Sousse and Sfax, where, we are told, better cloth was made than in Alexandria (no small compliment at the time) and by the same methods. Copper articles were manufactured in Kairouan and ceramics in Manṣūriya and Tunis: glass was made in Manṣūriya, Qal'a and later in Bougie. Kairouan had been displaced as the great commercial center by its suburb of Ṣabra, which under the name of al-Manṣūriya was chosen as the Fāṭimid capital in 948/337. From it roads led to Qal'a and Sijilmāsa, to Tripoli and the orient, and

[13] It is of course hard to determine whether the author mentions a plant or product because it is abundant or because its presence in the territory described is unexpected (the latter would seem to be the case with bananas, saffron and cotton in the region of Carthage and with sugar cane and cotton in the Ceuta region). Accordingly this literature is of value more for the general impression it gives than for detailed information.

to the port of Sfax which connected Ifrīqiya with Andalusia, Sicily and Egypt.

It was this commercial activity that made possible the munificence of the Zīrid and Ḥammādid amirs. Al-Bakrī tells us that in a single day the customs duties collected in the Zīrid capital amounted to twenty-six thousand dirham.[14] The Zīrid amirs preserved the Fāṭimid fiscal system based essentially on customs duties, pasturage and caravan taxes, and the revenues of the large estates. The Fāṭimids had instituted a land tax (no doubt justified in their eyes by the fact that they did not regard non-Shī'ites as true Moslems), and al-Mu'izz had advised Buluggīn never to abolish it, but in order to curry favor with the population and to symbolize the break with Shī'ism, Buluggīn reduced the kharāj, which was altogether abolished by Bādīs in 991/381. Thus the state was essentially dependent on commercial duties, which brought it into direct conflict with the Khārijite Zanāta, who had long controlled the commerce of the country. Be that as it may, the Zīrid amirs were rich, and since they had no great offensive designs, they were able to live sumptuously. Little by little they completed their apprenticeship as princes. Buluggīn appeared only rarely in Ifrīqiya, which he let an Aghlabid prince administer; his son al-Manṣūr first moved into the old Aghlabid palace in Raqqada, then established himself definitively in Manṣūriya, where he soon became known for his magnificence, displaying his wealth on every possible occasion: marriages, feast days, receptions of ambassadors from Cairo.[15]

Though less wealthy, the Ḥammādid princes tried to keep pace with their Zīrid cousins. Though the testimony of the chroniclers may seem exaggerated, it would appear to be corroborated by the excavations at the site of Qal'a, the capital of the Banū Ḥammād. In any event, both families intro-

[14] Equivalent, it has been estimated, to thirteen thousand gold francs (Al-Bakrī, *Al-Masālik*, p. 25, translation p. 58).

[15] These accounts all date from after the invasion of the Banū Hilāl and the fall of the dynasty; consequently nostalgia plays a large part in them.

duced a court life, which continued to thrive even at times when the political situation did not warrant it. It was this court life, so typical of classical Islam, that made possible the written Arabic literature which now developed. Previously all the men of letters except for the Mālikite jurists had been foreigners. Under the Zīrids two natives made their appearance: Ibn Sharaf (d. 1068), poet, literary critic and historian, author of a history of the Zīrids that was to serve all subsequent historians as a source, and Ibn Rashīq (d. 1064), poet and anthologer, whose *Kitāb al-'Umda* is still regarded as a classic of literary criticism. Other names could be cited, but the two we have selected became known far beyond the borders of Ifrīqiya, so demonstrating that their country had become an autonomous center of Arabic culture.[16]

A comparison between the two parts of the Maghrib in the middle of the eleventh century (end of the fifth century H.) reveals the same thriving agriculture and a similar level of commercial activity, except in the western part of the central Maghrib (the Sijilmāsa-Ṭāhart-Tlemcen axis), which undoubtedly suffered from the wars between the Fāṭimids and the Umayyads. The major consequence of the wars seems to have been not so much the westward migration of the Zanāta as the displacement to the east and west of this great commercial axis.[17] On this economic foundation two different political structures developed. The east was characterized by two unified states, the one urbanized and Arabized, attaining a high cultural level, the other moving vigorously toward urbanization; the west by a dispersion of political authority, though this decentralization was itself a mark of urbanization and an instrument of Arabization. The western Maghrib, however, was still far behind the

16 On the art of the Zīrid period, cf. Abd al-Wahhāb, *Waraqāt*, vol. II, pp. 207-224.

17 It should be remembered that at the time a trade route was simply a trail and involved no construction. Changes in itinerary could be easily made, and were hence frequent.

model of Arab civilization achieved in the east. Its largely peasant society remained untouched by urban culture and the handicrafts. All these states and city-states supported themselves by taxes levied on a flourishing trade with the Sudan, Andalusia, Egypt and Sicily.

The problem of the day seems to have been: who would unify the western Maghrib? The two kingdoms in the east seemed capable of doing so. The Zīrids tried and the Ḥammādids followed their example, their last expedition being that of Buluggīn against Fez (1062/454). More than by their own weaknesses or by the uncertainty of their relations with each other or with their suzerain in Cairo, they were thwarted by the opposition of Andalusia. The Umayyad caliphs would have had a still better chance of unifying the Maghrib, but they were interested only in northern Morocco, and just as success seemed to be within their reach in 1009/399, the caliphate entered on a period of crisis that was to culminate in its downfall. Instead of unifying the principalities of the Maghrib, Andalusia broke up into numerous principalities. Forty years later, the two emirates of the eastern Maghrib cast off their allegiance to the Fāṭimid caliphate. This independence might have fostered a strong western policy, but instead it weakened the two emirates irremediably, opening the road to outsiders from southern Morocco, the Almoravids. If we decline to take seriously the phantasm of the anarchistic and intractable Zanāti, dear to Gautier and his successors, the failure of the imperial movement from the east must be imputed to the balance between the Fāṭimid and Umayyad powers. By the time these two forces declined, the opportunity had been lost; Ifrīqiya had incurred economic ruin.

III

On the eve of the Almoravid conquest, the western Islamic states collapsed. The Cordova caliphate was first to go. Whatever the remote causes may have been, the process seems to have been accelerated by the arrival in the peninsula of all those who had been defeated in the Maghrib wars: Idrīsids, Ifranids and Maghrāwa. Those who had controlled the Saharan trade became soldiers of fortune, lusting for political authority. The fall of the Umayyads was marked by two phases: 1008-1016/299-407, when the crisis still had the aspect of an internecine struggle between members of the caliph's family, and 1016-1031/407-422, when the Idrīsid Ḥammādids entered the field. In 1031/422 the Umayyads were driven out of Cordova, which became an oligarchic republic. Throughout these turbulent years, which ended with the breakdown of Islamic Spain into fifteen principalities, the Berbers played a decisive role; the hatred that separated them, from the city-dwellers and the Saqāliba [Slavs, originally slaves from eastern Europe, who played the same role in Moslem Spain as the janissaries in the Ottoman countries] was a determining factor in the course of events. In 1013-1014/404, they began to carve out principalities for themselves, the Banū Zīrī in Granada and Elvira, the Maghrāwa in the north, the Banū Ifran in Jaén, the Banū Dummar in Sidonia, and so on. In a sense this was the revenge of the western Maghrib on the Umayyads, who had been able neither to unify it themselves nor to leave the task to Ifrīqiya.

The next breakup occurred in Ifrīqiya itself, under the impact of the Banū Hilāl. When in 1049/441 al-Mu'izz, after long years of preparation, declared his independence of the Fāṭimid caliph (al-Mustanṣir), the caliph, at the instigation of his minister al-Yāzūrī, decided to reconquer Ifrīqiya indirectly. Two Arab tribes, the Banū Hilāl and the Banū Sulaym, had taken part in the Qarmatian revolt against the 'Abbāsids in northeastern Arabia, but conducted themselves in such a way as to discredit the Shī'ite propaganda. Both before and after their establishment in Cairo, the Fāṭimids had been alarmed at their activities. The better to control them, they had moved them to the Upper Nile region and then, at the first opportunity, got rid of them by sending them to the Maghrib.[18] Land grants (*iqṭā'*) were distributed among their leaders. On the arrival of the Banū Hilāl—probably no more than two hundred thousand in number—in Ifrīqiya, the same process took place as with the German tribes at the end of the Roman Empire or with the Turks under the 'Abbāsids. The sovereign tried to neutralize them by incorporating them into his army, but an understanding proved impossible; a breakdown of authority resulted, and in the end each leader carved out a principality for himself. In 1052/443[19] the Zīrid army was crushed at Ḥaydarān, between Gabès and Sfax. The cities were occupied one by one; Kairouan held out until 1057/499, when it was taken and pillaged. Al-Mu'izz withdrew to Mahdiya, whose powerful ramparts protected it from the attacks of the Banū Hilāl. Once the central authority was destroyed, the inhabitants of the cities acknowledged new masters (the Banū Khurāsān established themselves in Tunis, the Banū Jāmī' in Gabès, the Banū Malīl in Sfax, the Banū al-Ward in Bizerte, etc.; some of these groups even took to minting their own coinage). The rural populations began to pay tribute to these new masters, so consolidating their power.

The Ḥammādids had expected to benefit by their cousins' difficulties. After al-Mu'izz's break with the caliph in Cairo, al-Qā'id had renewed his allegiance to the caliph and his territory could not be touched. But then one of his successors, al-Nāṣir, became involved in a conflict between sections

18 This is the rationalized version put forward by later historians. We are under no obligation to accept it even if it seems plausible. It is difficult to determine what part was played by chance, objective necessity, or deliberate policy in this development, and this explains why there is no general agreement among scholars as to when the Banū Hilāl arrived in Ifrīqiya. It seems probable that they arrived before 1048 and that there was no direct connection between al-Mu'izz's break with the Fāṭimids and the forced emigration of these Bedouins.

19 Another chronology is sometimes given, according to which the break between the Zīrids and Fāṭimids occurred well before 1049; the battle of Ḥaydarān, which was by no means decisive, would then have to be dated earlier. See Idrīs, *La Berbérie orientale sous les Zīrides*, pp. 213-214.

of the Banū Hilāl; he was defeated and obliged to let the Athbaj settle in the Constantine region. Thereupon he founded a city on the coast, an-Nāṣiriya (Bougie), which in 1104/498 became the capital of the last Ḥammādids. Thus all of the southern part of the Constantine region remained in the hands of the Banū Hilāl, who year after year were reinforced by new arrivals. The last contingent, the Ma'qil, went further west, one part of them branching off to the north and another heading for Tafilalt. The last Ḥammādids relied on the Zanāta of the Oran region to stop the Banū Hilāl in their westward march *(taghriba)*.

The account here given of the rise of the Banū Hilāl may be termed the classical version, though it presents a number of uncertainties. A widespread interpretation of it, put forward by contemporaries such as Ibn Sharaf, repeated by Ibn 'Idhāri and systematized by Ibn Khaldūn, was faithfully copied by Georges Marçais, utilized by Gautier, and most recently taken over almost textually by Idris,[20] who regards the coming of the Banū Hilāl as a turning point in the history of the Maghrib. This interpretation deals chiefly with the consequences, which are described as follows. As only a limited amount of pasture land was available, the Zanāta of the central Maghrib were driven westward beyond the Moulouya. In southern Tunisia, in the Tell region, and in eastern Morocco, farming gave way to pastoral nomadism. Urban life declined as a result of pillage and of the impoverishment caused by the fighting in the surrounding country; the big cities (Kairouan, Qal'a, Ṭāhart, Sijilmāsa), which had been created by the first Arab conquest, were ruined by this second one; urban life took refuge on the coast; the economy suffered from intense exploitation: a share of the wheat, date and olive crops was taken from the farmers, and trade was at the mercy of the Banū Hilāl, who either took it over directly or subjected it to their control. The cities, large and small, paid taxes to the Banū Hilāl

20 See *ibid.*, especially the conclusion.

chiefs in return for an illusory protection; according to al-Idrīsī (d. 1166/560), writing a century later, the great commercial highways described by al-Bakrī were no longer in use; political authority was dispersed among a large number of chiefs, among whom the last Zīrid amirs, who had taken refuge in Mahdiya, and the Ḥammādids, who had withdrawn to Bougie, enjoyed no special prerogatives; the constant conflicts between these princes served only to increase the power of the Banū Hilāl. This situation favored the newcomers to the Mediterranean, the Normans, who had no difficulty in conquering Sicily, which the Fāṭimids of Egypt had transformed into an emirate under the family of Ḥasan b. 'Alī al-Kalbī and which, unable to defend itself, could not count on help from al-Mu'izz, who had his hands full with the Banū Hilāl. Encouraged by their success, the Normans and the Genoese even attacked the ports of Ifrīqiya (Mahdiya was taken in 1087/480, and the amir Tamīm was obliged to pay a heavy ransom before the assailants would leave the city). Ifrīqiya now presented the same picture as Andalusia fifty years before, at the fall of the Cordova caliphate.

This account of the dissolution of the state cannot be contested; but then comes the question of responsibility. Playing on the pun *'Arab-A'rāb* as the classical scholars had played on the pun nomad-Numidian, colonial historians beginning with De Slane gave free rein to their anti-Arab passion. Naturally, the Arab chroniclers or Ibn Khaldūn himself could not have made so crude a blunder, for from early childhood they had learned in the Koran to distinguish between the two terms. The confusion could not long be maintained and the anti-Arab prejudice gave way to an anti-bedouin passion.

It was easy to show the one-sidedness of this traditional view.[21] Since the descriptions of the Zīrid splendor were the

[21] See Sahli, *Décoloniser l'histoire*, pp. 73-86; Lacoste, *Ibn Khaldoun*, pp. 87-105; Poncet, "Le Mythe de la 'catastrophe' hilalienne," pp. 1099-1120.

work of courtiers or nostalgics, we must allow for a good deal of exaggeration; the diatribes against the Banū Hilāl were all written by jurists or hagiographers belonging to the commercial bourgeoisie and opposed both to the Zīrid power and to the newcomers. From this literature itself, moreover, we can infer the existence of a grave political, financial and religious (the Shī'ite problem) crisis long before the coming of the Banū Hilāl. Actually the opponents of the traditional view, who do not deny the consequences of the incursion of the Banū Hilāl, try to throw light on the conditions that made these negative consequences possible and, intentionally or not, employ the arguments that have always been used to account for conquests. This is what Courtois attempted on behalf of the Vandal conquest and what several contemporary Arab writers have done on behalf of the first Arab conquerors. The theory is that every successful conquest presupposes conditions favorable to it in the country to be conquered. Accordingly this interpretation calls for a negative judgment on all conquered states (Roman, Byzantine, Aghlabid, and Zīrid Africa; Umayyad Andalusia, etc.). Each of these regimes, it is argued, exploited the population drastically and was imposed either by foreigners or by a small local minority. Thus the conqueror brought with him neither more injustice nor more destruction, since by discouraging production with its heavy taxation, its monopolies, and the cupidity of its officials, the exploiter state was already destroying the economy.[22]

Actually these two interpretations are equally abstract, for they utilize the same juridical, historical or hagiographical sources—which, as we have shown, are hostile to the Zīrid power for fiscal and religious reasons and to the new power for political and again for fiscal reasons. As a whole, this literature reflects the situation of a certain urban society and provides both sides with arguments. Thus the con-

[22] To be logical, this theory would have to be general; the argument of Courtois (who tries to draw distinctions between the Vandals and the Banū Hilāl) seems weak precisely because the theory is not general.

troversy can go on forever. In reality there are several factors, both exogenous and endogenous, that cannot be disregarded. First of all, the relation of forces in the Mediterranean: the almost concomitant decline of the western and eastern parts of the Moslem west, that is, of the two regions which were most urbanized and most Arabized, and for that reason most closely involved in the overall destinies of Islam, coincided with the decline of the Fāṭimid and ʿAbbāsid caliphates, soon to be symbolized by the success of the first crusade (1097-1099). The defeats in Andalusia, Sicily and the east must be seen in the context of a struggle for mastery of the Mediterranean. But thus far historians have contented themselves with noting the sudden imbalance between an expanding Western Europe and an Islamic world in crisis. Of course certain causes come to mind: demographic (probably the most important), economic (maritime commerce and its repercussions on the Saharan trade) and politico-religious (on the one hand, religious unity under the papacy, on the other, doctrinal dispersion); but all these factors and their effect on the situation in the Maghrib are obscured by the priority that has been given to internal phenomena. Some writers have gone so far as to deny the influence of events taking place in other parts of the Islamic world; neither the Ismāʿīlī crisis nor the ʿAbbāsid renewal with its vast implications have really been integrated with the historical development of the Maghrib. It is true that these phenomena are still far from being fully explained or understood, and indeed this is not the task of a historian of the Maghrib; still, it should be borne in mind that as long as we have no satisfactory explanation for such phenomena, any hypothesis concerning the history of the Maghrib is by definition incomplete.

Even the endogenous factors have not been isolated and analyzed in a satisfactory way; we encounter a constant confusion between social aspects (tribalism), economic aspects (pastoral mode of life), and the military and political aspects of nomadism. What really demands to be examined is the role of the nomad within specific overall structures and in specific historical conjunctures. To confuse the roles of the Musulāmi of the first century, the Luwāta in the third century, the Zanāta in the eighth and ninth centuries, and of the Banū Hilāl in the eleventh century is to be satisfied with formal explanations that explain nothing, and the geographer Gautier is the source of this confusion. In the present study we have had occasion to observe the nomad-in-spite-of-himself, driven beyond the *limes*, and the "Zanāti" who became the escort and controller of the Saharan trade; with the Banū Hilāl we encounter a third and entirely different type. It is certainly tempting to assimilate the role of the Zanāta in Andalusia to that of the Banū Hilāl in Ifrīqiya,[23] but to do so would be a mistake. There is indeed a relation between the two migrations, since it was the relative depopulation of the central Maghrib that attracted the newcomers and subsequently transformed tilled fields into pasture land (a process which, for lack of a strong political authority, could not quickly be reversed). But there was also a great difference between these "migrants": deprived of their privileges and of their profits on the central Maghrib trade, the Zanāta would try to recover the same privileges further west; no longer able to control the roads, they would take control of the cities, and when this was no longer possible, they went to Spain as soldiers and tried, as soldiers, to gain a share in the political power. Their old contact with cities (essentially as stopping places and markets) made it easy for them to integrate themselves with city life, and this they obviously did (except in years of famine) in Morocco and Andalusia; their behavior seems indistinguishable from that of the Idrīsids or the Saqāliba. The Banū Hilāl represented a new type, for they arrived

[23] Contrary to what Idris, "De la réalité de la catastrophe hilalienne," p. 395, seems to think, this is a classical thesis. Like earlier writers he speaks of *fitna barbariya*, forgetting that there was no Berber "invasion" and also failing to explain wherein this *fitna* of the Berbers differed from that of the Saqāliba generals.

with titles to property (*iqṭā'*). Whatever may have been the juridical significance of this term, its political meaning is clear: the Banū Hilāl appeared on the scene as heirs to the political power. We know next to nothing of the history of these Banū Hilāl. Originally perhaps they had suffered the same deterioration of status as the Zanāta (for it should be remembered that, surprising as it may seem, the great Arab conquests of the seventh century resulted in the impoverishment of the Arabian peninsula and the displacement of the major communication routes of the ancient world). But unlike the Zanāta, the Banū Hilāl remained for centuries in this inferior status, and as a result their social (tribal) structure was fixed and became a determining factor, producing wealth through the political supremacy it generated. True, this in itself does not adequately explain their behavior in Zīrid Ifrīqiya; if they had found themselves masters of a territory endowed with flourishing commerce, they might easily have adapted themselves to an urban, sedentary life, but since they did not (and this is the essential point), they continued to play their parts as political leaders, that is, as ferments of decentralization. Of course the actual facts are not so simple, but there nevertheless seems to be an essential difference between the events of the western and those of the eastern sections of the Moslem occident. In the west a continuous flow of trade enabled the Zanāta to adapt themselves rapidly (and would later enable the Marīnids and Zayyānids to found relatively centralized states), while in the east the flow of trade was deflected at its point of departure and virtually blocked at its point of arrival (the Norman peril). Thus the Banū Hilāl were held to their role as soldiers of fortune in search of a political heritage. This helps us to understand the conflict between the urban population and the Banū Hilāl as essentially a more and more desperate competition for the profits of a waning trade. It resulted from a special situation, very different from that existing in such city-states as Ṭāhart, Sijilmāsa, Tlemcen, Aghmāt, where the profits of an active commerce were sufficient to satisfy both the masters of the roads and the masters of the cities. In the new situation created by the disintegration of a state into petty principalities, the political power disputed by the urban aristocracy and the Banū Hilāl was a substitute for the diminishing trade, and the smaller the stakes the fiercer grew the struggle. Thus the Banū Hilāl not only presented a new historical type of nomadism, but also created a type of principality different both from the relatively centralized state of the Aghlabids and Zīrids, but also from the city-states of the eighth and ninth centuries. If we fail to distinguish the different types of nomad arising in different historical conjunctures, we shall be reduced to representing an abstract social structure as the cause of totally different developments and faced with insurmountable contradictions such as the incomprehensible metamorphosis of the nomad destroyer of empires (Zanāta and Banū Hilāl) into a nomad founder of empires (Almoravids, Marīnids, Zayyānids). What might in the last analysis settle the controversy between the two interpretations we have discussed is concrete evidence concerning the development of long-range trade. And it is symptomatic that the only uncontestable documents regarding the commerce of Ifrīqiya (those of the Genizah in Cairo, studied by Goitein)[24] support the second hypothesis, according to which nomadism (in its socio-political sense) is far more a secondary, induced phenomenon than a determining cause.

[24] In a number of articles, reprinted in *Studies in Islamic History*, chap. 14, and in *Mediterranean Society*, vol. 1. In an article published in *Etudes d'orientalisme dediées à la mémoire de Lévi-Provençal*, vol. II, pp. 559-579, Goitein writes: "I am thinking . . . of those passages in letters from Kairouan deploring the general decline of the Moslem west in the thirties and forties of the eleventh century, long before the invasion of the 'Hedjazi' bedouins, though at the beginning of the eleventh century we can read striking testimonials to the flourishing state of the people of Kairouan" (p. 569).

7. Western Forces for Unity: The Almoravid Venture

While the eastern Maghrib was undergoing a process of fragmentation, the west, which had hitherto been a country of city-states, experienced a unification on the imperial model. We possess little precise information on socio-economic developments in the region, in particular on the influence of regular, long-range trade and the diffusion of currency. What seems likely is that as the defensive needs that had given rise to the Berber social units we have termed clans lost their urgency, the clans in some degree lost their cohesion under the combined influence of religion, trade, and the use of money. It was precisely because the social structure had become relatively homogeneous while communications between groups and regions remained meager, that the era of city-states gave way to the era of empires. In the eleventh century the Maghrib was an empty stage: the Umayyad and Zīrid states had disintegrated into weak principalities; the Byzantine and Moslem orient was in a state of decline, and Western Europe was only beginning to recover. These internal and external conditions gave the western Maghrib its chance: it was able to play an active role for two centuries and a half, precisely the time needed by Western Europe to make good its lag. The first expression of this positive action was the rise of the Almoravids.

For the study of the Almoravid dynasty, the first Moroccan dynasty to achieve importance for Europe as well as North Africa, we possess numerous written sources, but almost all of them concentrate on the role played by the dynasty in the struggle against the Castilians and concern themselves far more with Andalusia than with the Maghrib. Consequently, for lack of documentation we have little knowledge of the rise and fall of the dynasty, the underlying causes of which are to be sought in the Maghrib. Some day our knowledge of the Almoravids may be revolutionized by archeological finds in Mauretania and southern Morocco. For the present this period in the history of the Maghrib is no better known to us than those preceding it, despite the apparent abundance of sources and the number of studies that have been devoted to it.

Background

The Almoravids[1] made their appearance in the western Sahara. We have seen that the Arab conquest, in traversing the fringe of the Sahara, had reopened the desert to the activity of the Maghribis. The economic importance of the region became evident soon after the founding of the city of Sijilmāsa (757/140). That part of the Sahara was inhabited by camel-riding nomads known as Ṣanhāja,[2] who entered into contact with the blacks and gradually pushed them southward. Gaining control of the salt mines, they traded this essential product for gold dust. Of course we do not know when and under what circumstances this trade was initiated, but we do know that on this foundation the Ṣanhāja formed a confederation, which imposed its suzerainty on the black kingdom of Ghana and built a capital at Awdaghost. As often happens in such cases, the confederation alternated between consolidation and collapse because of intense competition for power among the member tribes. In its struggle with the blacks, the confederation met with both victories and defeats. This seems to have been the situation in the ninth and tenth centuries. Still, a number of questions remain open, for the texts do not

1 The word is the transcription of the Arabic *al-murābiṭūn*, inhabitants of a ribat, a kind of monastery. These "soldier-monks" seem to have been a response to the Shī'ite "*du'āt.*"

2 Those who believe, with Gautier, that the words Ṣanhāja and zanāta have an objective meaning presuppose a Zanāti invasion from Tripoli, in the course of which the Ṣanhāja split into two branches, the one taking refuge in the mountains of Kabylia and becoming sedentary, the other in the Sahara where they became nomads.

always agree: it is not certain that there was only one confederation or only a single trade route; there may have been two of each, and competition between the two confederations and the two trade routes may account for the defeats at the hands of the Ghana blacks. Nor is it absolutely certain that regular relations were maintained with the north.

It seems possible that this trade was not carried on directly (since the last stage was in the hands of the Zanāta) and that the wars of the tenth century in the middle Maghrib had enabled the Ṣanhāja of the south to take advantage of the migration of the Zanāta to Morocco and penetrate the markets of the north. It also seems possible that the ruin of Sijilmāsa and Ṭāhart, brought about by the continual wars in the central Maghrib, restored the importance of a western route crossing the Mauritanian Adrar, long controlled by the Lamtūna and Guddāla, who were thus brought into contact with the cities of central Morocco (Tāmdult, Nfīs, Tadla, and Salé, which were all Idrīsid or Ifranid principalities). These of course are mere suppositions based on details in the chronicles. Still, they seem to throw light on events that would otherwise be hard to explain.[3]

Perhaps it is this long absence, this lack of contact with the north that accounts for the renewal of the movement of Islamization. The crude, purely political Islam of the first conquest may have become still more rudimentary through contact with the blacks. But then in the tenth century the Ṣanhāja found in southern Morocco a more advanced form of Islam, which had developed thanks to the action of the Idrīsids and the trade with Andalusia. Hence the need for a second conversion, symbolized by the pilgrimage of Yaḥiā b. Ibrāhīm, chief of the western confederation. In the eleventh century an intense reaction against Shī'ism gave rise

[3] This economic aspect is brought out in Oliver and Fage, *A Short History of Africa*, pp. 81-83. For details see de Moraes Farias, "The Almoravids," pp. 794-878.

to a religious movement that was to formulate the tenets of the Sunnite orthodoxy to come. Three schools participated in three different spheres: Ḥanbalism, which concentrated on dogma and gained a large following among the urban lower classes; Shāfi'ism, specializing in juridical methodology and appealing chiefly to the aristocracy of the great commercial centers; and Mālikism, which concentrated on juridico-social organization and found its main following in the less developed communities. The new movement developed a counterpropaganda that was carried on, not by *dā'i* (professional agitators) like the Shī'ite propaganda, but by *'ābid* (ascetics), who taught by setting an example. Convinced that the Persians were hopelessly committed to Shī'ism, they concentrated on others, the Turks for example, for this was the period of the great conquests of Mahmūd the Ghaznavid. The Almoravids could well be regarded as the western counterpart to the Seljuks of the east;[4] both attempted to outflank the Fāṭimids, just as the Fāṭimids had outflanked the 'Abbāsid empire by their conquest of Persia and Ifrīqiya. While in the east Neo-Ash'arism prepared the way for the Seljuks, in the west this role fell to Mālikism as it developed in Kairouan. It seems possible that the Mālikite *fuqahā'* provided Yaḥiā b. Ibrāhīm with a spiritual guide, in which case the line from Abū 'Imrān al-Fāsī through Wājjāj to 'Abd Allah b. Yāsīn would be a line of Mālikite-'Abbāsid propagandists.[5]

Yaḥīa b. Ibrāhīm returned to his country accompanied by 'Abd Allah, his preacher; when the first sermons met with failure the two of them withdrew to an island and built a ribat; in time a small group of men gathered around 'Abd Allah and the new chief Yaḥīa b. 'Umar; they were to become the nucleus of the future state. All this was a replica

[4] This notion played an essential role in the political theory of al-Bāqillānī (d. 1013/404), who was the teacher of Abū 'Imrān al-Fāsī (d. 1038/430).

[5] The questions that Abū 'Imrān put to Yaḥiā, as recorded in the chronicles, suggest ulterior motives. See al-Nāṣīrī, *al-Istiqṣā*, vol. II, pp. 5-6.

of the genesis of the state in Medina; intentionally so, for therein lies the meaning of the *sunna*, i.e. conscious submission to a guiding image. There is no reason to doubt these facts, but their truth lies precisely in an identification with an image of the past.[6] The Almoravids took this identification with a man from the Shī'ites, the better to combat them, while rigorous ascetism (*takfīr bī-al-kabā'ir*) was taken from the Khārijites. Thus the Almoravid movement may be regarded as a phase in the communitarian (Sunnite) counteroffensive which after endless reverses finally triumphed under the Seljuks.

Establishment of the Dynasty

Three stages can be distinguished in the development of the Almoravid empire. First a base of operations was set up in the western Sahara; the Lamtūna confederation was reconstituted. Here we find a reminiscence of the submission of the Quraysh in the story of the Prophet, since the Lamtūna later became the nucleus of the Almoravid state. Then the confederation attacked the populations that controlled the southern and northern markets of the Saharan trade. Wājjāj, who lived in Sijilmāsa, addressed an appeal to the new chiefs, one which would later serve as a precedent. It encouraged the Almoravids' expansionist designs and at the same time justified the conquest of a principality which, though apparently Mālikite, seemed unreliable from the standpoint of the new ideology. After taking Sijilmāsa from the last of the Maghrāwa amirs in 1053/445, the Almoravids returned to the south and recaptured Awdaghost, which had fallen into the hands of the Ghana blacks in 1040/432. By

[6] Terrasse, who calls it the golden legend (*Histoire du Maroc*, vol. I, p. 216), fails to understand the profound meaning of this identification. It must be interpreted in relation to the Mahdism of the Shī'ites. The anti-Shī'ites declared that their Mahdī was the Prophet, whose life must be relived at every moment (*sunna*); it was held self-evident that every political movement must relive the beginnings of the history of Islam.

these two conquests the Almoravids reasserted their control over the Saharan trade.

The next step was the conquest of Morocco. Sijilmāsa, which had revolted in the meantime, was retaken in 1056/448. Next the army in command of Abū Bakr b. 'Umar, seconded by his nephew Yūsuf b. Tāshfīn, captured Taroudant, Māsa, and Tadla. In Aghmāt, Abū Bakr acquired, along with the city, the ruling Maghrāwa prince's wife, the famous Zaynab, whom he married; thanks to her knowledge of Morocco she was to play an important political role. In 1068/450 operations were begun against the Barghwāṭa; unlike other populations already softened by Mālikite propaganda, they offered stubborn resistance. 'Abd Allah b. Yāsīn, the ideologist of the movement, was killed and replaced by Sulaymān b. Ḥaddū, who, when killed in turn, was not replaced. In the face of this opposition the Almoravid army returned northward by the route skirting the foothills of the Atlas and leading to Sefrou and Fez. It should be noted that the direction of operations was determined by the trade routes as described by al-Bakrī. Once southern Morocco was conquered, a pause ensued, enabling Buluggīn the Ḥammādid to send an expedition against the Maghrāwa amirs in northern Morocco. Abū Bakr went back to the Sahara, leaving Yūsuf in the company of Zaynab. This step is hard to interpret. Did it signify a sharing of the territory? Did Abū Bakr go south to secure his rear? Did Yūsuf marry Zaynab right away? We do not know. In any event the new chief organized the conquered territory. In 1062/454 he founded Marrakech and fortified it; the new city, at the intersection of the trade routes, was to replace Sijilmāsa as the great gold market. Hitherto, coins had been minted in any number of southern principalities; now this activity was concentrated in Marrakech. He also reorganized the army, adding a corps of archers, and under his leadership, which was both political and religious, the third stage, the conquest of northern and eastern Morocco, was begun. A first attack on Fez was repulsed (1063/455). Little by little, he invested it by capturing the cities of the north, leaving the *fuqahā'* time to work on the minds of the inhabitants. The city surrendered in 1069/462. Then, between 1070/463 and 1080/473, the Almoravid army conquered the central Maghrib, beginning with Taza, Guercif, Oujda, Tlemcen and Oran, and stopping only at Algiers (Jazā'ir b. Mazghanna). Invoking the authority of Ibn Khaldūn, Terrasse claims that he stopped at Algiers because he was conscious of a racial solidarity with the Ṣanhāja in the east, that is, the Ḥammādids and the Zīrids,[7] which would mean that the Almoravid conquest would have been essentially a campaign against the Zanāta. But it would be difficult to prove that the territories to the west of Algiers were not under Ḥammādid suzerainty, since some years earlier Buluggīn had penetrated as far as Fez. The most plausible explanation, as the chroniclers themselves suggest, is that Yūsuf had received an appeal from the Andalusian amirs for help. Every new power in Morocco was faced with the same dilemma, a choice between the east and the north; the Almoravids chose the north.

The Almoravid State

At the end of the eleventh century (end of the fifth century H.), the western Maghrib from the Sahara to the Mediterranean was for the first time subject to a single political authority. This authority was twofold: military and religious. The army, which was the foundation of the state, was made up of contingents of diverse origin and varying ability and prestige. The nucleus was formed of members of the Saharan confederation (Lamtūna, Guddāla, Lamṭa); these were supported by auxiliaries drawn from the populations of southern Morocco (Jazūla and Maṣmūda) and from what remained of the armies of the defeated Zanāta princes; later they were reinforced by Turkish mercenaries (Ghuzz) and even Christians. Thus Ibn Khaldūn's enumeration (one

[7] *Ibid.*, p. 226.

hundred thousand horsemen belonging to the Ṣanhāja, Jazūla, Maṣmūda and Zanāta tribes, the Ghuzz and the archers) reproduces the order in which these groups were incorporated into the Almoravid army and perhaps also the actual organization of the army. The leaders on the battlefield were the traditional chiefs of the contingents, but sometimes a general of outstanding bravery was appointed without regard for his membership in any particular group. If we could determine precisely the initial structure of this army, it would no doubt help to explain a number of obscure points in the history of the Almoravids both in the Maghrib and in Spain. The colonial historians imagine they have defined this structure by calling it a tribal army, but armies organized on a tribal basis can differ radically from one another, and moreover, to judge by the texts, the term does not seem really appropriate in the present case. In any event, the Almoravids improved their armament and tactics in the course of their northward progress. When a city was taken, Yūsuf appointed a governor and left him a garrison that remained totally isolated from the population.

The religious authority was represented by the *fuqahā'* (doctors of Mālikite law); they received salaries, served in the amir's council, and accompanied him on his trips to the provinces. Those *fuqahā'* who lived in the provinces were empowered to review the sentences handed down by the local judges. In other words, the *fuqahā'* guided the amir in his general policies and saw that the Mālikite law was put into practice. We know nothing of how these *fuqahā'* were chosen and can only assume that they were selected from among those who had helped the Almoravids to take power in the various cities. What was the policy of the Mālikite doctors? We must distinguish three elements: their preaching of moral reform and ascetism, which was both the justification of their movement and their instrument of propaganda; their dogmatic teaching, which opposed overexclusive ideologies and aimed at a communitarian consensus; and lastly, the juridico-political aspect of their work, their contribution to the organization of public life. These three aspects were not of equal influence. In the field of dogma, the *fuqahā'* dealt the Shī'ite, Khārijite and Barghwāṭa schisms a mortal blow.[8] In the area of state organization, they brought about a return to the policy of the Prophet's state in Medina (which was by definition one of orthodoxy). All fiscal innovations were declared illegal and abolished. Apart from legal alms (the *zakāt*), to be spent for specified purposes, the state's sole sources of income were the head tax (*jizya*), the territorial tax (*kharāj*) on nonconverts, and a fifth part of the spoils of war. It seems that in Yūsuf's time the Almoravid state actually contented itself with these revenues. This tax reform, which was the first measure undertaken by the new masters in every city they occupied, was excellent propaganda, for freedom from taxation encouraged trade, so contributing to the prosperity of the cities. But such a reform was viable only in an expanding state, that is, in an empire still in the process of building. To repeat the history of the Prophet was also in the long run to repeat the difficulties and convulsions of the Arab empire, and it seems (for the chroniclers, most of whom were favorable to the Almoravids say nothing of this) that 'Alī b. Yūsuf, the second amir, was obliged to reintroduce taxes on commercial transactions (*qabālāt*).

The Andalusian Policy

In reality this policy was part of the religious policy, for there is every reason to believe that Yūsuf's original program did not provide for the conquest of Andalusia. Andalusia was going through a grave social and political crisis. The social crisis was due to increasingly heavy taxation; the inhabitants of the rural districts, more than half of whom

[8] They were far from extinct in Morocco. Rāfiḍism flourished in Taroudant and Barghwāṭism in the Ghomāra. See the case of the chamberlain, Saggūt al-Barghwāṭī, in al-Nāsirī, p. 28.

had probably remained Christian in the north, could only desire a weakening of the Moslem power, and the Arab or Arabized urban population found influential spokesmen in the *fuqahā'* and the *nussāk* (ascetics). This fiscal policy was a consequence of military weakness; the small size of the Arab principalities reduced them to a state of dependency on the neighboring Christian kingdoms, which for their part were strengthened by the revival of Western Europe, the crusading spirit, and the rise of a warlike feudalism; the Arab princes began to employ Christian mercenaries, a phenomenon that may be regarded as a disguised reconquest. Taking advantage of the social discontent and of the weakness and dispersion of the Moslem forces, the Christian kings launched a series of destructive expeditions (corresponding to those of al-Manṣur the Amirid in the tenth century), which can be explained only by the collapse of political power in the rural zones that had remained partly Christian. The Andalusian princes were reduced to paying tribute to the Christian kings, as previously the Christian kings had paid tribute to the caliph in Cordova. The consequence was a vicious circle: military weakness resulted in crushing taxation, which further weakened the political power. In 1082/475 a Christian army under Alfonso VI of Castile advanced as far as Tarifa, and in 1085 Toledo fell without a fight, its will to resist undermined by the conflict between its inhabitants and their prince, whom they judged to be incompetent and tyrannical. At this stage a Mālikite pro-Almoravid party sprang up, an expression of social discontent and the fear of Christian aggression. Under the increasing pressure of this movement, three princes (of Seville, Granada and Badajoz) went to Africa and appealed to Yūsuf, who felt obligated by his own ideology to help them rather than wage war on other Moslem princes: his own legitimacy was at stake. He undertook four expeditions to Andalusia. The first two restored the military situation in the peninsula for a time. In 1086/479 the Almoravids won a great victory at Zallāqa, but two years later a victory, almost won, slipped through their fingers because of differences with the Andalusian princes (instead of storming the fortress of Aledo, they allowed the enemy to evacuate it quietly, so saving the Castilian forces). From 1090/483 on, the amir combated the Moslem princes of Spain far more than the Christians. Opposition to the princes had grown so great that the public at large welcomed the Almoravid authority. A council of jurists handed down a decision, ratified by the scholars in the east and west (notably Ghazzālī), which justified the deposition of all the princes of Andalusia, except for the prince of Saragossa, who could easily have received help from the Castilians. From then on the Almoravid empire had two distinct parts, the one European, the other North African, and two capitals, Marrakech and Seville. In view of his brilliant achievement, Yūsuf could now lay claim to an imperial title. That of Amir al-Mu'minīn had been discredited by the Khārijites and Shī'ites; he could not take the title of caliph nor content himself with that of sultan. The jurists found a compromise solution by inventing the title of Amīr al-Muslimīn. This innovation shows the influence of the new constitutional theories (those of Baghdādī and Māwardī) tending to reinforce the communitarian position.[9]

The Almoravid Empire

The empire was made up of three distinct parts. First, there was the western Sahara, which seems to have recovered its autonomy after 1062/454. Under the leadership of Abū Bakr, who died in 1086/479, the Lamtūna confederation went on fighting the blacks of Ghana. This was a fatal mistake, the effects of which were soon to be felt. Then there was the western Maghrib, with its three historico-geographical subdivisions: south, north, and east, the last two of

[9] The letters of advice received by Yūsuf from Ghazzālī and Turṭūshī also indicate the concordance of the pro-Almoravid and pro-Seljuk movements.

which had been exhausted by the wars of the tenth century. The third area was Moslem Spain, the whole of which fell under Almoravid domination after the conquest of Valencia (1102/495) and Saragossa (1110/504), but continued to be torn by social and political conflicts.

This in every way heterogeneous empire had a theoretical capital, Marrakech, where the emir lived surrounded by his *fuqahā'*. He delegated his powers to viceroys: Sīr b. Abī Bakr in Seville and his son Tamīm in Granada. The Lamtūna governors were placed in charge of the local courts with their chamberlains, administrative secretaries and court poets. Feeling discriminated against, more and more of the Andalusians employed in the administrations left Spain for the Maghrib. This movement, to be sure, had begun in the tenth century; there had already been Andalusians at the Zīrid and Ḥammādid courts; but in the atmosphere of the Almoravid empire this amalgam of Andalusians and Maghribis did not yield satisfactory results; the requisite cohesion was lacking.

In view of the ideology that had given rise to the new dynasty, the latter had to have a policy that was effective both defensively and offensively; and it was condemned to being at all times just and strong, if it was not to incur the criticism of its own propagandists. Thus, since Andalusia was still in danger, war against the Christians became the main focus of Almoravid policy; it was essential both to hold the Maghrib and to defend Andalusia. A number of fortresses were built or rebuilt at strategic points. But it was difficult to raise armies; neither Andalusians nor Maghribis were available for recruitment, and it soon became necessary to reemploy the Christian mercenaries formerly in the service of the Andalusian princes. But since they could not be used in Spain to fight other Christians, they were garrisoned in the fortresses of the Maghrib. The military effort soon created a shortage of funds, for unlike wars of conquest the defensive war in Spain produced no spoils. It was found necessary to revert to non-Koranic taxes, which the population found all the more intolerable since they had just been abolished. The Almoravid system, as finally imposed by political necessities, could hope to survive only if the situation in Spain were radically improved; but the Christian kingdoms were supported by the whole of an awakening Europe, and the war went on with varying fortunes. Though the kingdom of Portugal in the west and León in the northwest were for the moment in no position to take action, Aragon persisted in its aggressive policy and took Saragossa in 1117. But even more than this external danger, the great problem confronting the Almoravids was to provide the populations of the empire with an ideology capable of uniting them. Having become a state institution, Mālikism was no longer able to express the grievances of the common people in the cities.

As we have seen, Mālikism was at once a juridico-social system, sufficient to the needs of a rudimentary society, and a theology aimed at establishing an orthodoxy, that is, a system of ideas free from all exclusivism. In the orient this last aspect had reached full maturity through fusion with the Ash'arite *kalām*, but in the Moslem west the traditional Mālikism of Kairouan had preserved its originality as a strict juridical system. Thus there was no true enrichment of Mālikism under the Almoravids, although dogmatic studies had previously flourished in Andalusia, witness the rich and original work of Ibn Ḥazm (d. 1064). From these the Almoravid amirs drew no benefit, and the dynasty was unable to unite the 'ulama around it as the Seljuks had done in the east. The pro-Almoravid party was always a minority and conducted itself as such, making war on the others, especially the Shāfi'ites, which accounts for the excommunication of the work of Ghazzālī in 1109/503; thus the policy of communitarian tolerance, which was to be the foundation of Sunnite orthodoxy, was repudiated. Nor was the social problem solved. The old ruling families of Andalusia were able to renew their intrigues, and the Almoravids began to conduct themselves more and more as mercenaries, that is, as soldiers contemptuous and jealous of those they were defending. The consequence was a segregation, symbolized by the edict forbidding Andalusians to wear the veil (*litham*) that was the emblem of the military nobility.

In this seemingly so imposing empire, neither the military problem nor the problem of state organization was solved; nor was a unifying ideology established. It is evident, however, that these were Andalusian problems and that if the Almoravids had confined themselves to the Maghrib they might not have had to face such staggering difficulties.

The Weakening of the Dynasty

The Almohad movement, which was to put an end to the Almoravid dynasty, made its appearance in 1124/518, during the reign of ʿAlī b. Yūsuf. In 1144/539, after the first great Almohad victories, Andalusia revolted, either under the influence of the dispossessed former princes, such as the Banū Hūd, encouraged and supported by the Christians, or, in the southwestern part of the peninsula, under the leadership of ascetics. After its failure to nip this revolt at the very heart of the empire in the bud, the dynasty never recovered. But why did the empire begin to collapse in Morocco rather than in Andalusia as one might have expected? The classical explanation was that the warriors of the Sahara had grown soft in the gardens of Cordova.[10] But this explanation must be interpreted, for it merely states the visible effect of divergent underlying causes. The Saharan trade does not seem to have declined or changed its routes. When he assumed the title of Amīr al-Muslimīn, Yūsuf continued to mint his gold pieces, which remained for a long time the principal currency of the western Mediterranean basin, and it is interesting to note that the Almohad conquest was also to be guided by the desire to control the trade route

10 Taken up by Georges Marçais, *La Berbérie musulmane*, pp. 237-251 and Julien, *L'Histoire de l'Afrique du Nord*, 2nd ed., vol. 2, pp. 76-92.

between the Atlas and the Mediterranean. In the classical explanation, the term "Saharan" relates to the structural differences within the empire, the "softening" to the necessity of a defensive war against the Castilians, and Andalusian luxury to the permanent social problem, which necessitated low taxes, hence a modest standard of living for the prince and his court. Essentially, this explanation raises three questions. First, that of manpower. Was it a mistake to have cut off all ties with the western Sahara, or did this region give the dynasty all the men it had to offer? This demographic problem is important, for in some cases, though we tend to forget it, the demographic aspect is more fundamental than the state of the economy. And to judge by the ease with which this region was repopulated by the Ma'qil Arabs a century later, it must have been bled white by the Almoravids. This brings us to the second problem. Having conducted themselves as mercenaries in Andalusia, the Almoravids were faced with a choice. They could either continue to play this role, or, if they wished to control the destinies of Andalusia, hire other mercenaries, which would necessitate a new system of taxation. They could not be at the same time both princes and mercenaries. True, they might have enlisted Maghribis and Andalusians in a common defensive effort, and here the third question arises, that of a unifying communitarian ideology. Gradually this ideological problem became paramount, and that is why at the outset the Almohad revolt was to be essentially ideological (the conditions of its success were of another nature). Far from being the expression of a "national Maṣmudian" will,[11]

[11] Terrasse, *Histoire du Maroc*, pp. 239-291. It is strange to note that this author, who refuses to recognize the national character of the struggle against the Portuguese in the sixteenth or even of the Moroccans' revolt against the French in the twentieth century, calls the twelfth century "Maṣmūda" a national movement because the Almoravids were nomads from the Sahara, but fails to explain why these same Maṣmūda did not revolt against the Zanāta who came from the east. Such inconsistency can be explained only by political prejudice.

it was an attempt to give the Moslem west the unifying ideology it lacked. The fundamental weakness of the Almoravids was their failure to understand that their rudimentary Mālikism was far from meeting the requirements of Andalusia and perhaps even of Morocco. It may be argued that they were prevented from doing so by the war, but they thereby condemned themselves to carrying on the war alone, and finally to losing it. Of course this argument is valid only if we avoid the error of the traditionalist chroniclers, who regarded Almoravid Mālikism as a final expression of Sunnite orthodoxy; it was only a rudimentary sketch, as we can see by reading the work of the qadi 'Iyāḍ from a historical point of view. This the modern Arab historians have not done, and that is what clouds their judgment of the Almoravids, to whom they are at the same time favorable because of their Mālikite policy and defense of Andalusia, and unfavorable because of their anti-Ṣūfist tendency; they forget that, although Mālikism and Ṣūfism were to converge later on, they were at one time very different.[12]

The ideological problem had become essential because it was the concentrated expression of all other problems: the endless war in Spain; the reduction of state expenditure (demanded by the inhabitants of the cities); the need to consolidate a political community rising on the foundations of the city-states and towns, since without the day-by-day support of a highly developed ideology, this community was in danger of being undermined by local forces. This problem had been already present in germ in Zīrid Ifrīqiya, but under the Almoravids it was exacerbated by the larger area involved and above all by constant warfare. It was to be the central problem of the Maghrib for many years to come.

Comparison with the Seljuk Turks, also newcomers to the Mediterranean scene, may help us to round out our picture of the Almoravids. The victory of Manzikert (1071) may be

[12] Hence the explanation that the fall of the Almoravids was caused by the anathema allegedly leveled against them by Ghazzālī.

taken as a parallel to Zallāqa (1086). The destinies of the two empires were very different, however, not only because the Almoravids were in the west, where the Christian nations were on the rise and not in the east, where the Byzantine empire was in the midst of its long death agony, but also because the Seljuks had behind them Turkish populations able to provide them with all the soldiers they needed and because the great orthodox movement rallied public opinion to the new champions of Islam. We may, if we choose, speculate with the chroniclers: the Almoravid movement might have produced more decisive and durable results if it had maintained ties with the south, or if a neo-Mālikism had created ideological unity, or if the Almoravids had contented themselves with unifying the Maghrib. Such judgments enable us not so much to clarify the Almoravid past by rewriting it as to understand the next phase of our history: the Almohad reaction.

8. Western Forces for Unity: The Almohad Venture

For a long time historians of the Almohads drew on texts originating many years after the events, many of them the work of authors hostile to the Almohads. Now scholars have begun to publish accounts by contemporaries, many of whom believed in the movement and its aims. These texts, most of which were used in manuscript by Lévi-Provençal, have become available, though in an incomplete and not always satisfactory form.[1] Now that we are beginning to see Almohadism from the inside, it is no longer impossible to write a religious and political history of the dynasty. Still, the available documentation presents two negative aspects. First, it stresses the wars and affairs of Spain to the neglect of Morocco, where the movement had its base. Second, it throws little light on the economic situation; the development of agriculture and trade, in particular the Saharan trade, and the monetary situation can at best be conjectured. Consequently our judgment on the organization and disintegration of the Almohad empire are subject to caution.[2]

Ibn Tūmart and the Almohad Ideology

The genesis of the ideology that Ibn Tūmart proposed to the Moslem west becomes understandable only if we recall that in his day esoteric (*bāṭin*) Shī'ism was still influential despite the political weakening of the Fāṭimids of Egypt, and that the forces for communitarian unification were still rela-

1 Chief among these accounts are: Ibn al-Qaṭṭān, *Juz' min kitāb Naẓm al-Jumān*; Ibn 'Idhārī, *al-Bayān al-Mughrib*; and Ibn Ṣāḥib al-Ṣalāh, *Tārīkh al-Mann bi-al-Imāma*.

2 In this connection, Terrasse, *Histoire du Maroc*, vol. 1, pp. 314-316, gives vent to all sorts of racial prejudices, and his judgments are taken over in Julien, *Histoire de l'Afrique du Nord*, 2nd ed., vol. 1, pp. 110, 120.

tively dispersed. The communitarian movement consisted of three currents that were still separate: a striving for ascetic purification, based on the study of the hadith, a systemization of the laws, and a theological movement based on refinement of the principles of al-Ash'arī. At the end of the eleventh century these trends had not yet merged into a unified doctrine; partial and hence personal syntheses were still possible: al-Bāqillānī (d. 1013/403) had combined theology with jurisprudence, Ibn Ḥazm (d. 1064/456) hadith and jurisprudence, and Ghazzālī (d. 1111/505) theology and asceticism, but their propositions were still far from gaining the unanimous support of the faithful. Ibn Tūmart was to elaborate a personal synthesis for the use of his native community. The Almoravid movement had turned away from its original ascetic aims and, succumbing to a sterile legalism, had combated the two other trends, theology and mysticism, which would later become integral parts of the communitarian doctrine; hence the excommunication of the works of Ghazzālī, who precisely offered a synthesis of the two. As to Ibn Tūmart's psychology, his practice, conduct and political rigor, before we attribute them to his Berber character, it will be well to remember the profound and often unconscious influence of esoteric Shī'ism even on those who combated it; Ibn Tūmart's biography provides us with the elements of his synthesis, differentiated not logically but according to the successive stages of his peregrination through the Islamic world. Leaving his native Sous (in the territory of the Hargha on the northern slope of the Anti-Atlas), he went to Cordova where, we are told, he became imbued with the teachings of Ibn Ḥazm, then to Iraq, where he met Ghazzālī and familiarized himself with his doctrine as well. Toward 1116/510 he returned westward by way of Alexandria, Tunis, Bougie, Tlemcen, Fez and Meknès, and settled for a time in Marrakech. (Note his coastal itinerary, contrasting with the inland route hitherto taken by most of the founders of states.) In the course of his long return journey he seems to have developed not so much his religious ideology as its temporal expression, or his "political theory." In any event, his missionary activity followed a rising curve: starting out as a critic of morals (a right that could hardly be contested in an Islamic country), he soon imposed his authority as a theologian (controversies with the jurists of Marrakech), then as the leader of a school in Aghmāt, and finally as the head of a political party and a candidate for power in the mountain town of Tinmall. To each of these stages corresponds an element of his future doctrine. Moral censure, which is not only an exhortation to the individual but also a criticism of the public authority, has always embarrassed Moslem jurists; accordingly as the critic limits his censure by submitting to authority or refuses to do so, he identifies himself as a conservative or as a revolutionary. The *fuqahā'* have always insisted on the need to preserve the social peace by recognizing the right of the supreme authority to regulate the exercise of criticism (and this is what gave rise to the function of *muḥtasib*); but new movements have always by necessity refused to recognize any limitation whatsoever on the right to criticism, thus carrying on the tradition of Khārijite opposition to the state. In the past, the two adversaries, Mu'tazilism and Ḥanbalism had resorted at different times to the same theoretical justification in comparable situations. Ibn Tūmart's thinking derived no doubt from the Mu'tazilite tradition, though his theology, the second component of his synthesis, was Ash'arite in essence, based on the rational elaboration by syllogistic reasoning of a definition of God and his attributes and the allegorical interpretation of the Koran. Perhaps we should situate him halfway between Ash'arism and Mu'tazilism, which would account for his choice of the term *muwaḥḥid* (unitarian), for the Mu'tazilites themselves called themselves *ahl al-'adl wa al-tawḥīd*. Furthermore, as head of a school, Ibn Tūmart was bound to uphold his right to personal interpretation and accept as basic texts only the Koran and under certain circumstances the hadith, to the exclusion of all commentaries or glosses. In this he benefited from the ẓāharism of Ibn Ḥazm, for contrary to what one might think, Ibn Ḥazm's literalism was the consequence and condition of a rationalist choice. In this point Ibn Tūmart is often contrasted with Ghazzālī, and yet the difference between the two resides in their personal circumstances. Ghazzālī was an ideologist of the Seljuk state; he had no thought of working for his own advancement, but he had developed a system of propaganda and indoctrination, a progressive pedagogy, a method relativizing the truth according to the intellectual capacity of his audience. Ibn Tūmart was to use the same method, but for his own benefit, and since he worked in a hierarchical and none too cultivated milieu, which the Shī'ite propaganda of the eighth to tenth centuries had familiarized with the idea of the Mahdi, he had no scruples about incorporating it into his system. Since the Mahdi was supposed to be descended from a Fāṭimid line, Ibn Tūmart made himself, or someone made him, an 'Alīd genealogy connecting him with the Idrīsid dynasty of southern Morocco.[3] A last element, finally, which we have already encountered in the case of Ibn Yāsīn, was the conscious and meticulous reproduction of the Prophet's Sīra. Ibn Tūmart's synthesis, we observe, was one possibility among many; the only element that was not accepted later on was his Mahdism, but as the founder of an empire he probably needed it. Had he contented himself with being the mere leader of a school, he would no doubt have dispensed with Mahdism. But it is not enough to study the Almohad ideology in itself, to admire its intellectualism that avoids any concession to mystical sentimentality. We must also place it in the general movement of Islamic theology, for then we perceive that what gave it its strength in the Maghrib, namely, its fidelity to certain older tendencies already expressed in Khārajism

[3] In this context the question of sincerity means little, since from the Mahdi's point of view the only objective proof of his authenticity was political success. See the letter of Abū 'Abd ar-Raḥmān b. Ṭāhir to 'Abd al-Mu'min, in Ibn al-Qaṭṭān, p. 50.

and Barghwāṭism, was to condemn it in the long run. Compared with the "Sunnite" universalism that was to win out in the end, it had a distinctly exclusive and provincial character and was to prove even less capable than Almoravid Mālikism of becoming a communitarian rallying point. On the other hand, it proved singularly effective in cementing the Almohad movement.

Between 1121 and 1124/515-518, Ibn Tūmart completed the formulation of his doctrine; he began by settling in his native territory and giving himself the title of imam, to make it clear that he was a candidate for power. His following increased rapidly. In 1124/518 he set up headquarters in the virtually impregnable mountain town of Tinmall and organized a militant party. Its structure was rather complex, but it consisted essentially of two groups: one representing the élite of the movement, specially trained for propaganda and ideological struggle, and a larger body whose chief aim was to work within the various clans and prepare them to cooperate in taking power. The hierarchy was as follows: the members of the Household (*ahl al-Dār*), i.e. the Mahdi's intimate circle; the Ten (*ahl al-'Ashra*), the first disciples who had accompanied him on his return journey:[4] chief among these were 'Abd al-Mu'min b. 'Alī (the future caliph), whom Ibn Tūmart had met at the gates of Bougie on his way to the east; 'Abd Allah al-Wansharīsī, known as al-Bashīr, also a native of the central Maghrib, who, up to the time of his early death in 1128/523, played an important part in the political growth of the movement; and Abū Ḥafṣ 'Umar al-Hintātī (we do not know whether this was his real name) who as a local chief exerted an enormous influence. These Ten were the real leaders of the movement in the first period of Almohad history. Next came the council of local chiefs, the Fifty (*ahl al-Khamsīn*), who deliberated on the most important political and military problems, and an assembly open to persons of lesser importance, the Sev-

[4] See *ibid.*, p. 77.

enty (*ahl as-Sāqa*). It is hard to determine to what degree this organization was an innovation on the part of Ibn Tūmart and to what degree it was derived from local tradition, nor do we know how much of it was purely theoretical and how much was put into actual practice. Since we are without information about the beginnings of Idrīs I among the Awriba or of Abū 'Abd Allah among the Kutāma, we tend perhaps to overestimate the innovating genius of Ibn Tūmart, but in the present state of our knowledge he would seem to have been the most methodical and efficient of all the founders of states in the Maghrib. The movement needed propagandists and soldiers. The Mahdi busied himself personally with the training of the *ṭalaba*, the ideologists of the nascent regime, and of the *ḥuffāẓ*, whose functions were both religious and military. To this end he wrote pamphlets in Arabic and Berber, among which a creed, a doctrinal treatise, and some letters of instruction have been preserved.[5] The political life of the Tinmall period remains obscure, but as described by the chroniclers it seems to have been a conscious replica of the Prophet's Medina period and should be judged as such. Just as Muḥammad's mission was called into doubt, so was the Mahdi's infallibility (*'Iṣma*); in both biographies we meet with a group of hard-headed skeptics (*munāfiqūn*); a purge (*tamyīz*) was judged to be necessary in Tinmall, and it was carried out by al-Bashīr, Ibn Tūmart's faithful companion. Thus purified, the community embarked on the conquest of power. The first expediton was nevertheless a failure, for it was directed against Marrakech, the capital. The Almoravid army, still powerful, inflicted a severe defeat on the Almohads in 1128/522. Al-Bashīr was killed and 'Abd al-Mu'min was seriously wounded. Ibn Tūmart died soon after this defeat (in 1130/524), but he left behind him an organization prepared for every eventuality. Like the Prophet

[5] The *'Aqīda* of Ibn Tūmart, from *Le Livre de Mohammed ibn Toumert*; Lévi-Provençal, *Documents inédits; idem, Un recueil de lettres officielles.*

he appointed no heir, and we can only conjecture that his successor was chosen in the course of negotiations between 'Abd al-Mu'min and Abū Ḥafṣ 'Umar.[6] In 1132/526, after an interregnum of two years, the former was recognized as caliph.

'Abd al-Mu'min and the Founding of the Almohad Empire

The Maghrib was conquered in three stages. The first was the conquest of Morocco. After the defeat of 1128/522 the Almohad army abandoned the plains and advanced over the mountain route leading from Sijilmāsa to Sefrou and Fez. The decisive encounter took place between Taza and Tlemcen; the local populations joined forces with the Almohads and the Almoravid army itself was disunited.[7] The victory of the Almohads was complete (1139/534) and there was no further obstacle to the capture of Tlemcen (1144) and of Fez (1145). Finally Marrakech itself fell in 1146/541. After the first victories many Moroccan and Andalusian cities changed sides and sent letters of submission (*bay'a*), especially after Ismā'īl b. 'Alī, the last Almoravid amir, was killed in the battle of Marrakech. Jerez had rallied to the victors in 1144/539, Cordova in 1148/543 after having been surrounded by the Castilians, and Meknès in the same year. The submission, however, seems to have been more apparent than real, a far cry from the immediate acceptance of the Almoravid conquest, the way for which had been paved by the *fuqahā'*. Now, as soon as a city found a leader, it rebelled against the new authority. In 1147/542 Māsa revolted

6 'Abd al-Mu'min was said to have benefited from the fact that he did not belong to any of the Maṣmūda clans, but this seems to be a rationalization after the fact, since the same explanation had been given for the election of Abū Bakr after the death of the Prophet.

7 Knowledge of the structure of the Almoravid army would help us to understand why the Masūfa contingents broke with the Lamtūna. For details, see Merad, "'Abd al-Mu'min à la conquête de l'Afrique du Nord," pp. 109-160.

under the leadership of Muḥammad b. Hūd and Ceuta under the influence of the famous qadi 'Iyad. Meknès also revolted. It was only in 1151/546 that order seems to have been restored. At that date 'Abd al-Mu'min received in Salé a delegation from Andalusia, imploring him to cross the straits and fight the Castilians. He preferred to look eastward, for in Ifrīqiya there was also a Christian threat: the Normans. In 1151-1152, and this was the second stage in the formation of the empire, he conquered the central Maghrib, putting an end to the Ḥammādid emirate. Residing in Bougie, the last Ḥammādids (al-Manṣūr, al-'Azīz, and Yaḥyā) had arrived at a modus vivendi with the Banū Hilāl, the new masters of the plateaus; they had developed trade, and profiting by the difficulties of their Zīrid cousins, were enjoying a period of renewed prosperity. 'Abd al-Mu'min organized his expedition with care, creating the impression that it was to be directed against Andalusia, and then suddenly heading eastward. Arriving at Bougie by forced marches, he took it without difficulty (Yaḥyā fled to Constantine), while another detachment took Qal'a, the old capital. The real power, however, was still in the hands of the Banū Hilāl. The Almohad army crushed them in the battle of Sétif in 1153/548. Five years later 'Abd al-Mu'min embarked on the expedition that was to complete the conquest of the Maghrib and for the first time unite it under a single authority. Ifrīqiya was then divided among the Normans, the last Zīrids and the last Hilālī princes; none of these had the power to resist a disciplined army and the imposing fleet that set sail from the Moroccan ports at the beginning of 1159/554. Tunis was taken from 'Alī b. Aḥmad b. Khurāsān, Mahdīya was besieged and taken from the Normans, who had occupied it twelve years before; Ḥasan b. 'Alī, the last of the Zīrids, who had lost all power and had himself invited the intervention of the new caliph, was reestablished in Mahdīya, but as a mere governor under the vigilant eye of an Almohad inspector. In 1161/556 'Abd al-Mu'min returned to Marrakech after having occupied Sfax, Sousse,

Gabès and Tripoli, and succeeded where all his predecessors had failed. He now felt that with a united Maghrib behind him he could turn to Andalusia, where the relation of forces was still favorable to the Christian kingdoms. He was deep in preparations for a large-scale Andalusian campaign when he died in Salé in 1163/558.

The conquests of ʻAbd al-Mu'min show that he must have been a skillful general and a consummate organizer, with a remarkable knowledge of the country. Nevertheless, he proved unable to hold both Ifrīqiya and Andalusia, and this failure was to be a constant of Almohad history. During his reign, moreover, the Maghrib proper seems to have shrunk; the south, whence the Almoravids had embarked on their conquests, and the Tell, which had been the scene of the great confrontations of the tenth century, are hardly mentioned in the chronicles; perhaps the new power had lost interest in these regions because they no longer had manpower or riches to offer.

At the death of ʻAbd al-Muʻmin the empire had the form it was to preserve until the end. We do not know at exactly what date he took the title of Amīr al-Mu'minīn; it may have been as early as 1130/528. In any event, this step meant a break with the *fuqahā'*, though the scandal provoked by a Berber assuming a title hitherto reserved for the Qurayshites appears to have been exaggerated later on for the needs of the orthodox cause. This title implied a political program, namely, the reconquest of the whole Islamic world. To have contented himself with a mere province while theoretically claiming to be the commander of all the faithful would have given ʻAbd al-Mu'min the appearance of a "Khārij-ite," that is, a divider of the Moslem community. The political structure established by al-Mahdi was modified; theocratic democracy gave way to hereditary monarchy. We do not know for certain what Ibn Tūmart would have done if he had become master of an empire, but we do know that as the Almohad conquests progressed, the equality of the first companions was discarded in practice. ʻAbd al-Mu'-

min consolidated his personal position in the Almohad army and political organization. At first he based his power on his compatriots from the central Maghrib (the Gūmiya), importing, we are told, some forty thousand of them toward 1161/557; then on the Banū Hilāl whom, after defeating them at Sétif, he incorporated into his regular army.[8] It was these Bedouin chiefs who in 1154/549, at his instigation, proposed the appointment of his eldest son as heir presumptive. The assembly of the Ten accepted but al-Mahdi's two brothers, 'Abd al-'Azīz and 'Isā, revolted; they were defeated and executed. The party organization was not destroyed but gradually lost its importance. What remained was the distinction between the two groups of the ruling class: the members of the caliph's family, who bore the title of sayyid and the Almohads, especially the family of Abū Ḥafṣ, to whom the title of shaykh was given. The Almohads, however, had inherited an administrative structure which little by little was integrated with the organization set up by Ibn Tūmart. This central government was composed of a prime minister (*wazīr*), often chosen from among the shaykhs, one or more secretaries (*kātib*) in charge of official correspondence, usually Andalusians or Maghribis educated in Andalusia, a chamberlain (*ḥājib*), whose functions were relatively obscure, a grand judge (*qādī*) who under certain circumstances performed the function of the *khaṭīb* (who reads the Friday sermon), and finally a *ṣāḥib al-ashghāl* (minister of finance in charge of the armies), who had the greatest responsibilities of all and whose counsels were probably most heeded by the sovereign.

In the provincial centers we find the same organization on a smaller scale. In 1154/549, on his return from his campaign in the central Maghrib, 'Abd al-Mu'min put his sons in charge of the principal provinces and assigned to each of them a shaykh, both to advise and to keep an eye on him.

[8] This point is in need of verification. Ibn Khaldūn may well have exaggerated his account to make it fit in with his general theory of *'Asabiya.*

Later on, the brothers and uncles of the caliphs and sometimes descendants of Abū Ḥafṣ were appointed governors; but the sovereign corresponded directly with the *ṭalaba*; when informed of any suspicious machinations on the part of the governors, he dismissed them and sometimes had their property confiscated. On his return from Ifrīqiya in 1160/555, 'Abd al-Mu'min is reported to have ordered a land survey (*taksīr*) of all North Africa from Barqa in Tripolitania to Nūl in southern Morocco; a third of the territory was written off as mountainous or otherwise unproductive, and the rest subjected to a land tax (*kharāj*) payable in money or in kind. We have no estimate of the amount of taxes raised, but it seems certain that no ruler of the Maghrib since the Romans had possessed such vast resources. The theoretical justification of this tax was no doubt that the inhabitants were not true unitarians and could therefore be assimilated to non-Moslems; but it seems more likely that the Banū Hilāl had already instituted a comparable tax in the eastern Maghrib and that 'Abd al-Mu'min had only to extend it to the rest of the territory and make use of the same Banū Hilāl to collect it. Here we perceive in its beginnings the role the Bedouins were to play in the state as soldiers and tax collectors.[9] Sometimes a tax was levied on buildings. When he took Tunis, 'Abd al-Mu'min let the inhabitants remain in their houses but made them pay rent. Advantage was taken of every possible means of replenishing the treasury. The traditional taxes, such as the quint and the *zakāt* (legal alms) were maintained, but we have no information about the taxes on internal commerce. The Almohad currency was strong (the Yūsufī dinar, named after the second caliph, was well known in the Mediterranean markets).[10] This system of taxation made it possible

[9] Al-Nāṣirī, *al-Istiqṣā*, vol. II, p. 153: "wa kāna li-l Muwahhadīna 'alayhim 'askarat wa jibāya."

[10] We are told that they minted a silver coin, the square dirham, in order to fulfill an old prophecy. "The day when we see a square dirham" seems to have been a proverbial expression comparable to our "when hens get teeth"; but the Almohad propagandists saw the profit the dynasty might derive from such an unlikely achievement.

to finance a large army and navy. The Almohad army was never unified; on the roster (*dīwān*), in parades, and on the battlefield, the contingents were disposed in a strict order, determined no doubt by complex political and technical considerations: the caliph's guard, the Almohads, the Hilālī Arabs, the Zanāta, the mercenaries, and volunteers. As time went on the army deteriorated, largely because infantry was gradually supplanted by cavalry, whose effectiveness depended on the degree of harmony prevailing between the various groups of which it was composed. The Almohads had a powerful fleet, probably the strongest in the western Mediterranean at the time, which they had taken over from the Andalusian princes and the Almoravids. In the Ifrīqiya campaign of 1159 'Abd al-Mu'min made use of seventy ships, and in 1163, in view of his projected Spanish campaign, he assembled four hundred units in the ports of Ma'mūra, Tangiers, Badis, Hunayn and Oran. Commanded by a captain who had once served under Roger II of Sicily, or occasionally by Andalusians such as Ghānim, the son of Ibn Mardanīsh who had long opposed the Almohads in Spain, the fleet won victories at Mahdīya in 1160/555 and at Lisbon in 1177/573, which accounts for the appeal of Ṣalāḥ al-Dīn of Egypt to Ya'qūb, the third caliph, for help.

Thus for the first time the rulers of the Maghrib (unlike the Fāṭimids of Ifrīqiya), were natives, who, also for the first time, organized a state that was not essentially dependent on commerce and the spoils of war. Once the Almohads had completed their conquest, one would have expected them to develop and reinforce their administrative apparatus, but this called for a degree of ideological harmony. Unfortunately, the exclusiveness of the Almohad ideology was a source of dissension. Faced with internal opposition and an external threat, the Almohad state was unable to consolidate itself.

The Almohad era may be divided into two periods; the first, characterized by relative stability, extended from 1163/558 to 1213/610; the second, marked by disintegration and decline, from 1213 to 1269/669.

The Period of Threatened Supremacy

Three caliphs reigned during this period: Yūsuf, Ya'qūb al-Manṣūr, and Muḥammad al-Nāṣir. Significantly, this first unified state in the Maghrib attained its political apogee at a time of economic decline. To realize this, one has only to compare al-Idrīsī's (d. 1177/560) description of the country with that of earlier geographers. One gets an impression of decadence in the north of Morocco. Only the ports of Ceuta, El-Ksar and Tangiers were still active; the central region, that of the Barghwāṭa, had at last been opened up, but it remained underpopulated and apart from the minor ports of Fedala and Anfa there were few towns. The eastern region and the city of Taza were also on the decline. True, the crafts were developing in the interior and in the vicinity of Fez and Marrakech, the old towns of Aghmāt, Nfīs and Nūl were still prospering, the mineral wealth of the Atlas was still being exploited,[11] and the Anti-Atlas was still deriving wealth from its olive and argan trees. It is clear, however, that the area of economic activity in Morocco had shrunk; for the most part it was now concentrated in two regions of the Atlantic littoral, which seem to have been thinly populated. The western Sahara had ceased to attract the curiosity and admiration of the traveler-geographers. It seems possible that the Saharan trade route had again shifted in favor of that from the bend of the Niger via Ouargla to Bougie. Sijilmāsa, in any event, had lost its importance. A similar situation prevailed in the central and eastern Maghrib, where all noteworthy economic activity had become concentrated in the coastal strip extending from Bougie to Tunis, Sousse and Tripoli. The maritime trade had come under the control of the Pisans and Genoese. 'Abd al-Mu'min signed a treaty with the Genoese in 1153/548 and re-

[11] In 1182/578 the caliph Yūsuf built a fort in the Atlas to protect a state-owned (silver?) mine that private persons were trying to take possession of (see al-Nāṣirī, *al-Istiqṣā*, vol. II, p. 137).

newed it in 1161/556; in 1168/563 al-Manṣūr granted the Pisans a twenty-five-year charter, which was renewed by al-Nāṣir in 1211. Little by little the Genoese became the masters of the Maghrib's commerce, just as the Venetians had gained control of the trade of the Moslem orient. These charters, which guaranteed the security of merchants and regulated trade by setting fixed import and export duties, were innovations in the economic life of the Maghrib, introduced during the decline of the Zīrid and Ḥammādid states. In inheriting the two eastern principalities, the Almohad caliphs also inherited these symptoms of disintegrating states. Although the balance of this trade was probably favorable to the Maghrib, the resulting inflow of currency, attested by the minting of counterfeit coins with Arabic inscriptions in Marseilles and Montpellier, marked a turning point in the monetary history of the Mediterranean. Throughout the history of the Maghrib, maritime trade, though often regarded as a mark of prosperity, has gone hand in hand with a weakening of political authority.

The unfavorable economic situation was accompanied by political instability, resulting from continual conflicts in the caliph's family and in the central and provincial administrations. 'Abd al-Mu'min had already been obliged to get rid of Ibn Tūmart's two brothers in 1154/549, and of Islītin, a relative, a year earlier. In 1158/553 he executed the two Ibn 'Aṭiya brothers, who had been viziers under the Almoravids and whom he had taken into his service; one of them, Abū Ja'far, had become a secretary, then a counselor under 'Abd al-Mu'min; he was replaced by 'Abd al-Salām al-Gūmī, who two years later forfeited the caliph's confidence and his life. In 1177/573 Yūsuf removed his viziers who belonged to the B. Jāmi' family, detested by the Almohad shaykhs. In 1188/584 Ya'qūb imprisoned and executed his brother 'Umar, governor of Murcia, and his uncle Suleyman, governor of Tadla. In 1209 al-Nāṣir, on his way to Spain, inspected his governors of Fez and Ceuta and, dissatisfied with their administration, had them executed.[12] Behind these events, which seemed so normal to the chroniclers that they are mentioned only in passing, we can discern a stubborn and violent rivalry between the old Almohad administration and the new government personnel bound by exclusive loyalty to the caliph. Some members of the Mu'minid family became involved in the struggle and lost their lives. The Almohad administration seems to have been at once harsh and unstable.

To make matters worse, the ideology of Ibn Tūmart, which had been the source of the Almohad power, soon became an element of weakness. The chief reason for this was the impossibility of reconciling the oligarchic, consultative structure of the movement with the autocratic monarchy necessary for the maintenance of the empire. 'Abd al-Mu'min had chosen his eldest son Muḥammad to be his successor; but Muḥammad proved incapable and soon had to be deposed. He was not replaced, however, and at the caliph's death his son Yūsuf was subjected to a probationary period of two years before the shaykhs, in particular Abū Ḥafṣ, consented to recognize him. But by the time Ya'qūb acceded to the throne, the shaykhs had lost much of their influence, and this seems to have led the new caliph to break with the Almohad doctrine. After excommunicating certain books of applied law (*furū'*), he reminded the doctors of the law that only the Koran and the hadith could be regarded as basic texts, to the exclusion of all others, meaning no doubt the books of the Mahdi himself. Throughout the history of Islam, dynasties—in the vain hope of establishing a new legitimacy—have disavowed the ideological movements to which they owed their power. In 1229/626 al-Ma'mun accused al-Manṣūr of trying to break with Almohadism, and under al-Nāṣir the violent recriminations of the shaykhs against the vizier Ibn Jāmi' were among the causes of the defeat of 1212. Like the Fāṭimids before them, the Mu'-

12 A significant account of this journey is to be found in Ibn 'Idhārī, vol. 3, p. 237.

minids wished to take their distance from the doctrinal extremism of their own movement, but since the doctors of the law were the mainstay of the dynasty, to weaken them was suicide. On the other hand, the doctrine itself was a source of weakness, as is shown by the revolts in the Maghrib and the difficulties in Andalusia. Seven important revolts occurred in Morocco between 1147/542 and 1213/610, either in the southern, Māsa region or to the north of the Ghomāra mountains. Both these regions, we are told, were inhabited by Ṣanhāja, but more important, Mahdism, a doctrine that was bound to encourage adventurers, had long flourished there. The most serious revolts, however, were those that broke out in Ifrīqiya with the support of the Mālikite doctors. In 1178/574 Gafsa rose up under the instigation of a member of the Bantū Rund, a collateral branch of the Zīrids, which had managed to carve out a principality after the invasion of the Banū Hilāl. The movement soon spread to the entire Jarīd and the caliph Yūsuf was obliged to take charge in person; it took two years to quell the revolt. But peace was not yet restored in Ifrīqiya. The next to revolt was a descendant of the Almoravids of Spain, whose grandfather, known as Ibn Ghāniya,[13] had been governor of the Balearic Islands. In 1184/581, immediately after the accession of Ya'qūb to the imperial throne, 'Alī b. Ghāniya, instead of submitting to the new power as all the other Almoravid leaders and his own elder brother had done, attacked Bougie and soon gained control of the whole central Maghrib. He found allies in Ifrīqiya among the Banū Hilāl, who had not accepted their own defeat, and in the person of Qarāqūsh, a Turcoman mercenary who had conquered Tripoli with the support of Ṣalāḥ al-Ḍīn. In all probability this vast coalition reflected a Mālikite reaction to heterodox Almohadism. When 'Abd al-Raḥmān b. Ḥafṣ,

[13] Ibn Ghāniya = Muḥammad b. 'Alī b. Yaḥiā al-Masūfī, appointed governor of the Baleaircs by 'Alī b. Yūsuf. It was his grandsons, Muḥammad 'Alī and Yaḥiā b. Isḥāq, who were to undertake the Ifrīqiyan adventure.

the caliph's cousin, failed to put down the rebellion, Ya'qūb himself was obliged to head an expedition. 'Alī was driven into the desert, where he died in 1189/585, but his brother Yaḥiā took his place and led the caliph a merry chase for years. When the caliph was in Spain, Yaḥyā reappeared in Ifrīqiya; then at the approach of the Almohad troops, he retrenched himself in the Jarīd and waited for a propitious moment to resume operations. In 1195/591 Ya'qūb was unable to reap the fruits of a successful Spanish campaign and was obliged to sign a five-year truce with the Castilians, because the ravages of Ibn Ghāniya required his presence in Ifrīqiya. Four years later in the caliphate of al-Nāṣir, Yaḥiā succeeded in capturing Mahdīya and Tripoli. In 1203/600 he entered Tunis and all Tunisia renewed its allegiance to the 'Abbāsids. At a time when Andalusia was seriously imperiled by the Castilians, the caliph was obliged to head a large expedition and embark on the reconquest of Ifrīqiya. In 1206/603 he defeated Yaḥyā, who managed, however, to escape. Realizing that the eastern province could not be defended from Marrakech, al-Nāṣir decided to appoint a viceroy and chose 'Abd al-Wāḥid, a son of the shaykh Abū Ḥafṣ, for the post. 'Abd al-Wāḥid accepted it after long hesitation but with stipulations that made him virtually autonomous. The long and tenacious resistance of Yaḥyā b. Ghāniya at the height of the Almohad power can be explained only by the active support of public opinion, influenced by the Mālikite doctors, who preferred Ibn Ghāniya's Bedouins to the Almohads, just as they had preferred Abū Yazīd's Khārijites to the Fāṭimids. The dynasty fared no better in Spain, where the situation was even more precarious than at the end of the eleventh century. Almohad authority was at no time as firmly implanted as that of the Almoravids had been. Because of doctrinal opposition, the Almohads were constantly fighting on two fronts even in Spain. For many years Ibn Mardanīsh had a firm hold on Valencia and Murcia; he entered into an alliance with the Castilians and from his redoubt launched attacks, sometimes victorious (Carmona) and often dangerous (Cordova). 'Abd al-Mu'min was unable to defeat him, and Yūsuf was obliged to sign a truce with the Castilians in order to besiege him. It was only after the death of Ibn Mardanīsh in 1171/567 that his sons handed over the Levant to the caliph in return for commanding positions in the Almohad armies. A few years later a new opposition movement arose in the Balearics. In 1187, after 'Ali b. Ghanīya's successful attack on Bougie, his brother 'Abd Allah landed in Majorca and took possession of the island; after several unsuccessful attempts the islands were finally recovered in 1207/604 by al-Nāṣir's uncle. The Andalusians and the Almohads were seldom truly united in the war against the Christian kingdoms; it was lack of coordination that prevented Yūsuf from winning what seemed a certain victory over Alfonso IX of León in 1184/580 at Santarem; and distrust between Andalusians and Almohads was again partly responsible for the grave defeat of 1212/591. Conversely, the victory of Alarcos in 1195/591 was due in large part to coordination between Almohads and the Andalusians under an able captain, Ibn Ṣanādīd. When we recall the pressure exerted by the Mālikite doctors on the Andalusian princes to prevent them from intriguing with the Christian kings and make them incline to the aims and methods of the Almoravids, we can account for the instability of the Almohad régime only by their failure to win over the religious leaders, who held that the services the Almohads could render in the wars against the Normans and Castilians did not compensate for the danger to the community of their overly exclusive doctrine.

And yet, despite the unfavorable economic situation, despite the unstable government and contested ideology of the Almohads, their reign was a period of splendor. It was then that the Berbers of Morocco adopted the model of Arab civilization we observed in Zīrid Ifrīqiya two centuries earlier, but on a much larger scale. The Almohad government was much more Berber than that of the Almoravids; Berbers from all over the Maghrib were attached to the court as counselors, secretaries, poets, physicians, and ministers of finance, and no longer merely as governors and generals. Concomitantly, the population was for the first time being Islamized in depth, under the influence of a Ṣūfī movement that first developed under the protection of Almohadism and later undermined it. This movement, which for the first time provided the Maghrib with a truly popular ideology, was to define the essential features of western Islam and to reveal unsuspected strength at a time of danger. Also for the first time, a city of the Maghrib, Marrakech, attained the level of the great centers of Arab culture, Baghdad, Cairo and Cordova. Leading lights of Arab thought and science lived and died in Marrakech. And finally, transcending the influences that inevitably make themselves felt in an explicitly universalist culture, Maghribi art, as exemplified by the Kutubia, attained under the Almohads a grandeur and harmony it would never again equal. Like Ibn Tūmart's prose, with its restrained violence, it showed an uncompromising vigor, sobriety and delicacy that may in a certain degree be attributed to the psychology of the Berbers as molded by centuries of bitter struggle against oppression. It may be said, however, that just as Ṭāhart had to be destroyed before Āshīr could be populated, Kairouan sacked before Qal'a could take on new life, and Qal'a ruined before Bougie could prosper, so Ifrīqiya had to decline and Andalusia disintegrate before Marrakech could become a capital. Seen from Morocco, the Almohad period appears to have been an apogee; seen from elsewhere, it was an Indian summer. Almohad prosperity had its source not in the Maghribi economy of the twelfth century, but in the wealth accumulated by the Zīrids, the Almoravids, and before them by the Andalusian princes. The splendor of the Almohads was based on the consumption of wealth they had not produced. This explains why they fell so quickly and why the country, as they left it, was so hard to rebuild.

The Fragmentation of the Empire (1213-1269/610-668)

After the defeat of 1212, known to Moslems as the battle of al-'Uqāb and to Christians as that of Las Navas de Tolosa, the caliph al-Nāṣir returned to Marrakech in haste, appointed his son Yūsuf (al-Muntaṣir) as his heir, and shut himself up in his palace, where he died in 1213/610. Ibn 'Idhārī's account of the long preparations for the campaign throws light on the causes of the defeat: a disastrous economic situation (the author dwells at length on the high cost of living), incompetent administration, and political crisis (the conflict between the Almohad shaykhs and the caliph's advisers). Al-Muntaṣir was barely sixteen at his accession. During the ten years of his reign the enemies of the dynasty remained inactive, waiting to see if it would recover. The year 1223/620 was the beginning of a headlong collapse, marked by the same sort of tragi-comic events as took place in Cordova and Cairo before the downfall of the Umayyad and Fāṭimid caliphates. Among the last eight Almohad rulers, two showed a certain energy, Idrīs al-Ma'-mūn (1227-1232/625-630) and his son 'Alī al-Sa'īd (1224-1248/640-646), but their attempts to restore the situation were doomed to failure; the causes of disintegration were too numerous and profound.

The most obvious cause was the weakening of the army, whose structure was identical with that of the state. The chroniclers put the strength of al-Nāṣir's army in the Spanish campaign as six hundred thousand: startling as it seems at first sight, this figure is probably not exaggerated, for the chroniclers would have tended to minimize a Moslem defeat by underestimating the size of the army. An army of this size can almost be regarded as a mobilized society, so that the conflicts to which the defeat gave rise within the army became the conflicts of society as a whole. The financial power and political stability of the dynasty went hand in hand with its military strength, which suffered from external as well as internal factors. The Moslem victories in the orient worked against western Islam, for when defeated in the east many of the crusaders went to Spain to fight. And at a time when the Christian armies were becoming larger and more united, the Almohads were weakened both by their inability to impose their doctrine and by the intense hostility between the Mu'minids and the Almohad shaykhs. This internal crisis deepened after 1223/620: the shaykhs took advantage of the situation to reassert their power and avenge themselves on such ministers as Ibn Jāmi', but they no longer had an uncontested leader as in the days of Abū Ḥafṣ (d. 1175/571) and his sons. Al-Ma'mūn resolved to rid himself of this troublesome aristocracy. In 1229/626, after solemnly renouncing the Almohad doctrine in the grand mosque of Marrakech, he had the shakyhs (four hundred in number, we are told) thrown into prison and executed. By these acts he condemned his dynasty, for they deprived it of all legitimacy. From then on he based his power on Christian mercenaries rented at an exorbitant price from the king of Castile, and on contingents of Hilālī Arabs. When he died in 1232/630, his son 'Abd al-Wāḥid al-Rashīd was barely fourteen; the shaykhs took advantage of his youth to make him disavow his father's policy and to recover their own power, but they had ceased to be anything more than a small privileged group clinging to an illegitimate dynasty.

The consequence was a power vacuum, and as usual in such cases, the struggle to fill it was waged by conflicting factions within the army. At the height of the empire, the constant wars in Spain and Ifrīqiya had created a need for more and more men. The Almohad caliphs appealed to two warlike groups, the Banū Hilāl in the central Maghrib who, having been defeated in 1152 and 1187, had been transferred by Ya'qūb to the Atlantic plains (the Riyāḥ to the Habt and the Jusham to the Tamesna) and the Marīnids of eastern Morocco, who had made common cause with the dynasty from the start. These two groups provided the cavalry of the Almohad army. The colonial historians attach great importance to the fact that they were both nomadic, but in reality it was as mercenaries and not as nomads that they played their role in the disintegration of the empire;[14] the significant fact was their position in the army and not their original mode of life. At first they supported the members of the Mu'minid family, and it was only gradually that instead of fighting for Almohad pretenders they themselves became claimants of power. It was the illegitimacy with which the Almohad authority was tainted that made the mercenaries aspire to fill a power vacuum that they themselves had not created.

Ifrīqiya was the first province to break away from the empire, and no doubt it was the long resistance of Yaḥiā b. Ghāniya that enabled the descendants of Abū Ḥafṣ to found a dynasty there. By 1206/603 the Ḥafṣid 'Abd al-Wāḥid had obtained what amounted to de facto autonomy. When he died in 1221/618 without having defeated Yaḥyā, the Almohads of Ifrīqiya chose his son 'Abd al-Raḥmān as his successor. The caliph al-Muntaṣir opposed this appointment and sent his own great-uncle, Idrīs b. Yūsuf, to replace him, but neither he nor his son and successor 'Abd al-Raḥmān won a decisive victory over Ibn Ghāniya. The caliph al-'Ādil decided to appoint a Ḥafṣid, 'Abd Allah b. 'Abd al-Wāḥid, who was helped by his brother Abū Zakariyā', governor of Gabès (1223/620). Abū Zakariyā' took power in 1228/625 with the help of the Almohads; in 1233/631 he finally succeeded in capturing and executing Ibn Ghāniya, so becoming master of all Ifrīqiya. By then the Almohad power was contested everywhere. Already in 1230 Abū Zakariyā' had refused to go along with al-Ma'mūn's ideological revolution, broken off all ties with him, and caused the *khuṭba* to be said in the name of the Mahdi. In the course of time he became a pretender to the throne. In 1236/634 he had the *khuṭba* said in his own name, and in 1244/642 was recognized as a caliph by Seville, Ceuta, Tlemcen and

[14] Terrasse goes so far as to accuse 'Abd al-Mu'min and Ya'qūb of treason against their race (*Histoire du Maroc*, vol. II, pp. 220, 235).

even Meknès. It was this sudden rise of the Ḥafṣid that obliged all the Almohads to rally around Alī al-Sa'īd in his attempt to restore the empire (1242-1248); it failed and Abū Zakariyā' remained master of Ifrīqiya.

The loss of Andalusia was a repetition of events familiar since the beginning of the eleventh century. The Almohad governors among whom the authority was dispersed were replaced by Andalusians, who first appealed to the Christian kings for help and after a time submitted to them. The revolt began in the Mu'minid family itself. In 1223/620, when 'Abd al-Wāḥid, the son of al-Nāṣir, quite in spite of himself, was appointed caliph in Marrakech, his uncle 'Abd Allah, governor of Murcia (who later became the caliph al-'Ādil), refused to recognize him and under the influence of his counselor Ibn Yarjān, a notorious intriguer according to the chroniclers, put forward his own candidacy; he was immediately recognized by his brothers, Idrīs (in Cordova), 'Alī (in Granada) and Abū Mūsā (in Malaga), and by one of his cousins 'Abd Allah al-Bayāsī (in Jaén), but al-Bayāsī's brother refused to recognize al-'Ādil, won over al-Bayāsī to his point of view, and appealed to the Castilians for help. Al-'Ādil left his brother Idrīs, the future al-Ma'mūn, to fight them, and proceeded to Marrakech, where he was killed in 1227/624. Wishing to avenge his brother, Idrīs refused to recognize Yaḥyā al Mu'tasim, who had just been appointed caliph. In 1229/626 he obtained an army from the Castilians and crossed over to Morocco but was no more successful than his brother. These continual struggles between Mu'minids opened the way to the descendants of the old local dynasties such as the Banū Hud and the Banū Mardanīsh. In 1230/628 the Almohads were driven from Spain, and the various provinces recognized the suzerainty either of the 'Abbāsids (up to the fall of Baghdad) or of the Ḥafṣids of Ifrīqiya. One after another the cities of Spain were taken over by the kings of Castile or of Aragon.

At the center of the empire, as the Almohad pretenders continued to fight one another, the role of various groups within the army became preponderant. These were the Hilālī Arabs, who controlled the road between Fez and Marrakech, the Marīnids, who controlled the road between Meknès and Taza, and the Zayyānids, who controlled the road to Ifrīqiya. These groups provided the Almohad army with cavalry and collected taxes in the territories under their control. As intermediaries between the peasant populations and the Almohad government, they thus became autonomous powers. Because of their small number and because they divided their forces by supporting different Mu'minid pretenders, the Banū Hilāl could not hope to inherit the Almohad authority. The Marīnids, on the other hand, soon rallied around a leader, began to keep the taxes they collected,[15] and prepared to replace the crumbling dynasty. Their central position gave them an advantage over the Banū Hilāl in the west and the Zayyānids in the east.

Among the Zayyānids (also known as the Banū 'Abd al-Wād), it looked as though the leadership would fall to the Muṭahhar family, which had achieved a certain prominence during the reigns of 'Abd al-Mu'min and Yūsuf. In 1230/627 one of its members, Jābir b. Yūsuf, was chosen as chief, but he failed to establish his authority and his son Ḥasan was no more successful. When Ḥasan's uncle failed in turn, Abū 'Izza b. Zayyān was elected, but the Banū Muṭahhar refused to recognize him. Killed in battle in 1235/633, he was succeeded by his brother Yaghmurāsin. Up until then the Almohad sovereignty had been recognized. To establish his autonomy the new leader decided to recognize the Ḥafṣid Abū Zakariyā'. After the caliph 'Alī al-Sa'īd was killed at Tlemcen in 1248/646, the Zayyānids had nothing more to fear and remained firmly in control of all present-day Orania.

Meanwhile the Marīnids proceeded in the same way in the west. As early as 1216/613 they showed their strength by defeating the governor of Fez. The caliph then tried to

[15] See al-Nāṣirī, *al-Istiqṣā*, vol. II, p. 220.

reduce them by enlisting the help of the Banū Hilāl. Not yet sure of themselves or of the weakness of the Almohads, one group of the Marīnids submitted. Another carried on the struggle under their leader 'Abd al-Ḥaqq and gained the upper hand. At his death, 'Abd al-Ḥaqq was succeeded by his son Abū Bakr. In 1238/636 Meknès fell to the Marīnids and they, too, recognized the suzerainty of the Ḥafṣids. After a pause coinciding with the reign of 'Alī al-Sa'īd they resumed their conquest of northern Morocco. Under 'Umar al-Murtaḍā (1248-1267/646-665), the Almohad state disintegrated completely. The Sous in the south and Ceuta in the north broke away. In 1255/653 the caliph made a last attempt to retrieve the situation but, defeated by the Marīnids, contented himself with holding his capital. In 1262/660, after conquering the Tamesna, Abū Bakr's brother and successor Ya'qūb the Marīnid defeated the caliph's last Almohad troops and Bedouin mercenaries on the Um al-Rābī' and surrounded Marrakech. Al-Murtaḍā offered to pay him tribute, but Abū Dabbūs, a great grandson of 'Abd al-Mu'min revolted and appealed to Ya'qūb for help, promising to cede him half the territory he had conquered. Al-Murtaḍā was defeated, but Abū Dabbūs refused to carry out his promise, whereupon Ya'qūb laid siege to Marrakech and captured it in 1269/668. Al-Murtaḍā's brother Isḥāq, the last of the Almohads, escaped with his shaykhs to Tinmall, where he died in 1275/674. There was nothing to prevent the Marīnids from assuming a royal title.

Thus the death agony of the Almohad empire was long and pitiful. The process of disintegration was slow because the contenders for power were numerous and weak. Whereas the Almoravids and Almohads, like the Fāṭimids before them, had embarked on their conquests with new forces, now the contenders were components of the Almohad empire itself. The official thirteenth-century historians described the festivities of the ruling families in detail and exaggerated the importance of their essentially mediocre feats of arms; they should not be taken too seriously. In the last analysis the struggles between Banū Hilāl and Marīnids, between Marīnids and Zayyānids, and their conflicts with the Almohad caliphs, reflected little more than rivalry between groups of mercenaries, all intent on appropriating as much tax money as possible; the urban and rural populations cared little to whom they paid their taxes, and that is why the struggle went on with shifting fortunes for so many years. The downfall of the Almohads must be attributed primarily to the failure of their doctrine, to the disintegration of an army under difficult economic conditions, and to an unfavorable external situation. The empire was doomed because its center had been weakened both agriculturally and commercially. The removal of the Banū Hilāl to the west and the preeminence of the Marīnids can be explained only by the fact that the Atlantic regions had already been half ruined by the preceding wars. It seems possible that in transplanting the Banū Hilāl the Almohad caliphs had intended to colonize the western territories, but since the state had as much need of soldiers as of farmers, the newcomers had chosen to become soldiers, so aggravating the economic decline. The small part played by the south in Almohad history suggests that the Saharan trade had either died out or been diverted. But if the center of the empire was impoverished, war on the frontiers (Andalusia and Ifrīqiya) ceased to be a luxury or a mistake and became a necessity, since it was the only means of obtaining the funds needed to support a large army and navy and maintain peace between the Almohads and the clientele of the caliphs. But the exploitation of these two provinces could not go on forever, and once they were endangered the collapse may well have been inevitable. The strength of the dynasty rested on military victories, but in Spain the war was endless and the relation of forces soon became unfavorable. The Christian armies steadily improved their equipment and tactics, and little by little the Church imposed a unity that contrasted sharply with the dispersion of effort in the Moslem camp and the profound distrust between

Andalusians and Maghribis. The Almohads had put forward an ideology aimed at a consensus, and therein lay their greatest failure, for the majority rejected this ideology. Ṣūfism developed first outside of Almohadism and then against it. Without legitimacy and hence without strength, the Almohad authority was bound to crumble, even if its successors did nothing to hasten its downfall. The Marīnids did not, like the Almoravids and Almohads, set themselves up as champions of a doctrine. By representing themselves as the involuntary heirs to a defunct dynasty, they were to gain the sympathy of the *fuqahā'*, so leaving orthodoxy free to develop on its own. The Almohads, it is sometimes said, were wrong to expend so much energy in Spain. But had they any choice? And without the wars in Spain could the western Maghrib have overcome its provincialism and acquired a political model, a culture and a faith that would enable it subsequently to endure by identifying itself with a tradition?

9. The Failure of the Imperial Idea

There is no better indication of the importance of the Almohad empire than the fascination it has exerted on all subsequent rulers in the Maghrib. Every one of them tried to take over some part of the heritage and develop it; for lack of resources or favorable circumstances none was successful. The Maghrib split into three states whose borders gradually came to resemble those of the present day. None felt satisfied; all aspired to expand if not to restore the imperial unity. One nearly succeeded, but that failure put a definitive end to attempts at unification. In the thirteenth century a precarious balance of power was established between the Christian and Moslem states of the western Mediterranean. For a brief period it looked as though this peaceful coexistence, reinforced by diplomacy, trade and the employment of mercenaries on both sides, might last. But then the crusading spirit revived and changed the situation completely, especially in the Maghrib. The protagonists were Portugal, Castile, Aragon, the two cities of Genoa and Pisa, the kingdoms of Granada, Fez, Tlemcen and Tunis. Of the three states that constituted the Maghrib, two enjoyed a period of prosperity, the Marīnid kingdom in the west and the Ḥafṣid kingdom in the east, whereas the Zayyānid kingdom in the center, lacking the cohesion and strength to remain truly independent, was alternately dominated by one of the other two.

I

In the period extending from 1229/626, when the caliph al-Ma'mūn broke with the Almohad ideology, so enabling the Ḥafṣids of Ifrīqiya to become autonomous, to 1358/759, when the Marīnid sultan Fāris al-Mutawakkil (Abū 'Inān)[1]

[1] It should be recalled that Moslem sovereigns bore a name (ism), a *kunya,* by which they were commonly called, and an honorific title;

died, three phases can be distinguished: one of Ḥafṣid preponderance, one of stalemate, and one of Marīnid preponderance.

The Ḥafṣid preponderance (up to 1277/676) was more religious than political; the new dynasty had set itself up from the start as heir to the Almohad caliphate, for which pretension it had excellent justifications to offer. Abu Ḥafṣ 'Umar was as influential as 'Abd al-Mu'min; the two families had shared the highest administrative and military posts both in Morocco and in Andalusia, on an almost equal footing. Before embarking on the campaign of 1212, al-Nāṣir had asked (though not taken) the advice of the Ḥafṣid 'Abd al-Wāhid.[2] During the long struggle between Idrīs al-Ma'mūn and Yaḥyā b. al-Nāṣir, the Friday prayer was recited in Ifrīqiya in the name of the Mahdi and his faithful successors. In 1236/634, the Ḥafṣid Yaḥyā I had consolidated his position and caused the prayer to be recited in his own name, though he had not taken the title of caliph. Among all the pretenders to the Almohad throne it was he who offered the most plausible claims, and Andalusia, Tangiers and Ceuta, Meknès, and the Marīnids recognized his sovereignty. Taking advantage of this unexpected prestige at a time when the Marīnids and Zayyānids were still busy liquidating the Almohad empire, Yaḥyā patiently reconstituted Zīrid Ifrīqiya. Having nothing more to fear from southern Tunisia after the death of Ibn Ghāniya (1233/631), he took possession of Constantine, Bougie and Algiers, and imposed a payment of tribute on Tlemcen. As the most powerful sovereign in the Maghrib at the time and as the successor of the Zīrids and Ḥammādids, he entered into relations with the Mediterranean powers, renewing the Zīrid treaties with Venice, Pisa, Genoa, and the kingdom of Aragon. His successor Muḥammad al-Mustanṣir (1250-1277/648-675) took

the chroniclers make use of all three interchangeably. I shall use the name and honorific title for reigning sovereigns and the name and *kunya* for pretenders and sovereigns of doubtful legitimacy.

[2] See al-Nāṣirī, *al-Istiqṣā*, vol. II, p. 196.

the title of caliph and, after the fall of Baghdad to the Hūlāgū and the demise of the 'Abbāsid dynasty, was recognized by the sharīfs of Mecca in 1259 and the Mamelukes of Egypt in 1260. This sudden glory lasted no more than a year, for in 1261 Baybars resuscitated the 'Abbāsid dynasty, which was to maintain the fiction of the caliphate in Cairo until 1517. But for a brief moment a scion of a Berber family from the High Atlas was recognized by almost the entire Islamic world. To be sure, he claimed descent from 'Umar b. al-Khaṭṭāb and by then the title itself had little practical importance.[3] Still, his prestige was such that embassies were sent to him from countries as distant as Kanem and Bornu (1257/655) and Norway (1262/661). The city of Tunis seems to have developed impressively during the reign of al-Mustanṣir. It was his fame no doubt that made Louis IX undertake a crusade against him in the belief that by defeating him or obtaining his conversion he would become master of the orient. Though al-Mustanṣir came close to losing his capital and though the crusading army was defeated more by sickness than by force of arms, the failure of the crusade enhanced his prestige. The war ended in a compromise; al-Mustanṣir agreed to double his payments of tribute(?) to the Angevins of Sicily and accorded privileges and guarantees to French, Sicilian and Navarrese merchants. Al-Mustanṣir died in 1277. By then the overall situation had changed. The unity of Ifrīqiya was soon to be shattered as rival claimants disputed the throne. In the west the Marīnids were on the ascendant.

Until 1269/668 the west was the scene of indecisive struggles among Marīnids, Zayyānids, Hilālī mercenaries (especially the Riyāḥ settled in the Gharb) and Almohads reinforced by Christian contingents. The Zayyānid Yaghmurāsin allied himself with the Almohads in an attempt to acquire a degree of autonomy; it was he who in 1244 helped the caliph 'Alī al-Sa'īd to retake Meknès, which had served the Marīnids as a capital, and he also helped Abū Dabbūs. This

[3] Ibn Khaldūn makes it clear that he was recognized by default.

jockeying for power explains the general lack of interest in Andalusia. Then in September 1269, the Marīnid Ya'qūb entered Marrakech and took the title of Amīr al-Muslimīn, partly to dissociate himself from the heterodoxy of the Almohads and partly to show that he was taking over their authority. In 1274/673 he captured Sijilmāsa and subdued the Ma'qil Banū Hilāl, who for a century, under the nominal suzerainty of the Zayyānids of Tlemcen, had imposed themselves as the sole political power in southwestern Morocco. He was then in a position to turn either eastward or northward; since he had no other title to the Almohad succession than force and his sympathy with Mālikite orthodoxy, he was obliged to prove that his accession to power would not weaken western Islam. His choice was further determined by the fact that Muḥammad al-Faqīh, the amir of Granada, was under attack by the Castilians and Aragonese. Ya'qūb concluded a truce with Yaghmurāsin and crossed over to Spain; in all he waged four campaigns to save Andalusia, but under infinitely less favorable conditions than his Almohad predecessors. One three-cornered conflict (Almohad caliphs, kings of Castile and Banū Ghāniya) had given way to another (Marīnids, Castilians and Zayyānids), but this one was even more complicated and the scene of action was smaller. Nevertheless, the Marīnid achieved his purpose, namely, to gain a certain recognition by the doctors of the law. In 1275/674, near Ecija, the Marīnid army won a great victory, which was regarded as a revenge for the defeat of 1212. And four years later an important naval battle for mastery of the Straits ended in another Marīnid victory. In 1282/681 Ya'qūb even managed to play a part in Castilian politics. Alfonso X appealed to him for help against his son and gave him the crown of Castile as a pledge. These achievements may seem meager, considering that Andalusia was doomed in any event.[4] Nevertheless

[4] Terrasse tends to minimize the importance of all the Maghribi victories in Spain by stressing the ultimate downfall of Moslem Spain; by this method any victory can be made to look meaningless.

Ya'qūb al-Manṣūr acquired a certain prestige in the Maghrib, for he alone was in a position to help Andalusian Islam. His Spanish campaigns, however, gave the other two Maghribi dynasties a breathing spell, of which Yaghmurāsin took advantage to consolidate his emirate. Thanks to his energy and political sense, Tlemcen became the commercial and intellectual capital of the central Maghrib. He realized that the Marīnid victories were bound to have long-term consequences and, we are told, advised his successor 'Uthmān (1283-1303/681-703) to look eastward. 'Uthmān took his advice and exploiting the breakup of the Ḥafṣid kingdom attacked Bougie (1286/685). But he did not have time to gain his ends, for the Marīnids had just changed their policy. The new Marīnid amir Yūsuf al-Nāṣir (1286-1307/685-706) resolved to disengage himself from the affairs of Andalusia, where the intrigues of the amirs of Granada (Banū al-Aḥmar) were becoming more and more complex. (In 1291 Tarifa was taken by the combined forces of Granada and Castile; in 1306 the amir of Granada fomented a revolt in Ceuta.) In 1295 began the great duel between the Marīnids and the Zayyānids. The first siege of Tlemcen, the Zayyānid capital, went on for eight years (1299-1307). Yūsuf conquered the whole Maghrib as far as Algiers, built a new capital and patiently waited for Tlemcen to surrender. The Zayyānid amir Muḥammad I (1303-1308) was on the point of surrendering when Yūsuf the Marīnid was murdered and a truce was signed. The first attempt of the Marīnids to impose their hegemony had failed.

Meanwhile in Ifrīqiya the pretenders continued their struggle for the cities of Tripoli, Tunis, Bougie and Constantine. Abū Isḥāq Ibrāhīm revolted against his nephew Yaḥyā al-Wāthiq (1277-1279) and seized the throne. Whereupon Abū 'Umāra, an adventurer representing himself as the son of al-Wāthiq, revolted in Tripoli. The outcome of these struggles was that in 1284/683 the kingdom was divided between al-Mustanṣir II, who reigned in Tunis, and

Yaḥyā b. Ibrāhīm, who reigned in Bougie; Ifrīqiya was reunited in 1309, but this did not restore peace.

The Marīnid kingdom was also somewhat weakened between 1307 and 1331; 'Āmir (Abū Thābit) and Sulayman (Abū Rabī') occupied themselves chiefly with taking Ceuta (1309/708), and 'Uthmān II (Abū Sa'īd) was kept busy by the rivalry of his son 'Umar (Abū 'Alī), who set up an autonomous principality in Sijilmāsa. During this brief period, while the two neighboring kingdoms were torn by dynastic struggles, the Zayyānid kingdom of Tlemcen gained in strength and was even able to carry on an aggressive policy; according to Ibn Khaldūn the amir Mūsā I (1308-1347) went so far as to call himself king. His son 'Abd al-Raḥmān, judging the situation favorable in the Ḥafṣid kingdom, where Abū Bakr al-Mutawakkil (1317-1347) was trying in vain to defend his throne against all the members of his family who had banded against him, decided to seize Bougie and Constantine. The desperate Ḥafṣid appealed to the Marīnid amir and to seal the friendship between their two families gave one of his daughters in marriage to 'Alī (Abū al-Ḥasan), the eldest son of his ally. It was while on his way to meet his future daughter-in-law that 'Uthmān II died.

In consequence of these events, the Marīnids gained preponderance under the two amirs 'Alī (Abū al-Ḥasan) and Fāris (Abū 'Inan) 1331/732 to 1357/758. The former revived the ambitious projects of the Almohads. He unified the kingdom by taking possession of the principality that had formed in Sijilmāsa and the Sous, then turned back to attack Tlemcen, which fell in 1337. The Zayyānid 'Abd al-Raḥmān (Abū Tāshfīn), who had tried to enlarge his kingdom, lost both his throne and his life. Next 'Alī, who had retaken Algiers in 1333/733, led an expedition to Spain. Now in 1340 his navy, aided by that of his father-in-law Abū Bakr al-Mutawakkil, won a great victory in the Straits and laid siege to Tarifa. The city resisted, however, with the help of the Genoese, and the expedition ended in a Marīnid defeat. Four years later Algeciras fell to the Castilians, reinforced by knights from England, France and Italy. This was the last Maghribi campaign in Spain. In 1347, at the death of his father-in-law, 'Alī, summoned by the chamberlain Ibn Tāfrāgīn, moved into Ifrīqiya and took Constantine and Tunis without difficulty. The days of 'Abd al-Mu'min seemed to have returned, and 'Alī himself was conscious of walking in the Almohad's traces. His success, however, was short-lived, for he encountered 'Abd al-Mu'min's old adversaries, the Banū Hilāl, masters of the plains, who this time instead of being defeated were victorious at Kairouan (1348/749). Thereupon the whole edifice collapsed. In Morocco, Fāris (Abū 'Inān), believing his father dead, declared himself amir; the Zayyānid 'Uthmān II returned to Tlemcen and the Ḥafṣid princes to Bône, Constantine and Tunis, all the while continuing to fight among themselves. 'Alī (Abū al-Ḥasan) tried in vain to recover his throne and died in misery in 1351. He lacked neither energy nor intelligence, but the balance of forces in the Maghrib and the Mediterranean had changed, and ambitious ventures were doomed in advance. Of this his son and successor Fāris (Abū 'Inān) was unaware. Disregarding the affairs in Spain, he, too, attempted the conquest of Ifrīqiya. He took Tlemcen in 1352, executed the Zayyānid 'Uthmān II, captured Bougie, and in 1356 mustered a powerful expedition with a view to conquering all Ifrīqiya. His failure was due not to the Banū Hilāl but to his own soldiers, who refused to go beyond the central Maghrib. Abū 'Inān returned to Morocco and the territory he had conquered was soon lost. In 1359/760 the Zayyānid Mūsā II was reestablished in Tlemcen and the Ḥafṣid Ibrāhīm II, still counseled by the powerful chamberlain Ibn Tāfrāgīn, who lived until 1364/766, returned to Tunis after recapturing Bougie.

The mid-fourteenth century may be regarded as a key period in the history of the Maghrib, for in the course of the following century the same forces remained at work, though in a reduced area. The rulers of the day were undoubtedly influenced by nostalgia for the Almohad era; the two Marīnids, Yūsuf and ʻAlī, who had the greatest resources at their disposal, tried to transform this nostalgia into reality, but behind their nostalgia lay the same imperious necessity that led the Almohad state to defend its two distant provinces, Andalusia and Ifrīqiya. These wars were at once necessary and exhausting. ʻAbd al-Mu'min had confronted a multitude of principalities; ʻAlī, the Marīnid, had to contend with two kingdoms having the same structure as his own. It was this similarity of structure that made his efforts so futile, though he could hardly have helped combating the tendency to decentralization. Everywhere autonomous principalities were springing up: in Ifrīqiya around Constantine, Bougie and Tripoli; in the central Maghrib around Oran and Tlemcen; in Morocco around Ceuta (in 1306 and 1326 under the patrician al-ʻAzafī family), in the Sous and in Tafilelt. In each province the power rested on three foundations: taxes on trade, the *makhzen* (administrative personnel), and a force of mercenaries supplied largely by the Banū Hilāl who were dispersed throughout the Maghrib. The governors tended to rebel against their sovereigns, whom as a rule they regarded as in no way superior to themselves. The Marīnid ʻUthmān II sent his son Abū ʻAlī to Sijilmāsa. Thereupon ʻAlī raised an army with the help of the Maʻqil Bedouins, took possession of Tuāt and Gurāra, and minted coins. In 1322 he entered Marrakech and set up a principality, which survived until 1333. Similarly in the east, Khālid (Abū al-Baqā') reunified Ifrīqiya in 1309-1311 after a dismemberment of twenty years; no sooner had he appointed his brother Abū Bakr governor of Constantine than Abū Bakr declared his independence. Homogenization of structures, decentralization, and continuous struggles went hand in hand; the reason for this must be sought in the very nature of Maghribi society at that time.[5]

[5] Obviously Ibn Khaldūn's theory of the two Zanāti epochs is based on the similarity between the situation in the fourteenth century, which he knew perfectly, and that prevailing in the tenth century.

II

The homogeneity of Maghribi society in the thirteenth and fourteenth centuries is discernible not only in the political structures but also in the artistic and cultural life of the day. On the surface the various sovereigns differed in status. The Zayyānids were only amirs, without religious or political pretension outside the territory under their effective control; the Marīnids (in memory of the Almoravids no doubt) had taken the more ambitious title of Amīr al-Muslimīn; 'Alī (Abū al-Ḥasan) considered taking the title of caliph; his son did so at a time when the step was no longer justified, and the last Marīnids kept the title; the Ḥafṣids had preserved the structure, symbols and formulas of the Almohad empire. In reality the authority of these rulers was usually precarious and their honorific titles meaningless from the religious and juridical point of view; the only reality was effective power. With a view to consolidating their dynasties, the amirs chose their successors from among those associated with the exercise of authority; the heir apparent was endowed with all the royal prerogatives, a counselor (*wazīr*), secretaries, and a personal guard. This attempt to reinforce the dynasties was unsuccessful, not only because of the unfavorable economic conditions, but also because of the balance of power between several kingdoms. The princes, of whom there were always many, served the kings as means of pressure against each other. In 1324/724 the Zayyānid 'Abd al-Raḥmān I incited Ibrāhīm b. Abū Bakr I against the Ḥafṣid Abū Bakr II; in 1353/754 the amir of Granada, allied with the king of Castile, incited Abū al-Fadl against his brother the Marīnid Abū 'Inān. These diplomatic intrigues made the interims between reigns extremely dangerous. Yet despite continual political agitation, the emirates of this period developed an administrative structure (the

---

Consequently, the genesis of Ibn Khaldūn's theory can be explained on the basis of historical events, but historical events cannot be explained by Ibn Khaldūn's schematization.

makhzen), which in Morocco, for example, endured down to the twentieth century. This makhzen, reflecting a sophisticated etiquette and an increasingly subtle formalism, became uniform, apparently unaffected by the intrinsic weakness of the states.[6] Almost everywhere the state structure was tripartite. The actual control of domestic and foreign policy was vested in a council of two or three *wazīrs* or *ḥājibs*, who owed their position to their political influence on a section of the population or to their proved fidelity to the sovereign. Often they were freed slaves or foreigners, an advantage since as such they represented no danger to the throne. Once decided on, measures were formulated at the chancellery with its highly specialized *kātibs* (different categories of *kātib* attended to correspondence with different classes of persons; sometimes one *kātib* was entrusted with the writing [*inshā'*] and another with the signature [*'alāma*] of a document). The financial and economic functions of government were supervised by treasurers and intendants (*ashghāl* and *a'māl*). The fiscal administration was closely bound up with the army, which collected the taxes. Taxes in kind were stored in depots and served to feed the army.

The distinction between the three branches of government was not codified; the terminology changed from one kingdom to another, but the system was everywhere the same, even in the large provincial cities. Three groups shared unequally in the political power: the freed slaves, the Hilālī Bedouins, and the Andalusian émigrés; the friction between these groups was the principal cause of failure to find an adequate solution to the problems of taxation, army organization, and administration. Theoretically the treasury was replenished by rural taxes, duties on land and sea trade, and the revenues from farms and monopolies (the old taxes paid by Moslems and non-Moslems had largely lost their importance). In practice, rural taxation depended on the army and the other categories on the administration.

[6] This Maghrib is described in detail in al-'Umarī, *Masālik al-Abṣār*, pp. 131-153.

If the amir's authority was recognized, taxes poured into the treasury, the army and administration were paid, and the government functioned; otherwise those responsible for the collection of taxes were paid irregularly and kept the larger part of the state revenues for themselves. The only taxes that were easy to keep account of and collect were the duties on maritime trade, and this led the amir to make increasing concessions to foreign merchants; but in so doing he earned the hostility of the local merchants and of the religious leaders under their influence. Thus the problem of the army was inseparable from that of taxation. In their need of reliable troops, the amirs resorted to the Banū Hilāl, who had exerted political power since the eleventh century. The Fāṭimid decision of 1048 had provided a juridical instrument for this mobilization of Bedouins. This was the *'iqṭā'*, or delegation of political authority, which empowered the Bedouins to levy farm taxes and collect custom duties and land rents in the region under their control, in return for which concessions they raised other taxes for the sovereign and supplied him with soldiers. The situation of these Banū Hilāl deteriorated with the general economic situation. As commercial duties and farm rents declined, the Banū Hilāl resumed the nomadic mode of life, to escape which they had left the Hedjaz and Upper Egypt. From soldiers they became soldier-shepherds and then plain shepherds, who were not always available for military service; but it was still as soldiers in search of better remuneration that they took part in the political struggles of the day. The whole subsequent development in the Maghrib was determined by the increasing role of cavalry, hence increasing reliance on Bedouins, while everywhere else in the world the accent was shifting to infantry, that is, essentially, to the peasantry. The Zayyānids were highly dependent on the Banū Hilāl; Yaghmurāsin was helped by the Sulaym, Mūsā II by the Dawāwida. Thanks to their Almohad contingents, the first Ḥafṣids were able to dispense with the Banū Hilāl and even to subjugate them, especially during the reign of al-Mustanṣir I, but from the end of the thirteenth century on the Almohad army ceased to exist, the struggles among pretenders became more intense, and the Banū Hilāl recovered their autonomy. They helped al-Mustanṣir II, who in 1284 granted them an *'iqṭā'* for the first time. After the Marīnid intermezzi they restored 'Umar II and Ibrāhīm II to the throne and so regained all their influence. The Marīnids resisted this tendency the longest, because they themselves had been mercenaries in the service of the Almohad caliphs. They were able to keep at a distance the Banū Hilāl whom Ya'qūb al-Manṣūr had moved to Morocco, but in the middle of the fourteenth century they were obliged to come to terms with the Ma'qil, the most recent among the Banū Hilāl arrivals, who profited from the strategic position of their territory between the Marīnid and the Zayyānid kingdoms. In 1334, when the sultan 'Alī (Abū al-Ḥasan) took Marrakech and Sijilmāsa, he granted them an *'iqṭā'*. Thus the Banū Hilāl became everywhere an autonomous force, since all the states needed them for their self-defense.

Still another group played a leading role: the Andalusian émigrés. Everywhere, in Tunis, Bougie, Tlemcen, Fez and in cities of lesser importance such as Constantine and Marrakech, they introduced court etiquette, formalism and diplomacy. Their influence was especially felt in Tlemcen, where the Zayyānids were without a royal tradition, whereas the Marīnids had inherited the makhzen and the Ḥafṣids the state organization of the Almohads. Specialists in administration, the Andalusians went from the service of one prince to that of another, becoming secretaries, financial advisers and sometimes even viziers. But since they were an alien body in society, their strength and often their security depended on the sovereign's weakness and their own good relations with the Banū Hilāl. This situation had already existed in Andalusia, whence the émigrés derived a political tradition that they adapted to the Maghrib. They not only introduced the subtle intrigues and tortuous calculations underlying the alliances and counteralliances of the states and substates of the fourteenth-century Maghrib; they also revolutionized the whole concept of politics, relaxing its ties with society and religion. In their view political power no longer required serious religious justification. The consequence was a radical break with the Fāṭimid, Almoravid and Almohad past. The Andalusians regarded religion as a private concern (hence the concomitant growth of an individualistic and somewhat philistine Ṣūfism)[7] and as an ideological justification for the ambition of princes, a far cry from the view held in the preceding centuries. This autonomy of politics opened the way to a "laicization" of power, which might have had favorable effects in a country with a flourishing economy, but proved disastrous in the Maghrib of the fourteenth century. The amirs, Banū Hilāl, and Andalusians, who had become the pillars of a state divorced from society, helped each other to defend special and ephemeral interests, so preparing the way for a general and lasting decadence.[8] Yet though the politics of the fourteenth century had its source in the traditions of an Andalusia in distress, it also corresponded to the development of Maghribi society and was in a sense the theoretical expression of a real decadence. Whatever view we may take of the continuity of political forms from the city-states of the eighth century to the kingdoms of the fourteenth century, there can be no doubt that the developments of the fourteenth century created a real and lasting breach between the state and society. The one ceased to reflect the other; the sovereign ceased to symbolize the potential unity of society, his power ceased to be anything more than the formal expression of the in-

[7] The typical example is Ibn al-Khaṭīb, master of intrigue and Ṣūfism.

[8] This is the foundation of Ibn Khaldūn's theory. There is every reason to regard Ibn Khaldūn's point of view as that of the Andalusian group in their opposition to the Hilālī mercenaries. This does not mean, however, that his theory is entirely ideological; in many of its aspects it has nothing to do with ideology.

terplay between two permanently conflicting social groups. And the same dualism can be observed in the realms of religion and culture.

The fourteenth century was a period of cultural flowering, in which for the first time all parts of the Maghrib participated. After years of sectarian exclusivism, an orthodox doctrine had taken form. Combating the Fāṭimids and Almohads with their own weapons, the Sunnites propagated their doctrine in madrasas, or schools, which were first developed in the Seljuk territories and later adopted by the Marīnids. Fez, Tlemcen and Tunis each had several madrasas, some of which are still in existence. A new Mālikite movement, faithful to the teachings of the past but taking the needs of the new times into account, arose in Fez and Tunis. This educational effort completed the Arabization of Ifrīqiya and resulted in the almost total Arabization of the central Maghrib and the Moroccan plains (reflected in the fact that from then on most of the qadis were recruited locally). The madrasas also served to educate the numerous Maghribi historians who enable us to study the political life of the period in detail. Every dynasty had its historians, some of them of high ability. Art flowered no less than literature and theology; most of the monuments we admire today in Fez, Tlemcen and Tunis were the work of Marīnid or Ḥafṣid sultans.

If we confined ourselves to written documents, we should be tempted to conclude that the fragmentary activities of earlier times found their completion and culmination in the period under discussion. It would be closer to the truth to characterize the art and culture of the thirteenth and fourteenth centuries as borrowed splendor. If Marīnid art no longer has the grandeur of Almohad art, if it excels chiefly in detail, the reason is that this was the art of dying Andalusia. If the Zayyānid Abū Hammū Mūsā II wrote a book on politics,[9] it was because he had been educated in Spain. If an Ibn al-Khaṭīb was unable to found a literary school,

[9] *Wāsiṭat al-sulūk.*

it was because his work was that of a dying era. Thus the culture of the fourteenth century, that seems so rich, was a last flowering of waning Andalusia. It was not firmly rooted in the society that sustained it and did not express the historic experience of the Maghrib. Like the state which it served to glorify, it was polarized according to the interests of the two antagonistic groups we have described. Though the orthodoxy diffused by the madrasas gave theoretical support to the state authority, it was strongly influenced by the spirit, traditions, and interests of the Andalusian party in the makhzen.[10] Arabization was promoted by two different forces; on the one hand by the orthodoxy of the madrasas and on the other by the political influence of the Banū Hilāl. And that is why when the movement of Islamization and Arabization seemed on the point of completion, it stopped and perhaps receded. An abstract state and an isolated cultural life went hand in hand; both had lost the power to express or unify society, which was later to find an answer to its aspirations in popular Ṣūfism. This accounts for the immediate and lasting success of the *zāwiyas*.

III

The preceding developments can be explained only by the weakness of the economic base, and that perhaps is where we should have begun. But it seems preferable to begin with what one knows rather than with what one can scarcely conjecture.

Though our documents say nothing of the demographic situation, it seems probable that the population of the Maghrib continued to decline in the thirteenth and fourteenth centuries. Nāṣirī speaks of the disastrous effects of the defeat of 1212; he might have said the same of all the Andalusian campaigns, for the Maghrib went on supplying the

[10] This of course cannot be entirely true of a religious ideology with a universalist perspective, but these humanist potentialities are developed only when an opposition group rejects the accepted interpretation.

kingdom of Granada with soldiers long after the Maghribi amirs had abandoned all territorial ambitions on the peninsula. The decline in population can also be inferred from the relatively small size of armies under the Ḥafṣids and Marīnids. Because of constant revolts, the most populous regions, the Rif and Sous in the west, the region of Bougie in the east, were beyond the reach of the central authority. Depending on the period under discussion, the decline in the population may have been as much a cause as a consequence of fragmentation, political weakness, the enhanced role of the Banū Hilāl, and their reversion to nomadism.

We also have no direct knowledge of the agricultural situation. Those who with Terrasse infer that the extension of nomadism caused a decline in agriculture fail to consider that the contrary is equally plausible; the increase in nomadism may just as well have been brought about by the decline in agriculture, and the fact that the *'iqṭā'* (grants) of the thirteenth and especially of the fourteenth century were nowhere explicit seems to favor the latter interpretation. We can never be sure whether these grants concern transit duties or taxes on farmers,[11] and the consequence would not be the same. The situation of agriculture would be defined by the initial relation between the two kinds of *'iqṭā'* and by subsequent modifications in this relation. Under these conditions nomadic life became extremely unstable and was perpetuated only by the weakness of the state and the decline in the population. It is certain that arboriculture suffered most. The vast wooded areas of earlier centuries as described by traveler-geographers seem to have gone out of existence. Yet despite a certain instability, cereal production seems to have been maintained at a high level.[12] The commercial situation had improved. The Saharan trade appears to have

11 We often read the formula: "wa-qtaṭa'ū jibāyatah."

12 Emerit observes: "Whatever the geographers may think, invasions lead the population to abandon cattle-raising (since flocks are too vulnerable) and are far less detrimental to the production of cereals, since grain, once harvested, is easy to hide" (*Annales E.S.C.*, September-October, 1969), p. 1171.

revived; at its point of arrival it was now controlled by the Ma'qil, who had gradually taken possession of the southwestern Maghrib. The eastern route remained active and the western route had recovered, as is demonstrated by the sudden importance of the principality of Sijilmāsa, founded by the Marīnid Abū 'Alī b. 'Uthmān II, and by the diplomatic relations of the Ḥafṣid al-Mustanṣir I and the Marīnid 'Alī (Abū al-Ḥasan) with the kingdoms of Kanem and Bornu. Thanks to the friendly relations between the Zayyānids and the Ma'qil, it was probably Tlemcen that benefited most from this trade. Tlemcen and Ḥunayn, its port, became flourishing centers. It was the Mediterranean trade, however, that developed most strikingly during this period. The Ḥafṣids were the first to promote it. The treaties made by Yaḥyā I (Abū Zakariyā') with the Italian cities were renewed. The merchants lived in fonduks administered by their consuls. Duties were fixed once and for all at ten percent and paid to the Diwān al-Baḥr. In 1353 the Pisans, taking advantage of the amir's extreme weakness and urgent financial needs, persuaded him to recognize the personal liability of each merchant in case of conflict. Pisan merchants established themselves in Bône, Bougie, Sfax, Gabès, and Jerba, importing and exporting the same articles as in the days of the Zīrids and Almohads. The same situation prevailed in the west. The Genoese monopolized the trade of Ceuta, where they often engaged in espionage for the benefit of the Aragonese and Castilians. In principle the Venetians sent a fleet to Bādīs, which had become virtually the port of Fez, once every two years; trade relations also developed with Aragon, which in 1357 signed a friendship pact with Fāris (Abū 'Inān). The foreign merchants chiefly frequented the Mediterranean ports; on the Atlantic they went no further than Salé. Morocco exported slaves, leather, carpets, cereals, sugar and coral; it imported, as did Ifrīqiya, wines, cloth, and metals. These goods were carried largely by European ships, for in the course of the fourteenth century the Europeans achieved naval supremacy in the western Mediterranean. It was to compensate for this inequality and also to combat the frequent duplicity of the Spanish and Italian merchants, that the North Africans, especially those of Bougie, began to engage in piracy.

The maritime trade of this period is often represented as a mark of prosperity. In reality it enriched only the amirs and their entourages; in this it differed radically from the Saharan trade, which traversed the interior and involved the whole country. The significant fact is not that the one was operated at a profit and the other at a slight loss, but rather that the one unified the country while the other divided it. The new Mediterranean trade favored the autonomy of the makhzen by providing it with regular revenues and by encouraging its monopolistic policy. The makhzen entered into a de facto alliance with the foreign merchants, who thus became a force in internal politics. By favoring the autonomy of the amirs, the merchants helped to divorce the makhzen from the community and created dissension. In the long run the autonomy of the amirs might have been beneficial and helped to reinforce the state, but the general situation in the Mediterranean did not permit the maritime trade to expand sufficiently for that. Under the circumstances its effect was purely negative: it merely sustained a weak power, putting it more in opposition to society as a whole. This was only a beginning, but in it we can already perceive a certain stability bearing within it the seeds of stagnation and decay.

As we have said, the middle of the fourteenth century (end of the eighth century H.) was a critical point in the history of the Maghrib. This is particularly true because Ibn Khaldūn (1332-1406), who lived in that period, reconstructed the previous history of the Maghrib beginning with the seventh century. He drew from his work a theory of history that was both sociological and judgmental (i.e. based on a pessimistic view of history). He was thus both the consciousness and the victim of his time. It seemed to him that he was living at the end of a world. He felt this and described his feelings with such poignant intensity that no Maghribi writer since has been able to free himself from a sense of impending doom. Ibn Khaldūn's thesis is that there is a cleavage between political power and civil society: the one is related to the other as nomadism is related to city life (any anteriority is a logical rather than a chronological one). The course of history is determined by political power. But political power depends on a force (tribal cohesion or, more generally speaking, group consciousness) that is not constant but on the contrary is bound to spend itself. From this follows the value judgment that the decline of civilization, assimilated to city life, is similarly ineluctable. The process is repeated over and over again, in cycles.[13] Obviously this theory is a rationalization of the events we have just related, a schematization of the three imperial ventures. Ibn Khaldūn makes no attempt to explain history before the eleventh century, except by modeling the Zanāta of the first period on those of the second. And he offers no perspective on the future. Nowhere does he say that tribal structure and nomadism go hand in hand and that consequently the Hilālī nomads might resume on their own account the earlier efforts of the Berbers. He seems to have thought that the Arab race had long been exhausted and that consequently the weakening of the Berbers meant the end of all civilization, that there was no possibility of a renewal from within, and that the history of the Maghrib was at an end. Thus his work, far from being a rational interpretation of history, is a philosophy of history arising from an abstract analysis of a historical sequence. Like Machiavelli it reflects a profound crisis, but explains nothing and offers no solutions.

[13] A bibliography of Ibn Khaldūn would be almost endless. The reader is referred to Lacoste, *Ibn Khaldoun*; Nassar, *La Pensée réaliste*; Rabi', *Political Theory*; Lahbabi, *Ibn Khaldoun*. These recent studies in no way detract from the value of Mahdi, *Ibn Khaldūn's Philosophy of History*.

From Ibn Khaldūn the colonial historians borrow only what he has to say about the role of the Bedouins, into which, as we have seen, they inject their own racial prejudices by playing on the ambiguity of his Arabic vocabulary. Divesting the Khaldūnian concepts of all their subtlety, Gautier reduces the history of the Maghrib to an incessant struggle between nomads and the sedentary population. He distinguishes three attempts to build a state. The first was undertaken by the Aghlabids and Idrīsids, representing according to him the sedentary population, in opposition to nomadic Khārijism; it saved the legacy of Roman civilization, but brought no decisive result. Next the sedentary Kutāma, under the ideological cover of Shī'ism resumed the struggle against the nomadic Zanāta; they won important victories, but on the brink of defeat the Zanāta were saved by the Banū Hilāl. The third and last attempt was that of the sedentary Almohads of the Atlas, who gained the upper hand over the allied Zanāta and Banū Hilāl and might have triumphed completely if not for the political blunder of moving the Banū Hilāl to the Atlantic plains. From then on the Bedouins were everywhere and dominated the political scene; the consequence was general and lasting anarchy. It is not hard to see that this theory is alien to the thinking of Ibn Khaldūn, which it purports to clarify. In Ibn Khaldūn, *'aṣabīya* (group feeling) is a condition for the exercise of power and has nothing to do with nomadism; for Gautier it becomes a purely harmful force. Moreover, Gautier's theory ignores the facts it cannot explain, such as the success of the undoubtedly nomadic Almoravids or the Marīnid contribution to civilization. In general it may be said that Gautier fails to clarify what is obscure in Ibn Khaldūn (the period from the eighth to the eleventh century), but succeeds perfectly in obscuring what is clear in Ibn Khaldūn (his account of the imperial ventures). In spite of its numerous weaknesses, Gautier's theory was taken over in simplified form by H. Terrasse and C.-A. Julien (R. Le Tourneau), for whom the Bedouin becomes a deus ex machina who turns up when needed to account for the inevitable failure of the successive dynasties.

As for the Arab writers, they are afraid either to accept or to reject Ibn Khaldūn; in general they take a highly abstract view, stressing victories and quickly passing over defeats, so leaving the field to Gautier's disciples.

Perhaps the time has come to place the problems outside the Khaldūnian framework, though at present there is little hope of arriving at solutions. It cannot be doubted that a crisis occurred in the mid-fourteenth century, but to study this crisis we shall have to determine its internal and external causes, and this is impossible within the frame of Ibn Khaldūn's thinking, because he knew nothing of the history of the other Mediterranean nations and failed to define nomadism, which according to the circumstances can be an external or internal factor, either both at once or alternately. The internal causes cannot be reduced to the conflict with the Bedouins. The Bedouin problem was a secondary phenomenon, resulting from the demographic situation and the situation of agriculture and the Saharan trade. If these are beyond our knowledge, we shall do better to confess our ignorance than to mistake secondary for determining causes. But of course we cannot stop there. Taking the general decadence as a working hypothesis, we can use Ibn Khaldūn's reflections as indications of the problems confronting Maghribi society at the time: essentially those of political organization and of the army. The first was primarily a question of legitimacy; after the Shī'ite, Almoravid and Almohad experiments, an orthodox doctrine took form and imposed itself at the very moment when the state was losing its ideological militancy. It was no accident that the *fuqahā'* readily accepted and often justified the duality of a theoretical caliphate and of a sultanate whose legality depended entirely on its ability to defend itself. This was the climate that suited them best; but if authority had become purely a matter of force, the problem of legitimacy could no longer be solved. The dynastic state of the thirteenth and fourteenth centuries, responding solely to social and psychological trends, had become its own justification. Thus, looking back at the past, Ibn Khaldūn came to regard all religious doctrine as pure political ideology. It was in the light of a lost legitimacy that *'aṣabīya* took on its meaning, for if there had been a legitimacy, the various elements within the group would have curtailed their ambitions; they would have developed an ethos of submission and sacrifice, or vied with one another in producing positive complementary works. For lack of this self-imposed limitation (*wāzi'*), they could only destroy each other. The second problem was the impossibility of organizing a permanent police force or army; hence the recourse to mercenaries, the preeminence of the Banū Hilāl, and the stagnation of military technique; the army had ceased to be a force for organization and progress. This development of course was connected with the absence of legitimacy and still more with the decline in the population. It can nevertheless be analyzed as a problem in itself. Thus the decline of the Almohads takes on a special significance, because the Almohad army was a national nucleus and as such anticipated subsequent developments.

Legitimacy, national army—these two notions become meaningful only if we consider the Maghrib in relation to the general history of the Mediterranean region. The period from the eleventh to the fourteenth century was marked by a weakening of the eastern Mediterranean countries—Byzantium and the Islamic world—and a strengthening of Western Europe. At first this benefited the Maghrib but soon produced the contrary effect; hence the ambiguities of the Almohad apogee. It is quite possible that the three cyclic sequences described by Ibn Khaldūn resulted in the last analysis from military defeats, caused in turn by divergent developments in the realms of commerce and political organization on the two shores of the Mediterranean. In any event, the increasing strength of Western Europe accelerated the internal decay of the Maghrib. The de facto alliances between the Banū Hilāl and the Normans against the Zīrid state and between the Marīnids and the Castilians against the Almohad empire were no accident. Up to the fourteenth century, there was a certain balance of power. This made possible attempts to build empires and provided favorable conditions for cultural development. At the beginning of the fifteenth century the balance of power was shattered and the decline began. Its mechanism is easily described: increase in the power of the Bedouins, impoverishment of the state, struggles among pretenders, economic and cultural regression. The relations between these different aspects are complex and ambivalent, rich in theoretical possibilities; they provide the substance of Ibn Khaldūn's thinking. But despite his acute analysis of the situation, he takes no account of the causes that produced it. His vision is static rather than genetic. Unless this is recognized, we cannot hope to understand the history of the Maghrib.

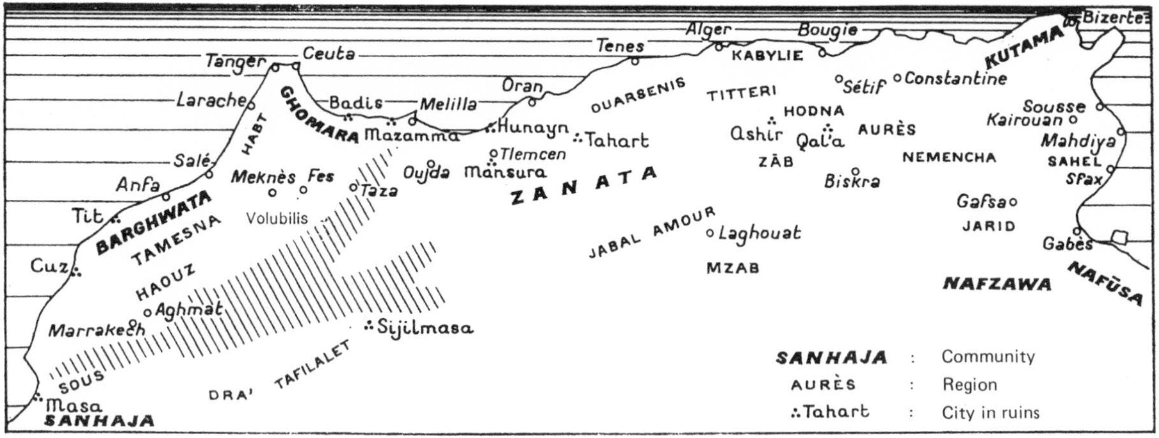
Bizerte
KUTAMA
Alger
Bougie
Tenes
KABYLIE
Tanger
Ceuta
Sétif
Constantine
Oran
OUARSENIS
TITTERI
Larache
Badis
Melilla
HODNA
Sousse
Kairouan
GHOMARA
Mazamma
Hunayn
Tahart
Ashir
Qal'a
AURÈS
Mahdiya
HABT
Tlemcen
ZĀB
NEMENCHA
SAHEL
Salé
Meknès
Fes
Taza
Oujda
Mansura
Biskra
Sfax
Anfa
ZANATA
Gafsa
Tit
BARGHWATA
Volubilis
JARID
TAMESNA
JABAL AMOUR
Laghouat
Gabès
Cuz
MZAB
HAOUZ
NAFZAWA
NAFŪSA
Aghmat
Marrakech
Sijilmasa
SOUS
TAFILALET
DRA'
Masa
SANHAJA
SANHAJA : Community
AURÈS : Region
∴Tahart : City in ruins

PART III
Institutional Stagnation

10. The Western Crusade

The two centuries between the death of the Marīnid sultan Abū 'Inān and the defeats of the Spaniards at Tunis (1574) and of the Portuguese at El Ksar (1578) are a period of deep-seated regression, which for this very reason may well be one of the most significant periods in the history of the Maghrib. As we shall see, its history shows a marked resemblance to that of the nineteenth and even the twentieth century in certain parts of the Maghrib. This resemblance has been interpreted as an indication that the history of the Maghrib has been a static history, and as such reflects the fundamental structure of the society and its collective psychology. It must be pointed out, however, that this structure did not simply exist, without beginning or end, but came about as a consequence of a specific development. Ibn Khaldūn's disenchanted view of his period seems fully justified: with its disintegrating state, declining agriculture and stagnant internal trade, the Maghrib seemed almost to be inviting the conqueror in, from near or far. The life of the cities was dying out; power was being increasingly dispersed among the leaders of the mercenaries, who first became feudal barons, then, with the decline of agriculture, mere tribal chiefs interested only in feeding themselves and their followers.

This weakness encouraged foreign intervention, which in turn only aggravated and perpetuated the state of disequilibrium and was in the end decisive. The Maghribi attempts at recovery, however successful temporarily, were ultimately condemned by this foreign presence, regardless of whether it was imposed by force or called in by the Maghribis themselves. Nothing is more indicative of the decadence of this period than the extreme aridity, and even futility, of contemporary historiography.[1] As long as the monarchies survived, the court writers and poets went on devoting pompous poems and rhymed prose to feats of arms hardly worthy to be mentioned in family chronicles. Disregarding out of ignorance the threats that were taking form on the other side of the Mediterranean, these hack historians affected enthusiasm for the illusory victories of the last Marīnids or Ḥafṣids over the increasingly helpless Zayyānids. Consequently they tell us nothing about the condition of the declining Maghrib. The more the state disintegrated, the more the historians concentrated on local matters; every tribal chief and every religious leader had his own historian to celebrate his achievements.[2] This literature, taken in conjunction with the works on practical jurisprudence (*fiqh*),[3] which flourished at the time, is our only possible source for the politico-social conditions of the period; unfortunately it has not yet been studied systematically. The European accounts growing out of the Iberian expeditions are no more reliable than the works in Arabic;[4] they provide a kind of golden legend of the Spanish and Portuguese aristocracy and only marginal information about life in the Maghrib. They tell of local chiefs, but give us a distorted view of their words and actions. An adequate interpretation of these Iberian sources requires a knowledge of the Arabic juridical literature. The most informative work on the period is that of

[1] This observation applies also to Ibn Khaldūn's histories (cf. the reign of Ibrāhīm Abū Sālim, whose private secretary he was), and a fortiori to such writers as Ibn al-Aḥmar or Ibn Abī Dīnār (*al-Mu'nis*). See also Muḥammad al-Karrāsī, *Arūsat al-Masā'il*.

[2] E.g. Ibn 'Askar, *Dawḥat al-Nāshir*, and its English translation; or al-Qādirī, *Nashr al-Mathānī*, and its French translation.

[3] E.g. the *Mi'yār* of al-Wansharīsī, which has not yet been studied from the point of view of social history.

[4] For particulars, see *Sources inédites de l'histoire du Maroc*, ser. 1, pt. 1 (Portugal); various bibliographic articles by Ricard in *Hespéris*, some of which are reprinted in *Etude sur l'histoire des Portugais au Maroc*; Braudel, "Les Espagnols en Algérie," especially pp. 234-250; Brunschvig, *Deux récits de voyage inédits en Afrique du Nord au XVe siècle*.

Johannes Leon Africanus.[5] His life is symbolic of the fate of a certain isolated, desperate, and skeptical Maghribi élite. Born in Granada, he was brought up in Fez. Captured by Mediterranean pirates, he was sent to Rome and baptized. There he wrote a remarkably accurate description of a good part of North Africa, which was consulted by all European explorers and conquerors down to the nineteenth century. His book is extremely useful, especially for the light it throws on the fifteenth century, but should be taken as a picture not of a static world but of a phase in a process. This unfortunately has not been the case since Massignon's study, written more than half a century ago. The older Maghribi writers tended to avoid this period, as do also those of today. Yet until it is adequately studied, we cannot hope to understand what is meant by "tribal structure," which was characteristic of the period of decadence in the Maghrib.

I

(A) Decadence and the Iberian offensive are the major elements in the history of the Maghrib during this period. That history unfolds in two stages. The first is characterized by the decline of Marīnid Morocco and the preeminence of Portugal in the expansion of Iberian power; the second, by the general disintegration of the Maghrib and by the preponderance of Spain.

The second half of the fourteenth century (eighth century H.) was characterized by an equilibrium among the three weakened monarchies. In the fifteenth century, the Marīnids and Zayyānids continued to decline, while Ifrīqiya experienced a recovery which saved it for a time from foreign intervention but perhaps also prevented it from finding the

[5] *The History and Description of Africa.* See the introduction to L. Massignon, *Le Maroc dans les premières années du XVIe siècle*; al-Hajawi, *Ḥayāt al-Wazzān al-Fāsī;* Mauny, "Note sur les 'Grands Voyages' de Léon l'Africain."

internal resources necessary for its defense when the foreigners, whose strength had vastly increased in the meantime, finally attacked.

In Marīnid Morocco the tendency to fragmentation was aggravated during the last decades of the fourteenth century by two new factors: the preeminent role of the viziers, due to family ties and their *'iqṭa'*, and the continued intrigues of the Zayyānids, the amirs of Granada, and the Spaniards. The vizier al-Fūdūdī finished off the dying Abū 'Inān (1358/759) in order to insure the accession of his own candidate; another vizier, Ibn Māsāy, put forward another candidate, but it was a third candidate, Ibrāhīm (Abū Sālim), who finally won out, thanks to the help of Pedro el Cruel, king of Castile. He dismissed al-Fūdūdī, but soon another minister, 'Umar b. 'Abd Allah,[6] with the support of the commander of the Christian mercenaries, deposed Ibrāhīm in favor of Tāshfīn, one of his brothers, who was totally unfit to rule because long captivity in Castile had affected his mind. In 1366/768, under 'Abd al-'Azīz, an attempt was made to remedy the situation. The ambitious viziers were executed or dismissed; al-Hintātī, the powerful and quasi-independent lord of the Atlas, was subdued in 1370, and Tlemcen occupied. By 1372 the Marīnid kingdom was reunified, but the sovereign died that year and under his son, al-Sa'īd, the rivalry between viziers resumed. The Naṣrid intrigues culminated in the accession of Aḥmad al-Mustanṣir, who became a mere tool in the hands of Granada. But this did not prevent the Andalusian amir, under the influence of the banished vizier Ibn Māsāy, from raising up a rival against Aḥmad. Aḥmad withdrew, but returned in 1387/789, recovered his throne with the help of the Ma'qil who controlled the Sijilmāsa region, and executed Ibn Māsāy. He rewarded his Ma'qil allies by giving them access to the Atlantic plains while leaving them their privileges in southern Morocco. At the death of al-Mustanṣir in 1384/786, the

[6] He, too, bore the ethnic appellation al-Fūdūdī. The name of the first was Ḥasan b. 'Umar (cf. al-Nāṣirī, *al-Istiqṣā*, vol. IV, pp. 3 and 37).

struggle among the viziers was renewed, and in the end one of them, a member of the Waṭṭāsid family, took 'Abd al-Ḥaqq, the last Marīnid amir, under his protection and governed in his place.

During this entire period the Marīnids, despite their weakness, continued to exert direct or indirect control over the neighboring Zayyānid kingdom. Thus the same political forces were at work in both countries. Thanks to his long reign and the difficulties of Abū 'Inān's successors, Mūsā II had managed to reorganize his kingdom. In 1360, however, he was attacked by Ibrāhīm (Abū Sālim) and obliged to evacuate his capital. In 1370 it was again taken by 'Abd al-'Azīz. When the amir of Fez was too weak to intervene directly, he put a vassal Zayyānid prince on the throne. Two of these vassal princes were Abū Tāshfīn II, who took power in 1388/791, and Abū Zayyān II, who mounted the throne in 1394/797. These vassal princes never remained loyal for long, but the Marīnids always had a fugitive prince available, whom they could quickly transform into a serious pretender by supplying him with money and troops. When this was impracticable, it was always possible to capture Tlemcen. Aḥmad al-Mustanṣir did so during each of his two reigns. The last attempt at direct government was that of 'Uthmān III; after various ups and downs he succeeded in 1411/814 in imposing 'Abd al-Wāḥid (Abū Mālik), who tried to find a way out of his hopeless situation by turning eastward. Unfortunately for him, Ifrīqiya was in the midst of a revival, and in escaping from Marīnid tutelage the Zayyānid kingdom merely became subject to its Ḥafṣid neighbors.

Several times during this period the southern part of the Marīnid kingdom had declared its independence, and the Marīnids' control over Tlemcen was never secure. Both these developments are explained by the increasing importance of the Ma'qil, who had become the main power in the central Maghrib before extending their domination southward to the western Sahara. Meanwhile conditions in

Ifrīqiya had become relatively stable. After the departure of Abū 'Inān, Ibn Tāfrāgin reigned as absolute master until 1364-1365/766. At his death the struggles among Almohads, Andalusians and Arabs were intensified, and all the governors declared their independence. Ibrāhīm II and his son Khālid II made no attempt to oppose this fragmentation. Finally the governor of Constantine, Aḥmad, the nephew of Ibrāhīm II, revolted against his cousin and captured Tunis in 1370/772. He put some order into the kingdom, reduced the autonomous cities of Sousse, Mahdiya and Gabès, reconquered Jerba and the Jarīd, and revoked all the territorial grants. Succeeding where the two Marīnid sovereigns had failed, he prepared the way for the recovery that was to take place under 'Abd al-'Azīz (Abū Fāris) at the beginning of the fifteenth century.

(B) While the Maghrib was destroying itself in futile struggles, Aragon, Castile and Portugal, aided by the Italian city-states, gained in economic and military strength. The crusades in the east had ended in failure, but on the whole had been economically profitable, and above all they had struck a fatal blow at the Mediterranean trade of the Moslem countries. Everything impelled the Christian states to continue the struggle against Islam. The crusading spirit was still alive. Foreign campaigns served both to fill the royal coffers and to keep the Church and the aristocracy busy. In 1326 the Turks had taken Brusa and in 1337 made their first serious attack on Constantinople. When it failed, they undertook a vast flanking movement, crossing over into Europe and gradually isolating the Byzantine capital. Alarmed by the Turkish advance into Europe, the Pope sent out an appeal for a crusade. The Iberians received it with sympathy, but rather than fight the Moslems so far from home they preferred to attack western Islam, which still had a foothold on their peninsula. After 1340 the Marīnids were no longer able to send expeditions to Spain, though they continued to supply the amir of Granada with mercenaries, who made up the bulk of his army.

The consequence of this state of affairs was a series of attacks on the seaports of the Maghrib. Ifrīqiya had experienced such attacks under the Zīrids, but the Almohads had put an end to them. They resumed during the first period of Ḥafṣid decline, especially after 1270. During the reign of al-Mustanṣir II the Sicilian fleet under the admiral Roger de Lauria made several attacks on the island of Jerba and finally occupied it in 1286; it was liberated only in 1335, under Abū Bakr II. The Kerkenna islands were also taken and Mahdiya was attacked several times, though unsuccessfully. In the west, two incursions coinciding with grave political crises had marked the beginning of the new era. In 1234/632, during the reign of the Almohad al-Rashīd, the Genoese laid siege to Ceuta and withdrew only after receiving a large payment of ransom.[7] In 1260/658, at a time of indecisive conflict between the Almohads and the Marīnids, the Castilians attacked Salé and held it for several weeks. At the end of the fourteenth century, Christian incursions became more frequent both in the east and west. In 1355 the Genoese attacked Tripoli and occupied it for a short time; in 1390 Mahdiya was attacked by a Franco-Genoese expedition; in 1399 the Aragonese attacked Bône, and the Castilians destroyed Tetuán. In the fifteenth century the recovery of Ifrīqiya discouraged such attacks, while the increasing weakness of the western Maghrib invited out-and-out conquest.

The organizers of these first incursions (thirteenth and fourteenth centuries) were well informed on the political situation in the Maghrib. Attacks became more frequent in periods of crisis. They owed their information to the relations between the Christian powers and the emirate of Gra-

[7] The city, which was autonomous at the time, was obliged to pay four hundred thousand dinars. Despite obvious exaggerations, the *Ikhtiṣār al-Akhbār* of al-Anṣārī gives an idea of the wealth of Ceuta.

nada, and to the activity of the Genoese merchants, whose vital role in the reconquest of Spain is often passed over in silence. The raids seem at first sight to have been made haphazardly, but they all served a definite purpose: to gain control of the Mediterranean. When the Italians and Iberians achieved their end, the Maghribis, unable to defend their own commerce, resorted to piracy, just as the English did two centuries later in combating the Spaniards. This piracy, centering chiefly on Bougie, was a form of warfare, the response of the Maghribis to the Christian monopolization of the Mediterranean trade. In passing judgment on the piracy of later centuries, we must not forget its original causes.

It was to make their control of the Mediterranean still more complete that the Italo-Iberians began to seize the ports of the Maghrib, which had been greatly weakened by the stagnation of trade in the fourteenth century. The Portuguese took the first step. Incited and advised by the Genoese, but also impelled by political and economic self-interest (competition with the Castilians), King John I organized an expedition against Ceuta, which presented little difficulty in view of the political weakness of the Marīnids in 1415/318.[8] The first attempts to recover it—undertaken by 'Uthmān III in 1419—were unsuccessful, and Ceuta, which had so often revolted against its Moroccan sovereigns, went the way of Andalusia. In capturing it, the Portuguese must have acquired considerable spoils. Otherwise, the place itself was of little use to them. Emptied of its inhabitants, isolated from its hinterland, the once flourishing port became a dead garrison town and an increasingly heavy drain on the Portuguese treasury. The aim, however, had been to

[8] The Portuguese version (of Zurara, for example) should be compared with al-Nāṣirī's account (*al-Istiqṣā*, vol. IV, p. 92) of the agreement made years before the fall of Ceuta by the amir with the Genoese and Portuguese merchants, granting the merchants complete freedom within the limits of the port, so placing them beyond the control by the local authorities. This of course facilitated the conquest.

bar the Maghribis from the Mediterranean. The conquest of Ceuta was not followed up until the end of the fifteenth century, when Spain and Portugal made an agreement, allotting to each its "sphere of influence." From then until the first part of the sixteenth century, their control over the coast of the Maghrib was uncontested. Today it is difficult to characterize the North African policy of the Iberian powers. Was it an early form of colonialism? A continuation of the crusades? Or the mere consequence of an upset in the balance of power, exploited almost in spite of themselves by the more powerful states? Good reasons have been adduced for all these analyses, which are at the same time value judgments. Undoubtedly economic motives played a part, but those of the Portuguese are more evident than those of the Spaniards. The upset in the balance of power is also undeniable, as is shown by the diplomatic intrigues and politico-military alliances of the time.

Nevertheless, the determining motivation seems to have been religious, and the Iberian assault on the Maghrib must essentially be regarded as a crusade, a reaction to the failure of the crusades in the Holy Land and to the new Turkish threat in eastern Europe. It was made possible by the weakness of the Maghribi states; its instrument was commercial imperialism (monopoly on the Mediterranean trade and asphyxiation of the North African ports); but its inspiration was religious. This western crusade attained its apogee during the first third of the sixteenth century. The Maghribi reaction was not a religious response to economic aggression, but a countercrusade—belated to be sure—against what was clearly conceived as a crusade.

II

Before the disintegration of the Maghrib became general and before the Iberian offensive developed its full force and scope, Ifrīqiya enjoyed a period of recovery lasting three-quarters of a century, during which the Ḥafṣid amirs were in a sense the kings of the Maghrib. After the death of Aḥmad II (1393/796), the conditions of Aghlabid and Zīrid prosperity—energetic rulers, comparative peace, a unified territory, a flourishing trade—appear to have been restored. A modus vivendi had been arrived at with the Banū Hilāl, who again recognized the sovereignty of the state. 'Abd al-'Azīz (Abū Fāris, 1393-1434) subdued the Banū Sulaym; the Marīnids, to whom they appealed for help, were no longer capable of action so far from home. The revival of trade is indicated by the fact that the Ḥafṣid fleet, led by Raḍwān, was able to carry out successful expeditions against Malta and Sicily. The state treasury was full (the territorial taxes were being collected, and the duties on internal and maritime trade had increased). The amirs built fortresses and palaces, the remains of which can still be seen in Hammāmāt, or Rafrāf, for example, while in Tunis they repaired the mosques and aqueducts, and built a hospital (*māristān*). They were also able to take action in the west. The Zayyānid 'Abd al-Wāḥid, at first a client of the Marīnid amir, had broken with his protector, who had consequently deposed him and put Muḥammad II on the throne; whereupon the Ḥafṣid amir took Tlemcen and restored 'Abd al-Wāḥid to power (1427/831). Then the Ḥafṣid proceeded to Fez, where the Waṭṭāsid regent, who had not yet consolidated his position, hastened to recognize his (quite theoretical) suzerainty. The Ḥafṣid returned home satisfied, though in reality nothing was settled. Two years later Muḥammad II took Tlemcen again and executed his rival. In 1430/834, Abū Fāris sent a second expedition and enthroned Aḥmad al-'Āqil, who three years later declared his independence. Thus the political accomplishments of the Ḥafṣids were no more lasting than those of the Marīnids a century before, but at least they show that Ifrīqiya itself was at peace. The kingdom had indeed been unified. Tripoli was retaken in 1398, Tozeur and Gafsa in 1400, Biskra in 1402, Algiers in 1410. 'Uthmān, the second successor of Abū Fāris, took Nafta in 1441 and Tuggurt in 1449. The amirs of Ifrīqiya had never gone so far south since the early days of the Arab conquest. The Ḥafṣids maintained their protectorate over Tlemcen, though they had to bolster it up now and then by a show of force.

Still, the extent of the Ḥafṣid revival should not be exaggerated. Without resources, defended by an army of Bedouin mercenaries whose loyalty was more than doubtful, Tlemcen nevertheless managed on several occasions to hold the Ḥafṣid army at bay. The Ḥafṣid recovery seems real enough when compared to the fragmentation that had preceded it and the conditions prevailing elsewhere in the Maghrib. But despite their energy, the Ḥafṣid amirs of this period never attained the level of the Zīrids whom they took as models. At the death of 'Uthmān III, in any event, Ifrīqiya entered on a new decline. Yaḥyā III had to contend with revolts in Bône, Gabès, and Sfax, and none of his successors was able to retrieve the situation. Freed at last from its two contending protectors who had imposed their tutelage for three centuries, the kingdom of Tlemcen, unable to take advantage of its autonomy, disintegrated in turn and the struggle between the princes installed in Oran or Ténès and the ruling amirs of Tlemcen continued.

The situation in the west was still darker. Until 1458 'Abd al-Ḥaqq, the last Marīnid sultan, was governed by his Waṭṭāsid regents. The Portuguese had gone no further than Ceuta. After the fall of Constantinople, the Pope called for a crusade. Alfonso V, king of Portugal, raised an army, but instead of sending it eastward, he ordered an attack on al-Qsar, which was taken in 1458 and in the years that followed served as a base for raids on Tangiers. 'Abd al-Ḥaqq put the blame for these defeats on Yaḥyā, his Waṭṭāsid guardian, who unlike his father and cousins was incompetent, and setting an ambush for the Waṭṭāsids massacred them all. Only one, Muḥammad al-Shaykh, escaped by chance and shut himself up in Arzila. There he organized opposition to the Marīnid, who on his return from an expedition was taken prisoner by the population of Fez and executed as a renegade in 1465. After an unsuccessful attempt at an Idrīsid restoration, al-Shaykh concluded a truce with the Portuguese and entered Fez in 1471. Breaking the truce, the Portuguese occupied Arzila and Tangiers, which had been left defenseless. This was the end of the Waṭṭāsid dynasty, whose power had never extended beyond northern Morocco. In 1471 the Moroccan state, as founded by the Almoravids, ceased to exist.

At the end of the fifteenth century, the fragmentation became general. Tripoli, Bougie, and Constantine were independent of Tunis; Oran contended with Tlemcen; Marrakech had ceased to recognize the authority of Fez; the oases of the south from Tuggurt to the Dra‘ valley were controlled by various groups of Banū Hilāl. The long-range overland trade was disorganized; its point of departure was controlled by the reconstituted kingdoms of the Sudan,[9] and the caravan trails were at the mercy of independent Hilālī chiefs. The dissatisfaction of the populations with rulers incapable of defending them expressed itself in a profound religious crisis. The remnants of authority were dispersed among the councils in the coastal cities, the tribal chiefs, and the leaders of the religious brotherhoods, who were acquiring more and more influence.

The Iberians soon took advantage of this power vacuum. In 1494, two years after the fall of Granada, Spain and Portugal, at the instigation of the Pope, came to an agreement, specifying the respective zones of their future conquests. In 1496 the duke of Medina Sidonia persuaded Queen Isabel to send him to Mellila at the head of an army; after waiting in vain for help, the inhabitants evacuated the city which was occupied by the Spaniards. Some years later the powerful Cardinal Jiménez organized an expedition against Mars

[9] The reconstitution of these kingdoms in the western Sudan (Mali), whose wealth was symbolized by the gifts sent to the Marīnid amirs (including the famous giraffe, which arrived in Fez in the reign of Abū Sālim), must be seen as an indication of the weakening of the Maghrib.

al-Kabir (1505), which capitulated after three days. Oran, which had been fortified in haste by the Zayyānid Muḥammad V, was lost by treachery in 1509; Bougie was taken in 1510 from a Ḥafṣid prince who had long been independent. Algiers, Dellys and Ténès, all autonomous by then, surrendered to Pedro Navarro. In 1511 the Spaniards destroyed Tripoli, then ceded it to the king of Sicily. In 1512, Muḥammad V, amir of Tlemcen, went to Burgos and swore fealty to the king of Spain. At the same time the Portuguese took possession of those cities of the Atlantic coast that were independent of the amirs of Fez and Marrakech, with which they had already been maintaining commercial and even political relations. Safi was occupied in 1507/913, and Azemmour in 1513. Thanks to the fortresses of Santa Cruz de Aguer (in the harbor of Agadir), built in 1505, and of Mazagan, not far from the old Almohad ribāt of Tīt, which they occupied in 1515, the Portuguese now controlled the entire coast.

Thus the Portuguese and the Spaniards, at small expense to themselves, carved out an empire in the Maghrib and so consolidated their control of the maritime trade. They found no difficulty in occupying the cities, since they were already autonomous, so that even if a state had existed it would not have helped them. By their intervention in local politics, the Iberian leaders accelerated the disintegration of Maghribi society. In the Oran region, Pedro Navarro made pacts with the local leaders, so reinforcing them in their opposition to the amir in Tlemcen; similarly in the Ḥaouz region, the Portuguese armed Yaḥyā b. Ta'fūft, who was at war with al-Ḥintāṭī, the autonomous amir of Marrakech.

This general disintegration, which lasted until 1574 and is described in detail by Leo Africanus, was no more than an evolution of tendencies that had already been at work in the fourteenth century. But it was intensified by the Iberian offensive and so prolonged that subsequent attempts to halt it carried within themselves the seeds of dissolution. The Maghrib never really overcame this centrifugal tendency.

III

Certain characteristics deriving from this period survived until very recently. Lasting internal frontiers were established. The long and indecisive struggle between the Marīnids and Zayyānids resulted in a line of demarcation, which continued to undergo certain changes, but within increasingly narrow limits. Likewise in the east, the continual revolts of Tripoli, Bougie, Bône and Constantine showed that the central power could hope to control no more than the northern part of present-day Tunisia. There was always a greater and a lesser Ifrīqiya, and the latter was to constitute modern Tunisia. These two delimitations were to enable the central Maghrib to take form through the slow fusion of the old Ḥammādid and Zayyānid territories.

Here we have a geographico-political tripartism, superimposed on the old socio-historical tripartism which had been accentuated in every period of crisis, and which in the period under discussion took the form of an increasingly sharp cleavage between cities, the agricultural countryside, and the mountain regions. The fall of Granada, followed by the reign of the Inquisition and the decree of expulsion in 1502, brought a wave of refugees to the Maghrib. Since government employment worthy of their talents was no longer available, they turned to commercial undertakings and developed into a new middle class, in competition with the local merchants and artisans. The weakness of the governments inspired them with contempt and a spirit of independence which might have led to a kind of bourgeois revolution, if as outsiders they had not been isolated from the local population. As it was, their very existence was an obstacle to the development of a prosperous and self-reliant native middle class.

The plains had long been under the control of the Banū Hilāl, whose chiefs had steadily consolidated their authority. But they had ceased to be professional soldiers, their ties with the central authority had become almost nonexistent, and agriculture had declined in their territories. Thus the possibility of becoming feudal barons was no longer open to them. The essential under such conditions was the control, not of lands, but of the population. This they achieved by converting their tribal structure into a form of political organization and integrating the local population into their own tribal subdivisions. Thus what had started out as a biological or social structure became a form of administration or local government.[10] With the return of peaceful conditions, the revival of agriculture, and the emergence of a central power capable of gaining the loyalty of the local chiefs, the structure might have provided the foundation of a feudal system. For long years, however, all these developments were impeded by foreign pressure. The Hilālī chiefs continued to be warlords (a few of their names have come down to us); their position always depended on the fortunes of war and was never really consolidated.

The mountains were cut off from the central authority by these local powers who shared the plains. As at the end of the Roman period, the population consisted of three elements, at this epoch Moors, Arabs and Berbers. The distinctions they designate were not so much racial as socio-historical. In Ibn Khaldūn's time they still engaged in political rivalries, because the state still offered an arena for their quarrels. Once the state had disintegrated, the three groups merged in their common rejection of the outside world and settled down to a long period of isolation in which they developed their own traditions, religious practices, and manner of speaking.

[10] For the present this must be taken as a working hypothesis. Its main advantage is that it introduces a social dynamic into the history of the Maghrib. It goes without saying that the writings of ill-informed foreigners from the sixteenth century down to our own day cannot be used as arguments against it. The only sources that can legitimately be used to confirm or refute it are the legal texts (*fatāwā*). Hence the capital importance of al-Wansharīsī's *Nawāzil*. Until this compendious work is completed, everything that has been said about the social history of the Maghrib must be put down to prejudice or speculation.

Unlike the tripartism that marked the end of another historical era, this tripartism was confined to the middle Maghrib. The south had already been cut off (Tuggurt had its autonomous sultans, Sijilmāsa was no more than a memory), and now the coastal cities were lost. The great sovereigns of the ensuing centuries were to be those who at least for a time extended their power to the northern fringe of the Sahara. In losing the Sahara, the Maghrib lost the very knowledge of the source of its wealth.

The question to be asked is whether there were any internal possibilities of overcoming the crisis. An analysis of the situation in the fifteenth century and of the subsequent development shows that the decline had all the elements of permanence. The falling-off of trade impoverished the cities, making them reluctant to pay taxes and desirous of autonomy. The decline of the cities impoverished the royal treasury and weakened the army. This encouraged the local chiefs to break with the central authority, which further weakened it. The foreign invaders were well aware of this situation and made the most of it. Power was divided among three elements—the amirs, the virtually autonomous cities, and the local chiefs—each of which tended to negotiate on its own and accept vassaldom.

Thus at a time when the countries of southern Europe were experiencing the Renaissance, the great voyages of discovery, and colonial expansion, those of the Maghrib entered on a dark age that lasted until Portugal and Spain were replaced as dominant powers by Holland and England, which were not interested primarily in North Africa, and until new elements, military (the Ottoman empire) and religious (the Marabout movement), entered upon the scene.

11. Two Reactions, Two Powers

From the sixteenth century on, our sources for the history of the Maghrib become more and more abundant. Does this make for greater clarity? With the consolidation of the new —Sa'did and Turkish—powers, a new official historiography developed, which, it goes without saying, makes much of victories over the Spaniards and Portuguese. But since the diplomatic game became exceedingly complicated in the middle of the century, a number of important points are passed over in silence or misrepresented, especially in the pro-Sa'did literature.[1] The local and family historiography that sprang up under the last Waṭṭāsids and Zayyānids enables us, however, to correct or complete the official versions. This family literature was much studied at the beginning of the present century,[2] but the political aim of the scholars engaged in studying it was to establish the historical titles of certain religious and social notables as a means of winning them over to French policy. This led them to stress the religious aspect and to disregard the essential problem, namely, the dialectical relation between the Marabout movement and the restructuring of society on the model of the Hilālī tribe. To what extent did the former supersede the latter? At what time did the latter movement, which had been halted for a time, resume, and why was it able to annex the former? An answer to these questions is essential for an understanding of the eighteenth century, but they were neglected because they had no bearing on the aims in hand. The sixteenth century was a century of contacts,

[1] The essential point of course concerns Al-Ghālib's negotiations with the Spaniards, his cession of Vélez (Bādīs) in 1564 and his role in the revolt of the Moors. The unfavorable version is given in Colin, *Chronique anonyme*.

[2] Studies by E. Michaux-Bellaire, A. Coure, A. Bel, R. Basset, and M. Bencheneb, synthesized by Lévi-Provençal, in his *Historiens des Chorfas*, and by Berque, *Al-Yousi*.

both pacific and warlike, between the countries on either side of the Mediterranean. These contacts gave rise to a literature in European languages,[3] from which, despite its obvious flaws (religious prejudice and feudal outlook), the standard works on the history of the precolonial Maghrib have derived the bulk of their material. The archival sources for the sixteenth century are also more abundant and more accessible than for the preceding period.[4]

Although the foreign sources have not yet been exploited to the full, it seems necessary to draw attention to their major fault. Apart from their ritual and obviously exaggerated accounts of Christian slaves in the Maghrib,[5] they put too much stress on piracy (a Mediterranean and not specifically Maghribi phenomenon), on commerce (which was marginal), on diplomacy (which in view of its futile and ephemeral aims was hardly deserving of the name), and on local chiefs (petty condottieri). To be properly understood, this copious literature would have to be interpreted in the light of the dynamic of Maghribi society as a whole. But since this is largely inaccessible to us, the literature in question is reduced to a mass of meaningless or opaque information.[6] Unfortunately many present-day Maghribi historians allow themselves to be dazzled by these false riches and

3 It includes numerous accounts of missions and captivities, histories such as that of Diego de Torres on the Morocco of the Sharifs, of Father Dan of Haedo on Algeria, among others. See the references in Julien, *Histoire de l'Afrique du Nord*, 2nd ed., vol. 2, pp. 342, 346, and Fisher, *Barbary Legend*, p. 97.

4 Despite the work done on Morocco in *Sources inédites*, on Tunisia by G. Grandchamp, and on Algeria by E. Plantet, it seems clear that much remains to be done in connection with England (Fisher, *Barbary Legend*), the Italian cities (Braudel, *The Mediterranean and the Mediterranean World*), and especially Turkey (Mantran, "L'Evolution des relations entre la Tunisie et l'Empire ottoman du XVIe siècle au XIXe siècle."

5 Fisher, pp. 102, 103.

6 This is the principal defect of the studies of Lacoste, Noushi, and Prenant in *Algérie passé et présent*, and of Gallisot, "Essai de définition," which rely too often on eighteenth-century accounts and fail to note the basic fact that only contemporary Arabic works might throw light on the crucial problems of Maghribi social structure.

judge the greatness of a king by the number of ambassadors he sent to the court of England or Spain.[7] If we are not to lose ourselves in irrelevant detail, we must consider the available data in relation to the essential questions, which are: the degree of cleavage between society and state, the nature of the local authorities, the level of culture and technology.[8] These questions, it might be argued, are alien to the spirit of the times and therefore incommensurable with the data at our disposal. But how, unless we at least raise these questions, can we hope to perceive the history of the Maghrib in its dynamic and continuity or to understand the objective causes of the "traditionalism" that was gradually to engulf it?

Two Reactions

The Marabout Movement and the Sa'did Power

As we have seen, the beginnings of the Ṣūfist movement date back to the Almohad period. Its essential aim was to democratize and deepen the Islamic faith. It flourished during the thirteenth and fourteenth centuries thanks to the encouragement of the Marīnids and Zayyānids, who hoped through the Ṣūfīs to establish a certain degree of legitimacy. Their attempt to channelize it by setting up madrasas where the study of orthodox theology and law would counteract its radicalization was unsuccessful, for as the central power grew weaker the Ṣūfist movement developed and formed autonomous groups. The formal organization, oriental in origin, is well known: a group of disciples (*ṭālib, murīd*) gather around a master (shaykh) and undergo a long process of initiation. When a student is judged capable of teaching,

[7] E.g. the accounts of the diplomatic activities of the Sa'did al-Manṣūr and of Muḥammad III. See Muḥammad al-Fāsī's introduction to Ibn 'Uthmān al-Miknāsī's *Al-Iksīr*.

[8] Several technical innovations imputed to the Arabs in Spain and Sicily seem to have been unknown in the Maghrib. If they had been used for a time and then forgotten, at what date were they reintroduced? E.g. the wagon (*kariṭa*) in Ibn Abī Ḍiyāf, *Itḥāf*, vol. II, p. 31.

he becomes the nucleus of a new initiatory group (*zāwiya*). The consequence is a decentralization of religious teaching, compensated by an oath of fidelity which by binding the disciples to the master makes for unity and continuity. This form of organization played an essential role in certain parts of the Maghrib down to the beginning of the twentieth century. Its functions were fourfold: religious, social, political and military. From the start the character of the movement reflected both its origins and its aims. Moderate, avoiding the esotericism of similar oriental and Andalusian movements, it made no attempt to replace the orthodox teachings but represented itself as their optional complement, so disarming the suspicions of the *fuqahā'*. Free from the individualism of the Ṣūfī extremists, it stressed the needs of the community and thus attracted a popular following. In regions beyond the control of the central authority, the *zāwiya* became the center of community life. The people took to rewarding the Ṣūfīs with gifts (*ziyāra*) for their public service, including the education of children. In the face of the Iberian threat, the *zāwiyas* became centers of defensive warfare (*ribāṭ*), which explains why this popular mobilization independent of the state is often referred to as the Marabout movement. At first the movement was not directed against the central power, but the state was too weak either to suppress it or to preempt it, and in the end the Sharīfs took it over. Indeed, its internal logic (the preeminent role of the master, the supernatural gifts conferred by piety, the concept of occult knowledge) made the movement receptive to legitimist claims. But though it ultimately converged with Sharīfism, Maraboutism preserved certain specific traits, remaining an educational movement and a force for decentralization. The two movements are symbolized by two men. Al-Jazūlī (d. 1465/870),[9] who carried on a vigorous campaign against all those of his compatriots who had commercial or political dealings with the Portuguese on the Atlantic

[9] See the article "Djazūlī" in *EI*[2] and references. See also and especially Muḥammad al-Mahdī al-Fāsī, *Mumti'*.

plains,[10] became the spiritual master of the Marabout movement; Muḥammad al-Sa'dī, a descendant of Sharīfs who had come from the Hedjaz in the middle of the thirteenth century and settled in the Sous, undertook to make war on the Portuguese in the south. To this end he set up headquarters near Taroudant and gave himself the title of al-Qā'im bi-Amri Allāh, with its distinctly Shī'ite ring. From the start he tried to identify himself with the Jazūlite anti-Portuguese movement. In 1511, he sent his two sons to Fez to obtain an authorization to levy troops. In 1512/918 he established himself at Afughāl, al-Jazūlī's old *zāwiya*. He died in 1517/923, but his two sons, Aḥmad al-A'raj and Muḥammad al-Mahdī, succeeded, thanks to the intense Jazūlite propaganda, in driving out both Yaḥyā b. Ta'fūft, who had allied himself with the Portuguese, and the Hintātī amir of Marrakech. By 1529 the two brothers had taken possession of the southern half of Morocco, which they divided between them, the one residing in Marrakech, the other in Taroudant. These victories alarmed the Waṭṭāsids in Fez and war broke out in 1536, but the ulama interceded,[11] and the autonomy of the kingdom of Marrakech was recognized. Then a decisive event occurred, which tipped the scales in favor of the Sa'dids. For years English ships had been putting into the ports of the Sous in an attempt to break the Portuguese monopoly on the African trade. In 1541[12] Muḥammad al-Mahdī, having obtained artillery from the English, attacked and captured the fortress of Santa Cruz. (The unexpected consequence of this first victory over the Portuguese was the

[10] It seems likely that the decision to occupy Safi and Azemmour after a long period of protectorate was due to the virulence of this campaign. The occupation would then coincide with a deterioration in the political position of the Portuguese.

[11] A significant fact, which proves the existence of a public opinion capable of thwarting dynastic ambitions. The days of Khaldūnian policy were over.

[12] See Willan, *Studies in Elizabethan Foreign Trade*. The ships, owned by Englishmen, Dutchmen and even Portuguese smugglers, were based at Antwerp. The earliest voyage for which there is a written record was made in 1551.

evacuation within ten years of all the towns they had occupied, except for Ceuta, Tangiers and Mazagan (today El Jadīda), which they kept for fiscal reasons.[13] The prestige of the Sa'dids was thereby greatly enhanced and in 1545/951 Muḥammad al-Mahdī, who in the meantime had taken the lead over his brother, was proclaimed sultan in Marrakech; the road to Fez was open. But from the outset the Sa'did power was dependent on three elements—foreign trade (with England and later the Netherlands), the political support of the *zāwiyas*, the patriotic or religious fervor of the population.[14] The first of these was not always compatible with the other two. A centralizing dynastic policy based on foreign support and conspicuously indifferent to the liberation of the cities occupied by the Iberians was bound to provoke strong opposition.

Turkish Condottieri and Ottoman Power

Before the western Mediterranean became the scene of a bitter struggle between the two world powers of the sixteenth century, the Ottomans and the Spaniards, several Turkish adventurers arrived in the Maghrib in quest of principalities. One of these, 'Arūj, who had made a name for himself by helping the Andalusian victims of the Inquisition, established himself in Djidjelli in 1514 and acquired great prestige with the population and its religious leaders by his attacks on Spanish ships. Seeing a possibility of throwing off the tutelage of the Spaniards, the city of Algiers sent for him. There he quickly consolidated his position and had himself proclaimed sultan despite the opposition of the traditional chiefs. The Spaniards tried to dislodge him, but he defeated them and easily took possession of Miliana, Médéa and Ténès. Thereupon Tlemcen revolted against Abū

13 On the causes of the Portuguese débâcle, see Lopes, "Les Portugais au Maroc," pp. 337-368. Terrasse, *Histoire du Maroc*, vol. II, pp. 118-122, still prefers to put the blame on their "limited occupation."

14 For a nationalist interpretation of the Marabout movement, see Muḥammad Hajjī, "L'Idée de nation au Maroc aux XVIe et XVIIe siècles."

Hammū III, its Zayyānid amir and opened its gates to him. Abū Hammū joined forces with the Spaniards of Oran and besieged him. Finally, in 1518/942 'Arūj was defeated and killed. Thus this first Turkish venture ended in failure, but by then the Ottomans were in Egypt; already they dominated the eastern Mediterranean and were looking west. The Ottoman sultan Selīm conferred the title of pasha beylerbey on 'Arūj's brother Khayr al-Dīn and provided him with artillery as well as an army of six thousand men with which to fight the Spaniards. Little by little he conquered northeastern Algeria. In 1529 he took the Peñon and began at once to build the port of Algiers. Then, taking advantage of a revolt against the Ḥafṣid al-Ḥasan he invaded the neighboring kingdom and entered Tunis without difficulty in 1534/941.[15]

The two new powers had developed along similar lines, attacking the Iberian invaders and their allies with a new or foreign army and a new weapon, artillery. Their clearly expressed ambition to reunite the country was violently opposed by those who had benefited by the years of chaos. Both the Turks and the Sharīfs met with strong resistance in the more or less autonomous cities (Marrakech, Fez, Algiers, Tlemcen) and among the local chiefs who, intent on preserving the fiefs they had won by diplomacy or force, were prepared if need be to support the ousted Ḥafṣid, Zayyānid and Waṭṭāsid princes on pretext of loyalty to their hereditary sovereigns.[16] Nevertheless, despite serious difficulties, the new powers were victorious with the help of the religious leaders grouped around the *zāwiyas*.

As we have seen, there were two reactions to the Iberian invasion. The difference between them was not primarily geographic but resided in the character of two élites—on the one hand the leaders of the *zāwiyas*, on the other the autonomous local chiefs. Both groups strove to restructure

[15] The date given in the Arabic texts is 936/1529. The chronology is inexact. See al-Jādirī, *al-Zahra al-Nā'ira*.

[16] See Ibn Abī al-Ḍiyāf, *Itḥāf*, vol. II, p. 21.

a disintegrated society. In the western Maghrib the religious leaders had the field to themselves. In the east, however, a movement to restructure society on the Hilālī model had been at work for three centuries. In geographical terms, the social difference between the two movements created a cleavage between Ifrīqiya with its predominantly Hilālī structure and the western Maghrib with its structure determined by religious brotherhoods. For forty years various systems based on alliances and counteralliances were to succeed one another and overlap. In the great Turco-Spanish confrontation the dynasties, the *zāwiyas,* and the local powers were to side with one or the other camp according to the circumstances. Needless to say, the fate of the Maghrib was decided elsewhere, that is, in Europe. But once the battles of Tunis and El Ksar had put an end to the ambitions of the Iberian conquerors, the structural difference here described exerted a determining influence on the new powers.

Two Powers

The world-shaking events of the mid-sixteenth century (1534-1578) had repercussions in the Maghrib.[17] The African campaign of Charles V—Tunis was taken in 1535 and Tlemcen in 1543 after an unsuccessful attack on Algiers in 1541—resulted in the restoration of the Ḥafṣid (Ḥasan) and Zayyānid (Muḥammad VI) princes, but under such conditions that the populations longed fervently for the return of the Turks. The Spanish victories benefited the new Sa'did power. The Waṭṭāsid amir could no longer hope for direct help from the Turks, to whom he appealed in 1548 when Muḥammad al-Mahdī was proclaimed sultan of Morocco. With the support of the Jazūlites, al-Mahdī easily conquered the north, entered Fez in 1549, and went on to besiege Tlemcen. This development was welcomed by the Span-

[17] See Braudel's fundamental work, *La Méditerranée et le monde méditerranéen sous Philippe II,* esp. pp. 723-760 and 963-984 (for an English translation, see bibliography).

iards, for from their point of view it was preferable to have the Turks opposed in western Algeria by a Sharīf whose prestige was still intact than by a discredited amir. The consequence was a tacit alliance between the Sa'dids and the Spaniards.[18] In Tunis, the Turks, exploiting the popular discontent, helped Aḥmad to revolt against his father. In 1556 Darghūt, following in the footsteps of 'Arūj, captured Gafsa, and two years later entered Kairouan. In the west, taking advantage of the weakness of the Sa'did army (which in 1551 had incurred a defeat due to poor tactics and lack of artillery) the Turks intervened in behalf of the Waṭṭāsid Abū Ḥassūn whom they enthroned in Fez in 1553. Nevertheless, their position was weak and they were restrained by the sultan in Constantinople, who had other preoccupations. The following year the Sa'did recaptured Fez and encircled Tlemcen. It was not until 1557 that Ḥasan Corso, the interim beylerbey, succeeded in getting rid of him, and then by assassination. With the appointment of 'Ulūj 'Alī[19] as beylerbey of Algiers they embarked on a more aggressive policy. By then Tlemcen was in the hands of a Turkish governor. In 1569 Aḥmad II was driven from Tunis and replaced by the qaid Ramḍān, the beylerbey's right-hand man. After their victory at Lepanto (1571) the Spaniards took Tunis—for the last time. The Turks countered with a powerful expedition and in 1574 recaptured it for good. 'Ulūj 'Alī then prepared to attack the Sa'did 'Abd Allah al-Ghālib, who had been negotiating with the Spaniards with a view to a joint attack on Tlemcen. At this point al-Ghālib died, leaving the throne to his son Muḥammad. The late king's two exiled brothers, 'Abd al-Mālik and Aḥmad, had long been serving in the Ottoman army. The beylerbey decided to help them take power. The Turkish army made its way to Fez without difficulty, Muḥammad surrendered

[18] This convergence of interests made an alliance almost indispensable, even though neither side could afford to set down its terms in writing.

[19] Even in the old manuscripts the Arab spelling of the name varies; the most frequent versions are 'Alūj and 'Alj, which mean renegade.

after the first skirmishes, and 'Abd al-Mālik was made sultan (1576) under Turkish suzerainty. His submission, however, was short-lived, and the beylerbey was contemplating the conquest of Morocco when once again the Iberians embarked on a crusade. After trying in vain to win Philip II to his cause, Muḥammad, the ousted Sa'did, persuaded Sebastian, the young king of Portugal, to send a large expedition. At first 'Abd al-Mālik made concessions in the hope of averting the danger, but Sebastian was fired with enthusiasm and wanted his war. The battle was fought south of Arzila. The invading army was large and well equipped, but 'Abd al-Mālik had won the support of the Jazūlites, who mobilized public opinion. 'Abd al-Mālik was killed but immediately replaced by his brother Aḥmad, and the outcome was a great victory for the Moroccan army (August 4, 1578).[20] Morocco was now delivered once and for all from the tutelage not only of the Iberians but also of the Turks, who abandoned their plans for conquest. The equilibrium thus established was enduring. Of all the Iberian conquests, only Oran, Mars al-Kabir and Melilla remained in the hands of the Spaniards; Ceuta, Tangier and Mazagan in those of the Portuguese. Morocco with its present boundaries had escaped from the Turkish orbit and was to remain independent from then on. After 1587 Algiers, Tripoli and Tunis became the capitals of three provinces, each governed by a pasha beylerbey. Thus the fate of the Maghrib had been decided on the Mediterranean, to which it no longer had access. But by then, as Braudel writes, history had left the Mediterranean behind. Here we may ask what the impact of these events and those that followed was on the Maghrib. For if we rely wholly on official or foreign historiography, we are unable to explain a number of glaring contradictions: a terrifying political instability and the impressive wealth of the cities; the diplomatic and military prestige of the three Maghribi sovereigns side by side with

20 See Bovill, *The Battle of Alcazar.*

economic and social stagnation; a noteworthy cultural and artistic development despite the fragmentation of society. How are we to account for them? The explanation is that once again our historians have confused the state with society and the seaports with the interior, while ignoring the marks left by the decadence of the fourteenth and fifteenth centuries. It is true that there were now two powers in the Maghrib, the Sharīfs in the west, the Turks in the east. But rather than dwell on this geographical and political dualism, which is none too illuminating, the historians would have done better to concentrate on the dualism between the state and society. It had played a dominant role since the thirteenth century, and now in the sixteenth it had attained full force. There were two economic systems, two partial societies, two political powers existing side by side, ignoring, when not combatting, one another. Apart from the city-states, inhabited by foreigners living by piracy and commerce, and the mountain regions, which were almost always isolated and where the nature of the life pursued remains largely a mystery, the history of this period is reduced to an uninterrupted conflict between the army and the local powers.

Autonomous city-states developed in Algiers, Tunis and in lesser degree in Tetuán and Salé, all sharing in the Mediterranean economic system. Their population was cosmopolitan, and moreover, their principal source of revenue, piracy, was a phenomenon unrelated to the central problems of the Maghrib.[21] It was carried on by renegades. Their armament and equipment were of foreign origin, and most of the profits went to foreign intermediaries. The commerce to which piracy gave rise involved only a small minority of the population, and the diplomatic relations it engendered

[21] Unfortunately Hubac's often suggestive book, *Les Barbaresques*, sometimes verges on fiction. But its main idea, that piracy was a European phenomenon, caused by the economic asphyxiation of the southern countries by the great national states of the north, is sound. See also Fisher, p. 139.

are hardly deserving of the name.[22] It must be regarded as a phenomenon of purely local interest, without long-term effects.

The great novelty in the Maghrib of this period was a new type of army. Largely foreign, made up of Turkish volunteers periodically recruited in Anatolia, it was organized along democratic lines. Toward the end of the century it assumed direct power, reducing the pasha, who represented the sultan in Constantinople, to a figurehead. It was a self-contained society, isolated from the population, and its internal history (intrigues and assassinations) had little effect on the overall development of the Maghrib. In the Sa'did kingdom, the core of al-Manṣūr's army (which occupied the Sudan) consisted of freed renegades, Andalusians, Turks and Zwāwa from the mountains of Kabylia. This army imposed itself both on the city-states and on the rural populations and became the sole intermediary between the two social and economic systems. The grain collected by way of taxes was exchanged for arms and equipment that were passed on to the pirates, whose activities swelled the population of slaves who tilled the fields outside the cities while waiting to be ransomed. But this army met with the opposition of the local powers, so weakening the state it supported and making it passive and conservative.

As for the central and eastern Maghrib, the historians have dwelt at length on the relations between the representative of the Ottoman sultan—the pasha, the spokesman of the corsairs—the chief of the Ṭā'ifa, and the army's elected representative—the dey. But the conflicts between the dey and the bey, who was in close contact with the rural population, are passed over in silence. There may be a certain justification for this in the case of Algiers, which was oriented definitively toward the sea. Thus any idea of non-Turkish society must be based on the study of the local histories of Constantine

22 The importance that has been attached to these very modest diplomatic relations is explained by the nineteenth-century notion of "historic rights."

and Orania, taking the former as representative of western Ifrīqiya and the latter as representative of the region coinciding with the old kingdom of Tlemcen. Despite the introduction of a new administrative boundary, the old social and historical dividing line (roughly, the meridian of Algiers) had not been effaced, and the conditions prevailing at the time in the two parts of the central Maghrib were approximately the same as in Ifrīqiya, on the one hand, and in Sa'did Morocco, on the other.[23]

The determining factor in the history of Ifrīqiya at the end of the sixteenth century and in the seventeenth century was the continuous struggle between the deys and the beys. Though they were both Turks, the conflict between them masks the resistance of the local shaykhs to the central power, by then appropriated by the Ottoman army (*ūjāk*). The majority of these shaykhs had been pro-Ḥafṣid, hence pro-Spanish, and unlike the inhabitants of the capital they had not suffered greatly from the atrocities of the Spanish soldiery (the sack of 1535). With the Turkish victory they found themselves in a difficult position. With the support of the local religious leaders, the Turkish administration proceeded to punish them for their pre-Spanish stand. Under 'Uthmān, the first dey, the famous Ramḍān Bey (d. 1613) waged war on the shaykhs of the Abī al-Layl, the Awlād Ḥamza, the Awlād Sa'īd, and even on such mountain tribes as the 'Amdūn. But in the course of this warfare it occurred to the bey that the shaykhs could be used as a means of pressure on the dey and the Turkish army. Ramḍān's successor, the freed slave Murād, obtained the honorific title of pasha from the dey and founded a dynasty of beys. The dey soon ceased to be anything more than the administrator of the capital and of the Turkish militia. The bey's army changed in structure, absorbing more and more local elements. The struggles between the Murādid family and certain of the deys of Tunis

[23] Only in the local histories of Tlemcen and Constantine will it be possible to find data throwing light on the social structure of the central Maghrib.

and Algiers from 1675 on reflected the determination of the Turks to recover control of the state and that of the local shaykhs to regain their former prerogatives.[24] When the people of Kairouan rebelled under the bey Murād III, he forced them to destroy their own houses. His assassin and successor Ibrāhīm al-Sharīf, who was both bey and dey, resolved to eradicate the "Arab" mode of life in the country.[25] This had the effect of rallying the whole population to the local shaykhs, who at least were restrained by a traditional communitarian morality. The evolution was thus complete; the Hilālī structure was now firmly established; the former mercenary leaders had become the acknowledged representatives of the people, and their despotism was found to be infinitely preferable to the unrestrained tyranny of the Turkish soldiers. The power of the Turks could not be destroyed, but now at least it was counterbalanced by the existence of a local authority. Once again the Hilālī structure had changed in character. This transformation was brought about by the inability of the new regime to identify itself with the nation, not the contrary as has too often been asserted. The new beylical dynasty of the Ḥusaynids drew the consequences and arrived at a modus vivendi with the local shaykhs.

The development in the west was roughly the same. The Sa'did power was largely dependent on a new army, which required a full treasury, hence regular and generalized taxation. The Marabouts had already established a system of taxation, which served to ransom prisoners and to support the war against the Iberians. Thus there was a source of friction from the start. The mountain regions refused to pay any new taxes and found effective support in the *zāwiyas*. Muḥammad al-Shaykh tried to conquer the Atlas, which had formerly submitted to al-Hintātī, but was not entirely successful. In 1547 he summoned the heads of the

[24] Ibn Abī al-Ḍiyāf, *Itḥāf*, vol. II, pp. 47 and 59.
[25] *Ibid.*

zāwiyas to Marrakech and massacred them. Weak and threatened by the Turks, 'Abdallah al-Ghālib was more modest in his ambitions. He won the support of some of the shaykhs by granting them privileges, so incurring the hostility of the others. Under Aḥmad al-Manṣūr (1578-1603), thanks to unusually favorable circumstances, a compromise was arrived at. The victory of al-Qasr (Wādī al-Makhāzin for the Arab chroniclers) had cemented the alliance between the Marabout movement and the Sa'did dynasty, in part by solving the fiscal problem for the moment. The large amount of war materials taken sufficed to equip al-Manṣūr's army, while the troops were paid out of ransom collected for the numerous Portuguese nobles who had been taken prisoner. Al-Manṣūr's entire policy consisted in finding outside sources of income, at which the local authorities could not take umbrage. The sugar trade of Chichaoua was farmed out to English merchants, who enjoyed a strict monopoly from which the Moroccan population was excluded.[26] The principal goal of al-Manṣūr's reign, the conquest of the Sudan, undertaken despite the unanimous opposition of the ulama,[27] was envisaged from the start as a source of taxes and loot—taxation of the salt mines and control of the gold mines.[28] Similarly al-Manṣūr's great project of an anti-Spanish alliance with Queen Elizabeth was motivated by the calculation that he would receive arms and subsidies from the English but would take his time about meeting his contractual obligations. Small wonder that the Queen's ambassadors accused him of cupidity and bad faith. It is not our intention to belittle the qualities of al-Manṣūr, who was the first and perhaps the only ruler of Morocco before the twentieth century to conceive a modern national policy, nor do we deny the power and magnificence of the Sa'did

[26] See Paul Berthier's documented study, *Les anciennes Sucreries du Maroc*, pp. 221-265.

[27] Fishtālī, *Manāhil al-Safā* (partial edition).

[28] *Ibid.*, p. 55.

monarchy, the numerous contemporary witnesses to which cannot all have been blind or naive.[29] But in order to understand the period that followed al-Manṣūr's reign without resorting to psychological interpretation, we must remember that the sources of the wealth were not indigenous and that the power resulted from a compromise with local authorities. These two facts are clearly indicated by the secrecy with which al-Manṣūr surrounded his projects. Was he so beset by Spanish and Turkish spies that he had to devise a code?[30] Or was it the leaders of the *zāwiyas* that he mistrusted? Be that as it may, as soon as the outside sources on which al-Manṣūr counted to replenish the treasury and supply the army dried up (Moroccan sugar was driven from the English market by Brazilian competition; the Sudan stopped sending gold; and with the simultaneous dwindling of the Turkish and Spanish threats, alliances with Morocco ceased to be of interest to anyone), the state collapsed like a house of cards for all al-Manṣūr's efforts to reorganize the administration on the Almohad model, updated with Turkish costumes, titles and etiquette. The army disintegrated, al-Manṣūr's sons appealed to foreigners to support their claims to the succession (Zaydān to the Turks, al-Ma'mūn to the Spaniards). Again the kingdom was divided between Marrakech and Fez, and behind these ludicrous conflicts, which recall those of the last Marīnids, the local powers regained their preponderance. Chief among these were the city-states such as Tetuán and Salé, which negotiated directly with the English and the Dutch, condottieri such as al-'Ayāshī (d. 1641), who fought the Iberians, and above all the *zāwiyas*, the most important of which, that of Dilā', came close to reunifying Morocco.[31] This quick resurgence of the local powers makes it clear that even in al-Manṣūr's time they

[29] See Bovill, *The Golden Trade of the Moors*, p. 180, where a letter written in 1594 by Lawrence Madoc, an English merchant residing in Marrakech, is quoted: "This king is like to be the greatest prince in the world for money if he keeps this country [the Sudan]."

[30] Fishtālī, *Manāhil al-Safā*, pp. 160-161.

[31] See Hajjī's study, *Al-Zāwiya al-dilā'iya*.

had not disappeared but had merely accepted a compromise with the dynasty in the interest of the struggle against the Iberians.

Thus in both the east and west of the Maghrib, under the Turks and under the Sharīfs, the state was strong only when it was independent of society and maintained its power only by recognizing the legitimacy of the local powers. In both cases, it was a mere shadow of a state, because it was not rooted in the soil of the Maghrib. In its basic structure, this state, which at first seems to have introduced significant novelties, was only a faint copy of the thirteenth- and fourteenth-century states. In the west the legitimacy of the state was contested by the Marabout movement and in the east by the Hilālī shaykhs. This difference was fraught with consequences.

Conclusion

Was this development inevitable? Those who ask this question immediately divest it of all interest either by demanding superhuman clairvoyance of the Maghribis (foreknowledge of the consequences of the absolutism of Queen Elizabeth or of Henri IV of France), or by imputing to them an incurable psychological defect (apathy or lack of curiosity).[32]

Let us limit ourselves to noting certain facts. A number of Andalusian refugees, we are told, went to Tunis at the beginning of the seventeenth century, and the dey 'Uthmān gave them lands. They built cities, introduced new farming methods and opened roads suitable for wagons (*karīṭa*), which they alone used.[33] All these "innovations," however, had been known centuries before, but forgotten. After 1541, and especially during the reign of Aḥmad al-Manṣūr, the

[32] Terrasse, *Histoire du Maroc*, vol. II, p. 103; Monlaü, *Les Etats barbaresques*, p. 116.

[33] See also Ibn Abī al-Ḍiyāf, *Itḥāf*, vol. II, p. 12, on the cannon mounted on wheels used by Khayr ad-Dīn in his attack on Kairouan.

English came to the coasts of the Sous to buy saltpetre, indispensable to them because the secret of producing it artificially, discovered in Germany, was well guarded. Years later the English had no further need for it, and the Moroccans not only made no progress in the manufacture of gunpowder but forgot what little they knew. Similarly, the Moroccan sugar industry died out once the collapse of the Sa'did state had put an end to the English monopoly. In the matter of both technical progress and technical regression, the determining factor is to be sought not in contact with foreign countries or the ingenuity of individuals, but in the structure of political power. In the situation that concerns us here, progress would have strengthened the local authorities (armaments, trade duties, etc.). Consequently the "state" regarded progress as a threat and did everything possible to discourage it.

On the other hand, the consolidation of the local authorities, Maraboutic in the west and "tribal" in the east, did not signify an increase in exploitation; that is, it did not aggravate the misery of the population or impede cultural development. On the contrary, independence from the central authority and the cities made for a paternalistic egalitarianism and a wider distribution of culture. After the profound decadence of the fourteenth and fifteenth centuries, Moslem culture spread through the whole country, even, by means of the small rural schools and the *zāwiyas*, to the mountain regions.[34] Thus centralized power was by no means a condition of social or cultural progress, or a guarantee of civil rights. Yet this culture, the product of an urban civilization, was too diversified for the society that was trying to assimilate it, and many of its elements were unresponsive to internal or local requirements. The thinking of the Turkish and Sa'did rulers had been molded by Constantinople and Almohad Marrakech; the culture of the thirteenth century was the highest aspiration of these men of the sixteenth and

[34] Al-Sūsī, *Sūs al-'Ālima,* cites two hundred schools in the province of Sous alone.

seventeenth centuries. How could they have been expected to discover anything new when relearning the past was in itself a kind of progress? The inhabitants of the inland cities (Fez, Tlemcen, Kairouan), who had no means of participating in the commercial life of the seaports, were obliged to seek a new social role. This they did by integrating themselves with the movement of "culturation" led by the *zāwiyas*.[35] This, and not the shortsightedness of the rulers or the people's lack of curiosity, was the actual basis for the lapse into traditionalism.

[35] It is in this light that we must interpret the development of mysticism in the cities (Fez, Salé, Tlemcen, Constantine, etc.) and the rise of large Maraboutic communities such as the Qādiryīn, Fāsiyīn, and Nāṣiriyīn. This development provided a new social role for an élite that had ceased to find occupations in the administration or in commerce, but it also diverted and paralyzed their energies for a long time to come.

12. The Eve of Foreign Intervention

During the eighteenth century the city-states lost much of their autonomy with the falling-off of piracy, which had been their main source of revenue. Especially in the western Maghrib, agricultural production did not increase appreciably. The struggle between the central power and the local powers continued unabated. The maritime trade developed to some extent, but since it was still under foreign control and benefited primarily the ruling minority, it could not become a force for the unification of society. Little by little the military threat of Europe gave way to economic infiltration. But the various regions of the Maghrib did not react uniformly to these developments, and this accentuated the differences between them.

The Ḥusaynid Beylicate

The system tended slowly toward both stabilization and "nationalization," which took the form of a return to the Ḥafṣid tradition.

After 1711 the regime took on the character of a hereditary monarchy, though as in the suzerain Ottoman dynasty the principle of primogeniture was not explicitly adopted. In theory the bey held absolute power. But the army, which was the mainstay of this power, was Turkish only in part. It consisted of three elements: the janissaries, who were always imported from Turkey; the *makhāznīya*, a kind of police force made up of local elements; and the *mazārqīya*, contingents levied among the population as the need arose. Though the Turks remained predominant in the higher echelons, the governing class tended in the course of the century to absorb more and more local elements. The janissaries, who had lost their preeminent position, revolted in 1743 under 'Alī Pasha, and later under Ḥammūda II and

Maḥmūd. They were finally disbanded by Ḥusayn II. The development was even more pronounced in the administration. At the end of the eighteenth century Ḥammūda II instituted a kind of cabinet. The old Ḥafṣid titles and functions—vizier, high chancellor, and lord of the treasury—were revived, and once more Arabic became the predominant language of the internal administration. One consequence of this reconciliation between the government and the urban population was a movement of internal colonization. The principalities of central Tunisia were absorbed and the nomads were pushed further and further south.

This Ḥafṣid renaissance accounts in large part for the relations between Tunis and Algiers. Since the preceding century the deys of Algiers had looked with misgiving at the weakening of the deys of Tunis and the concomitant takeover of the beys, which to them meant the end of Turkish absolutism. To block this development, they intervened whenever possible, taking advantage of family quarrels. But in the course of time their intervention changed in character. First Algiers helped Ḥusayn I's nephew ʿAlī, who revolted when the bey who had appointed him heir to the throne transferred the succession to his own newborn son. With the help of the dey Ibrāhīm (1732-1745), ʿAlī won out and in 1735/1148 took power in Tunis, promising to pay tribute to Algiers. As often happens in such cases, relations between the dey and his protégé deteriorated, and in 1746/1159 the dey switched his support to the sons of Ḥusayn I, who had been carrying on intrigues in Constantine where they had taken refuge. It was not until 1735, however, that they won their father's throne. After that the nature of the conflict changed. Its chief cause was now the expansionist policy of the bey Ḥammuda II, who first recovered the island of Jerba and then attacked Tripoli and Constantine. Under ʿAlī Pasha, the two beys of Tunis and Constantine competed for the allegiance of the border populations. Seen in perspective, all these events seem to indicate a slow but sure Ḥafṣid restoration, the essential reason for which was a rapprochement between the beylicate and the traditional élite of Tunis. The same tendency may be observed in the slow transformation of diplomatic relations with European countries, which little by little began to revolve around commerce rather than piracy. Tunis had a considerable navy, which participated in the Turkish wars, but the main confrontations between the beys on the one hand and France and Venice on the other resulted not from piracy but from commercial conflicts. In 1740 the bey 'Alī Pasha, to prevent the French and Genoese from developing their direct trade with the surrounding populations,[1] attacked their factories. And in 1784 the bey Ḥammūda attacked Venetian ships because Venice had refused to idemnify some Tunisian merchants whose wares, transported under the Venetian flag, had been seized in Malta. Piracy did not resume until during the Napoleonic wars, when the European countries set the example. Throughout the eighteenth century the ruling class—beys and viziers, Turks and non-Turks—was involved in the maritime trade, just as the élite of the Ḥafṣid emirate had been in its time. A series of treaties were negotiated with the leading European powers between 1710 and 1728, and subsequently renewed. As usual, the chief products exported were wheat and oil, while luxury articles and manufactured goods were imported. Increasingly this commerce was controlled by the French, who in 1781 set up a factory on Cape Bon, which soon dominated the Tunisian coastal trade. It was only in the nineteenth century that the English, needing Tunisian wheat to supply Gibraltar and taking advantage of their superior power in the Mediterranean, began to compete seriously with the French. This trade put the beylical élite and the urban élite into contact with foreign countries and encouraged them to undertake the internal colonization referred to above.

The Ḥafṣid renaissance was also manifested in the cultural and artistic fields. Enriched by trade, the beys, and even

[1] Cf. Ibn Abī al-Ḍiyāf, *Itḥāf*, vol. II, p. 124.

such ministers as Yūsuf Ṣāhib al-Ṭāba' built mosques, madrasas, and charitable institutions. It is significant to note that when the bey Ḥammūda built the palace of dār al-Bāy, he did not resort to the Turkish style but revived the Andalusian tradition. Whether or not he employed Moroccan artisans, as has been said, his desire to reestablish ties with the local past is evident. As to the new madrasas of al-Ḥusayniya or an-Nakhla, we find nothing very novel in the teaching they dispensed. But considering the total decadence of the early sixteenth century, which was not as in the west accompanied by a Maraboutic movement, we are inclined to regard this restoration as preparation for a potential renaissance.[2]

To sum up: Despite dynastic crises and the intervention of the deys of Algiers, Tunisia recovered its stability during the eighteenth century. The country was less wealthy than it had been, but the foundations of a wider development had been laid, for though the enlarged ruling class was still involved in the Mediterranean trade, it was beginning to take an interest in the interior. This development shows a certain parallel with Egypt. Tunisia took the lead, but then in the following century derived inspiration from the enlightened despotism of a Muḥammad 'Alī. And it was this development that made it receptive to the reformist ideas that made their appearance in the Ottoman world at the beginning of the nineteenth century. If in those days Tunisia looked eastward rather than to its neighbors of the Maghrib, the reason may be that it was already undergoing a "restoration" which would soon enable it to go beyond the stage of "traditionalist reform." Though this period has not yet been analyzed in depth, it seems reasonable to suppose that after the slow evolution of the two preceding centuries the return to Ḥafṣid cadres under the bey Ḥammūda was the first sign of a modern Tunisian nationalism.

[2] One indication of this cultural renewal was the rejection in Tunis of Wahhābism, which enjoyed a certain following in Fez. See Ibn Abī al-Ḍiyāf, vol. III, pp. 64-75; al-Zayyānī, *Al-Turjumān*, pp. 396, 402.

The Regime of the Deys of Algiers

The vast literature on eighteenth-century Algiers is concerned chiefly with the city-state, its politico-economic system, community life and foreign relations. In a world dominated by absolute monarchies, contemporary observers were struck by the special character of this military oligarchy, but the literature is no great help to the reader in search of an overall view, for it deals almost exclusively with the life of the Turkish minority and of the Europeans and Moorish emigrés from Spain who were associated with them in the administration and in commercial undertakings.[3] Far more important is the organization of the interior, for it was stabilized during this period and remained unchanged until well after the French conquest. The essential facts of the eighteenth century were the impoverishment of the city of Algiers and the concomitant consolidation of the local powers of the interior. The strongest indication of this is that the beys of Constantine and Orania became increasingly independent of the dey. In many respects the wars with the beys of Tunis and the sultans of Morocco recall the struggles between Zīrids and Hammādids or Marīnids and Zayyānids. Muḥammad b. 'Uthmān (1766-1791), the most capable of the deys of the time, tried to counter the political autonomy of the beys and to make himself king of Algeria, but the isolation of Algiers and its Turkish minority had become so deep-seated over the years that his efforts were doomed to failure.[4] The beys, especially the bey of Constantine, derived their strength from their direct contact with

[3] European foreigners in the eighteenth century, when absolute monarchy was the dominant form of government in Europe, took a considerable interest in the government of Algiers, no doubt because it appeared to them as the remnant of an outmoded regime. The dey was compared to the king of Poland, the Stathouder, or a secular pope. See Fisher, *Barbary Legend*, p. 330. Apart from purely formal accounts, however, we have little information concerning the real life of Algiers because it has never been studied in depth.

[4] Cf. the nationalist interpretation of al-Madanī, *Muḥammad 'Uthmān Pāshā*.

the local shaykhs. True, the qaids, former members of the *ūjāk,* were for the most part Turks, appointed by the bey at the suggestion of the agha, or commander of the local militia. But their power was contingent on the consent of the shaykhs. By and large the Turkish functionaries preferred a quiet life, and consequently the authority of the shaykhs increased from year to year. It was they who presided over the distribution of lands, collected taxes, and maintained order. Since the local history of the time has not been sufficiently studied, we know little of how the shaykhs acquired their authority. The new communities in the west seem at first sight to have been Maraboutic in origin, unlike those of the east that were based primarily on military power and wealth. But in reality religious prestige and economico-military power were everywhere present in varying degrees, and in view of the similarities in the social development of Tunisia and the beylicate of Constantine, on the one hand, and, on the other, of northern Morocco and Orania, the two types of local community attained their full maturity in the central Maghrib, largely because of the weakness and isolation of the central power. The ʿAlawite sultans were able to subdue, though not to destroy, the *zāwiyas;* the beys of Tunis allied with the urban élite succeeded in limiting the autonomy of the local communities by pushing them southward; but such measures were beyond the power of the deys or beys of Algiers. Even the army was affected more and more by this duality of power. It became more difficult to recruit men for the Turkish militia, whose strength decreased from twenty thousand in the early eighteenth century to four thousand a hundred years later—too few to man all the garrisons and fill the various administrative posts. The half-castes (*kurughli*), who never attained full equality with full-blooded Turks, were admitted to subordinate positions, but this measure further weakened the Turkish authority. The same causes increased the importance of the auxiliary troops, the *makhāznīya* (settlers on state lands surrounding strategic points and as such liable to military service) and the *gum*, contingents levied in time of need by the autonomous governors of Kabylia and the south, though they were far inferior to the Turkish militia in quality. What is significant from our point of view is the change in the relations between the two elements. As the army, the symbol of Turkish authority, lost its power of intimidation, force gradually gave way to diplomacy in the relations between the Turks and the indigenous population. The economic decline of Algiers made this development all the more inevitable.

The city-state lived by piracy and trade. The dey kept for himself all the tribute money,[5] the ransoms paid for prisoners, and a fifth part of the pirates' prizes. These resources dwindled throughout the century. Merchant vessels were better armed, and European pirates began to compete seriously with those of Algiers, so that negotiations resulted in an exchange rather than a ransoming of prisoners.[6] The falling-off of piracy was not compensated by trade. Customs duties and profits from concessions were small. Apart from wheat, which was in short supply in southern Europe, there was little foreign demand for the products of the Maghrib. As Algiers declined in wealth and population, the Turkish minority became increasingly dependent on the exploitation of the interior. The tithe on farm produce, the *zakāt* on herds, rents on makhzen lands, investiture taxes of all kinds, fines (*gharāma*), irregular taxes (*lazma*) on the autonomous populations of Kabylia and the south, were collected more and more strictly and regularly. Despite the show of strength that accompanied the two annual tax-collecting expeditions (*maḥalla*), the results depended on the prestige of the beys, which in turn hinged on their relations

[5] It is too often forgotten that these payments of tribute were the counterpart of a commercial monopoly. It was from the standpoint of modern free trade that they came to be regarded as discriminatory.

[6] The Turks of Algiers refused to ransom non-Turks; the Moroccan sultan Muḥammad III often ransomed Algerian captives. See Ibn 'Uthmān al-Miknāsī, *al-Iksīr*, p. 165.

with the local chiefs, for these chiefs, whether Marabouts or not, had their own systems of taxation. Thus the Turkish policy was contradictory, for on the one hand peace could be maintained and taxes collected only with the cooperation of the local shaykhs, while on the other hand the use of force drove these same shaykhs to head popular revolts on pain of being discredited with their populations.

The Turkish authority suffered from the resultant instability. Under the dey Ibn 'Uthmān the Kabyles revolted with considerable success; the end of the century witnessed the great revolts of Orania and of northern Constantine. During the Napoleonic wars a resurgence of piracy brought in fresh funds and the revolts subsided for a time, but they resumed in 1810 and continued until the French invasion of 1830. Certain Moroccan and Tunisian groups participated, responding to the call of local leaders with whom they were traditionally bound by fellow membership in the brotherhoods (*darqāwa*) or by alliances such as that of the Ḥanānisha of Constantine with the Shabbī of southwestern Tunisia. The only result of the belated attempt of Algiers to become the capital of the central Maghrib was to enhance the prestige of the local leaders, whose descendants were to distinguish themselves in the war against the French a century later.

Why did this unstable dual power endure as long as it did? The determining reason is probably the permanence of the foreign, chiefly Spanish, threat. Today the danger may seem to have been minimal, but at the time it was taken very seriously, and there is no doubt that it often enabled the Turks to gain the support of the religious leaders, who were far from giving their blessing to all the rural revolts.[7] Piracy was still represented as a form of warfare, and the tribute paid by the various countries (England's American colonies, Holland, Portugal, the Scandinavian

[7] The urban Islam of the *fuqahā'* usually favored the prevailing authority, regardless of its nature; the importance of the Algerian pro-Turkish historians should not be exaggerated.

countries) was regarded as *jizya*. Moreover, hostilities with Spain had not ceased. In 1708 the Turks took Oran and Mars al-Kabir after a long siege that was facilitated by the political anarchy in war-torn Spain. The new Bourbon dynasty resolved to avenge the affront, and in 1732 Philip V sent out an expedition which recaptured the still depopulated Oran. In 1775 O'Reilly attacked Algiers and suffered a disastrous defeat. In 1783 and 1784 Algiers was bombarded by the Spanish fleet. In every case the beys of the west and of Constantine, the Kabyles, and sometimes the Moroccans sent contingents. All these general mobilizations added to the prestige of the Turks.[8] But in 1792 the Spaniards evacuated Oran for good, and in the following year it became the capital of the western beylicate. The foreign peril was blunted, for the deys regarded France, which was to take over the North African interests of Spain, as an ally.

At the beginning of the nineteenth century the weakness and isolation of the deys had become evident. True, the Turkish minority had begun to take an interest in the interior of the country, but only with a view to the forcible collection of increasingly heavy taxes. Support for the brotherhoods and the building of mosques were sponsored as a way to appease the population but with no thought at all of any educational return. This inability to merge with the local population made the Turks cling to piracy, even when its meager proceeds had ceased to compensate for the international complications it involved. The weakness of the deys was well known to the European states, which had their resident or itinerant spies. The idea of replacing one foreign minority by another was familiar to the Spaniards and no doubt to their French allies as well. Small wonder then that the power of the deys, the most perfect example of the dichotomy between state and society in the Maghrib, was the first to collapse.

8 Cf. the anecdote about the bey Ibrāhīm's successor Muḥammad (Aḥmad), who, whenever anyone spoke to him of attacking Tunis, replied: "Let us first attack Oran." (Cf. Ibn Abī al-Ḍiyāf, vol. II, p. 146).

The 'Alawite Power

During the greater part of the seventeenth century Morocco was divided into autonomous principalities. None of the princes accepted this situation; each wanted to reunify the country for his own benefit. Territorial and political unity had become imperative, but the form it would take was a problem. The fall of the Sa'dids had shown that an overcentralized state resting on sheer force could not endure for long. The autonomous principalities were of various kinds: *zāwiyas*, such as those of Dilā' or of Abū Ḥassūn al-Jazūlī in the south; city-states such as Salé and Tetuán; estates organized by such military leaders as al-'Ayāshī and Ghaylān, his lieutenant and successor, in the north; and finally, Hilālī shaykhdoms such as the *Shbānāt* of Marrakech.[9] In Tafilalt, the local power was held by the 'Alawites, a family of sharifs, cousins of the Sa'dids, who had come from the Hedjaz at the same time. As sharifs, they were able to oppose the expansionism of the Dilā'ites in the north and of Abū Hassūn in the east. Their shaykh in 1631 was the Sharif 'Alī b. Yūsuf. The power of the 'Alawites, however, was not of Maraboutic origin like that of the Sa'dids. As related in the chronicles, their conquest of Morocco, first undertaken unsuccessfully by Muḥammad b. 'Alī between 1635 and 1659, then successfully by his brother al-Rashīd between 1666 and 1671, resembles all the preceding conquests since that of Yūsuf b. Tashfīn.[10] One is struck by the paltriness of their military effort. Al-Rashīd's adversaries seem to have collapsed under their own weight. The weakness of Ghaylān and the Dilā'ites and the constant conflicts between the former and Fez and the latter and Salé appear to have been caused by the decline in the Anglo-Dutch trade,

[9] It is necessary to differentiate these diverse powers. Those who see a state of anarchy in seventeenth-century Morocco fail to do so. An important distinguishing feature is the role played by foreign commerce in the consolidation of certain of these powers.

[10] For the beginnings of the 'Alawite dynasty, see al-'Alawī, *al-Anwār al-Ḥasanīya*, which has served all subsequent historians as a source.

which for a century had dominated the Moroccan scene and greatly reinforced the local powers by providing them with both revenue and arms.

At the same time, al-Rashīd's ambitions were considerably favored by the French commercial enterprises on the Rif coast, which were then just beginning and could be easily controlled. For the moment he was relatively free from foreign interference, a circumstance eminently favorable to his reunification of Morocco. His successors learned the lesson and consistently maintained that control of foreign commerce was indispensable to the territorial integrity of the country. Whatever may have been the determining cause of al-Rashīd's success, he achieved his ends. When, at his death in 1672, he was succeeded by his brother Ismā'īl, the new power owed nothing to the Marabout movement; its foundations were armed force and sharifian prestige. Ismā'īl, who reigned from 1672 to 1727, tried to consolidate his brother's achievement and found a new solution to the problem of the weakness of the central authority. His policy may be summed up as follows: the building up of a new army, the destruction of the influence of the brotherhoods, and imposition of a system of heavy taxation. This was a negative reaction to the policy of al-Manṣūr, for the *zāwiyas* had been discredited in the seventeenth century by their dealings with the Iberians, and al-Manṣūr's attempts to support the state with funds derived from foreign sources had proved a failure. Ismā'īl did not entirely repudiate the old organization of the army. It still included Hilālī contingents as in the days of the Marīnids; the Ma'qil, long the mainstay of the Zayyānid dynasty, banished for a time beyond the Atlas but now settled on the Atlantic plains, were now employed as mercenaries, as their cousins had been under the last Marīnids. As tenants of state lands, they were exempt from taxes but liable to military service. Renegades were also used, chiefly in the artillery and the corps of engineers. But Ismā'īl's great idea, borrowed indirectly from the Ottomans, was that the army should have ties with no one social group. Bound to the sovereign's person by an oath of fidelity, it was supposed in theory to be the living guarantee of dynastic continuity. The only way of implementing this idea at the time was to utilize slaves, who were made to swear fidelity to the sovereign, hence the name 'Abīd al-Bukhārī, from the book on which the oath was sworn. The 'Alawite king first sought out the descendants of the slaves al-Manṣūr's army had brought back from the Sudan after the campaign of 1591; then, since there were not enough of these, he enlisted all the slaves, even those belonging to private persons. Assembled at al-Maḥalla near Sidi Sliman, they were soon separated from their children, who were sent to Meknès to learn a trade and then after a brief training period enrolled in the army. At its height this system yielded an army of thirty to fifty thousand. This method of recruiting, with its obvious resemblance to the janissary system, was a tacit avowal that the ever-widening gulf between the state and society made it impossible to enlist a loyal army among the free population. To support this army, a system of crushing taxation was instituted and mercilessly applied. Not only were the legal taxes, the *'ushur* and the *zakāt*, maintained, but in addition the *nā'iba*, a war tax in money or in kind, originally levied with a view to liberating the territories under foreign occupation, was made permanent, and both foreign and internal trade were subjected to indirect taxes, which had always been regarded as illegal (*mukūs*). The reorganized army collected these taxes with increasing regularity, not only by force but sometimes with the help of politico-religious arguments. Sharifism served as a counterweight to Maraboutism, while juridical orthodoxy, as in the days of the Marīnids, was brought to bear against the mystical pretensions of the chiefs of the *zāwiyas*. The Marabout movement suffered two decisive blows, first when all the brotherhoods were ordered to transfer their headquarters to Fez (since their strength had resided in their presence throughout the country), and second when the new army laid siege to the towns under foreign occupation, since the results—the evacuation by the Spanish of al-Ḥalq (Ma'mūra) in 1681 and Larache in 1689, and of Tangiers by the English in 1684—were in glaring contrast to the long and ineffectual efforts of the Marabouts. The sharifian policy sometimes involved the sutlan in hopeless and obstinate ventures, such as his struggle against the Turks. True, the Turks had supported the Dilā'ites in their revolt of 1677 under Aḥmad al-Dilā'ī, just as they had helped the condottiere Ghaylān ten years before. But the essential reason for the conflict was that the 'Alawites, who regarded themselves as caliphs, demanded equal status with the sultan of Constantinople in their dealings with foreigners. Hence their fruitless attempt at an alliance with France, and hence their unsuccessful expeditions against Tlemcen. This foreign policy, however, was a mere accessory to a military policy aimed at a strict centralization.[11] In spite of dynastic and local revolts fomented by the Turks, Ismā'īl succeeded in reconstituting the "historical Morocco" of the Marīnids. But this policy was not universally accepted, and the sultan tried on several occasions to justify it. Whatever personal motivations there may have been behind the opposition to Ismā'īl, it reflected a reality, for by and large Ismā'īl's solutions were to prove disastrous. By sending the slaves to the army, he struck a severe blow at agriculture in the southern oases and in the environs of the cities (hence the bitter opposition of the *fuqahā'* of Fez). Long in a state of decline, agriculture might have revived with the return of peace, but this was made impossible by the lack of manpower. Another negative effect of his policy was political. The religious brotherhoods had come into being at a time when the state was disintegrating. Their principal role had been to preserve a certain territorial unity. By destroying

[11] It is clear that Ismā'īl concluded an alliance with the jurists of Fez to combat the Marabouts; this had already been the Waṭṭāsid policy; but the economic and social situation of the urban élite did not permit either partner to play the game to the full. See "Lettres inédites d'Ismā'īl," *Hespéris*, special issue, 1962, especially letter 10.

them, Ismā'īl removed the one force capable of saving the state from utter shipwreck in the event of its losing its principal support, namely, the army. And the isolation of the new army from society, which Ismā'īl regarded as a guarantee of the state's permanence, was on occasion to have the opposite effect, for the *'abīds,* who were bound by no loyalties whatever, were quite capable of serving anyone who paid them. Thus every crisis of the army became a crisis of the state, and that is what happened after the death of Ismā'īl. His two chief political acts—creation of a personal army and destruction of the *zāwiyas*—led to thirty years of disorder. Apart from the distressing conflicts[12] between factions within the army, between the army and the sultan ('Abd Allah b. Ismā'īl) as well as the population, and between the sultan and various rivals, the main reason for the 'Alawite sultan's failure was the incompatibility between his policy and the economic condition of the country, which was no longer capable of supporting an enormous centralized, and moreover parasitic, state apparatus. The steady impoverishment of the country called for a return to a certain decentralization, and this was the solution ultimately adopted.

Between 1727 and 1757 the sultan 'Abd Allah was deposed five times. The events of this period served as a lesson to his son Muḥammad III (1757-1790), who rebuilt the 'Alawite power on new foundations. Putting the accent more and more on his function as a religious leader, he reorganized the government on a more decentralized basis, contenting himself with investing local chiefs chosen or supported by the population. In recruiting his army, he relied above all on contingents provided by the tax-exempt communities settled on state lands. He tried to dispense with taxes on agriculture by developing trade, so that customs duties would provide the minimum required for the functioning

12 See the interesting observations of Ibn Zaydān at the end of his biography of the sultan 'Abd Allah b. Ismā'īl, in *Itḥāf a'lām al-Nās,* vol. IV, pp. 475ff.

of the state. Thus he revolutionized the political equations: instead of trying to increase tax collections and reinforce the state by means of a powerful and independent army, as his grandfather had done, he tried to dispense with a powerful army by developing an independent system of taxation. This accounts for his well-known interest in commerce. In 1757 he signed a treaty with Denmark (which there was no reason to fear, since it was a small country without great ambitions), according it a monopoly on trade in the port of Safi; then in 1765, with a view to controlling the smuggling that was flourishing on the southern coast, he decided to concentrate the whole Atlantic trade in a single port. Choosing the site of Mogador (Essaouira), he employed foreign engineers to build a modern port, where the consuls of the leading powers were invited to take up residence. From then until the beginning of the twentieth century customs duties made up the greater part of the state revenues. The prosperity and indeed the very existence of the state thus became directly dependent on an activity dominated by foreigners. Muḥammad III was the veritable architect of the "modern" Morocco described in numerous nineteenth- and twentieth-century accounts, and this in itself constitutes a judgment on his work. Little by little the 'Alawite power became stabilized; the dynastic struggles and local revolts lost their virulence precisely because of the more and more religious—that is, abstract—nature of this power.

Sultan, caliph and sharif, Muḥammad III maintained cordial relations with the sharif of Mecca and at the same time abandoned the violently anti-Turkish policy of his grandfather. Sole repository of the spiritual power, he opposed every attempt at a revival of Maraboutism.[13] One of his successors, Sulaymān (1792-1822), diverted the activities of the *darqāwā* and *tijāniya* to Orania and West Africa. This policy found a certain indirect justification in Wahhābism,

13 The relations between the Marabout movement and the process of feudalization have not yet been studied seriously and are still obscure.

the reform movement that made its appearance in Arabia in the eighteenth century. If not for the opposition of certain Mālikite *fuqahā'* and the violent campaign of the Wahhābites against the sharif of Mecca, Muḥammad III and Sulaymān would probably have institutionalized it.[14] The reinforcement of the sultan's prestige was accompanied by a reorganization of the government departments. Though certain Sa'did reforms were preserved, the essence of this reorganization was definitely a return to the Marīnid makhzen.

The *wazīr* (or vizier), the sultan's personal adviser and right-hand man, was from then on a kind of prime minister; his chief function was to maintain contact with the local authorities; the increasingly complex relations with foreign countries led to the appointment of a foreign minister (*wazīr al-Baḥr* or "minister of the sea," since all diplomacy revolved around piracy and commerce). The most striking innovation, however, was in the financial field. The treasury was reorganized and a strict accounting system introduced. The financial structure was headed by an *amīn al-umanā'*, to whom the *umanā'* of the ports and big cities were responsible. The old functions of *ḥajib, kātib,* chief qadi and *muḥtasib* were maintained. As in Marīnid times, the high political and military posts were given to persons having important clienteles in the various regions, while the financial and judicial positions went to members of the great commercial families of the Andalusian cities. This reorganized central government did not exert direct authority over the whole country. A considerable degree of decentralization was recognized, and the choice of the qaid in charge of a circumscription usually resulted from a compromise between the will of the sultan and that of the population. The qaid himself had absolute power. The degree of decentralization varied from region to region. Some were gov-

[14] Nevertheless Zayyānī, who served both these sovereigns, criticizes Wahhābism—after his defeat by the army of Muḥammad 'Alī of Egypt, to be sure.

erned by mere functionaries subject to recall, others by veritable princes who merely recognized the sultan as their suzerain. The dividing lines between the two were fluid, but little by little the status of independent prince became more frequent, for even in the days of Muḥammad III the sovereign's means of pressure were very limited. His army was little more than an armed police force; remnants of the older armies were still in service, but more and more the sultan relied on the contingents provided by the communities settled on state lands and those sent occasionally from the Haouz region.[15] In the unsettled state of his finances he could afford no more. With such an army the most he could expect was a modicum of obedience from the local authorities. Often long negotiations were necessary to avoid open revolts necessitating costly and risky expeditions such as those of 1764 and 1787. In his foreign policy he strove for a balance between the national ambitions implicit in his sharifian ideology and his more realistic desire for peace. Muḥammad III fortified several ports. In 1769 he besieged and liberated Mazagan, the last town held by the Portuguese; in 1774 he besieged but failed to take Melilla and in 1790 his successor al-Yazīd besieged Ceuta with no greater success. In the main, however, the sultans were extremely cautious in their dealings with foreign powers. In 1765 the French bombed Larache and Salé and in the following year moved up the estuary of the Loukkos, but this did not prevent Muḥammad III from signing a treaty with them in 1767. He carried on negotiations with all the European powers and signed numerous trade and friendship pacts, which were several times renewed in later years. Similarly Sulaymān, though he took advantage of the Turks' difficulties in Orania to recover Oujda in 1797 and appoint governors in the Saharan regions that had belonged to the kingdom of

[15] Why this region remained relatively calm has not yet been explained. There is no better indication of how much research still remains to be done than these obscurities concerning a period (the reign of Muḥammad III) about which so much has been written.

Morocco under al-Manṣūr and Ismā'īl, refused to occupy Tlemcen, though the population asked him to do so in 1803.

As reorganized by Muḥammad III, the 'Alawite regime did not command; it negotiated—both with foreigners and with the local authorities, using the army only to hasten negotiations. In this respect he achieved a certain success, but all in all his solution of the problem of operating a state under unfavorable economic conditions amounted to combining in one and the same person a king and an emperor, a military and a religious leader. From then on the dual power discussed above was embodied in the sovereign himself. But the balance thus achieved was unstable and ceased to function once a foreign element entered in. That is what happened at the beginning of the nineteenth century. The system already contained within itself the seeds of foreign intervention, for it depended more and more on foreign commerce that was dominated by foreigners. When foreign intervention became more direct, the system managed to survive, but on the basis of a very different balance. The diplomacy of the 'Alawite sultans succeeded with the foreigners as it had with the local authorities—if delaying the inevitable can be termed success.

Despite secondary divergencies, all the countries of the Maghrib seem to have undergone the same general development. The eighteenth century was characterized by an unstable balance of internal as well as external forces. The sovereigns tried to preserve this balance at all costs. For this reason what has often been termed a period of transition was in reality a period of stasis. The struggle against foreign occupation begun in the previous century was continued; most of the towns still held by the Iberians were retaken. But this movement of "national liberation" was illusory, for the interests of Spain and Portugal in the Maghrib had become marginal. Certain appearances to the contrary, the 'Alawite power was not Maraboutic in essence, and the Turks of Algiers had long since lost their aggressive spirit.

The struggle against foreign powers had ceased to be anything more than an ideology in the service of a contested authority. The conflict between the new dominant powers, England and France, was being carried on in other parts of the world and only its distant echoes reached the Maghrib. Thus conditions favored an improvement of the internal situation.

It did not improve. At best, the old sclerotic structures were preserved. Since resources of foreign origin (the gold of the Sudan, Mediterranean trade) had declined, the essential problem became financial, and this problem gave rise to continual conflicts between regionalism and centralism, or in the last analysis between the state treasury and the living standard of the individual or the community. Simultaneously or successively, the rulers of the different countries of the Maghrib attempted the same solutions, but with different results. The beys of Tunis succeeded in winning the confidence of the urban leaders, so effecting a symbiosis between the foreign and local élites, the most palpable result of which was a concomitant development of commerce and agriculture at the expense of the seminomadic groups. The deys of Algiers, inclined to an excessive use of force, provoked continual revolts which in the long run reinforced the position of the local leaders, who came to be regarded as the defenders of their communities. The sultans of Morocco resorted to a subtle blend of force and diplomacy, and tried to subsist on the proceeds of foreign trade. They did not entirely gain the support of the urban élite, but neither did they entirely lose their prestige in the eyes of the local leaders.[16]

In any case the solution was temporary. The power of the Turks in Algiers dwindled steadily, and even without the invasion of 1830 we cannot be sure it would have survived.

16 It would be highly instructive to compare the ideologies of the religious élites of Tunis and of Fez, for the Fez community preserved strong ties with the Marabout movement, whereas that of Tunis took an increasing interest in the "profane sciences."

In Tunisia and Morocco the breakdown of authority and the lack of resources invited foreign intervention. Without capital, neither the beys nor the sultans were able to change the structure of their governments or to exert effective control over foreign trade. Dependent on those who financed and directed this trade, they were its victims rather than its beneficiaries. And yet despite the poorness of the studies dealing with this period, one perceives a certain will to make a *fresh start,* to overcome the failings of the Turco-Sa'did century and the effects of the long crisis of the fourteenth and fifteenth centuries and to reestablish a bond with the Ḥafṣid and Marīnid monarchies. This striving is reflected not only in the forms adopted by the courts and governments but also in the cultural revival that was taking place. Restoration, to be sure, means a reinforcement of tradition, but it also means a resurgence of public spirit; hence the local historiography that flourished in Fez and Tunis. The renascence of an urban élite, which set itself up as the guardian of tradition and a force for political reform, was of course a threat to the Maraboutic élite, even though the two groups long remained closely linked. Once politically defeated, Maraboutism changed its character. Formerly the cement of society, it became the servant of central power and of the urban élite. It duplicated and sometimes replaced the commercial ties between cities and country. Losing their preeminent position in the capital, the Marabouts took refuge in the provinces (chiefly those of the southern Maghrib), putting themselves under the protection of the local leaders who were thus enabled to "feudalize" themselves,[17] that is, to concentrate in their hands a politico-administra-

[17] I use this word as indicative only, for both the colonial and the Maghribi historians exaggerate the unity of the Marabout movement, failing to see that it changed its function and character between the fifteenth and the nineteenth centuries, just as they fail to see any difference between the Hilālī mercenaries of the fourteenth, the condottieri of the seventeenth, and the qaids of the eighteenth century. Only when we have a clearer idea of the "status" of these social groups shall we begin to understand the dynamics of Maghrib history.

tive power, a military command, and a religious influence as supporters of the local shaykh. The development of a "fief" was only a matter of time.

The development here described is by no means self-evident, but can be inferred from the historical and hagiographic writings of the day. Before we can pass from the realm of subjective interpretation to that of scientific hypothesis, we must elucidate the following points: the influence of foreign trade on the central power structure and on the rise of an urban élite; the exact relations between this élite and the rulers; the role of the Marabouts in the service of the sovereigns and of the local leaders; and finally the relation, in the ideology of the urban élite, between juridical education and Maraboutic mysticism. These are highly complex problems. The long delay in formulating them clearly is all the more regrettable.[18]

Thus the successive eras of principalities, empires and kingdoms were followed by an era of military states. Though state organization is not the determining factor, we have taken it as the basis of our classification, because our sources consist primarily in dynastic histories and because history as commonly written is the history of states. Actually priority should be given to other factors—economic, social and ideological. But for lack of systematic and precise studies, we can present these factors only as methodological imperatives.

Nevertheless, on the strength of what we know of the primary socio-economic structures, we discern a logic in the sequence: principalities, empires, kingdoms, though it is usually masked in the dynastic histories. After the crisis of the fourteenth century which condemned the kingdoms to an inglorious death, a return to the coexistence of the primary social cells was impossible. Larger, more structured

[18] They have been posed and in some degree answered by Berque. In his study on *Al-Yousi,* he shows the way. It remains only to complete his work.

and more hierarchized units came into being, and because they were larger and more complex, they could no longer coexist or be subordinated one to the other. At that point a foreign organism, based essentially on an army distinct from the population, imposed itself on all. In time this foreign character, which prevented the state from being an organic expression of society, provoked a vigorous reaction on the part of the older units, which tended, though in new forms, to impose their implicit dialectic. Of course we can imagine other forms of state that would have been more in harmony with the social structure; we can even condemn the form which ultimately imposed itself on the Maghrib. But on this purely formal level all judgments must remain subjective; let it suffice to note the facts. It is evident that the states were at no time able to create a consciousness of legitimacy which would have provided an inviolable principle governing the transmission of power; the social contract was constantly being called into question; allegiance was always personal. Never was the principle of sovereignty completley disjoined from the person of the sovereign.[19] None of the states ever succeeded in creating a legitimist ideology. Islam always remained the common possession of the community, and under its protection. All Shī'ite or semi-Shī'ite legitimist strivings from the Fāṭimids to the Sa'dids were failures. Here again let us for the moment content ourselves with noting the facts. For want of a legitimist ideology these states were always dependent on force; but what force? We have discussed Ibn Khaldūn's theory and concluded that tribal cohesion could establish but not perpetuate a state. The mainstay of the state was the army, which collected taxes, which in turn secured the unity of the army. All the state structures we have discussed seem to have depended primarily on outside resources: gold from the Sudan, rents from Andalusia, Mediterranean piracy, and so forth. Since we have no means of evaluating these rev-

[19] If, as a historian should, we distinguish between sultanate and caliphate.

enues directly, we are obliged to infer their importance from the life of the courts, cultural development, or the monuments built. But was this economic situation unique? Is it not, rather, a constant in the genesis of states?

Seen from this angle, the last period, the period of the military states that arose with the decline of outside resources, takes on a capital importance. And here we note two significant developments: the organization of the "makhzen tribes" and the priority given to foreign commerce. These developments were not new; the novelty consisted in the dominant position they assumed in public life. Despite the inconsistency of the rulers, despite their meager achievements and ultimate failure, we cannot help seeing an attempt to provide the state with firm foundations by setting up a local army and by making taxes on commerce the main support of the treasury. Moreover, these policies resulted in a revival of the cities, so that in two different ways organic ties between the state and society were reconstituted. True, this development was not carried to its ultimate conclusion, yet what did subsequent history do but carry out this program of providing a society with a standing army and a middle class when the society itself was unable to do so? In part it is the attempts to correct the deficiencies of the day that call our attention to the deficiencies themselves. And yet in many areas historical research is still in its beginnings. Have we a right to judge before its investigations have borne fruit? And above all, are we justified in replacing real problems with pseudoproblems?

Yet this is what the colonial historians have done constantly. They see the history of the Maghrib as hinging on the dates 1830, 1882 and 1912 and, reluctant to speak of French aggression, they prefer to hold the Maghribis responsible for what happened. Terrasse puts the blame on Islam, and Julien on the Berber race.[20]

In their view history is made by kings and its course is

[20] C.-A. Julien, *L'Histoire de l'Afrique du Nord*, 2nd ed., vol. 2, p. 306; Terrasse, *Histoire du Maroc*, vol. II, pp. 445-470.

determined by whether these kings happen to be Christians or Moslems. They counter the golden legend of Arab historiography with a black legend. Thus they study the history of the Maghrib never as itself but only as the negative counterpart of some other history, which they often forget to identify. It is true that these two histories cannot be isolated from each other, since they interact at every step. But that is no reason to draw comparisons based on preconceived bias.

The major fault of colonial historians is to dissimulate, voluntarily or not, their frame of reference. Obviously they have the occident in mind when they speak of a world in ferment, of world-shaking transformations, and so on. But at what stage? For not all comparisons are legitimate. The only legitimate comparison for the period that concerns us would be between absolute monarchies. The existence of an absolute monarchy seems to be contingent on a state of balance between a feudal aristocracy and a merchant class. The monarchy imposes itself as the guarantor of the rights and privileges of both these classes; it is enabled to play this role of arbiter by establishing itself as an autonomous force based on an army composed of aristocrat officers and peasant soldiers and on an administration drawn from the merchant class, the whole financed by outside resources (conquest) and a system of regular taxation. This social balance guarantees the continuity of the monarchy, legitimized by the blessing of the Church. Other factors no doubt played a part, but let us confine ourselves to essentials. In this light, the points requiring discussion are these: Was there a feudal aristocracy in the Maghrib, and if not why not? What was the impact of foreign trade? Why was there no dominant legitimist ideology?

Since these questions cannot be adequately answered at the present time, all value judgments are premature. Nevertheless, we can note three facts that would seem to circumscribe the discussion. First, it was inevitable that Western Europe and the Maghrib, which could not simultaneously achieve power and wealth in the Mediterranean, should develop in different directions. Secondly, from the sixteenth century on the Mediterranean ceased to be the center of the historical stage. And finally, in the eighteenth century the Maghrib began to develop a balance of the type needed for absolute monarchy. If despite the reservations expressed above, we still wish to speak of failure, it can only be a very relative failure, due to a general conjuncture over which men, and the sovereigns least of all, had little control and in which external factors seem to have played the largest part.

Putting aside these judgments and counterjudgments, let us consider the lasting achievements of the period thus far discussed, achievements that gave the Maghrib its present face. First of all its work of civilization, symbolized by a religious faith and a language. At every step we have noted the deepening of the one and the extension of the other. Khārijism colonized the Sahara, Shī'ism introduced the dialectic of religious controversy and the model of the 'Abbāsid state; Almohadism implanted systematic education and doctrinal propaganda; popular mysticism democratized religion and gave it a patriotic character. Arabization, imposed with remarkable perseverance by the Berber sovereigns, gave the people of the Maghrib models of expression. If we find signs of opposition, it is only in the period of decadence and in connection with a political struggle the content of which is hard to define.[21] True, when the Arabic literature of the Maghrib is really local it seems arid, compared to that of Andalusia or Iraq, but it has barely begun to be studied by scholars and already appears to deserve something better than the contempt in which it has thus far been held.[22] In any case, it is far from being mere folklore, which would

[21] E.g. the revolts of Aït Umālū against Sulaymān. See al-Zayyānī, *al-Turjumān*, p. 75; al-Nāṣirī, *al-Istiqṣā*, vol. VIII, pp. 134-137. But according to the chroniclers themselves, this was a struggle for the control of the makhzen, exacerbated by the sultan's obstinacy.

[22] See Gannūn, *al-Nubūgh al-maghribī*.

have been the fate of Maghribi culture had it not adopted the Arabic language.

These are the two elements which, in conjunction with racial uniformity and similarity of social structure, gave the countries of the Maghrib a basic unity. The last centuries, however, witnessed the beginnings of a regional individualization, marked among other things by slight differences in dialect. The boundary lines became relatively set, separating distinct political entities. The national consciousness of the three states crystallized under different conditions. Morocco gained self-awareness in its struggles against the Iberians and the Turks, in the strivings of its religious brotherhoods, and through its fidelity to the heritage of Andalusian Islam. Tunisia integrated its foreign rulers and without forgetting the former splendors of Kairouan, opened itself to all the influences of the Mediterranean Orient. And Algeria, despite its divergent Zayyānid and Ḥammādid traditions, achieved individuality through a common awareness of the segregation imposed by the Turkish regime.[23]

This development, subject of course to many shadings, did not take on its definitive form until the nineteenth century, but there is no doubt that from the sixteenth century on new and distinctive elements were at work. In the nineteenth century, however, all three countries of the Maghrib were united in their deficiencies; none had a strong national army and all lacked capital. For this reason they were all to suffer the same foreign occupation.

23 On Turkish despotism, cf. "Lettres inédites," *Hespéris*, special issue, 1962, the reply to Ismā'īl of the Banū 'Āmir, who had allied themselves with the Spaniards of Oran against the Turks and who are the subject of al-Marshafī's satire, "L'Agrément du lecteur."

PART IV
The Colonial Maghrib

For the general reader the Maghrib entered modern history at the beginning of the nineteenth century, because for the ensuing period sources for a scientific historiography are available: public and private archives, diplomatic and political records, legislative and administrative texts, general and local budgets, investigations, eyewitness accounts, and so forth. The positivist historian finds at last the precision of dated events. But is the Maghrib of this period actually better known? One would think so to judge by the overwhelming mass of literature on the subject. In fact, the clarity that seems to result is misleading because of the meticulous care with which "true history" (that of the conquerors) has been distinguished from "subhistory" (that of the conquered). The former is recorded and analyzed in detail, the latter is lightly ignored or only cautiously touched upon. The motives of the diplomats and generals, the grievances of the colonial merchants and farmers are examined under the microscope, while the problems of the Maghribis, the transformation of the countryside, the social disintegration and spiritual uprooting, are mentioned in passing or treated as undecipherable enigmas.

Here of course I am referring to "colonial history," its scope and authority. Celebrating the exploits of Europeans outside of Europe, it long claimed to be the only possible history. Finally challenged by events it was unable to foresee, it has tried to overcome its one-sidedness in two ways: (1) it now concerns itself with the local populations, either by interpreting the familiar sources in a new way or by looking into hitherto untapped sources, and so arrives at a kind of social history of a colonial society;[1] (2) it has begun to collect material reflecting the reactions of the in-

1 The best example thus far is that provided by Nouschi, *Enquête* and *La naissance*, pp. 13-29.

digenous population: songs, folk tales, local chronicles, oral traditions, legal texts.[2] Without prejudging the advantage that traditional colonial history may derive from these researches, we cannot help seeing that what is being written about the Maghrib today still suffers from two basic defects: the overestimation of diplomatic and military affairs, the most immediate result of which is to show reason at work on one side and empirical bungling on the other, and the restriction of the historical field to the so-called "modern" —i.e. capitalist—world and its exclusively foreign protagonists. The phenomena that are of direct concern to Maghribis—the resistance movements, proletarianization and nationalism—are apprehended negatively, hence abstractly. The Maghrib "is always seen in profile."[3] Thus the task of decolonizing history is even more urgent for this period than for those that preceded it.

Foreign historians, as we have said, divorce "history" from the underlying social realities; Maghribi writers, on the other hand, usually distinguish the fundamental from the contingent. While the former put the accent on diplomacy and economics, the latter confine themselves to psychology and ethics, drawing almost exclusively on partisan witnesses (the nationalist press, diaries, political notes, apologias—often posthumous—and the like).[4] Thus an historic episode is seen only as it appeared before or after the event to one of the protagonists. Obviously such history is superficial. Unconcerned with objective causes, it requires interpretation to give it meaning.

But how are we to understand this history—written or yet to be written—of the colonial period? The historians of both camps are obliged to answer certain questions. What is the relation between colonial history and the previous

[2] See Charnay, *La Vie musulmane.*

[3] The expression is that of P. Nora in his review of Julien, *Histoire de l'Algérie contemporaine,* in *France-Observateur,* December 24, 1964.

[4] Several examples are given in Ibn 'Ashūr, *Al-Ḥaraka al-Adabīya wa-al-Fikrīya fī Tūnis*; reduced to the absurd in Muḥammad al-Bāqir al-Kattānī, *Tarjamat al-Shaykh Muḥammad al-Kattānī.*

history of the colonizing and colonized countries? What degree of integration did colonial society achieve? In the structure and ideology of the present-day Maghrib, which is preponderant: continuity or discontinuity? The historians of the two camps take diametrically opposed attitudes: the one wholly identifies the destinies of the colonized people with the action of the colonists; the other rejects this identification. The one claims to be writing the history of the French Maghrib when according to the other he is merely writing the history of Frenchmen in the Maghrib. But can everything be explained by either of these two approaches alone? Isn't the colonial period a self-contained field in which the determinations of the two nations' precolonial pasts and the contradictory forces implicit in colonial action itself are all simultaneously at work, sometimes reinforcing, sometimes annulling one another?[5] The question is meaningless, at best premature, the positivist historian would say. But he answers it nevertheless, if only by the periodization he chooses.

In colonial history one should judge only results, never intentions. Beyond the motives and justifications of the colonizers and colonized alike, it is the logic of the world market that makes colonial history understandable. A particular colonial society may be more or less integrated—the Maghrib was less so in the 1880-1930 period—but at all times the same laws are at work. Consequently colonial policy, virtually dictated by the requirements of the world economy, shows a striking continuity, even though the ideological justifications are continually changing. This continuity is expressed not in newspaper articles or in parliamentary speeches, but in the behavior of the bureaucracy, which remained unchanged throughout the period. It provides an objective concept of colonial history. If we concern

[5] Berque formulates the problem in this way in *French North Africa* and *Egypt, Imperialism and Revolution*, but goes on to expound an anthropological and philosophical doctrine without clearly stating his methodological premises.

ourselves with finalities, with intentions, we leave this domain for a very different one and should say so; otherwise we shall always be the victims of subjective judgments and counterjudgments.[6]

Remaining within the framework of colonial history, we need attach no great importance to the fact that all the countries of the Maghrib did not succumb at the same time. The year 1830 did not affect Algeria alone. The neighboring states felt the repercussions immediately. For forty years, moreover, the colonization of Algeria was of a mild, preimperialist type, in which Roman reminiscences, religious passions, the notions of honor, glory and suzerainty, in short an ancien régime ideology, played a large part; thus the difference between the policy pursued in Algeria and that pursued in the pseudoindependent countries was minimal. During the great imperialist period the extension of the colonized area was accompanied by intensified exploitation. Methods and ideas changed; though the agricultural base retained its importance, commerce, speculation and finance gained the upper hand. Algeria maintained a certain individuality, but underwent the same development as the two other countries. After the crisis of 1930 the imperialist system disintegrated rapidly and, as one might have expected, the countries of the Maghrib liberated themselves in the inverse order of their submission.

[6] See below, chapter 14, n. 28, and introduction to chapter 15.

13. Colonial Pressure and Primary Resistance

At the beginning of the nineteenth century, conditions in the Maghrib made it eminently vulnerable to European pressure. Increasing dependency on foreign trade had isolated the state and transformed it into a tool of foreign interests. This development was retarded by the Napoleonic Wars, but after 1815 Europe, to which the long negotiations in Vienna had given a common political consciousness, was ready to intervene in the name of the new deity: freedom. Free the slaves, suppress piracy, free trade—these were the slogans of the day. Despite the rivalries between European powers that would soon make themselves felt, especially between France and England, there was fundamental agreement on the principles of European action, and it was these principles which in the end decided the fate of the Maghrib. This development, however, took time; in other parts of the globe the preparations required no less than fifty years. In the Maghrib, however, the movement was accelerated by an "unforeseen" event. While in the course of the nineteenth century the Moroccan and Tunisian states suffered a long death agony, the collapse of the Algerian state was sudden and violent. No doubt the precariousness of the dey's power makes such an end readily understandable. But the policy chosen by France, which today seems retrograde compared to that of England, is explained by the structure and status of French society at the time—retarded industrial revolution, disparity between north and south, political reaction. The Algerian expedition would have been hardly more than a new version of the Iberian raids or Napoleon's Egyptian campaign if southern France had been prosperous enough to support its population and if there had not been a capitalist class eager to engage in land speculation. As long as we confine ourselves to diplomatic or military history, everything about the Algerian venture seems accidental and unforeseen, and it is because the diplomats and military men involved in the conquest looked no deeper that their picture of it is bathed in a golden haze recalling the world of Charles V and the partition of Africa. But over the years Algeria lost this special character and the ancien régime aspect lost its explicative value. From the form we must distinguish the substance, which can be summed up as the destruction of the traditional states throughout the Maghrib. The methods may have varied, the results were everywhere the same.

Destruction of the State by Violence

Conflict with the French

In its beginnings the conflict between the French government and the dey was generally regarded as a replica of the crises between Algeria and Spain, and the campaign for which preparations were slowly being made was likened to O'Reilly's expedition. No one made any serious attempt to interfere—neither Turkey to put pressure on the dey to take a more conciliatory attitude, nor England to dissuade France, nor the bey of Tunis nor the sultan of Morocco to help their endangered neighbor. When the French army of thirty-seven thousand won an easy victory over the six thousand ill-trained soldiers of the *ūjāk*, when the people of Algiers opened the city gates and the dey withdrew, leaving the victor enough spoils to defray the expense of the expedition, no one regretted the Turkish regime,[7] except of course the envoy of the Sublime Porte, who had waited in vain off La Goulette for permission to disembark and continue on to Algiers with a view to deposing the dey. This relative lack of interest is explained by the fact that for a long time Algiers had been without authority over Algeria as a whole. Even after their victory, it was believed,

[7] See the judgment of Ibn Abī al-Ḍiyāf, *Itḥāf*, vol. III, pp. 167-168; Part IV, Nāṣirī, *al-Istiqṣā*, vol. IX, p. 27 (second letter of the inhabitants of Tlemcen to 'Abd al-Raḥmān).

the French would confine themselves to the old Spanish policy, and no one imagined that the interior could be of the slightest interest to them. As it happened, the French went looking for vassal princes. First they thought of the bey of Tunis and offered him Oran. When this scheme failed, partly because its purpose was too obvious but above all because of the military and financial weakness of Tunisia,[8] the invaders approached the two leaders of local resistance, the bey Aḥmad in Constantine and the amir ʻAbd al-Qādir in Orania, but with no greater success. Traditional historians stress the differences that arose between the French government and the army of conquest, and later on between the army and the *colons*, who began to arrive in increasing number. From the Algerian point of view, these divergencies mattered very little, for the policies of all the parties concerned made for the same result, an extension of the area under French economic domination. Actually this necessitated the destruction neither of the Algerian state (total conquest), nor of Algerian society (the assimilationist policy favored by the colons). The establishment of a vassal state open to French businessmen would have sufficed. This was the colonial policy of England, the most advanced power of the day. If in the end France decided on a different course, it was because of the specific ideological situation in France between 1815 and 1871.[9] Thus it is futile to examine the motives of a Bugeaud or a Lamoricière or to try to call into play the policies of Napoleon III or of the Arab Bureaus; the determining causes are elsewhere and the only distinction that counts is that between ideology and form. Both soldiers and colons were steeped in ideology, the former in the Spanish, the latter in the Roman, myth.

Clearly the leaders of the French army disagreed on strategy, and all of them changed their minds in the course of

[8] Ibn Abī al-Ḍiyāf, *Itḥāf*, vol. III, pp. 175-178.

[9] The French political system clearly lagged behind the economic structure; hence a lasting revolutionary situation in which economic, moral or literary realism seemed dangerous.

operations, but the memory of the Spanish presence on the coasts of Africa played both a positive and a negative role in their thinking. The Spanish experience showed that a partial occupation could not succeed. The French could either vindicate the Spaniards and decide on a total occupation or impute the Spanish failure to a lack of gallantry and restrict their own occupation to the coastal strip. Military operations alternated with negotiations with the two leaders of the resistance, at least one of whom, it was hoped, would accept the status of vassal. When the sultan of Morocco refused to intervene in his traditional sphere of influence, the Tlemcen district, 'Abd al-Qādir b. Muhī al-Dīn al-Mukhtārī, the descendant of a leading family of Marabouts, was chosen by the population to carry on the war. From the start he showed superior qualities as a leader and trainer of men.[10] Desmichels, the new commandant of Oran, finally signed a treaty with him, recognizing him as independent sovereign of Orania. Allowing for possible divergencies between the two (Arabic and French) texts and the probable duplicity of the French negotiator, it is obvious that the treaty could benefit the French only if, in exchange for French neutrality in Orania, 'Abd al-Qādir accepted the sovereignty of the conquerors over a part of Algeria. In reality, 'Abd al-Qādir could do no more than close his eyes to a foreign, Christian presence. This soon became evident and the treaty was denounced. But a first attempt to crush the amir (Trézel's defeat at La Macta, Bugeaud's minor victory at La Sikkak) fizzled out and a second treaty was concluded at Tafna on May 30, 1837. It was more explicit than the first and for that very reason less applicable in the long run, for it divided the Algerian territory between two authorities, so that they could hope to coexist only by helping each other, which was out of the question. In the meantime the bey Aḥmad had been approached in the same way.

10 Amir 'Abd al-Qādir has not yet found a biographer worthy of him. Elements may be found in al-Jazā'irī, *Tuḥfat az-Zā'ir*, 1st ed., vol. 1, pp. 96-317; and in Blunt, *Desert Hawk*.

Twice he was offered the status of vassal and attacked when he refused.[11] The first attack on Constantine in 1836 ended in a French rout; in the second (October 1837), the city was taken, but under deplorable conditions. 'Abd al-Qādir took this as a breach of contract.

The war resumed in October 1839. The French were determined to win a total victory. Unity and stability of command were assured by the appointment of Bugeaud as governor general (December 20, 1840), counterguerrilla tactics were devised, and what was a large army for the time (108,000 in 1846) was assembled. The aim was to destroy the state that 'Abd al-Qādir had built up. Thus the traditionalist policy of merely gaining formal sovereignty over Algeria and letting it subsist as a distinct entity was abandoned. But the idea long continued to have its supporters, especially in the army.

'Abd al-Qādir's State

It was no accident that the most effective resistance to the French was organized in Orania and directed by a member of a family of Marabouts, for under the Turks, as we have seen, it was Orania that had suffered the severest oppression and had consequently offered the fiercest resistance. 'Abd al-Qādir replaced the Turkish system of taxation by a tithe (*'ushur*) on the harvest. Basing his regime essentially on the religious aristocracy, he combated the communities that had collaborated with the Turks. But he maintained the territorial and administrative divisions as well as the military organization of the Turkish period. Thus the character of his state was determined at once by that of the Turkish regime in its last stage and by the reformist religious ideology which permeated nearby Morocco at the time and which had been used to undermine the legitimacy of the Turkish authority. The importance of this state has been much discussed in an attempt to determine whether or not an Alge-

[11] New elements on Aḥmad Bey have been brought to light by Temimi, *Recherches et documents d'histoire maghrébine.*

rian nation existed at that time.[12] It is true that 'Abd al-Qādir's authority did not extend to all Algeria, and that his system would not, without modifications, have been appropriate to Kabylia or the Constantine district. But this in no wise detracts from the symbolic value of his action, which proves that the Maraboutic revolts at the end of the Turkish period were both reformist and patriotic in character.[13] The French aggression helped to crystallize this sentiment, since later on 'Abd al-Qādir received help from all the Maraboutic communities of Algeria, and there was nothing to prevent other local organizations, different in structure and traditions, from forming a federation or some other form of union with the Oranian kingdom. For Algeria, 'Abd al-Qādir's kingdom meant that the slow development, which since the early eighteenth century had gradually voided the Turkish occupation of its content, achieved its fulfillment for a brief moment before a stronger and better armed conqueror stepped in. For the Maghrib, it meant that the reformist religious ideology, always the first to make its appearance in a Moslem state in time of crisis, was capable of yielding positive results provided that an organic unity between the rulers and the ruled could be attained. In a historical perspective, 'Abd al-Qādir's state seemed to resuscitate the kingdom of Tlemcen, but unlike the Zayyānid kingdom it succeeded in solving the two fundamental problems of taxation and the army, something Morocco proved incapable of doing throughout the nineteenth century. Be that as it may, the French occupation, which may have hastened its birth, could not permit it to survive. Even if a modus vivendi had been arrived at between the two authorities, the Algerian kingdom would in the long run have ended like its two neighbors—under an increasingly overt protectorate.

12 See Gallissot, "Abd el-Kader et la nationalité algérienne," and "La Guerre d'Abd el-Kader ou la ruine de la nationalité algérienne."

13 In his letter to the jurists of Fez (1836/1252) 'Abd al-Qādir speaks of the Algerian fatherland: "Watan al-Jazā'ir"; the context leaves no doubt as to his meaning (al-Nāṣirī, vol. IX, p. 45). Compare with his letter to the Ottoman sultan in Temimi, pp. 195-202.

"The Arabs must be prevented from sowing, from harvesting, and from pasturing their flocks," Bugeaud had ordered. This destructive policy was applied systematically when the subtler policy of trying to drive a wedge between the amir and his lieutenants failed. When the cities of Tlemcen, Ténès and Tiaret were taken, 'Abd al-Qādir's government became nomadic. Then, on May 16, 1843, his camp itself was captured. In November of the same year his ablest lieutenant was killed. 'Abd al-Qādir then decided to recognize Moroccan suzerainty and wage conventional warfare. But the sultan 'Abd al-Raḥmān was by no means inclined to let the Algerian leader extend his Oranian reforms to Morocco.[14] He received him as a mere subaltern officer who had failed in his mission. The Moroccans suffered a crushing defeat (Isly, August 14, 1844), and by the treaty of Tangier concluded on September 10, 1844, under the auspices of England, the French won what they had previously obtained neither from Turkey nor the local chiefs, namely formal recognition of their presence in Algeria. But this did not end the war; it was in fact then that the war became really merciless, for the French could now call it an insurrection and treat the enemy as rebels. The widespread resistance, which continued until the surrender of 'Abd al-Qādir on December 23, 1847, was of great significance for the future: from 1845 on, it was no longer a state but a society that was being destroyed.

Colonial Policy

It is also at this stage that we observe the opposition between the ancien régime ideology (political suzerainty) and the modern capitalistic system (liberation of the individual from community ties). Both systems implied colonization, but each gave it a different significance. As both programs reflected French realities, neither could exclude the other for the time being. They were put into practice simultaneously, each in a delimited sphere. In the territory

[14] Al-Nāṣirī, vol. IX, p. 51 (on the poor relations between 'Abd al-Qādir and the sultan's son, the future Muḥammad IV).

under civilian control, French law was applied and the Islamic juridical structure gradually broken down. In the territory under military control, which was gradually extended toward the southern oases, the old social and administrative structures were maintained with the collaboration, deliberately courted by the military, of the local aristocracy that had served the Turks.[15] Undue importance has been attached to changes in the formulation of official French policy. In its esssentials it never varied, despite differences of opinion as to the rate at which the civil sphere should be expanded.[16] This is clearly shown by the uninterrupted spread of colonization. All the legislative texts from the decrees of 1844 and 1846 to the Senatus Consult of April 22, 1863, used modern capitalistic interpretations of Roman law as a means of taking lands from their owners. By confounding pasturage lands and uncultivated lands, jointly owned and collective property, by unduly extending the limits of forest lands, the French administration confined the indigenous population to a smaller and smaller territory, and on this point the military thought no differently from the civilians. They merely wished to defend the inviolability of individual property (law of June 16, 1851) and left the modalities to the administration (letter of February 6, 1863, and Senatus Consult of April 22, 1863). In this way the gates of the future were opened wide to the colons.[17] In spite of all that has been said about the goodwill of Napoleon III toward the Algerian population, the true nature of his policy is shown by the fact that in 1866 1.2 million

[15] See Monteil, "Les Bureaux arabes au Maghreb (1833-1961)."

[16] The policy of Napoleon III represents a kind of revenge of reality over ideology, but it was very late and hesitant.

[17] The policy of setting aside public lands for the colons has been studied by Ruedy, *Land and Policy in Colonial Algeria,* who explodes certain traditional ideas on the subject. The decrees of October 1, 1844, and June 21, 1846, and the Senatus Consult of April 22, 1863, the main legal instruments through which the Algerian peasants were expropriated, are analyzed by Bernard, *L'Algérie,* Julien, *Histoire de l'Algérie contemporaine,* and Ageron, *Histoire de l'Algérie contemporaine.* These analyses support and complement one another.

hectares of land were set aside for colonization; the only difference between the emperor and his detractors was that, under the influence of the modern capitalist ideology formulated by Saint-Simonism, he dreamed of a capitalism on an American rather than a French scale for Algeria. By 1870, roughly 674,340 hectares of farm land and 160,000 of forest land had been appropriated by the colons. This in itself shows that the destruction of Algerian society was well under way, though not uniformly in all parts of the country.

Destruction by Economic Means

Toward 1870 the number of colons approached two hundred and fifty thousand. They lived on an economy organized for their benefit, served by banks, a produce exchange (April 1852), railroads and a postal service, and producing for the French market (partial customs union with France in 1851). Living in a dominated economy, the Algerian population were the losers, regardless of whether prices rose or fell. After 1864 the Algerian peasants, already in difficulty because of the reduction in their lands, were hit by a drop in prices and a series of crop failures (in 1867 production fell to one-fifth of what it had been in 1863). The result was a general famine. In all likelihood the number of victims was considerably greater than the three hundred thousand ordinarily cited.[18] The destruction of society by a combination of political and economic means was leading to physical destruction.

The Algerian Reaction

Under the Turks the real power had been held by the local authorities—the religious élite and the military aris-

[18] Even if we reject the figure of ten million Algerians in 1830 advanced by Habart, *Histoire d'un parjure*, and accept the usually advanced figure of five million, it would follow that Algeria had lost half its population between 1830 and 1871; this cannot have resulted entirely from natural catastrophes. See C.-A. Julien's article of February 13, 1961, in *Le Monde*, and Lacheraf, *L'Algérie: nation et societé*, p. 221, n. 27.

tocracy. 'Abd al-Qādir's state owed its power to a federation of these authorities, which for a brief time were united. After 1847 the French military tried to maintain the system while changing the personnel. The policy of *cantonnement* (confining the indigenous population to specified areas) and the suppression of the Islamic judiciary prevented a reconciliation between the traditional élite and the new order. The consequence was a series of revolts in the Aurès Mountains, the Hodna, the Oranian Tell, and eastern Kabylia, which went on from 1859 to 1871. As in the days of the Turks, the local chiefs were obliged to act as intermediaries between the French and the population. Their position was subtly equivocal, for they had to take account of their own interests. The French authorities flattered them and incited them to expenditures which had the effect of impoverishing the population.[19] Thus the people lost confidence in the traditional élite. Pending the appearance of a new élite, they were left with leaders strong in duplicity and weak in experience. This is amply shown by the revolt of 1871, in which more than two-thirds of the population participated. The behavior of the chiefs can perhaps be attributed to the defeat of France at the hands of Prussia or even to a plot by certain French generals to defend their position in Algeria. The peasants, however, were undoubtedly motivated by the policy of *cantonnement* and by the steady fall in prices and production over a period of four consecutive years. In any event the attitudes of the local leaders and of the peasants who fought under them were very different. The chiefs waited, negotiated, tried to save their privileges, and let the opportunity for a surprise victory pass. Aware of this duplicity, the peasants charged certain men, originally chosen to keep the peace in the countryside and prevent pillaging (*sharṭīya*), with keeping an eye on the chiefs.[20] Despite the

[19] The policy of the Arab Bureaus of improving farming methods drove the shaykhs to incur debt through prestige expenditures.

[20] These *sharṭīya* of 1871 should be compared with those of 1804 in Tunisia; the idea came from the east and not from the Paris Commune. Cf. Ibn Abī al-Ḍiyāf, *Itḥāf*, vol. v, p. 121.

precautions and courage of the insurgents, who though virtually unarmed held out for seven months, the revolt collapsed in 1872. The colons had been desperately frightened and were ruthless in their vengeance. The higher structures of Algerian society had been destroyed in 1847. The insurrection of 1871 showed that legislation and the workings of the economy had now destroyed the intermediate structures. The French policy revived an aristocracy, but an aristocracy without influence or prestige. Southern Algeria, a protectorate under military control, continued to be the refuge of the brotherhoods (the revolt of the Awlād Sīdī Shaykh was to continue until 1884). When order had finally been restored, the individual Algerian, outside of his home, was virtually alone and defenseless against his new master. For the next fifty years his sole duty was to survive.

The history of Algeria from 1830 to 1871 is made up of pretenses: the colons who allegedly wished to transform the Algerians into men like themselves, when in reality their only desire was to transform the soil of Algeria into French soil; the military, who supposedly respected the local traditions and way of life, whereas in reality their only interest was to govern with the least possible effort; the claim of Napoleon III that he was building an Arab kingdom, whereas his central ideas were the "Americanization" of the French economy and the French colonization of Algeria. The French policy in Algeria (during and after the conquest) would seem to be explained primarily by the backwardness of French (as compared to English) capitalism. The methods of colonization employed suggest a mixture of seventeenth- and eighteenth-century colonialism and nineteenth-century imperialism. The course of events is explained far better by this historical lag than by the Algerian climate or memories of the Roman proconsulate. Every colonial undertaking requires three forms of violence: military, juridical and economic. Here they were combined in a very special way. The first overshadowed the second and the first two the third, but only in appearance, for the economic factor (based on France) led both the legislators and the military beyond the aims they had originally envisaged. In 1830 the French had no intention of destroying the Algerian state, but intended merely to replace one sovereign by another. In 1847 they still had no intention of destroying Algerian society. Even in 1870 they had no thought of destroying the traditional ties between individuals. Yet all these things were done, and since the economy that demanded them was still weak, a resort to arms and legislation was necessary. At a later date, as the economy grew stronger, it might have been possible to dispense with these supports. This becomes apparent when we observe the experience of Tunisia and Morocco.

Destruction of the State by Diplomacy

Tunisia

In the nineteenth century Tunisia retained the special character that distinguished it from the rest of the Maghrib. But to the two elements, Turkish and local, which had long provided the background of socio-political events, two more were now added: (1) a growing European colony represented by its consuls, and (2) the increased political influence of Constantinople. Thus the situation, in which diplomacy played a large part, was exceedingly complex. Nevertheless the French were able to impose their policy after 1830, but, because of competition with England,[21] it was to assume a subtler and more modern form than in Algeria.

(1) The Diplomatic Situation. The determining factor was the rivalry between France and England. England tried to reinforce Ottoman sovereignty over Tunisia, while France—at first cautiously, then, under Napoleon III, more and more aggressively—played the card of independence. Surprising

[21] English competition found its expression in the Anglo-Turkish commercial treaty of 1838, which the English tried to apply to Tunisia as part of the Turkish Empire and which served as a model for the Anglo-Moroccan treaty of December 9, 1856.

as it may seem, the Turkish élite, headed by the bey, favored the French policy, while the local élite inclined toward England and the sultan.[22] The reason is simple: what we have termed the Ḥafṣid restoration, which augured the rise of a national consciousness, was closely bound up with the development of the urban merchant class, which was intent on reform.

Since the early nineteenth century Turkey had undertaken profound reforms (from the military reforms of Selīm III to the Hatt i Sharif of Gülhan, issued in 1839). Thus there was no incompatibility between national strivings and the desire for reform. The bey, on the other hand, regarded independence primarily as a means of keeping his absolute power. This suited the French perfectly, because absolutism weakened Tunisia internally while isolating it diplomatically. Still, France could not go very far in this direction, because, as events were to show, reforms were in its own interest. The result of these contradictions was an atmosphere eminently favorable to intrigue. The beys Ḥusayn II, Mustapha and Aḥmad Pasha maintained polite and even cordial relations with the French authorities in Algeria, with the avowed aim of avoiding the fate of the Caramanli, who had lost the pashalik of Tripoli as a result of their internecine struggles. In view of Louis-Philippe's caution, Aḥmad Pasha was obliged to make conciliatory gestures toward the sultan, as is shown by his participation with fourteen thousand men and several warships in the Turco-Russian war of 1854-1855. Little by little Tunisia resumed its place in the Ottoman Empire, as did Egypt after the death of Muḥammad 'Alī. Thus through a conjunction of Ottoman, British, and to a certain degree French influence, the situation was favorable to reform.

(2) The Reforms. The first reforms were purely imitative, either of Europe or of Turkey, e.g. the vestimentary reform under Ḥusayn, the introduction of decorations (*nayāshīn*)

[22] On the relations between Tunisia and Turkey, see Ibn Abī al-Ḍiyāf, vol. VI, pp. 13-30, especially p. 16.

and the minting of commemorative coins by Mustapha Bey;[23] in 1846 Tunis closed its slave market, chiefly to create a good impression in Europe. A few progressive steps were also taken in the cultural field, such as the reorganization of the Zitūna library and the establishment of an official newspaper.[24] Other reforms affected the army. As in Turkey, the old janissary system, long a mere relic of the past, was abolished at the beginning of the century. The army (*nizāmīya*) was reorganized, first by Ḥusayn, but more radically by Aḥmad Pasha, who instituted compulsory military service and raised an army of thirty thousand, well equipped with artillery. In 1840/1256 a military school with Turkish and European instructors was founded at the Bardo.[25] Tunisia also had a small navy. These reforms, like those of Turkey and Egypt, are hard to explain. Did the beys with a possible aggressor in mind (in this case, France) wish to strengthen the country's defenses? Did they wish to make a show of modernism? Did they merely succumb to the blandishments of the European merchants? All these factors must have played a part. The result in any case was a modern police force rather than an army. It served primarily to maintain internal order, a basic demand of the European colony and its spokesmen, the consuls.

The direct consequence of the new policy was a fiscal reform which immediately laid bare the contradictions of Tunisian society. Ḥusayn II tried to increase the proceeds from the land tax by replacing the evaluation of the agricultural yield before the harvest by a tithe reckoned after the harvest. Aḥmad II was obliged to institute customs duties and taxes on internal trade, to accord himself a monopoly on the sale of such things as salt, tobacco, soap, and above all, like many governments in financial straits, to farm

[23] See *ibid.*, p. 18, for disabused comments on these decorations.

[24] The language of this publication is extremely interesting because it highlights the progress that has been made since then.

[25] On the shaykh Qabādū, who taught Arabic there, see the comment of Ibn 'Ashūr, *Al-Ḥaraka*, pp. 14ff., who speaks of an alliance between the Zitūna and modern science.

out the land taxes. In these supposed reforms it is not hard to see the influence of foreign advisers in connivance with the merchants and interested primarily in immediate results. Not only did tax farming enrich individuals while increasing the state's indebtedness and impoverishing the population; moreover, the taxes on commerce made the welfare of the treasury dependent on the expansion of foreign trade, which, once it reaches a certain level, becomes incompatible with government monopolies.[26] Well aware of the hopeless contradiction that doomed all these reforms to failure, the bey Mḥammad II, Aḥmad Pasha's successor, decided to abolish both the army and the taxes that were supposed to finance it. He thought he had found a solution to his difficulties when in 1856/1272 he imposed a single tax (*i'āna,* to which the generic name *majba* was later given). If it had been possible to check expenditures, the reform might have been successful, but the pressure of the foreign merchants was too strong; any policy of austerity struck them as a mark of hostility. And indeed it was their steadily increasing number and influence that accounts for the political reforms.

The reform spirit itself, expressing the desire for good relations with foreign countries, and the increasing involvement of the state in commerce both favored the growth of the foreign colony,[27] which clamored more and more for guarantees and incentives. Their watchword, of course, was freedom; the enemy to be struck down was the Islamic legal system. Here there is no need to discuss the validity of the arguments raised against Islamic law; suffice it to point out their heterogeneous character. Some remained within the framework of the system and invoked the terms of the ca-

[26] See André Raymond, "La France, la Grande-Bretagne et le problème de la réforme en Tunisie," in *Études maghrébines,* pp. 146-147, n. 5.

[27] Ganiage cites the figure of twelve thousand five hundred in 1856; to this may be added a good part of the twenty-three thousand Jews, whom several of the consulates tried to win over to their cause by offering them protection (*Les Origines du Protectorat français en Tunisie,* p. 173).

pitulations; others were attempts to codify capitalist relations. The foreigners' main objection to Moslem law was its communitarian aspect, its defense of collective property and guarantee of fair wages.[28] In the past foreign merchants had been judged as individuals, by their own laws, but now that their number increased, their business operations required the extension of these laws to the whole population. This extension called itself reform. This was the true significance of the reform of September 10, 1857/1274, in Tunis, as it had been of the reform (*tanzimat*) in Turkey. After various disputes in which the consuls played a determining role,[29] the bey Mḥammad promulgated a security pact (*'Ahd al-Amān*) which was a reform of the judiciary system. Its eight articles guaranteed religious freedom to non-Moslems (Art. 4), equality before the law (Art. 8), equal taxation (Art. 3); it also prohibited commercial monopolies (Art. 9) and gave non-Moslems the right to buy landed property (Art. 10). Article 6 provided for a criminal court (High Court of the Shra') and Article 7 for a commercial tribunal with foreign participation. The pact was read at an imposing ceremony attended by consuls and high government officials, and the bey, whose absolute power it curtailed for the first time, swore to apply it faithfully. With the help of the consuls, whose demands had been supported by demonstrations of naval power, the foreign colony (which had associated the local Jewish colony with its interests and demands) had imposed a kind of liberal revolution. Despite a certain community of interests between the foreign colony and the Tunisian élite, which seems to have welcomed the reform, the fact remains that a group of resident foreigners had thus initiated a process of denaturing the beylical state and making it subservient to their interests. The Security Pact was later implemented by such mea-

28 In the reply of Robert Wood, the British consul, to Ibn Abī al-Ḍiyāf, vol. IV, p. 236, we see that the consul was opposed to Islamic jurisprudence as it had developed over the centuries and not to the moral principles of Islam, which obviously harm no one.

29 *Ibid.*, pp. 233ff.; Ganiage, pp. 71ff.

sures as the institution in Tunis of a city council, whose members were appointed from among the notables of the city. Mḥammad Bey died in 1858. His successor Muḥammad al-Ṣādiq set up the above-mentioned penal code, established a court of appeals (*Majlis al-Taḥqīq*), and appointed a grand council with sixty members, twenty of whom were high government dignitaries, which advised him on political and financial matters and functioned as a council of state. The rules governing the operation of these councils were formulated in a charter, the first copy of which was given to Napoleon III in Algiers in September 1860, in the course of a visit paid him by the bey at the insistence of the French consul in Tunis. This charter (*Qānūn al-Dawla*) was promulgated in January 1861, but not put into effect until April 2. It remained in force for three years. In the meantime, between 1858 and 1863, various decrees had been published, authorizing foreigners to acquire property in Tunisia and to engage in business activities of every kind. The most important text pertaining to the rights of foreigners was the Anglo-Tunisian pact of October 10, 1863/1280.[30] Aḥmād Pasha's military reform, which might have enabled Tunisia to resist foreign pressure if it had been accompanied by a corresponding politico-administrative reorganization, had failed because of fiscal difficulties. Mḥammad Bey believed that if he acceded to the foreign demands a strong army would be superfluous. In reality, the foreign pressure could have been countered only if internal order had been maintained, and Muḥammad al-Ṣadīq failed to see that the Tunisian population would react violently to reforms which favored the European colony at their expense. Apparently introduced in order to render direct European intervention superfluous, the reforms actually paved the way for it.

(3) The Crisis. The crisis was of a type that was to become frequent in the nineteenth century. Essentially it was

[30] Ibn Abī al-Ḍiyāf, vol. v, pp. 101-105.

brought about by the juxtaposition of a modern state with a society that did not recognize such a state as its own image and moreover could not support it financially.

In 1858 when the security pact was promulgated, the economic difficulties that had been building up for some years culminated in a monetary crisis.[31] The policy of modernization led the political élite to buy on credit large quantities of European goods imported by local European merchants; thus the Tunisians became heavily indebted to the merchants, and their debts increased by leaps and bounds because of an unusually high rate of interest. Since there was a shortage of exportable commodities (especially oil and cereals), the European merchants sent gold and silver coins out of the country. Commodity prices fell, as did the income of the rural population. The copper coinage, which alone remained plentiful, soon lost its value. Merchants ceased to accept it and the commercial circuit was disorganized. A covert devaluation was decided on, but this expedient failed when the foreign merchants bought up the copper coins at low prices and sold them to the state at the official rate before the deadline that had been set for the exchange of coins. The beylical state never surmounted this monetary crisis. Its social consequences were disastrous, for it doomed every attempt at tax reform to failure. The foreign merchants with their hoards of capital benefited by it, but never the indebted state. Since the state needed money and the tax base diminished from year to year, it resorted to organized theft, seizing merchandise, buildings, jewels, furniture, and the like, and selling them on an already glutted market; or else it encouraged the population to pile up debts with the banks and foreign merchants. Since the local and Turkish élites were also in debt, theft by violence or ruse became almost general.[32] The Mamelukes were more and more detested; the traditional urban élite, resentful of Turkish

31 *Ibid.*, pp. 253-255.

32 Those who put the accent on "thieving Bedouins" ought to ask who started the thieving.

domination and suffering from the competition of the European colony, moved both sentimentally and politically closer to the rural masses, who had come to regard the state as a mere instrument of pillage in the service of foreigners. But this alliance was temporary, and when after long patience the rural communities revolted, their rebellion was either anarchic or utterly irrational, since they put their hopes in the sultan of Turkey or even in the foreign consuls (especially the British consul). Thus economic forces had the same effect as the juridical reform; to undermine the Tunisian state from within by exacerbating its old tendency to isolation from society.

We discern this dynamic in the great insurrection of 1864, known as the revolt of ʿAlī b. Ghadhāhum.[33] Prevented by the pressure of the consuls from putting heavy taxes on foreign commerce, obtaining nothing from foreign loans, which proved to be pure swindles, and unable to reimburse them because the borrowed capital never went into productive investments, the bey doubled the rate of the land tax in 1863. Already hard hit by the crisis, the people knew that these taxes served chiefly to defray expenses the foreigners had imposed: prestige building, equipment for the army, the modernization of Tunis, political and administrative reorganization. Consequently they demanded the abrogation of all the reforms from the abolition of slavery to the establishment of criminal courts. The "reactionary" character of these demands has often been stressed, but the one question that seriously concerns us here is the question asked by the rebels: Who benefited by these reforms, and who was expected to finance them? Be that as it may, the economic crisis that caused the revolt doomed it to failure. The alliance with the Sahel bourgeoisie was shortlived. The general poverty made the leaders (and first and foremost ʿAlī b. Ghadhāhum) receptive to the bey's promises and made the troops impatient to go home to the

[33] Bice Salamah's monograph, *L'Insurrection de 1864 en Tunisie*, replaces all earlier studies.

harvests. The pusillanimity of the leaders, which prevented the insurgents from attacking the principle of the beylicate, as well as a vague fear that the French would take advantage of the disorder to occupy the country, resulted in a return to the status quo. In the years that followed, the situation was further aggravated by drought, famine and epidemics (cholera in 1865, typhus in 1867).

In 1869 a commission was appointed to administer the Anglo-French-Italian debt. For practical purposes the state had ceased to exist. The survival of formal independence has been attributed to the rivalry among the European powers; a more likely explanation is that the economic conditions then prevailing in the European countries made the occupation of Tunisia seem impracticable or too costly. Be that as it may, the second reform experiment, undertaken by Khayr al-Dīn,[34] changed nothing despite the ideological importance attributed to it in Tunisia (which in some respects it deserves, for at least it showed a certain open-mindedness). The Tunisian state continued to have no other function than to serve foreign interests. It is important to note that Khayr al-Dīn was called to power under the pressure of foreigners, whose interest he had aroused in 1867 by publishing a program in French. This program, several points of which were put into effect between 1873 and 1877, was entirely in line with the foreigners' demands. The reorganization of the fiscal administration, begun in 1869, served primarily to guarantee the servicing of the foreign debt (then estimated at 125 million gold francs); the establishment of a mixed commercial tribunal, the unification of legislation, the institution in Tunis of a council of health and city planning, were all calculated to win the confidence of the foreign colony. Even the measures which were to have the most beneficial effects later on—the distribution of state lands among the peasants, a twenty-year tax exemption

[34] See Leon Carl Brown, Introduction to the English translation of Khayr al-Dīn's *The Surest Path*; and Hourani, *Arabic Thought in the Liberal Age*, pp. 84-94. These are the best analyses of Khayr al-Dīn's thinking.

aimed at encouraging arboriculture in the Sahel, the founding of a modern secondary school (*al-Ṣādiqiya*) in 1876—prepared the way for the absorption of Tunisian society by the capitalist system and thus favored the projects of the foreign colony. Regardless of the motives that inspired Khayr al-Dīn and his following of enlightened men, who were to transmit their political ideal to the young Tunisians of the twentieth century, it cannot be denied that the success of his experiment depended on the confidence it inspired in the foreign powers. The moment they decided it was too slow and did not go far enough, it was doomed. The French soon began to intrigue against the reform minister as they had against his corrupt predecessor. In the meantime, the foreigners saw their economic interests increase and diversify, and this sharpened their desire to take the reformation of Tunisian society into their own hands and carry it on in their own way. What could have been more logical than such an attitude? And what difference did it make to the Tunisian peasant whether foreigners or pseudonationalists held the controls, since the aim was identical? Those who say that national sentiment in 1880-1881 was lukewarm (a notion far from being fully justified by the facts) should not forget the objective causes that deterred the Tunisians from defending to the death a state which was less than ever theirs. Economic, legal and military violence succeeded each other as in Algeria, though in the inverse order: the result was the same.

Morocco

From the Moroccan point of view, the French capture of Algiers meant above all the end of a tyrannical and violently contested regime. It also presented the possibility of renewing the policy of Ismāʿīl in the Tlemcen region. The sultan soon realized, however, that a new situation had arisen.

(1) Military Pressure. After the collapse of Turkish power, the inhabitants of Tlemcen put themselves under the protection of the sultan ʿAbd al-Raḥmān b. Hishām. The sul-

tan, who after the catastrophic end of Sulāyman's reign had barely had time to restore a semblance of order by reorganizing the army, reducing Muḥammad b. Ghazi, one of the chiefs of the Middle Atlas, to submission (1822/1238), installing energetic governors with unlimited powers in the difficult provinces of Marrakech and Oujda, and pursuing an anti-Maraboutic policy in the interior (siege of the *zāwiya* of Sharrādiya), was opposed to direct intervention. He consulted the jurists of Fez and obtained the negative advice he wanted. But the inhabitants of Tlemcen insisted, and in the end he was obliged to send a garrison, led by his cousin 'Alī b. Sulāyman. Disobeying his express orders, the soldiers, taking advantage of the resistance of the Kurughli and the Turks' former allies, pillaged the city. When the sultan recalled the troops, some of them revolted.

The sultan's analysis had been proved right: he was in no position to campaign in Algeria. In 1832 he promised De Mornay, the French ambassador, that in the future he would refrain at least from direct intervention. His relations with 'Abd al-Qādir are explained as much by this first experience as by the general principles of Islamic public law, which they both invoked. When the jurists of Fez inclined to 'Abd al-Qādir's arguments, the sultan provided him with arms, horses and subsidies. The consequence was a sort of alliance accompanied by a vague recognition of suzerainty, and that was as far as the sultan would go. But this state of affairs lasted only from 1839 to 1843. After that the amir was several times obliged to take refuge in Morocco, and sometimes the French army pursued him. 'Abd al-Raḥmān became involved in spite of himself. The relations between the two men changed completely. Once he had sent regular troops to Oujda, the sultan regarded the amir as a mere subaltern who had failed in his mission and had no further right to make demands. 'Abd al-Qādir, on the other hand, saw no further need to recognize the authority of a sultan who was unable to make use of his power.[35]

[35] See the subtly moderate judgment of al-Nāṣirī, *al-Istiqṣā*, vol. IX, pp. 51-58.

The Franco-Moroccan war was a disaster for Morocco, which was saved only by English intervention; by the treaty of Tangier (September 10, 1844) the sultan undertook to drive out or intern the amir. In other words, he objectively allied himself with the French army. He also resigned himself to accept, by the convention of Lalla Marnia (March 18, 1845), a vague definition of the Algero-Moroccan border, which provided the French with a useful means of pressure. These treaties, of course, were not binding on 'Abd al-Qādir, who obstinately continued the struggle. He appealed directly to the border population, who often gave him their support, so bearing witness to the steadily widening gulf between local interests and communitarian obligations. 'Abd al-Qādir's attitude was normal and right for the time, but his cause was hopeless and he accomplished nothing: the French gained territory, while the amir succeeded only in destroying property.[36] This was true in Morocco as well as in Algeria. The sultan's independence and the integrity of his territory were safeguarded not by the Moroccan army, which was disorganized and poorly equipped, but by the protection of the English.

After the death of 'Abd al-Raḥmān in 1859, the military pressure increased. Taking advantage of the vagueness of the border convention or pretexting situations of insecurity, the French sent an expedition against the Banū Isnāsin and pursued the Banū Guīl in the Figuig region. Their main purpose was to show that the sultan's power had become a fiction. Perceiving the feebleness of the Moroccan government, Spain took the offensive after years of inactivity, occupying the Chafarinas Islands and, by sending the sultan an ultimatum containing religious demands that he could not possibly accept, deliberately created the incident that culminated in the expedition of 1859. Under the command of O'Donnell, fifty thousand men, including adventurers of all nationalities, advanced on Tetuán. The Moroccan troops opposing them numbered only fifty-six hundred. Neverthe-

[36] *Ibid.*, p. 49.

less the advance was slow, for the guerrilla bands that sprang up from among the population offered stubborn resistance. But the sultan's only thought was to negotiate. The population revolted against his representatives and attacked Tetuán, which hastened to open its gates to the invading army.[37] This war of 1860 was in every way characteristic of the crisis that shook the state and society of Morocco in the nineteenth century. Under English pressure the Spaniards finally withdrew after a two years' occupation, in return for an indemnity of twenty million douros, which was paid in part by a loan from English banks, guaranteed by Moroccan customs receipts.[38] The Moroccan historians of the time saw this unprovoked war of rapine as the end of Morocco's dreams: a serious war against the European powers was no longer possible; the inequality was too great.

This military pressure, which attained its paroxysms in 1844 and 1859-1860 was not intermittent but permanent; it responded to European economic interests.

(2) Economic Pressure. The first step taken by the powers was to abolish one of the Moroccan state's main sources of income: piracy. It had first been forbidden in 1818. When 'Abd al-Raḥmān tried to revive it, the consequence was an incident with Austria in 1829, and the following year it was abandoned for good. Its last vestiges, the fees still paid by Denmark and Sweden, were abolished under French pressure in 1844. As we have seen, taxes on trade had been the most regular source of treasury receipts since the reign of Muḥammad III. In 1825 a treaty was concluded with Sardinia and in 1829 with England. From then on we observe a tendency toward stabilization of the rules governing foreign trade and toward conciliation of the interests of the Moroccan treasury with those of the foreign merchants. In

[37] See the account in Dāwud, *Tārīkh Tiṭwān*, vol. IV, pp. 203-205, and his judgment in the matter, p. 204, n. 1.

[38] The consequences have been studied on the basis of unpublished Moroccan documents by Ayache, "Aspects de la crise financière au Maroc."

1856, a trade and friendship pact was signed with England and the commercial privileges accorded to the British were later extended to other European countries by means of the most favored nation clause imposed by the powers on the sultan. Its basic principle was absolute freedom of trade between the two countries; the sultan's monopolies, except for those on tobacco and opium, were abolished. Import duties were set at ten percent ad valorem, and export duties, though specific, were reckoned at roughly the same rate. The sultan retained theoretical control over the importation of sulphur, gunpowder, arms and ammunition. Unrestricted exportation, especially of grain, had for years been a subject of controversy among Moroccan jurists. Imposed by the treaty of 1856, it was the most conspicuous indication of how radically the commercial relations between Morocco and the European countries had changed. Since the sultan was no longer able to regulate commercial relations as he saw fit or to impose new taxes on the foreign merchants, his only hope of adding to his revenues lay in an increase in the number of foreign merchants and in the expansion of their activities. In 1861 Spain obtained the same advantages as England, plus the authorization for Spanish subjects to acquire landed property in the environs of certain coastal cities. To this the local population was violently opposed. The makhzen tried to discourage prospective buyers by making it as hard as possible to obtain the required permits, but in the end the buyers were almost always successful. The foreigners, however, were no longer content with their immunity from Moroccan legislation; they wished to extend the same privilege to an increasing number of their Moroccan business associates. By 1856 the consuls were empowered to settle disputes between foreigners and Moroccans. Privileges were granted to Moroccan employees of the consulates, agents of business firms and partners in agricultural enterprises. The Franco-Moroccan treaty of August 17, 1863, which was soon extended to other powers, consecrated these extraterritorial privileges. The authority of the

Moroccan government no longer applied to the whole population or territory. No one having business dealings with the foreigners (farmers, herdsmen, merchants) could be pursued by law without prior notification of the consular authority. Every advantage accorded the foreign powers provided them with a permanent means of intervention. As in Algeria and Tunis, the slogan of freedom (of trade, of property, of the individual)[39] served to undermine the state from within and prepare the way for the introduction of the capitalistic system.

(3) The Crisis. Foreign pressure in all its forms resulted in a grave economic crisis, which exacerbated the political crisis that had been latent since the beginning of the century.

The economic crisis was of the ancien régime type. The prices of some commodities slumped and others were in short supply; the consequence was inflation and monetary confusion. Free exportation led to a rise in the prices of grain and wool; increasing imports from Europe created difficulties for the urban artisans; in need of cash, they flooded the market with their wares, the prices of which fell. Since coins of all kinds were in circulation (the dirham was the official currency) and the market was fragmented, there was a rapid succession of inflationary and deflationary cycles,[40] which benefited no one but the foreigners. To remedy the disorganization of the commercial circuit, the sultan reinstated the legal rate of exchange, first in 1852, and after the difficulties ensuing from the Spanish war, again in 1869. It goes without saying that the result was not at all what he had hoped.

The economic crisis had immediate political repercussions, for the people attributed all their misfortunes to the

[39] The religious minorities, especially the Jews, provided the foreign powers with an excellent pretext for intervening in Moroccan and Tunisian affairs when they saw fit. See Ibn Abī al-Ḍiyāf, vol. IV, p. 259; al-Nāṣirī, vol. IX, pp. 112-114.

[40] *Ibid.*, p. 54, and especially p. 163; Miège, *Le Maroc et l'Europe*, vol. III, pp. 97-106.

foreign penetration, and every concession to the consuls cost the sultan a part of his prestige and authority. Since the limited customs receipts went into servicing the foreign debts, the sultan was obliged to institute new taxes, which the urban population resented all the more because the foreigners were always exempted. In 1850/1266 taxes on leather sales and livestock were introduced, and in 1861/1278 city tolls on goods of all kinds. The resulting discontent in the towns was taken up by the *fuqahā'*, who invoked religious tradition and condemned all fiscal "innovations." The ferment in the cities increased when the crisis spread to the countryside, as in 1850 when the southern region suffered a serious famine, and after 1866 when the country was struck by a series of natural catastrophes and epidemics. Increasing opposition both to the foreign pressure and to the makhzen which failed to combat it effectively was reflected in a number of autonomist revolts.

(4) The Futility of Reform. Confronted by all these difficulties, the government could only hesitate and temporize. Old methods were applied to new problems. Once again traditional methods of taxation were tried. 'Abd al-Raḥmān had realized that in the face of increasing European pressure no reform could succeed. To gain time, he relied on the benevolent protection that England deigned to provide from 1830 to 1880.[41] But the British policy was contradictory. The English were willing to defend the power of the sultan provided he introduced "liberal" reforms, the effect of which was precisely to weaken him both morally and materially; they resulted in the rich paying no taxes while the poor were crushed by taxes; the rich favored reforms (which they refused to finance) so as to encourage enterprises disadvantageous to the poor—a vicious circle. The new army (*'askar*), originally designed to defend the country's independence, served in the end only to insure the

[41] See Flournoy, *British Policy towards Morocco in the Age of Palmerston.*

security of the foreign colony by putting down local revolts. 'Abd al-Raḥmān's policy of giving commands with broad powers to personal friends was the origin of the great families of qaids, who, since the foreigners courted them and loaned them money, became the faithful allies of European interests. Neither the personal qualities nor the good intentions (stressed by the Moroccan historians) of the sultans are subject to doubt; it was the dialectic of the situation that condemned their actions to futility and often led to results very different from those intended. Everything they did benefited the consuls.

This situation was to drag on for many years; the dénouement was long delayed, as in Tunisia, but by 1880 the Moroccan state had ceased to be anything more than a fiction maintained for reasons that were by no means purely diplomatic. Under 'Abd al-Raḥmān and Muḥammad IV, the situation was tragic, because these were able and well-intentioned men condemned by circumstances; it became tragicomic under Ḥasan I, who raced up and down the country trying to save a fabric that was unraveling on all sides; under 'Abd al-'Azīz it was frankly grotesque. The incidents that mark the disintegration of Moroccan society from 1894 to 1914 redound to the credit of no one, neither of the bankers who pulled the strings, the diplomats who carried on the intrigues, nor the cynical and compliant Moroccan rulers. But the Morocco of 1900 to 1912 was not eternal.[42]

Primary Resistance: An Attempt at Definition

The year 1860 marked the beginning of intensive colonization. Two years before the Kabyles had been subdued, the French had made a demonstration of naval power off

[42] That it was is implied in the vast body of literature that has made Morocco fashionable since 1880. See the works of Ludovic de Campou, Charles de Foucauld, John Drummond Hay, Budgett Meakin, Eugène Aubin, etc.; also Miège, vol. 1, Bibliography.

the coast of Tunisia, and preparations were under way for the Spanish-Moroccan war. Three years later the Senatus Consult of 1863 was promulgated in Algeria, and the Anglo-Tunisian and Franco-Moroccan treaties were signed; the following year witnessed the revolts of Rehamna in Morocco, of the Awlad Sīdī Shaykh in Orania and of the 'Urūsh in southern Tunisia. Then followed years of famine, epidemics and natural catastrophes until 1871. Such disasters were familiar, to be sure, but in this period their devastating effects were increased by the growth of European commerce, the appropriation of land by the Europeans, the rise in prices, and the monetary crisis. Regardless of differences in juridico-political status, all the populations of the middle Maghrib suffered the same disastrous conditions.[43]

This fact is seldom mentioned in the voluminous writings devoted to Europeans in the Maghrib. On the pretext that the Europeans left documentary evidence behind them, we are overwhelmed with the details of their activities. But who were they? Diplomats, soldiers, businessmen, dealers in agricultural products and livestock, farmers, educators, missionaries—all were intermediaries. Their activity was neither action nor, in the strict sense of the word, reaction, but simply an actualization of ideas conceived elsewhere. What was the center of action? What were the rhythm, form, methods and results of this action? It is up to economic history and economics to answer these questions, not by recapitulating the general laws of capitalism but by formulating laws specific to a given national capitalism exercised in a given colonized territory. To this end it will be neces-

[43] Is it by chance that the idea of an Arab kingdom in Algeria arose at a time when the colonial pressure on Morocco and Tunisia was being intensified? From the point of view of the Algerian colon, there was a great difference between the situations in the three countries, but it was not he who determined French colonial policy; he merely influenced it. From the standpoint of the big bankers, the diplomatic status of a country mattered little, and events have proved them right.

sary to discover "documents" that have hitherto remained secret or difficult of access, and to study them with a certain theoretical rigor. We still have a long way to go.

The "object" of the action was of course the common man of the Maghrib. From 1860 on, he was to feel its effects more and more deeply. Those who were above him and lived by his labor—the local chiefs, the Marabouts, the cultural or commercial élite of the cities, the government personnel—were also intermediaries whose reactions, relatively easy to study because they were stated in writing, were nevertheless indirect expressions of a deeper dissatisfaction. If we are not to rely on the picture presented by the colonizers themselves, we shall need methods still to be created or still to be adapted in order to analyze the impact of colonial pressures on the inner life of the Maghrib. In the meantime let us sketch the broad outlines of the situation.

The foreign colony, whatever its size, played the role of a middle class in the Maghrib. It imposed juridical reforms that amounted to a "liberal revolution"—a circumstance which then and later condemned the idea of liberal revolution in the eyes of the Maghribis. In so doing it deepened the cleavages between indigenous social groups, which are now definable only in terms of their relationship to the foreign colony. These cleavages were not new, but under foreign impact they were intensified, for the opposition of interests between groups now became manifest. The rural communities suffered, among other calamities, virtually confiscatory taxes; they dreamed of a just, austere, frugal and equitable prince. "The rampart that protects us," Ibn Ghadhāhum had proclaimed, "is that we are the victims of injustice."[44] In the past they had been able to set their grievances before the unjust or dissolute prince; this they could do no longer because it was the princes who suffered most from the military reform recommended by the foreigners. The rural communities resorted to intermediaries such as the chiefs and marabouts, who played a double game be-

[44] Ibn Abī al-Ḍiyāf, vol. v, p. 122.

cause they, too, had been impoverished by the crisis. Actually the rural revolt was an anachronism, for the "just prince" must be strong, independent, and rooted in his community, but no prince had possessed these qualities in a long time, and if by chance a prince retained some vestiges of them, the revolt itself dealt him the death blow. Hence the guilty conscience of the chiefs and the desperate hesitation of their followers.

In the long run, the mercantile élite of the cities was to benefit by the foreign penetration; for the present its members smarted under foreign competition and resented the fiscal advantages from which they were excluded. Occasionally they supported the rural revolts through the brotherhoods, some of which were of urban origin. But they nursed old grudges against the country people, they were well aware of the contrast between the urban and the rural mode of life, and above all feared that a successful revolt would endanger their property. This accounts for their attitude in Tetuán in 1860 and in the cities of the Tunisian Sahel during the revolt of 1864. The relations of this urban élite with the makhzen, with the foreign colony, and with the rural population were thoroughly ambiguous, as became strikingly apparent when the very families that would later set themselves up as guardians of the national tradition appealed to the foreign powers for protection. At the time, however, the basic result of this loss of status by the urban élite was cultural regression in the literal sense, that is, a return to the past. In an effort to oppose the sultan's system of taxation (*mukūs*), to do away with foreign competition (free trade and the right of foreigners to hold property), or to confine the rural revolts within the limits imposed by respect for private property, the "Islamic tradition" was invoked. Liberalism would never be recognized as a progressive ideology.[45]

[45] Those who expressed liberal leanings were the government personnel, who had been subjected to the arguments of the consuls. This was the case of Ibn Abī al-Ḍiyāf in Tunisia. Al-Nāṣirī involuntarily throws light

Finally, the ruling class, having lost all authority and influence, split into conflicting factions and wasted its energies in endless intrigues. Mutual distrust often enabled the consuls or foreign bankers to play the role of arbiters. The generals or governors, whose mission it was to defend the independence of the country, were "protégés" of the foreign powers, or indebted to the bankers. Caught between the two fires of foreign pressure and internal revolt, the rulers resorted to the weapons of the weak—diplomacy and guile—but in the long run they deceived no one.

Thus each of the groups that made up Maghribi society alternately advocated violence and compromise, but all agreed that the foreigners were the root of the troubles. Xenophobia has often been condemned as a negative reaction, and rightly so, but in the present case it had its objective causes. Nevertheless, it was ineffectual; resistance to foreign pressure may be called primary because everything—government reforms, urban unrest, Maraboutic agitation and rural insurrections—was, or seemed to be, initiated from outside, because everything that happened served foreign interests. It matters little that there were deliberate traitors; in the given situation treason was only natural. A chloroformed society was allowed to drag out its death agony until the foreign powers decided on its death. The decision came early in Algeria. It was delayed in Tunisia and still more in Morocco, but the ultimate results were very much the same.

---

on the obstacles to the understanding and adoption of the liberal ideology when he laments that this "liberty invented by the Franks" is undoubtedly the daughter of "atheism."

14. The Triumph of Colonialism

From 1880 until the world crisis of 1929 colonialism triumphed; its only limits were those it imposed on itself in line with the ideology of the "white man's burden" and economy of expenditure and effort. Its triumph had its counterpart in the reactions of its victims: resignation or hopeless revolt.

1881. The Algerian administration was attached to various ministries in Paris; Tunisia was occupied, at first without great difficulty; Morocco was placed under international control at the Conference of Madrid (second session, held in May). With the disappearance of the last autonomous state the process of destroying Maghribi society was accelerated. Maghribi society had always been able, in one way or another, to separate its destiny from that of the organized state. Now it was attacked from all sides. The aim, consciously or not, was to reduce the man of the Maghrib to his individual dimension. Side by side with a slowly disintegrating society, another society came into being, with its land holdings, its economic system and its administrative organization. When these two movements, following opposite courses, reached a certain point, the nature of the institutional problem changed. In the nineteenth century the foreigners had striven for a reform of Maghribi society that would enable them to carry on their activities. In the twentieth century the reform movement would take the opposite direction, becoming an effort on the part of the Maghribis to wrest a share of power and responsibility from the long-privileged foreigners.

Quite apart from the political disturbances that shook the foreign colony and the economic upsets that undermined its prosperity, the great crisis came when the historical weaknesses of Maghribi society, which the foreigners had long exploited so ruthlessly, ceased to work to their advantage, when the man of the Maghrib began to find strength in the very fact that he had been reduced to the "anthropological" level.[1] At that point the whole situation was reversed: reasons became pretexts, action degenerated into agitation, labor ceased to be productive; smugness gave way to fear, and optimism to anxiety. When did this change occur? In 1910? In 1920? In 1930? And what caused it? A reversal of the demographic development? Loss of prestige resulting from the defeats suffered in the First World War? The crisis brought about by the increasing preponderance of high finance? There is truth in all these answers, but they are partial and probably premature. Definitive answers will be possible only when figures can be translated into states of consciousness and patterns of behavior. In the meantime we have only intuition as a guide.

A New Society

The small foreign colony of the nineteenth century soon developed into a self-conscious society ready to demand administrative autonomy. It was largely constituted of people of Mediterranean background whose forebears had always had dealings—for the most part unfriendly—with the people of the Maghrib, and who preserved from the past feelings of rancor and antipathy, if not downright contempt. France, with her political authority, had succeeded in "naturalizing" the descendants of the immigrants, but only superficially. In 1926 the European population in Algeria numbered 828,000; in 1931 it numbered 195,000 in Tunisia and 172,000 in Morocco. Counting the Spaniards of northern Morocco, we can estimate the foreign population of the Maghrib in 1930 at 1.3 million.[2] This population was con-

1 Previous history is denied. All this man's good and bad qualities, his courage, integrity, simplicity, generosity, as well as his duplicity, covetousness, respect for force, and "pillaging instinct," are attributed to "human nature." Hence the ideology of permanence, which actually reflects a process of dehistorization.

2 See Despois, *L'Afrique du Nord*, 2nd ed., pp. 917ff. The total figure for 1951-1956 is 1,737,800.

centrated increasingly in the coastal cities (the proportion varying from two-thirds to three-quarters according to the country). Except in Morocco, immigration played only a small part in the growth of this population, which consequently tended to develop a marked character of its own.

Land Tenure

Encouraged by every possible means, the European population acquired more and more land. In Algeria the Senatus Consult of 1863, though rigorously applied, proved insufficient. The Warnier Law (passed in 1873 and amended in 1887 and 1897) provided a legal though infamous means of dispossessing Algerian landowners. The system has often been described:[3] any colon or speculator who managed by whatever means to lay hands on even an infinitesimal part of a jointly owned piece of land was permitted by law to call an auction, which resulted inevitably in ruining all the joint owners and enabled him in the end to buy up the land for a song. Though widely deplored, this abuse continued until 1890. At the same time new means were found for implementing the Senatus Consult of 1863. Additions to the public domain opened up new horizons to official colonization. From 1871 to 1900, 687,000 hectares were ceded gratuitously to colons; from 1880 to 1908, 450,000 hectares passed from Algerian to European hands under more than dubious circumstances. After a momentary halt during the First World War, when colonization came to a standstill, the movement resumed, and by 1930 Europeans owned a total of 2,350,000 hectares in Algeria.[4]

[3] See Bernard, *L'Algérie*, pp. 400-402; Sahli, *Décoloniser l'histoire*, pp. 120-121.

[4] The figures expressing the development of European colonization vary from author to author: some consider the land area taken away from Maghribis for purposes of colonization, others the land actually colonized at a given moment. Private colonization varied from year to year according to the positive or negative balance in the land transactions between Frenchmen and Algerians in the free market. The French administration sometimes padded the figures in order to encourage immigration or influence parliament and sometimes minimized them

The methods developed in Algeria served in Tunisia and Morocco. From 1882 to 1892 the French authorities, hampered by diplomatic considerations, confined themselves to encouraging free colonization of Tunisia by legislative and other methods. The result and probably the aim of the Torrens system of land registration introduced in 1885 by Paul Cambon, the resident general, was to legalize dubious titles;[5] the habus lands were leased in perpetuity to colons at nominal rents (May 23, 1886), and the leases were soon made transferable (1905). After 1892, when the protectorate status was clarified and confirmed, the French administration launched a program of official colonization, resorting to the same methods as in Algeria, that is, putting the broadest possible construction on public lands (January 13, 1896), forest lands (July 22, 1903), and collective lands (1904).[6] In 1913 official colonization and private colonization, which was highly concentrated and capitalist in structure, totalled 550,000 hectares; in 1937 the figure had risen to 724,741.

In Morocco one of the first dahirs, promulgated under the pressure of the new administration, introduced land registration (August 12, 1913). In this way the occupation of 30,000 hectares in the regions of Oujda and Casablanca during the military operations of 1907-1912, when the owners fled from the advancing French army, was legalized. In 1916 a colonization commission was set up, and in Feb-

---

in response to the criticism of the nationalists or anticolonialist liberals. In any case the variation from one decade to another is less than 100,000 hectares.

5 This system, conceived for thinly populated countries like Australia and designed for the settlement of disputes among the colonists themselves, was totally unsuited to Moslem countries. The courts set up under it meted out summary justice. They did not seriously examine titles to property, and they operated in French, so that their deliberations were largely unintelligible to the Maghribis. They always favored the colons and validated numerous expropriations.

6 On these laws, see the pertinent criticism of Sebag, *La Tunisie*.

ruary 1919, a commission was charged with inquiry into the public lands. This was an indirect way of confiscating lands that had been cultivated for generations by communities serving the makhzen. The dahir of April 27, 1919, authorized a survey of collective lands with a view to leasing them to colons.[7]

Since it was necessary to move fast in order to catch up with the head start of Algeria and Tunisia, measures were taken to encourage agricultural colonizaton. These included subsidies for clearing land (which often did not need to be cleared), tax exemptions, loans, and the establishment of cooperatives to provide equipment. As a result of these measures, calculated to prevent the periodic crises from which Algerian colonization had suffered, the Europeans quickly extended their land holdings. By 1932, free and official colonization accounted for roughly 837,000 hectares. As in Algeria, colons soon infringed on the private holdings of the local population. In Tunisia, from 1913 on, the authorities, on pretext of increasing their yield, leased the lands of the private habus to colons. In Morocco, from 1927 on, the *malk* (privately owned) lands were expropriated (62,000 hectares in the Tadla in two years) and ceded to Europeans. In the Maghrib as a whole 3,800,000 hectares[8]—roughly a third of the land under actual cultivation—had by 1930 passed into the hands of Europeans, who at no time made up more than a seventh of the total population.

This land policy was regarded as a political necessity, and in this respect the old "Roman" ideology retained its influence despite the Saint-Simonian propaganda and the "Arab kingdom" myth. After 1880 its political character became more evident, since there was more and more reason to

[7] Contrarily to its professed aim. To hold that the authors of the dahir acted in good faith, one would have to suppose that they were unaware of the consequences of Napoleon III's pro-Arab policy in Algeria—which is unthinkable.

[8] By 1950 this figure had risen to 4,500,000 hectares. See Despois, pp. 356f.

doubt whether it was profitable either from the Maghribi or from the French point of view.

The Economic System

During the imperialist era French colonialist policy underwent a change even in Algeria. Little by little Algerian agriculture came to be controlled by the banks and finance corporations. This development was even more manifest in Tunisia and Morocco, where the men of action were not military men and colons but bankers and speculators.

In 1851 the Bank of Algeria (which was not to be nationalized until 1947) was founded. Authorized to issue bank notes, it specialized in farm loans. The private French banks were quick to open branches in Algeria. At the end of the century, as cash crops (wine, cotton, tobacco) replaced cereals, bank capital took control of distribution (collection, storage, transportation and sale on the French market) and through it of production itself, especially after 1892 when the customs union with France was decreed. The infrastructure—railroads, highways and harbor facilities—developed slowly, because only the government was willing to finance it. Private capital took no risks and waited for the French parliament to vote credits or underwrite bank loans. From 1857 to 1881 the French railroad companies built rail lines totaling 1375 kilometers and twice that much in the next ten years. When the big profits of the early years dwindled, the companies tried to sell the lines to the government and in 1920 succeeded. The mines failed to attract private capital. The administration found no one willing to operate the Ouenza mines, and it was only in 1921 that the project was successfully revived. Thus the European economic sector was dominated by agriculture during the greater part of the colonial period; the great fortunes were made in the growing, processing and distribution of wine and tobacco. And despite the gradual turn to industry, the French interests continued to be based on Algeria; the power of decision remained in Algiers. The situation was different in Tunisia and especially so in Morocco.[9]

From the start Tunisia was thought to be richer and more prosperous than Algeria, no doubt because its affairs had long been in the hands of the metropolitan French banks. In 1883 their domination became even more marked when France took over the public debt, estimated at 150 million gold francs.[10] The servicing of this debt was for many years a heavy drain on the Tunisian budget (thirty-five percent in 1939). The Bank of Algeria was authorized to issue currency in Tunisia. In 1885 phosphate mines were discovered in the Gafsa region. Extraction and transportation were monopolized by the *Compagnie des Phosphates de Gafsa*, a branch of the *Banque de l'Union Parisienne*, which obtained a grant of thirty thousand hectares of land from the Tunisian government. From then on, phosphate, along with the traditional oils and cereals, played a leading role in the country's economic life. In 1898 France accorded Tunisia a preferential tariff agreement, and in 1928 a customs union was formed; duties continued to be paid only on wine, tobacco and salt. The French market absorbed seventy percent of Tunisian production. Despite the importance of the French colony, the economic life of the country was controlled by metropolitan French banks; thus in many respects the center of decision was Paris.

This was even more true of Morocco. In 1903, at the instigation of Eugène Etienne, the energetic deputy from Oran, a Morocco Commission was set up in Paris with the participation of several banks and corporations with interests in the Maghrib.[11] The crises of 1905-1906 and 1909-1911

[9] See *Economie et politique* (special issue, 1954): *La France et les trusts*, pp. 108-117.

[10] See Cambon, *Correspondance*, I, pp. 162, 170, 190.

[11] See Guillen, "Les Milieux d'affaires français et le Maroc à l'aube du XXe siècle." Certain conclusions (pp. 419-420), compatible with the prejudices of traditional diplomatic history, are questionable. The essential is to determine not whether the bankers or the politicians had

led to an agreement among the international banks regarding their respective shares in government loans and the financing of mining operations and public works.[12] Once this was done, the question of political domination became secondary, at least for the moment.

The sultan's loans of 1904 (62.5 millions) and 1910 (101 millions) had been provided by a consortium of banks. In 1913 the French parliament authorized the Protectorate administration to float a loan for the purpose of paying off this debt. Further authorizations followed: 170 millions in 1914, 70 millions in 1916, 744 millions in 1920, 819 millions in 1928. The entire economic activity of Morocco depended literally on these authorizations. The loans, guaranteed by the French government and serviced out of Moroccan budgets, served to finance public works—the construction of harbors, highways and railroads. Despite the Act of Algeciras and the vigilance of the British and Americans, most of the contracts were awarded to the big French corporations (Schneider, Hersent, etc.). It was precisely in order to exclude the claims of the English and Americans to a share in exploiting the phosphates discovered in the Marrakech region in 1907 that Lyautey, resident general from 1912 to 1925, established the Sharifian Office of Phosphates (O.C.P.) in 1920; his purpose was not, as has too often been claimed, to defend the interests of the Moroccan state.[13] During Lyautey's proconsulate and later, the big French corporations also acquired vast tracts of land.

Development capital was provided by French savings and by the budgets of France and the countries of the Maghrib, but administered by the French banks at no risk to themselves. The interest was paid out of the Maghribi budgets

the upper hand at a given moment, but whether the colonial policy as a whole is intelligible without an assumption of economic determinism.

12 Anderson, *The First Moroccan Crisis*; Taylor, "The Conference at Algeciras."

13 On all these points, see Ayache, *Le Maroc*.

and the loans were guaranteed by the French government. No attempt was made to keep down the costs, because contracts were automatically awarded to the big French corporations, so that there was virtually no competition. Since the European sector was increasingly dominated by the banks, speculation took the lead over production. The economy became more and more vulnerable, hence dependent on French government support. Geared to the French market, prices were determined without reference either to production costs or to the local market; costs were kept down by tax exemptions and forcibly imposed low wages. The colonial economy, so often described as modern and efficient, was increasingly subsidized by the French and Maghribi governments; it came to be an artificial, "political" economy.[14] As this tendency became more pronounced, the character of the foreign colony changed; abandoning the rural districts, the foreigners concentrated in the cities and devoted themselves to the tertiary sector. The number of intermediaries and white-collar workers far outweighed the number of actual property owners. As they began to feel more and more directed and dominated from the outside, they began to demand exclusive political power and a shift of the center of gravity from Paris back to the Maghrib. But for such efforts to achieve autonomy it was already too late. As the banks strengthened their hold on the Maghribi economy, the concentration of power in Paris increased, and meanwhile Maghribi nationalism was coming to the fore.

In the nineteenth century a small foreign colony, buoyed by an expanding economy, was able to impose a true liberal revolution. Fifty years later this foreign colony was much larger, possessed of vast tracts of land and a complex economic organization. Yet when it tried to impose its economic demands, it discovered that it was helpless, betrayed by the very economic forces that had brought it into being. After 1930 the foreign colony continued to increase in numbers;

[14] This point is stressed by Knight in *Morocco as a French Economic Venture.*

billions were invested in the Maghrib, and more land was acquired. Yet, though this seemed to increase France's chance of maintaining its power over North Africa, it diminished the likelihood of the foreign colony ever gaining autonomy.[15]

This was possible only in Algeria, and only for a brief moment, before the development we have just described actually got under way.

Administrative Organization

In order to develop its activities, the foreign colony required an administrative organization totally independent of the old local administration. In Algeria, the civil territory where French laws were applied grew steadily at the expense of the military territory. The French organization of departments and communes was extended to Algeria with negligible modifications. In application of the French law of April 6, 1884, the communes obtained the same autonomy as their counterparts in France. As their resources were inadequate, they annexed larger and larger areas. They also benefited by the taxes levied on the Algerians, while offering no services whatever in return. Hence the "underadministration" (or nonadministration) deplored by the French commissions of inquiry between 1892 and 1955. Half the funds of the district councils were supplied by taxation on the Algerians, who were represented only by six appointed assessors. In the municipal councils the number of Algerian councillors was limited to six, and they had no voice in the election of mayors (decree of April 7, 1884). Just when the Algerian element in local administration was reduced to a minimum, a movement toward autonomy with respect to France began to develop. This was favored by the system inaugurated in 1881, attaching the various branches of the

15 This would make possible a valid theory of colonial history as an independent field and no longer as an appendage to the economic history of the colonizing country.

Algerian administration to the corresponding ministries in Paris, for the result of this system was that no one in Paris really knew what was going on in Algeria. The Algerians were at the mercy of the colons, who at the same time, thanks to their deputies, obtained all manner of concessions from the French administration. The system was finally abolished on December 31, 1896, but by then the colons were in full control; the agitation of 1898-1900 served to consolidate their authority and gave it a legal basis.

By the decrees of August 23, 1898, an economic assembly, *les Délégations financières*,[16] was established and the High Council of Algeria reorganized. By the law of December 19, 1900, Algeria was recognized as an autonomous entity and no longer a mere extension of metropolitan France. At this stage the foreign colony believed that it no longer needed the myth of Algeria as an integral part of France. But this autonomy was purely administrative. The political rights enjoyed by the French population of Algeria were individual and, as it were, extraterritorial. The logic of the situation demanded that the colony should become a political force, distinct both from France and from the Algerians, but this never happened. The powers of the governor general became more and more extensive, and, in spite of appearances and the contentions of the jurists, the situation in this respect was comparable to that of the two neighboring countries.[17]

By the treaties of 1883 and 1912 the sovereigns of Tunisia and Morocco lost their power to propose laws. It was for the representative of France to introduce reforms, for the most

[16] These were made up of three sections: colons (24), delegates of other sectors (24), all elected directly; Moslems (21, including six Kabyles) elected by the members of the municipal councils, of the European communes and of the mixed communes. The sections met together only to vote.

[17] From 1900 on the governor general of Algeria was assisted by an administration as plethoric as those surrounding the resident generals of Tunisia and Morocco.

part administrative, juridical and financial—or precisely those that seemed likely to serve French interests.[18] The first obstacle the French got rid of consisted of the old capitulary rights. The powers made no difficulty about renouncing them in Tunisia; only Italy did not consent until 1896. In Morocco all, except England, abandoned their opposition after the introduction of the French legal system in September 1913. England retained its rights until 1937 when France agreed to similar concessions in Egypt. In both countries the resident general was the head of the European colony, which he administered directly. He also directed the new government departments, over which the Tunisian or Moroccan authority had no control whatever, and which, it goes without saying, concerned themselves chiefly with the affairs of the European colony. The only matters in which a certain collaboration with the local authority was necessary were Islamic justice and the habus. A high French official was charged with suggesting desirable reforms in these spheres.[19] In the local administration we find the usual distinction between civil and military territories. The latter were small in Tunisia but covered half the country in Morocco. In the cities municipal councils were established (in 1885 in Tunisia, in 1917 in Morocco) under the presidency of a mayor in Tunisia and of a pasha in Morocco. In reality this presidency was purely nominal, for in both cases the real power was held by the French vice-president. The European members, who always enjoyed a slight numerical superiority, took the lead in all deliberations. In the central administration, consultative assemblies enabled the foreign colony to air its grievances. The first was established in Tunisia in 1896, with members appointed by the resident general. It deliberated on financial problems, chiefly connected with

[18] On the true nature of the protectorate, see Cambon, *Correspondance*, pp. 166-167.

[19] Islamic justice and the administration of the habus were all that remained of the competencies of the three Tunisian and four Moroccan ministers retained by the French administration. The secretary of the Tunisian government kept a close watch on them.

the budget and the awarding of public works contracts. Similarly in 1919, a council of government, or "board of directors of the Morocco Company," as Lyautey called it, was instituted in Rabat; it comprised the presidents and vice-presidents of the chambers of commerce and agriculture, which had just been set up with appointive membership. At its bi-monthly meetings it examined the budget and the progress of public works projects.

From the start this administration was essentially designed for the benefit of the foreign colony, and despite minor adjustments after the First World War it underwent no real change until 1930. During this period the political problem was not clearly conceived. The foreign colony never demanded legislation consecrating its administrative autonomy and social separatism. Not until nationalism demanded a reform that would extend the administration to the whole of society was the question of sovereignty raised explicitly.

Why this lag in the political consciousness of a society that would cast off its timidity only when faced with nationalism, and then only for a short time? Here again we are reduced to hypotheses. One plausible explanation is that the colonists saw indigenous society disintegrating before their eyes. Could this have encouraged them to bide their time?

An Atomized Society

"In Algeria we found ourselves in the presence of an atomized, inorganic state of society . . . whereas in Morocco . . . ," said Lyautey,[20] forgetting that Bugeaud had spoken rather differently and failing to foresee that thirty years later observers would contradict him by describing Morocco as in a state of anarchy. It was at the end not at the beginning of the colonial period that the cliché—"a scattering of tribes killing each other"—became a reality, for such a state of affairs was the aim and purpose of colonialism, not its cause.

[20] Lyautey, *Paroles d'action*, p. 172.

The Senatus Consult of July 14, 1865, gave the Algerians a status intermediate between subject and citizen. To obtain the right of citizenship they were obliged to sign a statement renouncing the protection of Islamic law.[21] This was the very essence of the colonial process: to destroy indigenous society and then to accept individuals one by one into a new society organized by and for foreigners. In other words, the foreigners, after destroying most of the old society's functions, were kind enough to let it die in peace. In the two protectorates the pretext was fidelity to treaties that made no mention of political reform. The purpose, however, was the same: to control the Maghribis by maintaining their status as subjects. "I shall see to it . . . that the ranks and hierarchies are preserved and respected," Lyautey promised,[22] no doubt imagining that he was saying something new. Actually this had always been the attitude of the military when the number of Europeans was small, that is, at the beginning of the colonial era. Even under the civil regime in Algeria, the administrator of the mixed communes wore a uniform, no doubt to maintain the illusion of rank. Between the officials of Native Affairs and the populations there were always intermediaries (qaids, shaykhs) who interpreted and applied orders, and throughout the Maghrib the policy was to make the old local élites collaborate in the work of colonization by transforming them into a parasitic class. The power of the controllers and of their auxiliaries was always unlimited. In Algeria the law defining the status of natives (1881) identified forty-one offenses (reduced to twenty-one in 1890) and was designed essentially for the daily harassment and intimidation of the Algerians. The administration also had the power to intern anyone it pleased without putting him on trial. Most Alge-

[21] See the remarks of Sahli, *Décoloniser l'histoire*, pp. 110-111, on the motives of the French legislators. This regime seems comparable to that of the *Ahl al-Dhimma* in Islam, which has often been criticized; the critics, however, fail to add that there at least no one enjoyed the rights of citizenship.

[22] Lyautey, *Paroles d'action*, p. 173; also p. 243.

rians were forbidden to leave their place of residence without special authorization. In both protectorates the qaids enjoyed the same authority. As administrators and judges chosen by the French authorities for their docility, they had absolute power over the local populations. Administrative internment remained a current practice in Tunisia until 1934 and was never suspended in Morocco. It goes without saying that none of the usual civic rights (the rights of assembly, association, free speech, etc.) existed in the Maghrib. Once it gained authority, the foreign colony, which in the nineteenth century had criticized the despotism of the local authorities, which had imposed reforms in the name of freedom, or when that was impossible demanded "protection," invoked the old argument: Islam is contrary to democracy, the Moslem respects only the sword and the uniform. And indeed, throughout the colonial period the Maghrib was almost always under martial law (officially decreed in 1911 in Tunisia, it was maintained until 1935, and in the civil territory of Morocco it was suspended only during the period from 1924 to 1937). The result—and no doubt the purpose—of all these restrictions on the daily life of the individual was to drive the Maghribi out of public life. Let each man remain in his *douar*, or better still in his house, and go out as little as possible. The only public gathering place left to him was the mosque.

Every aspect of the Moslem juridical organization presenting an obstacle to the development of capitalism had already been done away with. By a series of decrees, the most important of which was that of April 17, 1889, the jurisdiction of the qadi was limited to private matters such as marriage, divorce, and inheritance. Everything else, and especially questions of land tenure, was transferred to the French courts. In Tunisia, the secularization of jurisprudence had begun long before the protectorate; thereafter the process continued. The dahir of August 12, 1913, specified that all civil suits involving both Moroccans and Frenchmen should be tried in the modern, i.e. French, courts. But it was not enough to banish Islamic law from the modern sector, where the Maghribi was at a disadvantage in any case; it was also necessary to break the hold of Islam on the population. A beginning was made with the Berbers, who—the authorities liked to believe—were only superficially Islamized. From 1874 the Islamic courts were abolished in Kabylia, and after 1914 the "Berber policy" was put into effect in Morocco, all Berber-speaking regions being removed from the authority of the makhzen and the *shar'*.[23] Even in Arabic-speaking districts the policy pursued consisted in a subtle falsification of Islam. Everything was done to win over the heads of the *zāwiyas*, and this was largely successful; at the same time an attempt was made to encourage all manner of particularisms, however absurd, so as to give popular religion a local, naturalistic and primitive character.[24] The old Koranic schools (*kuttāb* and *msid*), which were no longer financed by the habus, were closed down one by one. The French authorities did their best to discourage the pilgrimage to Mecca and to disrupt the old ties between the rural sections and urban Islam. It is no accident that European writers on the Maghrib in the 1920s spoke of a "primitive mentality." The ideal was an "unlettered people," and every attempt was made to achieve it. The Moslem schools were allowed to die out and sometimes, as in southern Morocco, they were closed, but no serious effort was made to replace them with French schools. As a rule, no more than two percent of the Maghribi children of school age went to school. This was the figure for Algeria in 1890 and for Morocco in 1939.

Thus the policy of *cantonnement* was extended to the whole of life. It was not enough to drive the Maghribi once again beyond the *limes* into the desert of camels, palm trees and *zāwiyas*; it was necessary also to deprive him of his

[23] See Ageron, "La Politique berbère du protectorat morocain de 1913 à 1934," in *Politiques coloniales.*

[24] Hence the spurious theory of the *baraka* so often invoked by pseudoauthorities on the Maghrib.

religion, language and historic heritage, so producing a man free from culture, who could then be civilized. Up to a certain point this policy was successful. Impoverished and "decultured," the Maghribi seldom left his house; when he did go out, he looked with an absent, empty gaze—the gaze that struck so many travelers and that we sometimes see today in the waiting rooms of France as well as the Maghrib—upon a land that was no longer his. Small wonder if at a time when his country escaped him, when he was losing the command of his language, when his religion was degenerating to meaningless gestures, the Maghribi should have begun to say to himself: my country, my religion, my language. Here indeed was an awakening, but at the historically lowest level.

The Logic of the Situation

There was always a discrepancy between the structural situation of the foreign colony in the Maghrib and its ideology and policy, between what a middle class—which objectively it was—would have said and done had it been indigenous and what this colony, because it was foreign, actually did and said. This discrepancy is discernible during the three periods (1830-1880, 1880-1930, 1930-1954), though at a higher and higher level.

In the middle of the nineteenth century, as we have seen, the foreign colony, still small in numbers, played the part of a middle class struggling for its freedoms. One might suppose that a Maghrib with a strong, disciplined, organized government might have drawn profit from this "liberal revolution" by controlling it, but the failure of Khayr al-Dīn shows that such a Maghrib was impossible, precisely because of the growing influence of the foreigners. In the period from 1930 to 1954, the foreign colony would play a similar role, though on a higher level. In a society outwardly unified by economic forces, it would oppose the bourgeois democratism of the nationalists with an equally bourgeois aristocratism. Having superimposed a second, more or less abstract Maghrib on the real one, it would try, in the name of this dualism and for the moment disregarding the question of sovereignty, to impose a system of "colonial corporatism." But this program was not clearly formulated until very late, and by then the structure it claimed to express had in part ceased to exist. In the intermediate period from 1880 to 1930 we observe a similar contradiction between the role played and the policy formulated by the European colony.

The Maghrib had produced neither a modern capitalism nor, it follows, a bourgeoisie. Colonial Europe lent it one, but on condition that this European bourgeoisie enjoy exclusive privileges, that bourgeois law, bourgeois freedoms, bourgeois economy and administration remain a closed sphere, forbidden to Maghribis. They have no need of them anyway, it was said. This policy, one might think, ought logically to have enabled two societies to coexist. But in the eyes of the colonial establishment the coexistence was essentially provisional, for after going through a phase of enlightened despotism,[25] the one society, it was thought, would transform itself into an adult bourgeois democracy, while the other, after a period of slow disintegration under the benevolent control of the military, would degenerate into an anthropological reservation. An aid to growth, on the one hand, a speeding up of regression on the other—this, the colonial ideologists tried to make themselves and others believe, was the judgment of history. The condemned society was expected to work to its last breath for the society that would survive it.

Because this social Darwinism did not succeed, it strikes us today as naive. But this does not detract from the rigor of its logic. The fact that for the moment at least we have

[25] In the historical sense, that is, considered as a regime which encouraged the growth of a bourgeoisie by providing the necessary juridical and cultural infrastructure before the bourgeoisie itself demanded it, and by supporting the rising class financially through a system of taxation weighing most heavily on the peasantry.

escaped it does not exempt us from the obligation to seek the causes of its failure, for it should not be forgotten that the exponents of this colonial Darwinism claimed merely to be acting on the lesson taught by our history. We have already said that colonialism seems to have adapted itself to the structures it found waiting, structures which had been building up, not continuously to be sure, but cumulatively since the sixteenth century. Cultural regression, the cleavage between urban and rural Islam, the contradiction between central authority and local liberties—all these factors betokened a structure of lasting decadence. Colonial violence merely severed the few remaining ties between the historical domain (states, cities, Islamic justice and ritual) and the infrahistorical (*zāwiyas*, rural communities, customs, folklore and private life). Insinuating itself between the two and in the name of history, it condemned the one to decay and oblivion, the other to regression and death. At what point and for what basic reason did the rationale of the decadent centuries, once it was reformulated in political terms,[26] divorce itself from, or reject, reality? Is the reason to be sought in demography? In economic forces? In an immanent justice, as the nationalists have always believed? Or must we be satisfied with noting the dangerous consequences of a continuing discrepancy between the political theory of the colonizers and the social evolution of the colonized and observe that the moment colonization became a reality its ideology (rooted in the realities of the precolonial period) became irrelevant, just as after 1930 the reforms inspired by the colonial ideology were merely a theoretical reflection of the reality experienced between 1880 and 1930. But all this is merely an admission of ignorance.

Be that as it may, the liberal critique of the system, despite the symbolic and sentimental value it may still retain in the

[26] Berque, *Le Maghrib entre deux guerres* (rev. ed.), p. 200, implies that at a certain time the very soil of the Maghrib refused to reward the new techniques that had been introduced. That would make the refusal total. But while listing the symptoms of this refusal, he never tells us what caused it or when it appeared.

eyes of certain nationalists and anticolonialists, was superficial. The critique stressed the scandalous double taxation of Algerians, which remained in force up to the reforms of 1919, and in general the flagrant injustice of taxing the Maghribis, who were undoubtedly poorer than the Europeans, more heavily and giving them less service in return;[27] it pointed out contradictions, such as trying to eliminate the social role of Islam and nevertheless trying to make it serve the aims of colonialism, blocking the development of Arabic schools while refusing to replace them by French schools, introducing inequitable personal legislation while condemning Islamic law for this very shortcoming, and asking the people of the Maghrib to sacrifice themselves in defense of the French establishment and French values while refusing them the rights of citizenship.[28] All these criticisms, timidly expressed in French liberal circles, taken over by the Young Tunisians and the Young Algerians, and later embodied in the program of the "moderate" nationalists, amount to a demand that the foreign colony keep faith with the nineteenth-century liberalism that had won it the support of international opinion in its conflict with the precolonial regime and that it complete its mission of "civilizing" Maghribi society. The flaw in this critique is only too evident: its proponents pretended not to see that the foreign colony amounted to an imported bourgeoisie which, true to its inherent logic, refused to serve the honor of Man or the glory of God without recompense, and that the foreign colony formed a separate society juxtaposed to another society which it was able to repress but not to revolutionize. This critique had meaning in the middle of the nineteenth century; it again took on meaning after 1930,

27 In 1912 the Algerians supplied forty-six percent of the various budgets, though they controlled only thirty-seven percent of the total capital. Similar observations on Tunisia and Morocco may be found in the cited works of Sebag and Ayache.

28 In the conclusion of *L'Afrique du Nord en marche*, 1st ed., pp. 395-409, Julien sums up all these arguments. The remedies he proposes are equality before the law and equal access to French culture.

when it became possible to represent proposed reforms as a simple means of enlarging the autonomous local market with the help of a local bourgeoisie that could still hope to find a suitable place in the colonial system. But in the intervening period, its abstract logic reduced it to absurdity. Why, indeed, should the foreign colony have tried by legislation and education to "bourgeoisify" a population which under the impact of economic forces was regressing into tribal primitivism? Patriarchal, personal justice, yes; abstract bourgeois justice, no—so said the Maghribis' other friend, the military.[29]

Thus for all its moderation the liberal critique of liberalism was illogical, while the radical critique, though silent at the time, showed a logic as rigorous as that of colonialism itself. It is no accident that liberal reformism and its appendage, moderate nationalism, proved ineffectual.

[29] Was colonial society a unified society or was it a dual one? Economists and historians postulate its homogeneity and integration as a basis for analysis. Psychologists, psychoanalysts and political pamphleteers necessarily deny this homogeneity and speak of two peoples, two societies, two psychologies, etc. Thus there is no simple, definitive answer; each method of analysis dictates its own specific answer.

15. The Renascent Maghrib

We now know that Maghribi society, cut off from its land and its past, nevertheless found a means of surviving. This knowledge obliges us, not to rewrite the history of the colonial period, but to isolate the determining factors that have been stressed in our analysis.[1] All colonialist history tends to stress the economic, if not the purely technological, contribution of colonialism. This bias may seem to find justification in the fact that the Maghribis have taken over the heritage of the foreign colony unchanged and appointed themselves its guardians without stopping to consider the social costs of their conservatism. Such justification, however, does not go very far, for there is no reason to suppose that the Maghribis will remain forever in awe of their former masters.[2] More serious is the fact that economic analysis will always see the Maghrib as a fading picture in the margin of an expanding capitalist system, granting it at best the possibility of being reborn at some future date as an integral part of this same system.

[1] Berque, in his books on the Maghrib and on Egypt (see bibliography), ridicules the mania of "foreseeing what has already happened." But might it not be said that events take on their relative significance only after they have taken place, and that to consider them all on the same plane on the pretext that none of them could be predicted before they happened is to segregate events arbitrarily from their consequences and to reduce all history to a kind of perpetual present, or more precisely, to relativism and meaninglessness?

[2] Many Marxist historians remain within the confines of this economic determinism (Nouschi's title "Le Sens de certains chiffres" [The meaning of certain figures] in *Etudes Maghrébines*, p. 199, is highly significant). Their approach is in fact typically bourgeois but accounts for the popularity of their works among colonial historians in the process of conversion. This whole movement (regardless of the good faith of its participants) may be said to contribute to the development of a neocolonialist ideology that is to be defined as a justification of colonization without the colonizers. Modern technology, they say, was unjustly monopolized by the colonizers; let us restore it to its original purpose. Obviously we have here a return to Saint-Simonism.

Thus seen in economic perspective the colonial period of the Maghrib shows a continuity with imperialist Europe and discontinuity with the local past. In the life of the Maghrib there is a zero point, a point at which man is reduced to his generic definition. But this is an anthropological or a philosophical point of view; the historian recognizes no such breaches of continuity; he is obliged to postulate continuous developments. Consequently he resorts to two other lines of analysis: the one, social—presupposing a direct influence of the foreign group on indigenous society (colonial activity, he says, creates a local bourgeoisie, which gains awareness of its interests, organizes, and comes forward as the spokesman of all exploited groups); the other, ideological—arrived at by reconstructing, on the basis of Maghribi testimonies, the successive reactions to colonialism from religious reformism to political activism. Neither of these approaches, however, confirms the presumed continuity, because in the first the changes in the social role of the various groups reveal a gap, less evident to be sure than in the case of economic determinism, but nonetheless real, and in the second the continuity is illusory, since the same ideology can serve different political aims.

We need be in no hurry to take a position in this controversy; suffice it to underline the heterogeneity of the three continuities we have postulated: that of statistics, that of social roles, that of professions of faith. The first refers to the activity of the colonizer; the second to the passive experience of the colonized; the third to a sphere that seems common to both. But can we hope to apprehend the total reality of the colonized society by setting the three determinants side by side or by reducing them all equally to merely symbolic value? It would not seem so; this at least is the impression created by numerous studies devoted to the reaction of the Maghribis to colonialism. Few of them rise above the level of facile journalism.[3]

[3] An example of overhasty theorization may be found in the brochure *Les Nationalismes maghrébins* by Louis-Jean Duclos (Morocco), Jean

I

In spite of these reservations, let us start by summing up the findings of social and ideological analysis.

Taken as a whole, the period under consideration shows contradictory features. Military resistance never ceased entirely; it continued in southern Tunisia, where several groups regularly crossed the Libyan border in either direction, in the Algerian Sahara, where revolts broke out sporadically, and in the greater part of Morocco. The last phase of this resistance, the Rifian war, was spectacular. Because it came late and the situation was more favorable to the rebels than it had been to Ibn Ghadhāhum in 1864 or to Moqrani in 1871, it might with outside help have developed into a war of liberation.[4] One can, to be sure, regard the

---

Leca (Algeria), and Jean Duvignaud (Tunisia), published by the *Fondation nationale des sciences politiques.* In the study devoted to Tunisia, ignorance of the most elementary facts leads to dogmatic assertions; the one on Algeria is an illustration of theses absolutely irrelevant to the problems of the Maghrib; the study on Morocco is a generalization based on partial (in both senses of the word) studies, many of them serving the purposes of the Residence or of the present government; the author goes so far as to repeat the old absurdities about demographic growth and the increase in the number of mixed marriages being manifestations of nationalism. In all three cases the use made of Berque's work is more than questionable; legitimate use of it would require profound knowledge of the Maghrib's past and culture, and this the authors obviously do not possess. Berque's work consists almost entirely of hypotheses; it cannot be regarded as a series of manuals summing up facts that have been demonstrated once and for all and that everyone is free to interpret as he pleases.

[4] Anyone who confines himself to the study of Morocco is struck by the coincidence between the end of the Rifian war (1926) and the beginning of the nationalist movement (1927), and between the end of "pacification" and the publication of the "Plan of Reforms" (1934). All the historians stress this concordance. But is it not illusory? For if we extend our perspective to the Maghrib as a whole, the war in the Rif recedes into the past and takes its place beside numerous rural and mountaineer revolts (the Rif had been in a state of revolt against the Spaniards since 1860), whereas the political phenomena relate to the overall nationalist movement in the Maghrib and the orient. In reality, initial resistance and political nationalism are separated by far more than the lapse of a year's time. The positivist historian's refusal to

rebel victories in the Rif as the brilliant rearguard actions of an already defeated army, and yet the battle of Anoual (July 1921) in which the Spanish army lost two hundred cannon and seven hundred prisoners, among them General Silvestre, and, above all, the fact that France and Spain were obliged to muster an army of half a million men supported by forty-four squadrons of fighter planes before Muḥammad b. Abd al-Karīm finally surrendered,[5] bear witness to the existence of a large reserve of untapped forces. At the time, the official authorities (makhzen) were unable to mobilize them; others would do so, for they would still be there when the time came.

The size of the French army stationed in the Maghrib, as well as the number of naval and air bases,[6] shows that the country was under military occupation. But up to 1927 we find no indication that the colonists were troubled by the price of such an occupation; they seemed to take it for granted as indispensable to the extension of French sovereignty (unlike the Spaniards who were never really confident in their mission and were driven into action almost in spite of themselves, first by the English and then by the French). But more significant than the colonists' optimism was the extremely cautious, not to say ambiguous, behavior of the Maghribis. The Maghrib fought beside France in the First World War. Algeria contributed 173,000 soldiers, whose courage was acclaimed in August 1914, and 25,000 of

---

accept this idea makes it difficult for him to interpret the successes and failures of 'Abd al-Karīm's army. On the Rifian war, of which there is still no satisfactory study, see Furneaux, *Abdel-Krim*, for the current bibliography, including works by journalists, diplomats, and civil servants; and the anthropologist, Coon, *Flesh of the Wild Ox*. Woolman, *Rebels in the Rif*, is disappointing.

5 These figures were long kept secret; see Ayache, *Le Maroc*, p. 232.

6 Wide variations on the strength of the colonial army as well as the frequent use of auxiliaries make it difficult to arrive at precise figures; between the two wars, the strength of the French forces in the Maghrib seems to have varied between 70,000 and 200,000 men. It is interesting to compare these figures with the small numbers of British soldiers in India or Egypt.

whom never returned; and moreover a third of the male population (119,000 men in 1919) went to France to replace drafted French workers in the factories. Despite its status as a protectorate Tunisia was obliged to contribute 56,000 soldiers, 12,000 of whom were killed. Even Morocco, the conquest of which had barely begun, sent soldiers who took part in the defense of Paris, and in 1916 Moroccan workers began to land in Bordeaux. Whatever may be said of the forced character of this military and civilian mobilization, of the revolt in the Aurès Mountains (1916), of Turkish intrigues in Tunisia and German intrigues in Morocco, the fact remains that the entire Maghribi élite[7] collaborated with the French authorities, postponing even its more moderate demands until later; as for the general population, it was largely passive.

How are we to account for this contradiction? Here it becomes necessary to analyze the changes that had taken place in Maghribi society. Beyond a doubt the section of the population that had suffered most from colonization was the peasantry of the plains and the high plateaus. These people were losing their lands and at the same time continuing to pay heavy taxes. Especially in Algeria, many were reduced to a state of beggary. Flocks diminished as the pasture lands shrunk. It has been estimated that in Algeria the number of sheep diminished from 8 million in 1865 to 7.7 million in 1885 to 6.3 million in 1900, and the number of bovines from 1,071,000 in 1887 to 846,000 in 1900.[8] During the same

[7] See the *fatāwa* with which Moroccan jurists (especially ‘Abd al-Haj al-Kattānī, Abū Shu’ayb al Dukkālī and Muḥammad Skiraj) responded to the Ottoman sultan's appeal for a *jihād, Revue du monde musulman,* December 1914, special number, and XXXIV (1917-1918).

[8] Compare these precise figures taken by C.-R. Ageron and others from official publications with the cautious generalization of Despois, *L'Afrique du Nord,* p. 250: "It was between 1885 and 1915 that the flocks were largest in Algeria; the average number of sheep was 10 million." Studies on the development of nomadism were the specialty of administrators with a military background. This decadence, they say, is to blame for everything, but there is nothing we can do about it. See the affair of the Marmoucha in Morocco (Berque, *Le Maghreb,* 1st ed., pp. 119, 123).

period the number of landless peasants, condemned by the new economic system to remain landless, increased steadily, until in 1919 fifty percent of the Algerian peasantry were landless. This development went hand in hand with the consolidation of a middle class of Maghribi landowners, openly encouraged by the French administration and bound by no customary obligation (*'āda*) to the dispossessed peasants. Maghribis who collaborated with the civil or military authorities were rewarded with large tracts of land. In a sense this class was a successor to the landed aristocracy which, as we have seen, made its appearance in the eighteenth century,[9] but in 1900 conditions were more favorable for its development and it gained unprecedented influence. In 1918, 60,000 hectares of land in the Constantine region were purchased from colons by Algerians who were certainly not small peasants. From 1921 to 1925 Frenchmen bought 135,000 hectares of land from Algerians, and Algerians 114,000 from the French. In 1930, one percent of the Algerian population owned more than one-fifth of the Algerian-owned land. A comparable development may be observed in Tunisia, where Khayr al-Dīn had already tried to consolidate the class of well-to-do landowners. The indigenous landowners found the same support in the administration of the Protectorate, especially when they associated themselves with French colonization, as in the Sahel. In Morocco, where Lyautey did everything on a large scale, the collective lands and habus lands, which supposedly belonged to the state, were divided among the large colons and qaids. In 1933, a third of the population was estimated to consist of landless peasants. Thus we observe the same social differentiation in the three countries, and it goes without saying that the big landowners, who were always favored by the

[9] There is still no serious study on this subject; the authors are satisfied with diffuse observations. Nevertheless we cannot endorse the opinion of Lacheraf that this class of feudal landowners was a pure creation of French colonialism. The men were new, but the social group had been long in existence. In the Maghrib the rule of a foreign or a weak government always favored the rise of a class of big landowners.

government whether or not they controlled the local administrations, were the chief instrument of the colonial authority in the rural districts. They even managed to divert the few reforms introduced by the French, such as the rural cooperatives (*Sociétés de Prévoyance*)—established in Algeria in 1893, in Tunisia in 1907, and in Morocco in 1921, and the Land Bank (*Crédit foncier*),[10] from their original purpose and turn them to their own advantage. But it was these circumstances that for a long time favored the big Algerian landowners and enabled them to get rich quickly. Until 1920 cereal prices remained high, and French demand steady. During the same period the dispossessed peasants were employed on public works projects or enlisted in the army.[11]

As for the urban population, the old merchant class, as we have seen, had disappeared almost entirely in Algeria. In 1886 only 6.9 percent of the Algerian population lived in cities, and in 1906 the figure had risen only to 8.5 percent. In Tunisia and Morocco, thanks to their capital and long experience, the merchants and master artisans managed to survive as a class. At first they even benefited from foreign immigration by renting their buildings, participating in the colonial trade, and so on. They also profited considerably from the situation created by the war. But after 1920 the circumstances became progressively worse. To understand the ambiguous reactions of this social group, we must remember that it had long enjoyed foreign protection. In the nineteenth century the same urban élite had been in a state of almost permanent revolt because its members were taxed heavily, while as a rule the rural masses were not. With the coming of the Protectorate the situation had been reversed, and despite the wounds to their pride inflicted by the new

[10] It was only in Tunisia that the small peasants (again in the Sahel) were able to benefit by the Land Bank (established in 1907) and of the rural cooperatives (thirty-six in 1909).

[11] This is particularly true of Morocco. It is generally known that numerous Maghribis participated in crushing the Rif revolt as well as the Syrian revolt of 1925.

regime, the members of the urban élite gave the regime credit for having restored what they regarded as the natural order of things. For a long time to come, they were not affected by the cardinal sin of colonization—the expropriation of land.[12]

We are now in a position to understand the contradictions referred to above. The armed revolts came at the end of a profound upheaval brought about by the land hunger of the colons. The revolting communities need not necessarily have suffered spoliation themselves; often they were merely swept up by one of the waves that every act of expropriation or *cantonnement* provoked in Maghribi society. It might even be said that the further away a community was from the sphere of actual colonization, the more likely it was to revolt, since it was less weakened, less overcome by despair, and less supervised. Since the traditional secular leaders saw by the example of others how much they had to gain by prompt submission, it was not they who commanded the most stubborn uprisings, but their eternal competitors, the religious leaders.[13] These revolts, which were regressive in the strict sense of the word, did not gain the support of the cities, for the old cleavage between urban and rural districts was further aggravated by the division of the country into civil and military territories. Often the

[12] We purposely disregard the observations that have often been made on the demographic development of the two—colonial and Maghribi—populations. The figures advanced are often questionable and always difficult to interpret. There may have been a physiological response to a politico-military aggression. But what was its mechanism? Until the demographers supply an answer, the historian will do well not to invent one.

[13] This is Berque's view. According to him, the marabout is explained by dislocated nomadism (*Le Maghrib*, 1st ed., pp. 114-116). The same hazardous judgment is applied to 'Abd al-Karīm (p. 174). Berque contends that 'Abd al-Karīm sided with the Mahdīs and marabouts, not with the traditional shaykhs (the majority of whom had become big qaids), but the information he makes use of is very doubtful. Cf. the equally hasty judgments of Ashford, *Political Change*, who makes 'Abd al-Karīm a Salafi, and of Jamil Abūn Nasr, *The Salafiya movement*, p. 102.

city-dwellers were not even aware of the importance of the rural uprisings. And in spite of these revolts, which though numerous were never general, the old merchant élites of Morocco and Tunisia, and the religious and feudal élites of Algeria, were induced by the benevolence of the administration and the apparent respect of the military to at least tacit collaboration. Thus the only social sector with a political vocation was the new intelligentsia, which was small in numbers and isolated, and moreover owed its very existence to colonialism. In part it was a fortuitous product of the contact between the foreign colony and Maghribi society, but it was also the outgrowth of a deliberate policy, since at the time the colonizing power needed an opposition for reasons that were both political (the problem of Algerian conscription) and diplomatic (rapprochement with the new leaders of Turkey after the 1908 revolution). Comprised of schoolteachers and low-ranking civil servants, this group recommended mild and gradual reforms and their tone was one of respectful timidity.[14] Thanks to the nineteenth-century development in Tunisia, it was there that the intelligentsia first came forward with its grievances, and soon made its influence felt in Algeria. A similar group existed in Morocco, but too late to distinguish itself from the subsequent nationalist movement.[15]

Though it may seem satisfactory at first sight, this analysis is too general to enable us to put our finger on the internal mechanisms of Maghribi society. Its major defect is, as we have said, that it postulates a continuity that is far from obvious. The traditional shaykh who becomes a landowner, the herdsman who becomes a farm laborer, the

[14] Several of the post-1930 nationalist leaders revolted as much against the pusillanimity of their fathers as against French policy. Hence the ambiguity of their attitudes: tactical activism and psychological revolt against a background of opportunism.

[15] The sons of makhzen families chosen by the Protectorates to play this role came of age toward 1930. Though swept up in the wave of nationalism, they represented a moderate element. Some of them later collaborated with the colonial regime.

middle-class merchant of Fez who about 1920 transfers his activities to Casablanca, the son of a chaouch who becomes a schoolteacher and political spokesman—all these change their social roles and from the point of view of a dominated society such changes cannot be regarded as "only natural." We lack both regional structural analyses and significant biographies. Only studies of this kind can give body to the sketch that has just been presented.[16]

II

The ideological, or what one might call the cultural or literary approach deals primarily with the genesis of political movements and relies chiefly on written documents, whether published or in manuscript. It takes little account of far more complex problems such as the social significance of certain words (e.g. *waṭan*) or concepts (*ḥurrīya, istiqlāl, shūrā,* etc.) or of the actual effect of certain actions or campaigns in the Maghribi mind. The most important facts are now beginning to be known,[17] and recent works in this field indicate above all a tendency to look further and further back into the nineteenth century in search of origins.[18]

In speaking of written documents, we have in mind chiefly books and newspaper articles as forms of political and cultural action. Thus from the outset our vision is confined to the men who act (or rather react to colonial action); and on principle a people's self-awareness is reduced to its nationalist manifestations. It is this reduction that gives Tunisia the honor of precedence, for it was in Tunisia that the work of a Khayr al-Dīn and the very nature of the Protec-

[16] There are no serious monographs on the bourgeois and feudal families. The few biographies of great qaids (Glaoui, Goundafi, Baghdadi, Raysuli) are fictionalized. Yet this was a classical form of Moslem historiography.

[17] See the works, cited above, of Julien and Le Tourneau in French and of 'Allāl al-Fāsī in Arabic.

[18] This is true of Ziyadeh, *Origins of Nationalism in Tunisia*; Merad, *Le Réformisme musulman en Algérie*; Halstead, *Rebirth of a Nation.*

torate itself had prepared the way for a degree of political expression.

What is commonly regarded as the first period in the rise of Tunisian nationalism ended with the outbreak of violence in 1911. This essentially cultural movement was a direct, though distorted consequence of the Khayr al-Dīn experiment;[19] direct, because some of its leaders, such as Muḥammad Sanūsī and Sālim Bū Ḥājib had been friends or collaborators of the reformist minister; distorted, because the failure of the reforms attempted in the independent beylicate made the movement receptive to French arguments in favor of a cautious gradualism.[20] Thus the activity of these first nationalists was limited to educational efforts, such as the founding in August 1888 of a weekly magazine, *al-Ḥāḍira* (which thanks to its moderation was permitted to continue publication until 1910, while another, more radical organ, *al-Zahra*, founded in 1890, was suppressed in 1896)[21] and the founding in 1896 of a cultural circle, the *Khaldūniya*, the president of which was a prominent youth, Bashīr Ṣfar, who, thanks to his moderation and the sympathy of certain French politicians, was to have a brilliant career. The articles published by these journals and the lectures delivered at the Khaldūnian circle emphasized the

[19] See Khaïrallah, *Le Mouvement évolutioniste tunisien*, which Ziyadeh summarizes at the beginning of his book. See also Bouali, *Introduction à l'histoire constitutionelle de la Tunisie*, vol. 2, notes to the section entitled "Voyage au bout de la nuit," pp. 159ff.

[20] This situation is parallel to that of Egypt. The similarity is symbolized, as it were, by the work of Muḥammad Bayram (V), who was a friend of Lord Cromer, and in the journeys of Muḥammad 'Abduh (also a friend of the English) to Tunis (1884-1885 and 1903). Cf. Chenoufi, "Maṣādir 'an Riḥlatai Muḥammad 'Abduh ilā Tūnis," *Annales de l'Université de Tunis* (3), 1966, pp. 71ff., which is in reality a study of the beginnings of the reform movement in Tunisia.

[21] References to these periodicals seldom indicate whether any issues still exist. More often than not titles are merely cited from articles that appeared at the beginning of the century in *Revue du monde musulman* (e.g. "La Presse marocaine," vol. II, 1907, p. 586, and "La Presse arabe au Maroc," vol. VII, 1909, p. 128). These are then requoted from book to book with no additional information. This is the case in al-Kattānī's book, *Al-Ṣiḥāfa al-maghribiya*, vol. I.

need for gradual reform, beginning with the education of the individual and improvement of the family environment. Occasionally the proponents of this moderate, philistine ideology ventured to speak of such remote aims as freedom and democracy, but insisted that they must first be deserved. Encouraged by the administration, this movement became increasingly French both in mentality and in language. In 1905 the young graduates of the Sadiki College (the former Ṣādiqīya, reorganized by a French principal) formed an association of their own, in which 'Alī Bash Ḥāmba soon imposed his leadership by his learning and energy. The road was now open to a cultural movement more faithful to the traditions of the country and more independent of the colonial authorities. Its natural center was the old Zitūna University. Its leader 'Abd al-'Azīz al-Tha'ālibī, whose thinking had been molded both by the local reformism of Qabādū and Muḥammad Bayram and by the new movement directed from Cairo by Muḥammad 'Abduh, also spoke of moral, social, individual and collective reform, but in a very different sense.[22] From 1895 to 1897 he published a weekly, *Sabīl al-Rashād,* but soon fell afoul of the administration, not so much because his ideas were revolutionary as because they owed nothing to western liberalism and because he addressed himself to those whom the colonial system could not assimilate. Under his influence, which despite, or because of, the hostility of the traditionalist professors at the Zitūna, became dominant after his return from the orient in 1902, the alumni formed an association of their own. The gulf between the Ṣādiqīya and Zitūna groups widened steadily; the one, influential with the old families of beylical officials whose sons had found employment in the French administration, tried by moderation to obtain a few concessions from the new masters, while the other,

[22] The ideologists of the two movements (of the Ṣādiqīya and of the Zitūna) have often been lumped together, but one can distinguish certain differences on the basis of models they often unconsciously invoke.

finding its most ardent partisans among those held outside the system, became increasingly radical in its opposition.[23] On certain occasions the moderate group was influenced by its rival, as in 1906 when the administration threw open the habus lands to the colons. Such measures revealed the true nature of the Protectorate even to such men as Bashū Ṣfar.[24] The administration tried to cultivate the friendship of the moderates. Muḥammad al-Aṣram and Hassūna al-'Ayāshī were invited to the colonial conference of Marseilles (September 1906), and Ṣfar and Zaouch to the congress on North Africa held in Paris two years later. The professors, journalists and high officials present praised the papers submitted by the Tunisians, for they were moderate, technical and well documented and above all did not question the French authority.[25] In 1907, between the two conferences, Bash Ḥāmba founded a French-language journal, *Le Tunisien,* to acquaint French public opinion with the grievances of his group, and the administration responded by appointing Ṣfar governor of Sousse in the hope of isolating the nonmoderates, but succeeded only in increasing their intransigence. In 1909 Tha'ālibī founded an Arabic *Tunisien* in opposition to the French *Tunisien,* and in 1910 the students of the Zitūna went on strike, ostensibly in support of their demands for university reform but in reality in opposition to the whole policy of colonial conservatism. Even the moderates were obliged to support them. The year 1911 was one of international crises over the still free territories of the Maghrib, Morocco and Libya. The resulting passions brought the two movements together; Bash Ḥāmba and Tha'ālibī joined forces to transform the Young Tunisian

[23] Here again the similarity with the Egyptian situation is striking. After 1906-1907 (the Danshwāy affair and the recall of Cromer), opposition to British occupation became more intense.

[24] Cf. the résumé of Ṣfar's speech (March 24, 1906) at the *Awqāf attakiya* association in Ziyadeh, *Origins.*

[25] At the congress Muḥammad al-Aṣram uttered these words: "The Tunisian Moslem, with his atavistic resignation, is well aware of his inability to modify the situation created by the events of 1881."

movement, which had been in the making since 1908, into a political party (the Evolutionist Party) with distinctly pro-Ottoman leanings (its organ was named *al-Ittiḥād al-Islāmī*). Incidents immediately followed, the best known of which was that of the Jallāz (November 7, 1911) from the name of the Moslem cemetery which the Tunis city council voted to expropriate, having first registered it in compliance with the land registration act of 1885. In the face of intense opposition the measure was cancelled, but the demonstrations were not called off. The police were submerged, and in restoring order the army killed a large number of Tunisians. Martial law was proclaimed. The riot had been chiefly between Tunisians and Italians, who were in keen competition in various spheres of economic life. This led to the second incident (February 1912) involving an Italian streetcar motorman and culminating in a general boycott of the streetcar lines. The discipline shown by the Tunisians in carrying out the boycott indicated the profound influence of the leaders of the Evolutionist Party and impelled the authorities to take extreme measures. The nationalist papers were suspended and the leaders exiled. The protest movement was driven underground. So ended the first round of the fight between the nationalists and the colonial administration. In the years that followed, the same scenario was to be several times repeated in Tunisia and elsewhere in the Maghrib: a brief period of rapprochement between the moderates and the administration, followed by brutal repression when the agitation of the less moderate elements had demonstrated the incompatibility between the interests of the two communities.

A similar development, strongly influenced by the Tunisian example, occurred in Algeria.[26] At a time when the old Islamic consciousness had ceased to exist except in the Tlemcen region, the first graduates of the French schools,

[26] See Ageron, *Les Musulmans algériens et la France*. The chapter on the Young Algerian movement, vol. II, pp. 1030-1055, is summarized in *Etudes maghrébines*, pp. 217-243.

many of them of Kabyle extraction, began to form cultural associations with the blessing of Governor Jonnart. In French-language weeklies (such as *Le Rachidi* and *L'Etendard algérien*) they expressed the same ideology of gradual, cautious reform as *Le Tunisien*. In June 1912, taking advantage of the French public's alarm over the increasing demographic and hence military imbalance between France and Germany, the movement published its Manifesto of the Young Algerians. They offered to support the French project of extending conscription to Algeria in return for abolition of the Status of Natives Laws and of the special taxes on Arabs, increased representation in the local Algerian assemblies, and the right to send deputies to the parliament in Paris. There are many who still characterize this program, then supported by French liberal circles, as assimilationist. It should be remembered, however, that at the time Algeria was already autonomous and such a program, if applied, could only have resulted in a change of majority, in other words, in an Algerian Algeria—not explicitly Arab or Moslem, to be sure, but at that stage the Young Algerians gave no more thought to the problem of national identity than did the Young Tunisians. In any event, the movement was weak (membership has been estimated at one thousand) and achieved none of its aims, except for the abolition of administrative internment. But its program formed the basis of the reforms of February-March 1919, imposed by Clemenceau on a reluctant Chamber of Deputies.[27]

Both subjectively and objectively the Young-Tunisian and Young-Algerian movements were modeled on the Young Turks. This same influence made itself felt in Morocco, but

[27] The number of Algerian Moslems eligible to vote was increased (421,000 for the local councils, municipal councils and *jmā'as*; 130,000 for the general councils and *Délégations Financières*; the proportion of Moslem municipal councillors rose from one-quarter to one-third, and they were now entitled to participate in electing mayors; the number of departmental councillors rose to one-quarter of the total. Access to French citizenship remained contingent on renunciation of the personal status. Cf. Bernard, *L'Algérie*, pp. 493-495; Ageron, *Algériens musulmans*, vol. II, pp. 1212-1227.

there, it would seem, directly. Before 1912, as we now know, there had been a constitutionalist movement in Tangiers and Fez. Its members were merchants, who were in close contact with England, and journalists, many of whom were of Syrio-Lebanese origin. The Constitutionalists opposed the machinations of 'Abd al-'Azīz, who since the Touat affair (1901-1902) had been increasingly dominated by French diplomacy; they took part in the revolt of 'Abd al-Ḥafīdh and drafted the still-born Constitution of 1908.[28] Unfortunately there is still much to be learned about this movement; in particular we know nothing of its relations with the contemporary reform movement which was based in the Qarawiyīn and which enjoyed greater influence in makhzen circles.[29]

The war of 1914 marked the end of the moderate, educational stage. Again it was Tunisia, encouraged by the activity of the Egyptian Wafd, that set the example for the Maghrib. Tha'ālibī, who had become the spokesman of Tunisian nationalism after the death of 'Ali Bash Ḥāmba in 1918 in Constantinople, tried to submit the Tunisian case against the Protectorate to the Congress of Versailles and, to acquaint the public with the facts, published (in collaboration with other militants) an important book in French, *La Tunisie martyre*. It describes the reformist Tunisia of the nineteenth century, the stagnant Tunisia of the Protectorate, and finally, the future as conceived by the nationalists. The entire book is impregnated with a liberal, constitutionalist spirit, so much so that the reader cannot help

[28] Arabic text in 'Abd al-Karim Ghallāb, *Difā' 'an ad-Dimuqrātiya* (Tangiers, 1966), pp. 195-208. French text published in Robert, *La Monarchie marocaine*; cf. the analysis in 'Allāl al-Fāsī, *al-Harakāt*, pp. 98-100, and the article reprinted in the group's paper, *Lisān al-Maghrib*. The same text may be found in Gannūn, *Aḥādīth 'an al-Adab al-Maghribī*, pp. 15-16. Analysis of this constitution shows both intellectual backwardness and a certain genuineness; it was the work of the urban commercial élite (comparison with the Tunisian constitution of 1861 is instructive).

[29] On this movement, see Halstead, "The Changing Character of Moroccan Reformism," p. 438.

wondering how much of it was written by Tha'ālibī himself. Faithful to this ideology, the party took the name of *Dustūr*, since it aimed to restore the Constitution of 1861. On March 7, 1920, a program was published and in May a delegation went to the palace of the bey Nāṣir (himself inclined to reform), bearing a petition with thousands of signatures—in this the example of the Wafdist *Tafwīḍ* (delegation) launched in Egypt in 1919 is evident. Though the Franco-Tunisian treaties of 1881-1883 were not overtly attacked, the Dustūr's direct contacts with representatives of the foreign powers and its stated aim of restoring the power to initiate reforms to the bey, represented an implicit attack on the treaties (despite the contrary opinion of the reputed jurists consulted by the Dustūr). In any event, such was the interpretation of the French government, which after some hesitation had Tha'ālibī arrested in Paris early in 1921. On April 5, 1922, the bey Nāṣir, who had declared his willingness to accept reforms, was called upon to retract (here the British attitude in Egypt was taken as an example). The crisis ended with the granting of minor reforms: the establishment of a ministry of justice under the presidency of Ṭāhir b. Khayr al-Dīn, and the institution in 1922 of a purely consultative grand council of Tunisia, in which the French enjoyed double representation and the Tunisian members, fewer in number, were elected indirectly.[30] This setback drove the leaders to despair and provoked a split in the Dustūr party. Tha'ālibī left Tunis in 1923. He did not return until 1937 and never regained his position of leadership.

In Algeria a similar political movement also ended in disillusionment. The reforms of 1919 had been bitterly attacked by the colons. Nor did they satisfy the majority of

[30] There were 56 members in the French section (22 appointed by the chambers of agriculture and commerce and 34 elected directly); in the Tunisian section there were 41 members (18 appointed by the chambers of agriculture and commerce, and 23 elected in accordance with a highly complicated system), which, except in the capital, amounted practically to the "appointment" of pro-French candidates.

the Young Algerians. Only a small minority who failed to realize what it meant to the Algerian masses to lose the personal status conferred by Islamic law were willing to play the game. Others accepted the electoral franchise, but only as a means of airing their grievances, and found a leader in the person of Khālid, grandson of the amir 'Abd al-Qādir. Elected municipal councillor of Algiers, general councillor and elected member of the *Délégations financières,* he took up the 1912 program and, carrying it to its logical conclusion, demanded the extension to Algerians of all the political rights enjoyed by the French. The way to do this was, to be sure, by assimilation, but the result could be revolutionary. This the administration understood and always regarded the new leader as a dangerous revolutionary. Receiving President Millerand in April 1922, in the name of the municipality of Algiers, he reiterated the demand for Algerian representation in the French parliament in a tone that some chose to regard as disrespectful. The colonial administration responded by bringing suit upon suit against the newspaper he directed and by putting pressure on his friends. Finally, in 1924, he was exiled from Algeria. After a period in Paris he went to Damascus, where he ended his days in isolation and disillusionment.[31]

These crises now strike us as insignificant. At the time, however, they had loud reverberations, because public opinion in Europe viewed them in the light of the socio-political upheavals of the postwar period. This was probably one of the reasons why Lyautey, despite strong opposition, continued his "liberal" policy in Morocco and maintained the fiction of an autonomous Moroccan state.[32]

In 1924-1925 a period of stabilization set in. There were signs of economic recovery, the political movements were under control, resistance in the Rif had been subdued, and

[31] See Ageron, *Politiques coloniales,* pp. 249-288, and Kaddache, *La Vie politique,* pp. 65-77.

[32] See Lyautey's speech at the Paris mosque in his *Paroles d'Action,* pp. 369-374; and the testimony of Spillmann, *Du Protectorat à l'indépendance,* pp. 22ff.

the French policies toward the Maghrib countries had been coordinated. (The first North African Conference was held on February 6, 1923.) Political action within the framework allotted by the colonial power had failed. At a time when the French were confident of a return to prewar prosperity, the political movements of the Maghrib went through a process of "traditionalization" or "nationalization." In appearance the period from 1925 to 1930 was calm; in reality it was marked by the deepening of both a national and a social consciousness, taking place simultaneously. The problems of national identity and social mobilization were treated both in the poetry of Abū al-Qāsim Shabbī and in the work of such publicists as Ṭāhir al-Ḥaddād.[33] In 1924, under the impulsion of Mḥammad 'Alī, the Tunisian nationalists turned their attention to economic questions. A mutual-aid society was founded with the blessings of Ṭāhir Ṣfar, but was swept away by the wave of strikes which, despite the opposition of the Dustūr and the French Socialists, culminated that same year in the founding of the C.G.T.T. (*Conféderation Génèrales des Travailleurs Tunisiens*). At the same time in Algeria the religious reform movement of the ulama, led by the shaykhs Ibn Bādīs al-'Uqbi, and Ibrāhīmī, propagated the idea of Algerian identity in the religious schools, and the Algerian workers in France (92,000 in 1923) organized the "Etoile Nord-Africaine" movement (1925), which proposed to carry Khālid's work to its logical conclusion, namely, Algerian independence. In Morocco the anti-maraboutic campaign of 'Allāl al-Fāsī and his Fez group and the more political efforts of Aḥmad Balafrej in Rabat and Abd al-Salām Bannūna in Tetuán (1927) all aimed at restoring Moroccan sovereignty. This process of "nationalization" was punctuated by symbolic actions, in reality reactions to the measures of an in-

[33] This connection has not yet been clearly formulated. See Sraieb, "Contribution à la connaissance de Tahir El-Ḥaddād (1899-1935)." Khalid, *Al-Ṭāhir al-Ḥaddād*, is more detailed.

creasingly tactless colonial administration, such as the Berber dahir of May 1930, and in the same year the Eucharistic Congress held in Carthage and the centenary of the French landing in Algiers. By 1937 full-fledged political parties had come into being and took the initiative from the colonial administration. The Popular Front tried to drive a wedge between the new forces and the urban bourgeoisie and sometimes succeeded. During the periods of intense agitation (1937-1938, 1945-1949, 1951-1954), the nationalists put the accent on national identity and the struggle against social exploitation.

In what perspective are we to view these facts? If we take each country separately, we can discern different sequences: in Tunisia, cultural reformism, political reformism, political activism; in Algeria, gradual assimilationism, accelerated assimilationism, religious reformism and political activism (the last two with autonomist aims); in Morocco, military resistance, religious reformism, and political activism. In other words the phases in the development of national awareness differed from country to country. Thus in trying to explain any one of them there is no need to go beyond a local sociological analysis or a simple exposé of the colonial policy in this one country. We can proceed as though each movement were born from the failure and repression of the movement preceding it. If on the other hand we take the Maghrib as a whole, our study of literary material seems to justify the following sequence: secular political reformism (moderate both in ideology and action); religious reformism (radical in ideology but moderate in action); and lastly, political activism (moderate in program, extremist in its methods of action).[34] If this sequence should prove correct, how are we to account for it, avoiding at the same time any artificial harmonizing of the facts? Thus far historians of Maghribi nationalism have shown no interest in such

[34] This was true of Bourguiba's Dustūr and of the League for Moroccan Action in 1934.

questions. Each is satisfied to state his particular conclusion with regard to a given country at a given time. Thus their studies, for all their richness, are limited in scope.[35]

III

In order to avoid the absolute relativism that would credit all the movements studied above with equal effectiveness, a general explicative theory is needed. Otherwise, on what shall we be able to base a statement that one school of thought derived from another, that one tactic was born from the success or failure of another? No causal sequence would be possible. Although more precise than social analysis, analysis of intellectual history is, in this respect, more deficient.

We find, nevertheless, that even pointillist historians usually arrive at a tripartite division; some refer to affective, ideological and political nationalism; others to protonationalism, nationalism proper and internationalist(?) nationalism; still others to religious reformism, bourgeois nationalism and popular nationalism.[36] The adjectives alone denote a conceptual imprecision that leads to a confusion of levels —the sociological (which deals with movements and parties), the ideological (which deals with matters of conscience) and the historical (which is concerned with evaluating one nationalism in the light of another, in the present case the nationalism of nineteenth-century Europe). Despite this imprecision, however, one reality seems to stand out; it can, at least hypothetically, be described as follows.

First, let us isolate (this is a methodological necessity) the

[35] See the conclusions of Ziyadeh, Ageron and Halstead; they make statements and are surprised by nothing. Is it true, for example, that laicizing thought preceded religious reformism in Tunisia? And, if so, how is this to be explained? Cf. the pages devoted to this subject in my *Idéologie arabe*, referred to earlier.

[36] On these definitions, see Duclos, Leca, Duvignaud, *Les Nationalismes maghrébins* (in which the notion of an impure, perverted internationalist nationalism is applied by Jean Leca to Algeria, pp. 63-72).

situation of the Maghrib in the nineteenth century, rejecting the illusion of a mechanical continuity, for if we succumb to it, philological study will always show a line of filiation between nationalism and movements in the more and more remote past and tend increasingly to underestimate outside influences, in particular the impact of colonial action itself. On the social level the nineteenth century witnessed the coexistence of a governmental élite (makhzen), an urban petite bourgeoisie, and a rural population; the same coexistence is discernible in the realm of feeling and conscience. The makhzen was the guardian of a historical tradition manifesting itself in historiography; the urban élite engendered a reformism that was both religious (dogmatic) and political (moderate liberalism), while the rural districts nurtured a local patriotism bound up with a religious renewal (in the realm of ritual). This situation seems to have prefigured others that were to follow. Nevertheless we must remember that it was a reaction to a definite form of foreign pressure. The total colonization of the Maghrib created a breach which for purposes of analysis must also be regarded as total. The zero degree of historic existence postulated by colonial economism never became a total reality, but undeniably the colonial situation tended toward this point and this made absolute continuity impossible. If the notion of absolute continuity survived in the minds of men, it was an ideological concept; philological analysis finds it, but the historian must not let it mislead him; methodology obliges him to reject chronological determinations.

When a colonial society insinuates itself between a traditional society and its land base, the determination becomes multiple and indirect. In studying the reactions of the dominated society, we must try to construct a model comprising all these determinations and, above all, symbolizing the general "regression" of the dominated society toward the zero degree mentioned above, that is, toward an objective and absolute negation of its historic past. In a colonial situation the individual is inwardly oriented, psychologically (infantilism), sociologically (traditionalism) and even geographically (exile in the desert and the mountains, in a symbolic journey to the heartland). One might say that in this totally repressed society, everything, even the ideal, was seen in retrospect. But colonial society did not stop with the repression of traditional groups; it engendered new groups which, though subordinate, experienced the world in the same way and looked out on the same horizon as the colonial bourgeoisie, though for them the horizon was closed. These groups saw things in a flat perspective that offered no view of a totally new future. This was the birthplace of "nationalism" in the usual sense of the term: caviling, making demands, but participationist, opposed to innovations. Unable to conceive of a postcolonial situation, these nationalists tried, long after the end of formal dependence, to reenact the colonial tragedy; the consequence is what is commonly known as neocolonialism. Thus before analyzing a movement's economico-social determinations, ideological themes, and models of organization, it is essential to relate it to the "model" that gives it its lasting significance. These "models" may be represented as follows:

I *(Old Maghrib)*	*European Colony*	II *(New Maghrib)*	III *(The New Nationalism)*
Traditional élite	Financiers and parliamentarians	New élite	
Petite bourgeoisie	Colonial bourgeoisie	Urban proletariat	
Peasantry	Agrarian colonization	Farm proletariat	

The old Maghrib (I) with its three main groups suffered a general regression. Each of the groups had its peculiar reaction: religious reformism, popular asceticism, siba (rural revolt); all their ideologies and activities were "negative" expressions, not because the groups were inarticulate, but because objectively they denied the past (for religious reformism twelve centuries of history were expunged) and because their positive aspects became effective only if other groups, belonging to the new system created by colonization, took them in hand and interpreted them. Colonial European society, which was also differentiated, secreted ideologies that found direct political expression (repression, integration or cosovereignty, formal independence). It was this colonial society that determined the scope of history, that separated the past from the future, the regressive from the progressive. In this it influenced the Maghrib profoundly, determining the thought and action of the new Maghrib society (II).

The ideologies (liberalism, populism, socialism), the organizations (clubs, parties, unions), the political opinions and slogans of this society may differ, but they all partake of tactics (which explains why the Maghribi leaders of the time have been complimented for speaking a modern political language). This is the focus both of nationalism in the restricted sense and of the future neocolonialism.[37] But insofar as this society lives in the realm of tactics, that is, of appearances, its true force arises from the negative aspects of society (I). Nationalism is nothing unless it takes upon itself the negative consequences of past history, and from 1934 on it did just that. But this attitude was itself tactical: the nationalists frightened their adversary by threatening him with the nihilism of others. But never at any time did they offer any positive expression of these negative attitudes,

[37] Hence the traditional criticism of their programs: too much social reform without regard to economic development (Julien, *L'Afrique du Nord en marche*, p. 154; Le Tourneau, *Evolution politique*, p. 191). This lack of realism, however, is the exact counterpart of the colonial situation. Colonialism established itself in the name of technology and development; thus it was up to the colonials to solve the economic problem. The nationalists regarded themselves as the spokesmen of a vast proletariat with social demands to present; they held that it was up to the colonial bourgeoisie to meet these demands in return for the enormous privileges they enjoyed. Thus the alliance between Maghribi nationalism and the French socialist movement was not fortuitous; they were brought together by an identity of attitude.

and even after independence there has been no true clarification. Yet if this possibility were realized, we should find ourselves in the presence of another model (III), expressed by a new kind of nationalism, a nationalism oriented toward the future and for this very reason taking over and transcending the demands of the nationalisms that preceded it; then we could speak of a true assimilation of the past.[38]

Of course it would be possible to study all manner of relations among the expressions of these three "models," but we can already be sure that they can be neither direct nor continuous. Just as between the retrospective model (I) and the colonial model (II) there is a breach, namely, colonization, so between model II and the not yet realized model III there will be a breach, namely, the revolution.[39]

Thus we arrive again at a tripartism, but instead of speaking of types of nationalism—affective, religious and political—we shall refer to different expressions—regressive, neutral[40] and prospective—of an identical reality (the reality of a dominated Maghrib which reacts). These expressions relate respectively to a society which undergoes colonization without understanding it, to a society which plays the game of colonization without fundamentally questioning it, and finally to a third society that will understand the mechanisms of colonization and transcend them along with its own compromises and weaknesses. If we, nevertheless, wish to retain the term nationalism, we will distinguish three kinds, characterized respectively by resignation, tactical acceptance and rational synthesis. This provides a frame of reference that will help us to place the various manifestations of na-

38 Nationalism, it goes without saying, ignores the history of the precolonial period and its own history during the colonial period.

39 These observations, of course, will gain cogency only when they are illustrated and tested in a special study. They are, however, the product of fragmentary studies on Moroccan nationalism, which I hope to complete soon.

40 Because it does not raise the question of the future and of communitarian identity, it accepts the colonial perspective.

tionalism, some of which have been summed up above and some of which, making their appearance after the Second World War, have survived down to our day.

IV

This discussion of nationalism permits us to stop at the period ending between 1930 and 1932. Since then Maghribi society has been taking its own destinies in hand, but this movement, revealed by symbolic events, has not yet run its course. The polarization that characterized Maghribi life at that date remained unchanged. From then on colons and nationalists confronted each other with two contending ideologies and two contending programs, the circumstances favoring now one, now the other, but most often favoring the nationalists.

The foreign colony defended itself vigorously. But unfortunately for the colonials, at the very moment when they hoped to obtain their autonomy, they found they needed the mother country, to which the center of decision had already shifted. Hard hit by the world crisis, the colonials violently criticized the local administration which had always been devoted to their interests but which they nevertheless held responsible for a situation that was largely beyond its control. They demanded more and more attention from the administration, which consequently neglected the Maghribi population, controlling it only superficially, through the police. By demanding assistance (price support, the closing of the French market to foreign products, government credits, debt relief, etc.), the colonials drew criticism in the French parliament. At the same time they suffered from the social contradictions of metropolitan France. Denigrated by the military in the Maghrib and by parliamentarians in France, betrayed by the bankers and industrialists, they became more and more unrestrained in their egoism, expecting the French government to support them economically, to palliate the evils they themselves had created (the social policy of colonization), and to defend them by force of arms. And in the name of what? Honor? The flag? Fidelity to the dead? Notions of another age!

Meanwhile the nationalist party, aided by its tactical orientation, wisely spoke the language of figures. Order, security, agrarian colonization, they declared, were costing too much; all sorts of economies could be effected, giving rise to "invisible" profits. They offered all possible guarantees and, to lend weight to their proposals, fomented revolts at the most sensitive point, in the cities. What difference did it make that the countryside remained calm, that the good Berbers were still smiling? That wasn't where fortunes were made. Whom could such language convince? Those capable of understanding it were in Paris.

Alibis and tactics! True, this had been the case in the Maghrib since 1830. The underlying elements had never found direct expression in politics. But now the roles were reversed. Nationalism was sustained by the logic of the modern age, while the foreign colony seemed to be a relic of the past, suffering from the same historical lag as the regime of the sultan or the bey in the nineteenth century. When the time came, the French army would fight to safeguard the interests and rights of the colony. And when it uttered the words "honor" and "glory" it would be booed. After 1830 the old Maghrib had lived on borrowed time; the same was true of colonization after 1930.

But did not the very logic that sustained nationalism subject it to limitations that it would never surpass? It is the importance of this question that impels us to stop at 1930-1932, for at that date, though certain signs of recovery were already apparent, the Maghrib was still very close to the theoretical point at which the old humanity of the Maghrib was destroyed forever, a point even more regressive than those described in the course of the foregoing pages: the end of the second millennium B.C., the first century B.C., the fourteenth century A.D., when the Maghribi individual, ex-pelled from history, was reduced to his anthropological dimensions. From this vantage point, we can gain a perspective on all preceding periods and present the problems in the form of demands, without involving ourselves in polemics by asking whether or not these demands have since been fulfilled.

What have we made of an atomized society, of a negated history? What should we do? It is by taking up this question that tactical nationalism can transcend itself and develop rational politics and a rational nationalism.

Conclusion
Heritage and Recovery

I

The colonial era is past. Some defend it ardently or half-heartedly, others castigate it in relevant or irrelevant terms. Some claim that it enriched nature and the individual; others call it a scar on the landscape and on the bodies of men. The argument about the colonial period never seems to end, probably because the period itself is not entirely ended. But the matter should be judged on a very different level.

Undoubtedly there is a grain of truth both in the theory that colonization came by chance and in the theory that it resulted from a sense of mission provoked by a historical disequilibrium and void. Without this grain of truth, neither theory would have the minimum of logic required to convince its proponents. It would be hard to deny that the colonization of the Maghrib was already implicit in the pseudosolutions applied to the crisis of the fourteenth and fifteenth centuries. The expansionism of modern colonialism would then be the logical consequence of another expansionism that had affected the same territories. It was not necessarily inevitable, but the possibility of avoiding it—and this is essential—depended on outside forces. Once decided on, it could have been stopped only by "economic calculation," but the calculators were a part of the expanding system. It is not the facts of colonization that should concern us, but the conditions under which it took place. Missed opportunity? Necessary failure? The Maghribi reaction of the nineteenth century can be discussed indefinitely. In any event it was inadequate. The ports could not be defended from the land side with a few old cannon bought from the enemy; the coastal plains, which had been ravaged for centuries, could have been rehabilitated only by intensive repopulation and intensive farming; perhaps the only true defense would have been to accept the risks of "opening up," that is, of precisely what seemed to signify defeat.

Yet the negative or insufficient results should not blind us to the existence of a striving for reform. Blind, misdirected to the point of aberration, it was nevertheless real, and it cannot be denied that such a striving was at work in Khayr al-Dīn and his friends, in 'Abd al-Qādir, and the 'Alawite sultans. Nor can it be denied that the strategic crux of all reform was modernization of the army. No improvement was possible without a strong army, designed, to be sure, not to defeat the enemy, but to conquer the interior of the country. The difficulty, which numerous attempts proved insuperable, was that this could not be done without "capital." It was there that the absence of a true aristocracy made itself cruelly felt. In the Maghrib, economic surpluses could have been requisitioned only by an army that remained to be organized, while elsewhere the state was enabled by one or more mechanisms—religious, social, political—to lay hands on such surpluses, to build up a modern army with their help, and through the army to institute a process of sustained growth by educating and disciplining the country.

In the case of the Maghrib the proximity of Europe undoubtedly exerted a negative influence. It prevented contradictory structures from gradually resolving their contradictions. But the determining factor was the weight of the past, that is, the past policies of the rulers and the past actions of the peoples of the Maghrib. European pressure and the cautious, self-interested conservatism of the Maghribis had the same stultifying effect, for colonial policy was conceived precisely on the basis of facts gleaned from the study of the Maghribi past. In the end colonization completed and consummated this past by providing the Maghrib with what for two centuries it had desperately tried to acquire: an army and an accumulation of capital. What followed from that point on was no more than the consequence, both in the material sphere and in the minds of men, of a comprehensive logic. Wherever it went, the army introduced an administration and a juridical system. Capitalist law, an impersonal administration, and a middle-class language opened the roads through which businessmen would pour. This was the abstract, unseen moment (which for this very reason aroused much less opposition after than before the conquest) intercalated between the conquest and the exploitation of the conquest.

What followed and changed the landscape—roads, mining enterprises, light industries, urbanization—was also the work of businessmen (agrarian colonization, as we have seen, was a relic of another age and denotes the backwardness of the French colonial mind in the Maghrib), and this is what condemned colonization in the long run. For this colonization was wholly dependent on buying and selling. In order to develop or even hold its own, it needed "primitive" people. When there were no more "primitives," or not enough of them, this middleman's colonization turned against itself and took flight into finance, which made it even more hideous than before, for now it began to exploit an increasing number of the colonials themselves.

Moreover, colonization became superfluous, since it is obvious that under these conditions high finance can dispense with a colony defined as physical presence in someone else's country. Quite a few observers realized at the time how large a part the ideologies of another age played in nineteenth-century expansionism, especially where the Maghrib was concerned.

But then diplomatic motives, which at first had been totally unrealistic, gradually took on content. Pacification, "civilization," security, territorial unification—these false justifications of colonial undertakings—produced more lasting results in the Maghrib than any technical improvements in agriculture or the crafts. Morocco provides a perfect example of this reversal of motives, of this new resurrection of the "ruse of reason," because it was there that the experiment was attempted last, after practice had purified the concepts of colonization. But it is also true in the Algeria of 'Abd al-Qādir and the Tunisia of Khayr al-Dīn. The true significance of colonial action was to generalize the presence of the army and to make taxation effective. This, however, was not evident to most people, since, once these results were obtained, everything stopped, whereas that was precisely where everything should have begun. What should have been the work of the nineteenth century was lovingly carried over to the twentieth. The consequences were the preservation of structures which were felt to be obsolete even by those who benefited by them and in several cases a geographical and psycho-sociological reduction of the population to still more archaic forms, the reappearance of which filled the colonist—who feigned innocence—with joy.

And that is the great crime of all colonization.

It not only stops historical evolution, but obliges the colonized people to regress. In principle every colonization is a condemnation to historical death. The old structures, the old habits, the old egoisms rise to the surface of minds and societies, and in misfortune everyone takes refuge in childhood. Then it becomes an easy matter, and politically expedient, to look on in ecstasy and exclaim: Look, nothing has changed in twenty centuries—without stopping to see that what has driven the subject people back into its remote past is precisely the colonist's presence. It is true that taken as individuals Jugurtha can be superimposed perfectly on 'Abd al-Qādir and Tacfarinas on 'Abd al-Karīm, because down through the ages man has only one childhood and one refuge. Colonization leaves only one alternative: revolt or death. The examples are innumerable. In Algeria the tradition of 'Abd al-Qādir was preserved, but coldly, without perspective; the brotherhoods were preserved, but diverted from their original purpose; the administration supported or occasionally created a supposedly aristocratic class of supine shaykhs, devoid of prestige. It hemmed the family in so closely that it became a prison of the soul, and when the work of destroying Maghribi society was almost complete, permitted individuals to enter French society one by one, after having made them acknowledge in writing that the old society was thoroughly dead. Clearly the reaction could only be a *return* to the land and to religion, the foundations of the old community, and condemnation of the social forms developed through the centuries. The example of Tunisia is still more conclusive: the reforms of Khayr al-Dīn, accepted by the Tunisians despite the conditions under which they were drawn up, were not carried out until a century later, after the demise of the Protectorate, whose only concern had been to oppose them. In Morocco, reduced to the condition of a vast "national park," tradition was defended against the traditionalists, monarchy against the monarchs, custom against its presumed beneficiaries. The longer colonization went on, the more the will of the dominated people weakened, the more its intelligence deteriorated, and the rarer became integrity. Those who say that colonization brings with it the seeds of its own destruction forget the wasted years, the lost opportunities, the energies squandered in the world of appearances, not to mention the waste of the nationalist struggle itself. Who can say what the energies wasted in forty years of sterile struggle against an obstinate, conservative administration might have done for the Tunisian people if used more profitably? Modern colonization leaves behind it a task infinitely more arduous than the one it prided itself on performing. It is more difficult to lift up a man reduced to the level of an animal and to teach him optimism than to build roads and dams.

But, one might ask, is it necessary to justify or to condemn colonization? Perhaps not. Quite a few writers have been trying to appeal the case of colonialism; to them it must be said that the case has thus far not been seriously tried, since on both sides the wounds are still too painful and too shameful.

II

On several occasions the social mechanism has stopped in the Maghrib. Individuals and groups have often concluded a separate peace with destiny. What can we do to prevent this from happening again, now that the end of colonization has offered us an opportunity to make a fresh start? The question may not be appropriate for a historian, but we ask it, because it is no accident that young Maghribis have been taking a passionate interest in the experience of nineteenth-century Europe but fall asleep if the subject of conversation is the medieval Maghrib. What do the words "time lag," "colonization," "blocked evolution," "unequal development" matter? What does it matter who is responsible? God, geography, or men? What each one of us wants to know today is how to get out of ourselves, how to escape from our mountains and sand dunes, how to define ourselves in terms of ourselves and not of someone else, how to stop being exiles in spirit. That alone is the Revolution, and it remains to be fought.

The words tripartism and dualism have recurred frequently in these pages; diversity changes its form and meaning from stage to stage, it does not vanish. In the last analysis the image we retain of the Maghrib is one of a pyramid with different levels: anthropological, linguistic, socio-economic, in short historical, and at each level lies the sediment of an unresolved contradiction. Every true revolution must necessarily be total, and deliberately so. Otherwise new sediment will pile up on the old, after long decay. In the meantime, and this is one precondition of such a revolution, let no one impose his creed on his fellow men. The historical corpus, which remains to be constituted, must be neutral. This neutrality will guarantee the neutrality of the state, but first we must achieve it in our own minds, for each one of us, seeing only a part of his society's past, terrorizes a part of himself. That will take time, but to hope for a political consciousness without such historic consciousness is a delusion.

The Maghrib has now been independent for a decade. Despite all the ideas popularized by government propaganda, the problem remains politico-cultural. Economic underdevelopment will never be overcome until social and cultural underdevelopment have been diagnosed and combated, and that calls for a questioning of the past. Here let us make three observations:

(1) Despite our sometimes justified harangues about democracy and justice in Islam, we must recognize that the political structure which Islam engendered, and which foreign pressure solidified or fossilized, was not equal to modern needs and never will be. Colonial preoccupation did not eliminate these needs, and thus far the postcolonial states have not been able to meet them. The age-old crisis of the Maghrib may be summed up as follows. We never had a true feudalism that would have imposed a sense of discipline and organized work, or a true bourgeois domination that would have unified society culturally, or, it follows, a true absolute monarchy which, enjoying subjective and objective legitimacy, would have dominated the two antagonistic classes in such a way as to make the competition between them further the progress of the nation. Those were the socio-political foundations of the modern economic revolution, and we experienced them, at best, in embryonic forms. The question of the internal and external factors that impeded such a development in the Maghrib can be debated ad infinitum. But this much is certain: it is now incumbent on the new states of the Maghrib, starting from the mostly negative, rather than positive, situations created by the two preceding (national and colonial) regimes, to complete simultaneously the tasks which elsewhere feudalism, bourgeois revolution, and absolute monarchy had plenty of time to carry out step by step. Let us neither lament nor rejoice over the gaps in our history, but merely take cognizance of this truth: because Maghribi society nev-

er ran the full course of this critical evolution, it was only marginally prepared for the modern era. Thus the essential task of contemporary nationalism is in some regions to undertake and in others to complete such preparation. Accordingly, cultural unification, politicization of groups, legitimization of the state order are the imperatives of any national policy.

(2) In the past, the reaction of the Maghribi populations has always been either submission or nonrecognition—in short, the attitudes that foreign observers have popularized under the names of fatalism or *siba*. In this sense nationalism was a general *siba* which, beginning with the crisis of 1934-1937, decreed the colonial system to be illegitimate. From then on, attitudes of rejection were regarded as virtues; withdrawal into private life, noncooperation, personal or family independence, lack of discipline, negligence, and finally destructive individual revolt came rightly to be seen as the only adequate response to foreign intrusion. But we must recognize that such a response, justified as it was in the face of an unjust and incompetent—national or foreign—authority, was valid only under specific circumstances, and that such habits, traditional in areas of historic repression, must be extirpated, not by violence of course, but by suasion, for everywhere the cynicism of the governing feeds on the despair of the governed.

(3) The worst of all policies is the traditionalist one of taking over the rules of government hallowed by preceding regimes, for though effective in the short term, since by legitimizing the action of the colonial power a posteriori it often obtains the assistance of that power, in the long run it is criminal, since it perpetuates the structures of decadence. Once solidified, these structures will stifle even those germs of progress that the foreigners introduced in spite of themselves. To defend tradition in the mountains and on the plains, to discourage urbanization and encourage emigration as a safety valve, is indeed to confirm the opinions the colonists have always held of us.

These three observations tend to define the historical

conditions of effective political action; in the last analysis they are subsumed in the question that has haunted this whole study: the question of legitimacy.

There are undoubtedly objective reasons for the "personal power" prevailing in the Maghrib today. In some respects it can even pose as "enlightened despotism"; but in the long run it can achieve legitimacy only if it prepares for, or allows others to prepare for, its replacement. If its principal activity is limited to nullifying the normal but revolutionary consequences of the few projects imposed on it by foreign pressure or the striving for prestige, then it is just as fundamentally illegitimate as the colonial regime it has supplanted.

The true problem, as we have said, is cultural (i.e. to unify the country beginning with the youth and to build a single organization capable of dissolving the historic distinctions which only too often add up to something very close to a caste system) and political (i.e. to encourage, beginning on the local level, the participation of all groups in public life, so putting an end to the negative attitudes inherited from the past and bringing about the long delayed fusion of the state and society). The future belongs to the cities. We must encourage urbanization rather than try to impede it for fear of the problems it engenders. But since urbanization will for a long time be a step ahead of industrialization, the new urban masses will have to be organized and work somehow found for them which, even if not economically profitable, will be socially educational. Administration! That seems to be the watchword today of every regime in the Maghrib, but it was also the watchword of colonialism with its offices for native affairs. Is the essential not rather to politicize the people, to make them into members of a single community? We hear constantly about a policy of development! But the colonists also tried to develop the country, and everyone agrees that their failure was due to the noncooperation of the population. We would do better to speak of social participation, for without it no form of industrialization can survive.

Yet nowhere is the "personal power" working toward that end with energy, continuity and good faith. Instead we find zones of transplanted industry as alien (an affront to the landscape, say the tourists) as the society built by colonization of the land. True, the situation is not uniform. Despite appearances, the most appreciable results in the right direction have been achieved in Tunisia, thanks to its nineteenth-century experience. The greatest hopes are still attached to Algeria, because of the upheavals caused by its war of liberation; the greatest danger of stagnation confronts Morocco, because of its long tradition. But everywhere the most essential need remains to be fulfilled: the fusion of the state with society, in short, the establishment of a true democracy. Our future depends on free dialogue among social groups. But, it is replied, social contradictions must be kept under control. The only effective and durable control must be based on a true legitimacy that is something more than formal recognition. Thus democratic participation becomes at once the precondition and the normal consequence of the legitimization of power.

In concrete terms, what must be done is to induce the victims of all the defeats and repressions of the centuries to come down from their mountains and in from their deserts. After centuries of decadence and foreign occupation, despite the unification accomplished by the brotherhoods, despite the renewal initiated by the political parties, and despite the comradeship experienced during the years of violence, the great revolution has not taken place; it is still on the order of the day, and will be first and foremost political. It alone can guarantee the depth and permanence of a future industrialization.

Before the Maghribi can become reconciled with his time and his country, he must first be reconciled with himself and his brother. The only legitimate government of the future is the government that will work toward this end with all its energies and with the authority conferred precisely by this intent.

Appendix

The rulers belonging to the principal dynasties are cited below as an aid in following the text. Principal seats of each dynasty are given with each name. For local dynasties the reader is referred to E. de Zambauer, *Manuel de généalogie et de chronologie pour l'histoire de l'Islam* (Hanover, 1927), which however should be checked against *Encyclopédie de l'Islam,* 2nd ed. In connection with the Maghrib, C. E. Bosworth, *The Islamic Dynasties* (Edinburgh, 1967) should be used with caution. I cite relationships only when a ruler is not directly descended from the preceding.

I. The Massyle Dynasty (Cirta = Constantine; then Cherchell)

—Gaïa	d. 206 or 203 B.C.
—Massinissa	202—148
—Micipsa	148—118
—Hiempsal I	118—116
—Adherbal (brother of the preceding)	118—112
—Jugurtha (son of Mastanabal son of Massinissa)	118—105
—Gauda (brother of Jugurtha)	105—88
—Hiempsal II	88—60
—Juba I	60—46
—Juba II	25—23 A.D.
—Ptolemy	23—40

II. Heads of Armies and Arab Governors (Kairouan)

CONQUERORS	DATE OF ARRIVAL IN IFRĪQIYA[1]
—'Abd Allah b. Sa'd	647/27
—Mu'āwiya b. Ḥudayj	665/45
—'Uqba b. Nāfi' (first period of command)	670/50
—Abūl Muhājir dīnār	674–5/55
—'Uqba (second period of command)	681–2/62
—Zuhayr b. Qays al-Balawī	688/69
—Ḥassān b. an-Nu'mān	692/73
—Mūsā b. Nuṣayr	705/86
GOVERNORS	
—Muḥammad Yazīd al-Qurashī	715/96
—Ismā 'īl b. 'Ubayd Allah b. Abī l-Muhājir	718/100

[1] Here we have adapted the chronology suggested after careful study by Sa'd Zaghlūl 'Abd al-Ḥamīd.

—Yazīd b. Abī Muslim	720/102
—Bishr b. Safwān al-Kalbī	721/103
—'Ubayd Allah b. al-Ḥabhāb	732 or 735/114 or 117
—Kulthūm b. Iyāḍ l-Qurashī	741/123
—Ḥanzala b. Ṣafwān	742/124

Descendants of 'Uqba

—'Abd al-Raḥmān b. Ḥābīb	745/127
—Ilyās b. Ḥabīb	755/137
—Ḥabīb b. Abd al-Raḥmān	756/138
—Muḥammad b. al-Ash'ath	759/142
—al-Aghlab b. Sālīm	765/148

The Muhallabids

—'Umar b. Ḥafṣ	768/151
—Yazīd b. Ḥātim	772/155
—Rawḥ b. Ḥātim	787–8/171
—Naṣr b. Ḥabīb	790/174
—al-Faḍl b. Rawḥ	793/177
—Harthama b. A'yan	795/179
—Muḥammad b. Muqātil al-'Akkī	797/181

III. The Aghlabids of Ifrīqiya (Kairouan)

	DATE OF PROCLAMATION
1) Ibrāhīm I b. al-Aghlab	800/184
2) 'Abd Allah I	812/197
Abū l-'Abbās	
3) Ziyādat Allah I (brother of the preceding)	817/201
4) Al-Aghlab (brother of the preceding)	838/223
Abū 'Iqāl	
5) Muḥammad I	840/226
Abū l-'Abbās	
6) Aḥmad (nephew of the preceding)	856/242
Abū Ibrāhīm	
7) Ziyādat Allah II (brother of the preceding)	864/249
8) Muḥammad II (son of Aḥmad)	864/250
Abū l-Gharāniq	
9) Ibrāhīm II (brother of the preceding)	875/261
10) 'Abdallah II	902/289
Abū l-'Abbās	
11) Ziyādat Allah III	903/290–909/296

IV. The Idrīsids of Fez

	YEAR OF PROCLAMATION
—Idrīs I b. 'Abd Allah	788/172
—Idrīs II	793/177 and 803/188

—Muḥammad	828/213
—'Alī (Ḥaydara)	836/221
—Yaḥyā I (brother of the preceding)	848/234
—Yaḥyā II	
—'Alī b. 'Umar b. Idrīs II	
—Yaḥyā III b. al-Qāsim b. Idrīs II al-'Addam	d. 904–5/292
—Yaḥyā IV b. Idrīs b. 'Umar b. Idrīs II	904–5/292 deposed 921/309
—Ḥasan b. Muḥammad b. al-Qāsim b. Idrīs II al-Ḥajjām	922/310
—al-Qāsim (brother of the preceding) Jannūn	d. 948/337
—Aḥmad Abū l-'Aysh	948/337–959/348

V. The Maghrāwa of Fez

Muḥammad b. Khazar
- 'Abd Allah
  - 'Aṭiya
    - *Zīri* 987/377 d. 1001/391
      - *al-Mu'izz* 1001/391–1026/417
        - Mu'ansar
          - Ḥammād m. 1043/435
            - *Mu'ansar* 1063/455–1067/460
              - *Tamīm* 1067/460–1069/462
    - al-Mu'izz
      - *Ḥamāma* 1026/417–1032/424 1037–8/429–1049/440
        - *Fatūh* 1060/452–1062/454
        - *'Ajīza* d. 1063/455

VI. The Fāṭimids of Ifrīqiya (Mahdiyya)

1) 'Ubayd Allah *al-Mahdī*	910/297
2) Muḥammad *al-Qā'im*	934/322
Abū l-Qāsim	
3) Isma'il *al-Manṣūr*	946/334
Abū al-Ṭahir	
4) Ma'dd *al-Mu'izz*	953/341–972/361
Abū Tamīm	

VII. The Zīrids (Ṣabra-Manṣūriya, near Kairouan)

1) Buluggīn (Yūsuf) b. Zīrī b. Manād	973/361
Abū l-Futūḥ	
2) al-Manṣūr	984/373
Abū l-Fatḥ	
3) Bādīs	996/386
4) al-Mu'izz	1016/406
5) Tamīm	1062/454
6) Yaḥyā	1108/501
7) 'Alī	1116/509
8) al-Ḥasan	1121/515–1148/543
	d. 1171/566

VIII. The Ḥammāmids (Qal'a of B. Ḥammād, then Bougie)

1) Ḥammād b. Buluggīn	1007/398
2) al-Qā'id	1028/419
3) Muḥsin	1054/447
4) Buluggīn b. Muḥammad Hammād	1055/447
5) al-Nāṣir b. 'Alā al-Nās b. Ḥammād	1062/454
6) al-Manṣūr	1089/481
7) Bādīs	1105/498
8) al-'Azīz (brother of the preceding)	1105/498
9) Yaḥyā	1121/515–1152/547
	m. 1163/558

IX. The Almoravids (Marrakech)

	DATE OF PROCLAMATION
1) Yūsuf b. Tāshfīn	1073/465
2) 'Alī	1106/500
Abū al-Ḥasan	
3) Tāshfīn	1142/537
Abū al-Mu'izz	
4) Ibrāhīm b. Tāshfīn	
5) Isḥāq b. 'Alī	1146–7/541

X. The Almohads (Marrakech)

1) 'Abd al-Mu'min b. 'Alī	1130/524
2) Yūsuf I Abū Ya'qūb	1163/558
3) Ya'qūb Abū Yūsuf al-Manṣūr	1184/580
4) Muḥammad al-Nāṣir	1199/595
5) Yūsuf II al-Muntaṣir	1213/610
6) 'Abd al-Wāhid b. Yūsuf I al-Makhlū'	1223/620
7) 'Abdallah b. al-Manṣūr al-'Ādil	1224/620
8) Yaḥyā b. al-Nāṣir al-Mu'taṣim	1227/624
9) Idrīs b. al-Manṣūr al-Māmūn	1227/624
10) 'Abd al-Wāḥid al-Rashīd	1232/630
11) 'Alī (brother of the preceding) as-Sa'īd	1242/640
12) 'Umar b. Isḥāq b. Yūsuf I al-Murtaḍā	1248/646
13) Idrīs b. Muḥ. b. 'Umar b. Abd al-Mu'min Abū Dabbūs	1266/665
14) Isḥāq (brother of al-Murtaḍā)	1269/668 d. 1276/674

XI. The Ḥafṣids (Tunis)

—'Abd al-Wāḥid b. Abī Ḥafṣ Abū Muḥammad	1207/603
—'Abd al-Raḥmān	1221/618
—'Abd Allah (brother of the preceding) Abū Muḥammad	1224/621
1) Yaḥyā I Abū Zakariyā'	1228/625
2) Muḥammad al-Mustanṣir I	1249/647
3) Yaḥyā II al-Wāthiq	1277/675
4) Ibrāhīm I b. Yaḥyā I Abū Isḥāq	1279/678

5) 'Umar (brother of the preceding)		1284/683
	al-Mustanṣir II	
6) Muḥammad II b. Yaḥyā II		1295/694
	Abū 'Aṣīda	
7) Abū Bakr I b. 'Abd al-Raḥmān b. Abī Bakr B. Yaḥyā I		(17 days)
	Abū Yaḥyā ash-Shahīd	
8) Khālid I b. Yaḥyā b. Ibrāhīm I		1309/709
	Abū l-Baqā' an-Nāṣir	
9) Zakariyā' I b. Aḥmad b. Muḥ. b. 'Abd al-Wāḥid		1311/711
	Abū Yaḥyā Ibn al-Liḥyanī	
10) Muḥammad III		1317/717
	Abū Ḍarba	
11) Abū Bakr II (brother of Khālid I)		1318/718
	Abū Yaḥyā	d. 1346/747
	al-Mutawakkil	
12) 'Umar II b. Abī Bakr		1346/747
	Abū Ḥafṣ	
13) Aḥmad I b. Abī Bakr		1346/747
	Abū l-'Abbās	

Marīnid Interlude 1347/748

14) al-Faḍl (brother of the two preceding)		1350/751
	Abū l-'Abbās	
15) Ibrāhīm II (brother of the two preceding)		1350/751

Second Marīnid Interlude 1357/758–1359/760

16) Khālid II		1369/770
	Abū l-Baqā'	
17) Aḥmad II b. Muḥammad b. Abī Bakr II		1370/772
	Abū l-'Abbās	
18) 'Abd al-'Azīz		1394/796
	Abū Fāris	
19) Muḥammad IV b. al-Manṣūr b. Abī Fāris		1434/837
	al-Muntaṣir	
20) 'Uthmān (brother of the preceding)		1435/839
	Abū 'Amr	
21) Yaḥyā III b. al-Mas'ūd b. 'Uthmān		1488/893
	Abū Zakariyā'	
22) 'Abd al-Mu'min b. Ibrāhīm b. 'Uthmān		1489/894
23) Zakariyā' II b. Yaḥyā III (?)		1490/895

24) Muḥammad V b. al-Hassan b. al-Mas'ud b. 'Uthmān	1495/899
25) al-Ḥasan	1526/932
26) Aḥmad III	1543/950–1569/976
Abū l-'Abbās	
27) Muḥammad VI (brother of the preceding)	

XII. The Zayyānids (Tlemcen)

1) Yaghmurāsīn	1236/633
Abū Yaḥyā	
2) 'Uthmān I	1282/681
Abū Sa'īd	
3) Muḥammad	1303/703
Abū Zayyān I	
4) Mūsā I (brother of the preceding)	1308/707
Abū Ḥammū	
5) 'Abd al-Raḥmān I	1318/718–1337/737
Abū Tāshfīn	
Marīnid Interlude	
6) 'Uthmān II b. 'Abd al-Raḥmān b. Yaḥyā b. Yaghmurāsin	1348/749
Abū Sa'īd	
7) Yūsuf (brother of the preceding)	
Abū Thābit	
Second Marīnid Interlude	
8) Mūsā II b. Yūsuf (nephew of the two preceding)	1359/760
Abū Ḥammū	
9) 'Abd al-Raḥmān	1388/791
Abū Tāshfīn II	
10) Yūsuf	1393/796
Abū Thābit II	
11) Yūsuf b. Mūsā II	
al-Ḥajjāj	
12) Muḥammad (brother of the preceding)	1394/797
Abū Zayyān II	
13) 'Abd Allah I (brother of the preceding)	1399/802
Abū Muḥammad	
14) Muḥammad I (brother of the preceding)	1401/804
Abū 'Abd Allah	
15) 'Abd al-Raḥmān	1411/813
Abū Tāshfīn III	
16) al-Sa'īd b. Mūsā II	1411/814
17) 'Abd al-Wāḥid (brother of the preceding)	1411/814–1423/827
Abū Mālik	1427/831–1429/833

18) Muḥammad II b. Abū Tāshfīn II 1423/827–1427/831
Abū 'Abd Allah 1429/833–1430/833
19) 'Aḥmad b. Mūsā II 1430/834
al-'Āqil
20) Muḥammad III b. Muḥ. b. Abī Thābit II 1461/866
Abū 'Abd Allah
al-Mutawakkil
21) 'Abd al-Raḥmān 1468/873
Abū Tāshfīn IV
22) Muḥammad IV (brother of the preceding) 1468/873
Abū 'Abd Allah
23) Muḥammad V 1504/910
al-Thābitī
24) Mūsā b. Muḥammad III 1517/923
Abū Ḥammū III
25) Abd Allah II (brother of the preceding) 1527/934
Abū Muḥammad
26) Muḥammad VI 1540/947
Abū 'Abd Allah 1543/950
27) Aḥmad (brother of the preceding) 1540/947–1543/950
Abū Zayyān III 1544/951–1550/957
28) Al-Ḥasan (brother of the preceding) 1550/957
d. 1554/962

XIII. The Marīnids (after taking the title of Amīr al-Muslimīn) (Fez)

1) Ya'qūb 1258/656
Abū Yūsuf
al-Manṣūr
2) Yūsuf 1286/685
Abū Ya'qūb
al-Nāṣir
3) 'Āmir b. 'Abd Allah b. Yūsuf 1307/706
Abū Thābit
4) Sulaymān (brother of the preceding) 1308/708
Abū Rabī'
5) 'Uthmān II b. Ya'qūb 1310/710
Abū Sa'īd
6) 'Alī 1331/731
Abū l-Ḥasan
7) Fāris 1348/749
Abū 'Inān
8) Muḥammad 1358/759
Abū Zayyān I
9) Abū Bakr (brother of the preceding) 1358/759
al-Sa'id I

10) Ibrāhīm b. 'Alī .... Abū Sālim	1359/760
11) Tāshfīn (brother of the preceding) .... Abū 'Umar	1361/762
12) Muḥammad b. Ya'qūb b. 'Alī .... Abū Zayyān al-Munṭaṣir	1361/763
13) 'Abd al-'Azīz I b. 'Alī .... Abū Fāris	1366/767
14) Muḥammad .... Abū Zayyān al-Sa'īd II	1372/774
15 and 19) Aḥmad b. Ibrāhīm (first reign)	1373/775
Abū l-'Abbās (second reign) .... al-Mustanṣir	1387/789
16) Mūsā b. Fāris .... Abū Fāris al-Mutawakkil	1384/786
17) Muḥammad b. Aḥmad .... Abū Zayyān al-Muntaṣir	1386/788
18) Muḥammad b. Abī l-Fadl b. 'Alī .... Abū Zayyān al-Wāthiq	1386/788
20) 'Abd al-'Aziz II b. Aḥmad .... Abū Fāris	1393/796
21) 'Abd Allah (brother of the preceding) .... Abu 'Āmir	1396/799
22) 'Uthmān III (brother of the preceding) .... Abū Sa'īd	1398/800–1420/823

Waṭṭāsid Regency

XIV. The Waṭṭasids (Fez)

REGENTS

—Yaḥyā I b. Zayyān .... Abū Zakariyā'	1420–1458/823–863
—'Ali b. Yūsuf b. Manṣūr b. Zayyān	c. 1458/863
—Yaḥyā II b. Yaḥyā Ier	killed in 1458/863

SULTANS

—Muḥammad al-Shaykh (brother of the preceding)	1471–1505/876–911
—Muḥammad al-Burtughālī	1505–1524/911–931
—'Alī (Bū Hassūn) brother of the preceding Abū I-Ḥasan	1524/931 1554/961
—Aḥmad b. Muḥammad al-Burtughālī Abū I-'Abbās	1524–1548/931–955 1548–1550/955–957

XV. The Sa'dids (Marrakech)

—Muḥammad al-Qā'im	1509–1517/915–923
—Aḥmad al-A'raj	Shaykhs in 1517/1548/923–955 Southern Morocco
1) Muḥammad al-Shaykh (brother of the preceding) al-Mahdī	
sultan of Morocco	1548–1557/955–965
2) 'Abdallah al-Ghālib	1557–1574/965–982
3) Muḥammad al. Mutawakkil al. Maslūkh	1574–1576/982–984
4) 'Abd al-Malik (uncle of the preceding)	1576–1578/984–986
5) Aḥmad al-Manṣūr adh-Dhahbī (brother of the preceding)	1578–1603/986–1012
—Zaydān	1603–1618/1012–1028
—'Abd al-Malik (in Marrakech)	1618–1636/1028–1046
—Muḥammad al-Shaykh II (in Marrakech)	1636–1654/1046–1065
—Aḥmad al-'Abbās (in Marrakech)	1654–1659/1065–1070
KINGDOM OF FEZ	
—al-Māmūn	1610–1613/1019–1022
—'Abdallah	1613–1623/1022–1033
—'Abd al-Malik	1623–1626/1033–1036
—Aḥmad b. Zaydān	1626–1641/1036–1051

XVI. The 'Alawites (Meknes, then Fez and Marrakech)

—'Alī b. Yūsuf Ash-Sharīf	1631–1635/1041–1045
—Muḥammad I	1635–1664/1045–1075
1) Al-Rashīd (brother of the preceding)	1664–1672/1075–1083
2) Ismā'īl (brother of the preceding)	1672–1727/1083–1140
3) Aḥmad al-Dhahbī 4) 'Abd al-Malik	1727–1728/1140–1141
— Aḥmad (second reign)	1728–1729/1141–1142
5) 'Abd Allah	1729–1757/1142–1171
Pretenders: 'Ali al-A'raj : 1735 Muḥammad II : 1736–38 al-Mustaḍī' : 1738–40 Zayn al-'Ābidīn : 1745	
6) Muḥammad III	1757–1790/1171–1204
7) Yazīd	1790–1792/1204–1206
8) Sulaymān (brother of the preceding)	1792–1822/1206–1238
9) 'Abd al-Raḥmān b. Hishām b. Muḥammad III	1822–1859/1238–1276
10) Muḥammad IV	1859–1873/1276–1290
11) al-Ḥasan I	1873–1894/1290–1312

12) 'Abd al-'Azīz	1894–1908/1312–1326
13) 'Abd al-Hafīdh (brother of the preceding)	1908–1912/1326–1330
14) Yūsuf (brother of the preceding)	1912–1927/1330–1346
15) Muḥammad V	1927–1961/1346–1381
16) al-Ḥassan II	——

XVII. The Murādids (Tunis)

—Murād Bey	1613–1631/1022–1041
—Hammūda Pasha Bey	1631–1659/1041–1067
—Murād II Bey	1659–1675/1067–1086
—Muḥammad Bey	1675–1696/1086–1108
—'Alī Bey (pretender)	1675–1686/1086–1097
—Ramḍān (brother of the two preceding)	1696–1699/1108–1110
—Murād III	1699–1702/1110–1114
Bū Bāla	
Interim: Ibrāhīm al-Sharif	1702–1705/1114–1117

XVIII. The Ḥusaynids (Tunis)

—Ḥusayn I b. 'Alī Turkī	1705–1735/1117–1147
—'Alī I b. Muḥammad b. 'Alī Turkī	1735–1756/1147–1169
—Muḥammad Bey b. Husayn Al-Rashīd	1756–1759/1169–1172
—'Ali Bey II (brother of the preceding)	1759–1782/1172–1196
—Ḥammūda Pasha II	1782–1813/1196–1229
—'Uthmān (brother of the preceding)	1813–1814/1229–1230
—Mahmūd Pasha b. al-Rashīd	1814–1824/1230–1239
—Ḥusayn II	1824–1835/1239–1251
—Mustapha (brother of the preceding)	1835–1837/1251–1253
—Aḥmad I Pasha	1837–1855/1253–1271
—Mḥammad Bey b. Ḥusayn	1855–1859/1271–1276
—Muḥammad al-Ṣādiq (brother of the preceding)	1859–1882/1276–1299
—'Alī Bey III (brother of the preceding)	1882–1902/1299–1320
—Muḥammad *Al-Hādī*	1902–1906/1320–1324
—Muḥammad *al-Nāṣir* b. Muḥammad b. Ḥusayn II	1906–1922/1324–1341
—Muḥammad *al-Ḥabīb* b. Māmūn b. Ḥusayn II	1922–1929/1341–1348
—Aḥmad II Bey	1929–1942/1348–1361
—Muḥammad *al-Munṣif* b. an Nāṣir	1942–1943/1361–1362
—al-Amīn	1943–1958/1362–1378

Bibliography

'Abd al-Ḥamīd, Sa'd Zaghlūl. *Tārīkh al-Maghrib al-'Arabī.* Cairo, 1965.

'Abd al-Wahhāb, Ḥasan Ḥusnī. *'Waraqāt 'An al-Ḥaḍāra al-'Arabīya bi-Ifrīqiya al-Tūnisīya.* Tunis, 1965. 2 vols.

Abū Ḥammū Mūsā II (King of Tlemcen, 1323-89). *Wāsiṭat al-Sulūk Fī Siyāsat al-Mulūk.* Tunis, 1862.

Abū Zakarīyā, d. 1078. Ed. Roger Le Tourneau. " 'La Chronique' d'Abū Zakariyyā' al-Wargalānī (m. 471 H = 1078 J.-C.). Traduction annotée," *Revue africaine,* vol. 105 (1961), pp. 117-176.

Abun-Nasr, Jamil M. *A History of the Maghrib.* Cambridge: Cambridge University Press, 1971.

———. "The Salafiyya Movement in Morocco: The Religious Bases of the Moroccan Nationalist Movement," *St. Antony's Papers,* no. 16 (1963), pp. 90-105.

Ageron, Charles Robert. *Les Algériens musulmans et la France (1871-1919).* Paris: P.U.F., 1968. 2 vols.

———. *Histoire de l'Algérie contemporaine (1830-1966).* Paris: P.U.F., 2nd rev. ed. 1966.

———. *Politiques coloniales au Maghreb.* Paris: P.U.F., 1972.

al-'Alawī, Aḥmad b. 'Abd al-'Azīz. Ed. 'Abd al-Karīm al-Filālī. *al-Anwār al-Ḥasanīya.* Rabat, 1966 (written in 1101/1690).

Albertini, Eugène. *L'Afrique du Nord française dans l'histoire.* Lyon and Paris: Archat, 1937.

———. *L'Afrique romaine.* Algiers: Imprimerie officielle, 1955 (1st ed. 1922).

———. "Un témoignage de Saint Augustin sur la prospérité relative de l'Afrique au IVe siècle." In *Mélanges Paul Thomas,* Bruges: Imprimerie Sainte Catherine, 1930, pp. 1-5.

Amin, Samir. *L'Economie du Maghreb.* Paris: Minuit, 1966. 2 vols.

al-Andalusī, Yaḥyā ibn 'Umar, d. 901. Ed. Maḥmūd 'Alī Makkī. "Kitāb Aḥkām al-Sūq li-Yaḥyā ibn 'Umar al-Andalusī." *Revista del Instituto Egipcio de Estudios Islamicos en Madrid,* vol. 4 (1956), pp. 59-151.

Anderson, Eugene Newton. *The First Moroccan Crisis, 1904-1906.* Chicago: University of Chicago Press, 1930.

al-Anṣārī, Muḥammad b. al-Qāsim. Ed. Evariste Lévi-Provençal. "Une Description de Ceuta musulmane au XVe siècle, *l'Iḥtiṣār al-Aḥbār* de Muḥammad b. al-Ḳāsim ibn 'Abd al-Malik al-Anṣārī: texte arabe," *Hespéris,* vol. 12 (1931), pp. 145-176.

al-Ash'arī, Abū al-Ḥasan, d. 935. Ed. Muḥammad Muḥī al-Dīn 'Abd al-Ḥamīd. *Maqālāt al-Islāmīyīn wa-Ikhtilāf al-Muṣallīn.* Cairo, 1950-54. 2 vols. in 1.

Ashford, Douglas E. *Political Change in Morocco.* Princeton: Princeton University Press, 1961.

Ayache, Albert. *Histoire ancienne de l'Afrique du Nord.* Paris: Editions sociales, 1964.

———. *Le Maroc, bilan d'une colonisation.* Paris: Editions sociales, 1956.

Ayache, Germain. "Aspects de la crise financière au Maroc après l'expédition espagnole de 1860." *Revue historique,* vol. 220 (1958), pp. 271-310.

al-Bakrī, Abū 'Ubayd, d. 1094. *Description de l'Afrique septentrionale, par Abou-Obeïd el-Bekri.* Tr. Mac Guckin de Slane (tr. and Arabic text of part of *Kitāb al-Mamālik wa-al-Masālik*). Paris: Adrien-Maisonneuve, 1965 (1st ed. 1859).

Balout, Lionel. *Préhistoire de l'Afrique du Nord, essai de chronologie.* Paris: Arts et métiers graphiques, 1955.

———. "Quelques problèmes nord-africains de chronologie préhistorique." *Revue africaine,* vol. 92 (1948), pp. 231-262.

Baradez, Jean Lucien. *Fossatum africae; recherches aériennes sur l'organisation des confins sahariennes à l'époque romaine.* Paris: Arts et métiers graphiques, 1949.

Barbour, Nevill, ed. *A Survey of North West Africa (the Maghrib)*. London and New York: Oxford University Press, 2nd ed. 1962 (1st ed. 1959).

Basset, Henri. *Essai sur la littérature des Berbères*. Algiers: Carbonel, 1920.

Bayram al-Khāmis al-Tūnisī, Muḥammad. *Ṣafwat al-I'tibār bi-Mustawda' al-Amṣār wa-al-Aqṭār*. Cairo, 1884-93. 5 vols.

Bekri, Chaikh. "Le Kharijisme berbère. Quelques aspects du royaume rustumide." *Annales de l'Institut d'études orientales*, vol. 15 (1957), pp. 55-108.

Belal, Abdel Aziz. *L'Investissement au Maroc (1912-1964) et ses enseignements en matière de développement économique*. Paris and The Hague: Mouton, 1968.

Bernard, Augustin. *L'Algérie. Histoire des colonies françaises*, vol. 2. Paris: Plon, 1930.

Berque, Jacques. *Egypt: Imperialism and Revolution*. London: Faber, 1972.

———. *Le Maghreb entre deux guerres*. Paris: Seuil, 1962, rev. ed. 1970. English tr.: *French North Africa; The Maghrib between Two World Wars*. New York: Praeger, 1967.

———. "Les Hilaliens repentis ou l'Algérie rurale au XVe siècle, d'après un manuscrit jurisprudential." *Annales: Economies, sociétés, civilisations*, vol. 25 (1970), pp. 1325-1353.

———. "Qu'est-ce qu'une 'tribu' nord-africaine?" In *Hommage à Lucien Febvre, Eventail de l'histoire vivante*, Paris: Colin, 1953, vol. 1, pp. 261-271.

———. *al-Yousi; problèmes de la culture marocaine au XVIIe siècle*. Paris: Mouton, 1958.

Berthier, André. *Le "Bellum Jugurthinum" de Salluste et le problème de Cirta*. Constantine: Attali, 1949.

Berthier, Paul. *Les anciennes Sucreries du Maroc et leurs réseaux hydrauliques. Étude archéologique et d'histoire économique*. Rabat: Imprimeries françaises et Marocaines, 1966.

Birebent, J. *Aquae romanae; recherches d'hydraulique romaine dans l'est algérien.* Algiers: Service des antiquités de l'Algérie, 1962.

Blunt, Wilfrid. *Desert Hawk; Abd el Kader and the French Conquest of Algeria.* London: Methuen, 1947.

Bono, Salvatore. *I corsari barbareschi.* Torino: ERI, 1964.

Bosch Vilá, Jacinto. *Los Almorávides; historia de Marruecos.* Tetuán: Editoria Marroqui, 1956.

Bouali, Mahmoud. *Introduction à l'histoire constitutionelle de la Tunisie.* Tunis: En-Najah, 1963-64. 2 vols.

Boule, Marcellin. *Les Hommes fossiles; éléments de paléontologie humaine.* Paris: Masson, 4th ed. 1952.

Bourguiba, Habib. *La Tunisie et la France; vingt-cinq ans de lutte pour une coopération libre.* Paris: Julliard, 1954.

Bovill, Edward William. *The Battle of Alcazar; an Account of the Defeat of Don Sebastian of Portugal at El-Ksar el-Kebir.* London: Batchworth, 1952.

———. *The Golden Trade of the Moors.* London and New York: Oxford University Press, 2nd rev. ed. 1968 (A rewriting of the author's *Caravans of the Old Sahara,* published in 1933).

Boyer, Pierre. "Des Pachas triennaux à la révolution d'Ali Khodja Bey." *Revue historique,* vol. 244 (1970), pp. 99-124.

Braudel, Fernand. "Les Espagnols en Algérie 1492-1792." In *Histoire et historiens de l'Algérie,* Paris: Alcan, 1931, pp. 231-266.

———. *La Méditerranée et le monde méditerranéen à l'époque de Philippe II.* Paris: Colin, 1949. English tr.: *The Mediterranean and the Mediterranean World in the Age of Philip II.* New York: Harper & Row, 1972-73. 2 vols.

Brémond, Edouard. *Berbères et Arabes, la Berbérie est un pays Européen.* Paris: Payot, 1950.

Briggs, Lloyd Cabot. *The Stone Age Races of Northwest Africa.* Cambridge, Mass.: The Museum, 1955.

———. *Tribes of the Sahara.* Cambridge, Mass.: Harvard University Press, 1960.

Brisson, Jean Paul. *Autonomisme et christianisme dans l'Afrique romaine de Septime Sévère à l'invasion vandale.* Paris: Boccard, 1958.

———. *Gloire et misère de l'Afrique chrétienne.* Paris: Laffont, 1948.

Brunschvig, Robert. *La Berbérie orientale sous les Ḥafṣides; des origines à la fin du XVe siècle.* Paris: Librairie d'Amérique et d'Orient, 1940-47. 2 vols.

———, ed. *Deux récits de voyage inédits en Afrique du Nord au XVe siècle par 'Abdulbāsiṭ b. Ḥalīl et Adorne.* Paris: Larousse, 1936.

———. "Ibn 'Abdalh'akam et la conquête de l'Afrique du Nord par les Arabes." *Annales de l'Institut des études orientales,* vol. 6 (1942-47), pp. 108-155.

———. "Justice religieuse et justice laïque dans la Tunisie des Deys et des Beys, jusqu'au milieu du XIXe siècle." *Studia Islamica,* vol. 23 (1965), pp. 27-70.

Cagnat, René Louis Victor. *L'Armée romaine d'Afrique et l'occupation militaire de l'Afrique sous les empereurs.* Paris: Leroux, 1913. 2 vols.

Cambon, Paul. *Correspondance, 1870-1924.* Paris: Grasset, 1940-46. 3 vols.

Camps, Gabriel. *Les Civilisations préhistoriques de l'Afrique du nord et du Sahara.* Paris: Doin, 1974.

———. "Massinissa ou les débuts de l'histoire (Aux origines de la Berbérie)." *Libyca* (série Archéologie-Épigraphie), vol. 8 (1st semester 1960), pp. 1-320.

———. *Monuments et rites funéraires protohistoriques (Aux origines de la Berbérie).* Paris: Arts et métiers graphiques, 1962.

———. "Les Traces d'un âge de bronze en Afrique du Nord." *Revue africaine,* vol. 104 (1960), pp. 31-55.

Camps-Fabrer, Henriette. *L'Olivier et l'huile dans l'Afrique romaine.* Algiers: Imprimerie officielle, 1953.

Capot-Rey, Robert. *Le Sahara français.* Paris: P.U.F., 1953.

Carcopino, Jérôme. *Le Maroc antique.* Paris: Gallimard, 2nd ed. 1943.

———. "Les Tablettes Albertini." *Journal des savants,* Oct.-Dec. 1952, pp. 145-169.

Charles-Picard, Gilbert. *La Civilisation de l'Afrique romaine.* Paris: Plon, 1959.

———. "Néron et le blé d'Afrique." *Cahiers de Tunisie,* vol. 4 (1956), pp. 163-173.

——— and Colette. *La Vie quotidienne à Carthage au temps d'Hannibal, IIIe siècle avant Jésus-Christ.* Paris: Hachette, 1958. English tr.: *Daily Life in Carthage at the Time of Hannibal.* London: Allen, 1961.

Charnay, Jean Paul. *La Vie musulmane en Algérie d'après la jurisprudence de la première moitié du XXe siècle.* Paris: P.U.F., 1965.

Chenoufi, Moncef. "Les deux Séjours de Muḥammad 'Abduh en Tunisie." *Cahiers de Tunisie,* vol. 16 (1968), pp. 57-95. Tr. of "Maṣādir 'an Riḥlatai Muḥammad 'Abduh ilā Tūnis," *Annales de l'Université de Tunis,* vol. 3 (1966), pp. 71ff.

Colin, Georges Séraphin, ed. *Chronique anonyme de la dynastie sa'dienne.* Rabat: Moncho, 1934.

Confer, Vincent. *France and Algeria: The Problem of Civil and Political Reform, 1870-1920.* Syracuse: Syracuse University Press, 1966.

Coon, Carleton Stevens. *Flesh of the Wild Ox; A Riffian Chronicle of High Valleys and Long Rifles.* New York: Morrow, 1932.

Cour, Auguste. *La Dynastie marocaine des Beni Waṭṭās (1420-1554).* Constantine: Braham, 1920.

———. *L'Etablissement des dynasties des chérifs au Maroc et leur rivalité avec les Turcs de la Régence d'Alger, 1509-1830.* Paris: Leroux, 1904.

Courtois, Christian. "De Rome à l'Islam." *Revue africaine,* vol. 86 (1942), pp. 25-55.

———. *Les Vandales et l'Afrique.* Paris: Arts et métiers graphiques, 1955.

Cruickshank, Earl Fee. *Morocco at the Parting of the Ways; The Story of Native Protection to 1885.* Philadelphia: University of Pennsylvania Press, 1935.

Dāwud, Muḥammad. *Tārīkh Tiṭwān.* Tetuán: 2nd ed. 1959– . 6 vols.

Demougeot, Emilienne. "Le Chameau et l'Afrique du Nord romaine." *Annales: Economies, sociétés, civilisations,* vol. 15 (1960), pp. 209-247.

Despois, Jean. *L'Afrique du Nord.* Paris: P.U.F., 3rd ed. 1964 (1st ed. 1949; 2nd ed. 1958).

Devisse, Jean et al. *Tegdaoust. Recherches sur Aoudaghost.* Paris: Arts et métiers graphiques, 1970.

Diehl, Charles. *L'Afrique byzantine; histoire de la domination byzantine en Afrique (533-709).* New York: Franklin, Burt, 1959 (repr. of 1896 ed.). 2 vols.

Djaït, Hichem. "L'Afrique arabe au VIIIe siècle (86-184H./705-800)." *Annales: Economies, sociétés, civilisations,* vol. 28 (1973), pp. 601-621.

Drague, Georges. See Spillmann, Georges.

Duclos, Louis Jean, Jean Leca, Jean Duvignaud. *Les Nationalismes maghrébins.* Paris: Fondation nationale des sciences politiques, 1966.

Doufourcq, Charles Emmanuel. *L'Espagne catalane et le Maghrib aux XIIIe et XIVe siècles.* Paris: P.U.F., 1966.

EI[1]: *Encyclopaedia of Islam,* 1st ed. Leiden: Brill, 1913-36. 4 vols.

EI[2]: *Encyclopaedia of Islam,* 2nd ed. Leiden: Brill, 1960–. vol. 4 in progress.

Economie et politique (vol. 1, nos. 50-56): *La France et les trusts; numéro special.* Paris, 1954.

Emerit, Marcel. *L'Algérie à l'époque d'Abd-el-Kader.* Paris: Larousse, 1951.

Etudes d'orientalisme dédiées à la mémoire de Lévi-Provençal. Paris: Maisonneuve et Larose, 1962. 2 vols.

Etudes maghrébines: Mélanges Charles-André Julien. Paris: P.U.F., 1964.

al-Fāsī, 'Allāl. *Al-Ḥarakāt al-Istiqlālīya fī al-Maghrib al-'Arabī.* Tangier, 1948 (1st ed. Cairo, 1947). English tr.: *The Independence Movements in Arab North Africa.* Washington, D.C.: American Council of Learned Societies, 1954.

al-Fāsī, Muḥammad al-Mahdī, d. 1109/1698. *Mumti' al-Asmā'.* Fez, 1895 (lith.).

Février, James G. "Que savons-nous du libique?" *Revue africaine,* vol. 100 (1956), pp. 263-273.

Fisher, Godfrey. *Barbary Legend; War, Trade and Piracy in North Africa, 1415-1830.* Oxford: Clarendon Press, 1957.

Fishtālī, 'Abd al-'Azīz, d. 1031/1621. Ed. 'Abdallah Gannūn. *Manāhil al-Safā fī Akhbār al-Mulūk al-Shurafā'.* Tetuán, 1964.

Flournoy, Francis Rosebro. *British Policy towards Morocco in the Age of Palmerston (1830-1865).* London: King, 1935.

Frend, W. H. C. *The Donatist Church; a Movement of Protest in Roman North Africa.* Oxford: Clarendon Press, 1952.

Furneaux, Rupert. *Abdel Krim; Emir of the Rif.* London: Secker, 1967.

Furon, Raymond. *Manuel de préhistoire générale, géologie et biogéographie, évolution de l'humanité, archéologie préhistorique, les métaux et la protohistoire.* Paris: Payot, 5th ed. 1966.

Gallagher, Charles F. *The United States and North Africa: Morocco, Algeria, and Tunisia.* Cambridge, Mass.: Harvard University Press, 1963.

Gallissot, René. "Abd el-Kader et la nationalité algérienne. Interpretation de la chute de la Régence d'Alger et des premières résistances à la conquête française (1830-1839)." *Revue historique,* vol. 233 (1965), pp. 339-368.

———. "Essai de définition du mode de production de l'Algérie précoloniale." *Revue algérienne des sciences juridiques, politiques et économiques,* vol. 5 (1968), pp. 385-412.

———. "La Guerre d'Abd el-Kader ou la ruine de la nationalité algérienne (1839-1847)." *Hespéris-Tamuda*, vol. 5 (1964), pp. 119-141.

———. *Le Patronat européen au Maroc: action sociale, action politique (1931-1942)*. Rabat: Éditions techniques nord-africaines, 1964.

Ganiage, Jean. *Les Origines du protectorat français en Tunisie (1861-1881)*. Paris: P.U.F., 1959.

Gannūn, 'Abdallah. *Aḥādīth 'an al-Adab al-Maghribī al-Ḥadīth*. Cairo, 1964.

———, ed. *Al-Nubūgh al-Maghribī fī al-Adab al-'Arabī*. Beirut, 1961.

Gautier, Emile Félix. *Le Passé de l'Afrique du Nord. Les siècles obscurs*. Paris: Payot, 1952 (1st ed. 1937).

———. *Sahara, the Great Desert*. New York: Columbia University Press, 1935. "Translated from the second French edition of E.-F. Gautier's *Le Sahara* (Paris, Payot, 1928) and from hitherto unpublished material supplied by the author."

Germain, Gabriel. "Qu'est-ce que le Périple d'Hannon? Document, amplification littéraire ou faux intégral?" *Hespéris*, vol. 44 (1957), pp. 205-248.

Ghallāb, 'Abd al-Karīm. *Difā' 'an al-Dimuqrāṭīya*. Tangier, n.d. [1967].

Goes, Damião de. *Les Portugais au Maroc de 1495 à 1521*. Rabat: Moncho, 1937.

Goitein, Solomon Dob Fritz. *A Mediterranean Society; the Jewish Communities of the Arab World as Portrayed in the Documents of the Cairo Geniza*. Berkeley: University of California Press, 1967–. 2 vols. (3rd vol. forthcoming).

———. *Studies in Islamic History and Institutions*. Leiden: Brill, 1966.

Golvin, Lucien. *Le Maghrib central à l'époque des Zirides; recherches d'archéologie et d'histoire*. Paris: Arts et métiers graphiques, 1957.

Grammont, Henri Delmas de. *Histoire d'Alger sous la domination turque (1515-1830)*. Paris: Leroux, 1887.

Gsell, Stéphane. *Atlas archéologique de l'Algérie.* Algiers: Jourdan, 1911. 2 vols.

———. *Histoire ancienne de l'Afrique du Nord.* Paris: Hachette, 1914-1928. 8 vols.

———. "Vieilles exploitations minières dans l'Afrique du Nord." *Hespéris,* vol. 8 (1928), pp. 1-21.

Guillen, Pierre. "Les Milieux d'affaires français et le Maroc à l'aube du XXe siècle. La fondation de la Compagnie marocaine (1902-1906)." *Revue historique,* vol. 229 (1963), pp. 397-422.

Habart, Michel. *Histoire d'un parjure.* Paris: Minuit, 1960.

Hajjī, Muḥammad. "L'Idée de nation au Maroc et quelques-uns de ses aspects aux XVIe et XVIIe siècles." *Hespéris-Tamuda,* vol. 9 (1968), pp. 109-121.

———. *Al-Zāwiya al-Dilā'īya wa-Dawruhā al-Dīnī wa-al-'Ilmī wa-al-Siyāsī.* Rabat, 1964.

al-Ḥajwī, Muḥammad al-Mahdī. *Ḥayāt al-Wazzān al-Fāsī wa-āthāruhu.* Rabat, 1935.

Halstead, John P. "The Changing Character of Moroccan Reformism, 1921-1934." *Journal of African History,* vol. 5 (1964), pp. 435-447.

———. *Rebirth of a Nation; the Origins and Rise of Moroccan Nationalism, 1912-1944.* Cambridge, Mass.: Harvard University Press, 1967.

Hazard, Harry Williams. *The Numismatic History of Late Medieval North Africa.* New York: American Numismatic Society, 1952.

Hespéris-Tamuda: Mulay Isma'il; numéro special, 1962.

Histoire et historiens de l'Algérie. Paris: Alcan, 1931.

Hopkins, J.F.P. *Medieval Muslim Government in Barbary until the Sixth Century of the Hijra.* London: Luzac, 1958.

Hourani, Albert Habib. *Arabic Thought in the Liberal Age, 1798-1939.* London and New York: Oxford University Press, 1967 (repr. with corrections of 1962 ed.).

Hours-Miéden, Madeleine. *Carthage.* Paris: P.U.F., 3rd ed. 1964.

Hubac, Pierre. *Les Barbaresques.* Paris: Berger-Levrault, 1949.

Huici Miranda, Ambrosio. *Historia política del imperio Almohade.* Tetuán: Editora Marroquí, 1956-57. 2 vols.

Hussein, Taha. *Al-Fitna al-Kubrā.* Cairo: vol. 1 (*'Uthmān*), 1947.

Ibn 'Abd Allāh, 'Abd al-'Azīz. *Tārīkh al-Maghrib.* Casablanca, n.d.

Ibn 'Abd al-Ḥakam, d. 870. *Conquête de l'Afrique du Nord et de l'Espagne (Futūh' Ifrīqiya wa'l-Andalus).*Text in Arabic and French. Algiers: Carbonel, 2nd ed. 1947.

Ibn Abī al-Diyāf, Aḥmad. *Itḥāf Ahl al-Zamān bi-Akhbār Mulūk Tūnis wa-'Ahd al-Amān.* Tunis, 1963-66. 8 vols. in 5.

Ibn Abī Dīnār, Muḥammad ibn Abī al-Qāsim, fl. 1690. *Histoire de l'Afrique.* Tr. by E. Pellissier and Rémusat. Paris: Imprimerie royale, 1845. Arabic edition ed. Muhammed Chammam, Tunis: Librairie al-'Atīqa, 1967.

Ibn Abī Zar' al-Fāsī, 'Alī ibn 'Abd Allāh. *Roudh el-Kartas. Histoire des souverains du Maghreb (Espagne et Maroc) et annales de la ville de Fès.* Paris: Imprimerie imperiale, 1860. Tr. of *Al-Anīs al-Muṭrib bi-Rawḍ al-Qirṭās fī Akhbār Mulūk al-Maghrib wa-Tārīkh Madīnat Fās.* Rabat, 1936.

Ibn al-Ahmar. *Histoire des Beni Merin, rois de Fès, intitulée Rawdat en-Nisrin (le jardin des églantines).* Text in Arabic and French. Tr. by Ghaoutsi Bouali and Georges Marçais. Paris: Leroux, 1917.

Ibn al-Qaṭṭān, fl. 1248. Ed. Muḥammad 'Alī Makkī. *Juz' min Kitāb Naẓm al-Jumān.* Tetuán, n.d. [1964].

Ibn al-Ṣaghīr. *Chronique d'Ibn Saghir sur les imams rostemides de Tahert.* Paris: Leroux, 1907.

Ibn 'Ashūr, Muḥammad al-Fāḍil. *Al-Ḥaraka al-Adabīya wa-al-Fikrīya fī Tūnis.* Cairo, 1956.

Ibn 'Askar, Muḥammad ibn 'Alī, d. 1578. *Dawḥat al-Nāshir li-Maḥāsin man Kāna bi-al-Maghrib min Mashāyikh al-Qarn al-'Āshir.* Fez, 1892. For English translation, see

Thomas Hunter Weir, *The Shaykhs of Morocco in the XVIth Century*. Edinburgh: Morton, 1904.

Ibn Ḥawqal, Abū al-Qāsim, 10th cent. *Configuration de la terre (Kitab surat al-ard)*. Tr. by J. H. Kramers and G. Wiet. Beirut: Commission internationale pour la traduction des chefs-d'oeuvre, 1964.

Ibn 'Idhārī, al-Marrākushī. *Histoire de l'Afrique du Nord et de l'Espagne musulmane, intitulée Kitāb al-bayān al-mughrib*. Arabic text. Leiden: Brill, new rev. ed. 1948-51. 2 vols. Vol. 3 of this text was published under the title *Al-Bayān al-Mughrib: tome troisième, histoire de l'Espagne musulmane au XIe siècle*. Paris: Geuthner, 1930. French tr.: *Histoire de l'Afrique et de l'Espagne intitulée Al-bayano'l-Mogrib*. Algiers: Fontana, 1901-04. 2 vols.

Ibn Khaldūn, 'Abd al-Raḥmān, d. 1406. *Histoire des Berbères et des dynasties musulmanes de l'Afrique septentrionale*. Tr. by *Kitāb al-'Ibar*. Paris: Geuthner, 1969 (repr. of 1925-56 rev. ed.). 4 vols.

Ibn Khurradādhbih, 'Ubayd Allah, d. ca. 912. Hadj-Sadok, Mahammed, ed. and tr. *Description du Maghreb et de l'Europe au IIIe-IXe siècle*. Arabic text and French translation. Algiers: Carbonel, 1949.

Ibn Ṣāḥib al-Ṣalāh, 'Abd al-Malik, 12th cent. *Tārīkh al-Mann bi-al-Imāma*. Beirut, 1965.

Ibn Tūmart, Muḥammad, d. ca. 1130. *Le Livre de Mohammed ibn Toumert mahdi des Almohades*. Arabic text. Algiers: Fontana, 1903.

Ibn Zaydān, 'Abd al-Raḥmān. *Itḥāf A'lām al-Nās bi-Jamāl Akhbār Ḥāḍirat Miknās*. Rabat, 1929-33. 5 vols.

Idris, Hady Roger. *La Berbérie orientale sous les Zīrīdes; Xe-XIIe siècles*. Paris: Adrien-Maisonneuve, 1962. 2 vols.

———. "De la Réalité de la catastrophe hilalienne." *Annales: Economies, sociétés, civilisations*, vol. 23 (1968), pp. 390-394.

al-Idrīsī, Muḥammad b. Muḥammad, d. 1166. *Description de l'Afrique et de l'Espagne. Texte arabe pub. pour la première fois d'après les man. de Paris et d'Oxford avec une traduction, des notes et un glossaire.* Leiden: Brill, 1866. Reprint of the Arabic text in Algiers: Maison des livres, 1957.

al-Ifrānī, Muḥammad Saghīr, fl. 1724. *Nozhet-Elhādi. Histoire de la dynastie saadienne au Maroc (1511-1670).* Paris: Leroux, 1888-89. Vol. 1: Arabic text; vol. 2: French tr.

'Inān, Muḥammad 'Abd Allāh. *Dawlat al-Islām fī al-Andalus.* Cairo, 1943-58. 3 vols. vol. 3: *al-Dawla al-amīrīya wa-Suqūṭ al-Khilāfa al-Andalusīya.*

al-Jādirī, Muhammad b. Muhammad b. Ruqayya. "al-Zahra al-Nā'ira" (written in 1780), *Revue d'histoire et de civilisation du Maghreb.* Algiers, vol. 2, 1967, pp. 2-32.

al-Jazā'irī, Muḥammad ibn 'Abd al-Qādir. *Tuḥfat al-Zā'ir fī Tārīkh al-Jazā'ir wa-al-Amīr 'Abd al-Qādir.* Beirut: 2nd rev. ed. 1964 (1st ed. 1903).

Julien, Charles-André. *L'Afrique du Nord en marche; nationalismes musulmans et souveraineté française.* Paris: Julliard, 1952, 2nd rev. ed. 1953, 3rd rev. ed. 1972.

———. *Histoire de l'Afrique blanche des origines à 1945.* Paris: P.U.F., 1966.

———. *Histoire de l'Afrique du Nord: Tunisie, Algérie, Maroc.* Paris: Payot, 1931; 2nd ed. 1951-52, 2 vols.; rev. 2nd ed. 1966, 2 vols. Tr. of vol. 2: *History of North Africa: Tunisia, Algeria, Morocco. From the Arab Conquest to 1830.* New York: Praeger, 1970.

———. *Histoire de l'Algérie contemporaine: la conquête et les débuts de la colonisation (1827-1871).* Paris: P.U.F., 1964.

Kaddache, Mahfoud. *La Vie politique à Alger de 1919 à 1939.* Algiers: SNED, 1970.

al-Karrāsī, Muḥammad, d. 1556/964. Ed. Ben Mansūr. *Arūsat al-Masā'il fimā li-Banī Waṭṭās min al-Faḍā'il.* Rabat, 1963.

al-Kattānī, Muḥammad al-Bāqir. *Tarjamat al-Shaykh Muḥammad al-Kattānī al-Shahīd.* n.p. 1962.

Kattānī, Zayn al-'Ābidīn. *Al-Saḥāfa al-Maghribīya, Nash'atuhā wa-Taṭawwuruhā.* Rabat, n.d. [1969]. Vol. 1 (1820-1912).

Khairallah, Chedly. *Le Mouvement évolutionniste tunisien, notes et documents.* Tunis: Imprimerie de Tunis, 1934-38. 3 vols.

Khālid, Aḥmad. *Al-Ṭāhir al-Ḥaddād wa-al-Bī'a al-Tūnisīya fī al-Thulth al-Awwal min al-Qarn al-'Ishrīn.* Tunis, 1967.

Khayr al-Dīn, Pasha. Ed. Leon Carl Brown. *The Surest Path; the Political Treatise of a Nineteenth-Century Muslim Statesman.* A translation of the introduction to *The Surest Path to Knowledge Concerning the Condition of Countries* by Khayr al-Dīn al-Tunisi. Cambridge, Mass.: Harvard University Press, 1967.

Knight, Melvin Moses. *Morocco as a French Economic Venture, a Study of Open Door Imperialism.* New York and London: Appleton-Century, 1937.

Lacheraf, Mostefa. *L'Algérie: nation et société.* Paris: Maspero, 1965.

Lacoste, Yves. *Ibn Khaldoun; naissance de l'histoire passé du tiers-monde.* Paris: Maspero, 1966.

———, André Nouschi and André Prenant. *L'Algérie passé et présent. Le cadre et les étapes de la constitution de l'Algérie actuelle.* Paris: Editions sociales, 1960.

Lahbabi, Mohamed. *Le Gouvernement marocain à l'aube du XXe siècle.* Rabat: Editions techniques nord-africaines, 1958.

Lahbabi, Mohamed Aziz. *Ibn Khaldūn. Présentation, choix de textes, bibliographie.* Paris: Seghers, 1968.

Laoust, Henri. *Les Schismes dans l'Islam; introduction à une étude de la religion musulmane.* Paris: Payot, 1965.

Laroui, Abdallah. *La Crise des intellectuels arabes; traditionalisme ou historicisme?* Paris: Maspero, 1974.

———. *L'Idéologie arabe contemporaine, essai critique.* Paris: Maspero, 1967.

———. "Marx and the Intellectual from the Third World; or The Problem of Historical Retardation Once Again." *Diogenes,* no. 64 (Winter 1968), pp. 118-140.

Latham, John D. "Towards a Study of Andalusian Immigration and Its Place in Tunisian History." *Cahiers de Tunisie,* vol. 5 (1957), pp. 203-252.

Legley, Marcel. "Les Flaviens et l'Afrique." *Mélanges d'archéologie et d'histoire,* vol. 80 (1968), pp. 201-246.

Leo Africanus, Johannes. *The History and Description of Africa and of the Notable Things Therein Contained,* tr. by John Pory and ed. by Robert Brown. New York: Franklin, Burt, 1963 (repr. of 1896 ed.). 3 vols.

Leroi-Gourhan, André. *La Préhistoire.* Paris: P.U.F., 1966.

Le Tourneau, Roger. *The Almohad Movement in North Africa in the Twelfth and Thirteenth Centuries.* Princeton: Princeton University Press, 1969.

———. *Evolution politique de l'Afrique du Nord musulmane, 1920-1961.* Paris: Colin, 1962.

———. *Fès avant le protectorat; étude économique et sociale d'une ville de l'occident musulman.* Casablanca: SMLE, 1949.

Lévi-Provençal, Evariste. *Documents inédits d'histoire almohade; fragments manuscrits du "Legajo" 1919 du fonds arabe de l'escurial.* Paris: Geuthner, 1928.

———. *Les Historiens des Chorfa; essai sur la littérature historique et biographique au Maroc du XVIe au XXe siècle.* Paris: Larousse, 1922.

———. "Naṣṣ Jadīd 'an Fatḥ al-'Arab li-al-Maghrib." *Revista del Instituto Egipcio de Estudios Islamicos en Madrid,* vol. 2 (1954), pp. 193-224. French tr.: "Un nouveau Récit de la conquête de l'Afrique du Nord par les Arabes." *Arabica,* vol. 1 (1954), pp. 17-52.

———. "Réflexions sur l'Empire Almoravide au début du XIIe siècle." *Cinquantenaire de la Faculté de Lettres d'Alger,* 1932, pp. 307-320.

Levi-Provençal, Evariste, ed. *Un Recueil de lettres officielles almohades; étude diplomatique, analyse et commentaire historique.* Paris: Larousse, 1942.

Levtzion, Nehemia. *Muslims and Chiefs in West Africa: a Study of Islam in the Middle Volta Basin in the Pre-Colonial Period.* Oxford: Clarendon Press, 1968.

Levy, Reuben. *The Social Structure of Islam.* Being the 2nd ed. of *The Sociology of Islam.* Cambridge: University Press, 1957.

Lewicki, Tadeus. "L'Etat nord-africain de Tāhert et ses relations avec le Soudan occidental à la fin du VIIIe et au IXe siècle." *Cahiers d'études africaines,* vol. 2 (1962), pp. 513-535.

Lézine, Alexandre. *Architecture de l'Ifrīqiya; recherches sur les monuments aghlabides.* Paris: Klincksieck, 1966.

Lhote, Henri. *A la Découverte des fresques du Tassili.* Grenoble: Arthaud, 1958.

Lopes, David. "Les Portugais au Maroc." *Revue d'histoire moderne,* vol. 14 (1939), pp. 337-368.

Lyautey, Louis Hubert Gonzalve. *Paroles d'action, Madagascar—Sud-Oranais—Oran—Maroc (1900-1926).* Paris: Colin, 4th ed. 1944.

MacMullen, Ramsay. *Enemies of the Roman Order: Treason, Unrest, and Alienation in the Empire.* Cambridge, Mass.: Harvard University Press, 1966.

al-Madanī, Aḥmad Tawfīq. *Kitāb al-Jazā'ir.* Algiers, 1931.

———. *Muḥammad 'Uthmān Pāshā wa-Khulāṣat Tārīkh al-Atrāk fī al-Jazā'ir.* Algiers, 1937.

———. *Qarṭajanna fī Arba'a Uṣūr.* Tunis, n.d. [1926].

Magalhães-Godinho. Vitorino. *L'Economie de l'empire portugais aux XVe et XVIe siècles.* Paris: SEVPEN, 1969.

Mahdi, Muhsin. *Ibn Khaldūn's Philosophy of History; a Study in the Philosophic Foundation of the Science of Culture.* London: Allen and Unwin, 1957.

al-Mālikī, Abū Bakr 'Abd Allāh ibn Muḥammad, fl. 967. *Kitāb Riyāḍ al-Nufūs fī Ṭabaqāt 'Ulamā' al-Qayrawān wa-Ifrīqiya.* Cairo, 1951.

al-Mannūnī, Muḥammad. "Waṣf al-Maghrib Ayyām al-Sulṭān Abī al-Ḥasan al-Marīnī." *al-Baḥth al-'Ilmī* (Rabat), no. 1 (1964), pp. 131-153.

Mantran, Robert. "L'Evolution des relations entre la Tunisie et l'Empire ottoman du XVIe au XIXe siècle." *Cahiers de Tunisie*, vol. 7 (1959), pp. 319-333.

Marçais, Georges. *La Berbérie musulmane et l'Orient au moyen âge*. Paris: Montaigne, 1946.

Marçais, William. *Articles et conférences*. Paris: Adrien-Maisonneuve, 1961.

al-Marrākushī, 'Abd al-Wāḥid, b. 1185. *Al-Mu'jib fī Talkhīṣ Akhbār al-Maghrib*. Cairo, 1929. French tr.: *Histoire des Almohades*. Algiers: Jourdan, 1893.

al-Marshafī, 'Abd al-Qādir. Ed. and tr. Marcel Bodin. "L'Agrément du lecteur: Notice historique sur les Arabes soumis aux Espagnols pendant leur occupation d'Oran, par Si Abd-el-Kader el Merchefi (texte et traduction)." *Revue africaine*, vol. 65 (1924), pp. 193-260.

al-Mashrafī, Muḥammad Muḥī al-Dīn. *Ifrīqiyā al-Shamālīya fī al-'Aṣr al-Qadīm*. Casablanca: 2nd ed. 1957.

Massignon, Louis. *Le Maroc dans les premières années du XVIe siècle; tableau géographique d'après Léon l'Africain*. Algiers: Jourdan, 1906.

Mauny, Raymond. "Note sur les 'grands voyages' de Léon l'Africain." *Hespéris*, vol. 41 (1954), pp. 379-394.

———. "Le Périple de la mer Erythrée et le problème du commerce romain en Afrique au sud du Limes." *Journal de la Société des Africanistes*, vol. 38 (1968), pp. 19-34.

Merad, Ali. " 'Abd Al-Mu'min à la conquête de l'Afrique du Nord (1130-1163)." *Annales de l'Institut d'études orientales*, vol. 15 (1957), pp. 109-160.

———. *Le Réformisme musulman en Algérie de 1925 à 1940. Essai d'histoire religieuse et sociale*. The Hague: Mouton, 1967.

Miège, Jean Louis. *Le Maroc et l'Europe, 1830-1894*. Paris: P.U.F., 1961-63. 4 vols.

al-Miknāsī, Muḥammad ibn 'Uthmān, d. 1799. Ed. Muḥammad al-Fāsī. *Al-Iksīr fī Fikāk al-Asīr.* Rabat, 1964.
al-Mīlī, Mubārak. *Tārīkh al-Jazā'ir fī al-Qadīm wa-al-Ḥadīth.* Constantine, 1929-32. 2 vols.
Monlaü, Jean. *Les Etats barbaresques.* Paris: P.U.F., 1964.
Monteil, Vincent. "Les Bureaux arabes au Maghreb, 1883-1961." *Esprit,* vol. 29 (1961), pp. 575-606.
Moraes Farias, P. F. de. "The Almoravids: Some Questions Concerning the Character of the Movement during its Period of Closest Contact with the Western Sudan." *Bulletin de l'Institut français de l'Afrique noire,* vol. 29 (1967) B, pp. 794-878.
al-Nāṣirī, Aḥmad ibn Khālid. *Al-Istiqsā li-Akhbār Duwal al-Maghrib al-Aqṣā.* Casablanca, 1954-56. 9 vols. in 4. French tr.: "Kitāb el-istiqça li-akhbar doual el-maghrib el-aqça (Histoire du Maroc)." *Archives marocaines,* vol. 9 (1906), pp. 1-399; vol. 10 (1907), pp. 1-424; vol. 30 (1923), pp. 1-302; vol. 31 (1925), pp. 1-238; vol. 32 (1927), pp. 1-283; vol. 33 (1934), pp. 1-621; vol. 34 (1936), part I.
Nassar, Nassif. *La Pensée réaliste d'Ibn Khaldūn.* Paris: P.U.F., 1967.
Nickerson, Jane Soames. *A Short History of North Africa: Libya, Tunisia, Algeria, Morocco, from Pre-Roman Times to the Present.* New York: Devin-Adair, 1961.
Nouschi, André. *Enquête sur le niveau de vie des populations rurales constantinoises, de la conquête jusqu'en 1919; essai d'histoire économique et sociale.* Paris: P.U.F., 1961.
———. *La Naissance du nationalisme algérien.* Paris: Minuit, 1962.
———. "Le Sens de certain chiffres. Croissance urbaine et vie politique en Algérie (1926-1936)." In *Études maghrébines. Mélanges C. A. Julien.* Paris: P.U.F., 1964, pp. 199-210.
Oliver, Ronald Anthony, and John D. Fage. *A Short History of Africa.* Baltimore: Penguin Books, 1962.

Poncet, Jean. *La Colonisation et l'agriculture européennes en Tunisie depuis 1881; étude de géographie, historique et économique.* Paris: Mouton, 1962.

———. "Le Mythe de la 'catastrophe' hilalienne." *Annales: Economies, sociétés, civilisations,* vol. 22 (1967), pp. 1099-1120.

Qādirī, Muḥammad. *Nashr al-Mathānī.* Fez, 1893 (lith.). French tr.: "Nachr al-Mathânî de Mouhammad al-Qâdirî." *Archives marocaines,* vol. 21 (1913), pp. 1-400; vol. 24 (1917), pp. 1-464.

Rabī', Muḥammad Maḥmūd. *The Political Theory of Ibn Khaldūn.* Leiden: Brill, 1967.

Rachet, Marguerite. *Rome et les Berbères. Un problème militaire d'Auguste à Dioclétien.* Brussels: Latomus, 1970.

Raymond, André. "Les Tentatives anglaises de pénétration économique en Tunisie (1856-1877)." *Revue historique,* vol. 214 (1955), pp. 48-67.

Revue du monde musulman. Numéro special, December 1914.

Ricard, Robert. *Études sur l'histoire des Portugais au Maroc.* Coimbre: Universidade, 1955.

Robert, Jacques. *La Monarchie marocaine.* Paris: Librairie générale de droit et de jurisprudence, 1963.

Rousseau, R. "Hannon au Maroc." *Revue africaine,* vol. 93 (1949), pp. 161-232.

Ruedy, John. *Land Policy in Colonial Algeria; the Origins of the Rural Public Domain.* Berkeley: University of California Press, 1967.

Sahli, Mohammed Chérif. *Décoloniser l'histoire; introduction à l'histoire du Maghreb.* Paris: Maspero, 1965.

Salamah, B. *L'Insurrection de 1864 en Tunisie.* Tunis: Maison tunisienne de l'édition, 1967.

Sallustius Crispus, C. French tr.: *Salluste. Conjuration de Catilina. Guerre de Jugurtha. Fragments des Histoires.* Tr. and ed. by François Richard. Paris: Garnier, 1933;

new ed. 1968. English tr.: *The Jugurthine War and the Conspiracy of Catiline.* Baltimore: Penguin, 1963.

Saumagne, Charles. *La Numidie et Rome. Masinissa et Jugurtha. Essai.* Paris: P.U.F., 1966.

———. "Ouvriers agricoles ou rôdeurs de celliers? Les circoncellions d'Afrique." *Annales d'histoire économique et sociale,* vol. 6 (1934), pp. 351-364.

———. "Un Tarif fiscal du IVe siècle avant notre ère (d'après des fragments épigraphiques découverts à Carthage)." *Karthago,* vol. 1 (1950), pp. 105-200.

Sebag, Paul. *La Tunisie; essai de monographie.* Paris: Éditions sociales, 1951.

Sources inédites de l'histoire du Maroc de 1530 à 1845. Ed. Henry de Castries et al. Paris: Leroux, 1905–. In progress. 1st series: *Dynastie saadienne (1530-1660)*; part 1, Portugal. 5 vols. (1934-53).

Spillmann, Georges. *Du Protectorat à l'indépendance, Maroc, 1912-1955.* Paris: Plon, 1967.

———. *Esquisse d'histoire religieuse du Maroc; confréries et zaouïas.* Paris: Peyronnet, 1951.

Sraieb, Noureddine. "Contribution à la connaissance de Tahir El-Ḥaddād (1899-1935)." *Revue de l'occident musulman et de la Méditerranée,* no. 4 (1967), pp. 99-132.

Stein, Ernst. *Histoire du Bas-Empire.* Paris: Desclée de Brouwer, 1949-59. 2 vols. in 3.

Stewart, Charles Frank. *The Economy of Morocco, 1912-1962.* Cambridge, Mass.: Harvard University Press, 1964.

al-Sūsī, Muḥammad al-Mukhtār. *Sūs al-ʿAlima.* Rabat, 1960.

Syme, Ronald. "Tacfarinas, the Musulamii and Thubursicu." In *Studies in Roman Economic and Social History in Honor of Allan Chester Johnson.* Ed. P. R. Coleman-Norton. Princeton: Princeton University Press, 1951, pp. 113-130.

Tablettes Albertini; actes privés de l'époque vandale (fin du Ve siècle). Ed. Christian Courtois, Louis Leschi et al. Paris: Arts et métiers graphiques, 1952.

Talbi, Mohamed. *L'Émirat aghlabide, 184-296, 800-909, histoire politique.* Paris: Librairie d'Amérique et d'Orient, 1966.

al-Tamīmī, Muḥammad ibn Aḥmad, Abū al-'Arab, d. 944. *Ṭabaqāt 'Ulamā' Ifrīqiya wa-Tūnis.* Tunis, 1968. French tr.: *Classes des savants de l'Ifrīqīya.* Algiers: Carbonel, 1920.

Taylor, A. J. P. "The Conference at Algeçiras." In *idem, Englishmen and Others,* London: Hamish Hamilton, 1956, pp. 88-107.

Temimi, Abdeljelil. *Recherches et documents d'histoire maghrebine; la Tunisie, l'Algérie et la Tripolitaine de 1816 à 1871.* Tunis: Université de Tunis, 1971.

Terrasse, Henri. *Histoire du Maroc des origines à l'établissement du Protectorat français.* Casablanca: Atlantides, 1949-50. 2 vols. Abridged English tr.: *History of Morocco.* Casablanca: Atlantides, 1952.

Tillion, Germaine. *Le Harem et les cousins.* Paris: Seuil, 1966.

al-'Umarī, Ibn Faḍl Allāh, d. 1349. *Masālik al-Abṣār fī Mamālik al-Amṣār.* Cairo, 1924. French tr.: *Masālik el abṣār fi mamālik el amṣār.* Paris: Geuthner, 1927.

UNESCO. *Nomades et nomadisme au Sahara.* Paris, 1963.

Valensi, Lucette. *Le Maghreb avant la prise d'Alger, 1790-1830.* Paris: Flammarion, 1969.

Van Norstrand, John James. *The Imperial Domains of Africa Proconsularis; an Epigraphical Study.* Berkeley: University of California Press, 1925.

Vanacker, Claudette. "Géographie économique de l'Afrique du Nord selon les auteurs arabes, du IXe siècle au milieu du XIIe siècle." *Annales: Economies, sociétés, civilisations,* vol. 28 (1973), pp. 659-680.

Von Grunebaum, Gustave Edmund. *Modern Islam; the Search for Cultural Identity.* New York: Vintage, 1964.

al-Wansharīsī, Aḥmad ibn Yaḥyā. Ed. Emile Amar. French tr. of *al-Mi'yār al-Maghrib*: "La Pierre de touche des fétwas de Aḥmad al-Wanscharīsī; choix de consultations juridiques des faqīhs du Maghreb." *Archives marocaines,* vol. 12 (1908), pp. 1-522; vol. 13 (1909), pp. 1-536.

Warmington, Brian Herbert. *Carthage.* London: Hale, 1960.

———. *The North African Provinces from Diocletian to the Vandal Conquest.* Westport, Conn.: Greenwood Press, 1971 (repr. of 1954 ed.).

Wendel, Henry C. "The Protégé System in Morocco." *Journal of Modern History,* vol. 2 (1930), pp. 48-60.

Willan, Thomas Stuart. *Studies in Elizabethan Foreign Trade.* Manchester: Manchester University Press, 1959.

Woolman, David S. *Rebels in the Rif; Abd el Krim and the Rif Rebellion.* Stanford: Stanford University Press, 1968.

al-Ya'qūbī, Aḥmad ibn Abī Ya'qūb, d. 897. *Kitāb al-Buldān.* Najof, 1918. Arabic text and Latin tr., ed. Michael Jan de Goeje: *Specimen literarium iuaugurale, exhibens descriptionem al-Magribi sumtam e Libro Regionum al-Jaqubii.* Leiden: Brill, 1860. French tr.: *Les Pays.* Cairo: Institut français d'archéologie orientale, 1937.

al-Zarkashī, Muḥammad ibn Ibrāhīm, d. 1525. *Tārīkh al-Dawlatayn al-Muwaḥḥadīya wa-al-Ḥafṣīya.* Tunis, 1966 (1st ed. 1872). French tr.: *Chronique des Almohades et des Hafçides attribuée à Zerkechi.* Constantine: Braham, 1895.

Zartman, I. William. *Morocco: Problems of New Power.* New York: Atherton, 1964.

al-Zayyānī, Abū al-Qāsim ibn Aḥmad. Ed. Octave Victor Houdas. *Le Maroc de 1631 à 1812, extrait de l'ouvrage intitulé Ettordjeman elmo'rib 'an douel elmachriq ou 'lmaghrib.* Arabic text and partial French tr. Paris: Imprimerie nationale, 1886.

———. *Al-Turjumāna al-Kubrā fī Akhbār al-Ma'mūr barran wa-baḥran.* Rabat, 1967.

Ziadeh, Nicola A. *Origins of Nationalism in Tunisia.* Beirut: Librairie du Liban, 1962.

Index

This index has been prepared especially for this edition by Richard Jones.

Library of Congress Cataloging in Publication Data

Laroui, Abdallah, 1933–
The history of the Maghrib.

(Princeton studies on the Near East)
Includes bibliographical references and index.
1. Africa, North—History. I. Title.
DT194.L3613 961 76-20679
ISBN 0-691-03109-6

DATE DUE

DEC 20 '82

MAR 17 1997

GAYLORD

PRINTED IN U.S.A.

DT
194
L3613

Laroui, Abdallah, 1933-
The history of the Maghrib : an interpretive essay / Abdallah Laroui ; translated from the French by Ralph Manheim. -- Princeton : Princeton University Press, 1977.
viii, 431 p. ; 23 cm. -- (Princeton studies on the Near East)
Bibliography: p. 401-422.
Includes index.
ISBN 0-691-03109-6

1. Africa, North--History. I. Title.

DT194.L3613 961
76-20679

SUPA B/NA A C0-667682 02/17/78